Mazda MX-5
Owners Workshop Manual

Martynn Randall

Models covered

(5565 - 256)

MX-5 Convertible 'Mk 1', 'Mk 2' & 'Mk 2½' (NA & NB Series) with 1.6 litre (1597cc) & 1.8 litre (1840cc) engines

Also covers most features of Eunos (Japanese import)
Does NOT cover models with turbocharged engines or automatic transmission
Does NOT cover 'Mk 3' (NC Series) introduced October 2005

© Haynes Publishing 2013

ABCDE
FGHIJ
KLMNO
PQRST

A book in the **Haynes Owners Workshop Manual Series**

All rights reserved. No part of this book may be reproduced or transmitted in any form or by any means, electronic or mechanical, including photocopying, recording or by any information storage or retrieval system, without permission in writing from the copyright holder.

ISBN **978 0 85733 565 4**

British Library Cataloguing in Publication Data
A catalogue record for this book is available from the British Library.

Printed in the USA

Haynes Publishing
Sparkford, Yeovil, Somerset BA22 7JJ, England

Haynes North America, Inc
861 Lawrence Drive, Newbury Park, California 91320, USA

Haynes Publishing Nordiska AB
Box 1504, 751 45 UPPSALA, Sverige

Contents

Illegal Copying

It is the policy of Haynes Publishing to actively protect its Copyrights and Trade Marks. Legal action will be taken against anyone who unlawfully copies the cover or contents of this Manual. This includes all forms of unauthorised copying including digital, mechanical, and electronic in any form. Authorisation from Haynes Publishing will only be provided expressly and in writing. Illegal copying will also be reported to the appropriate statutory authorities.

Contents

The Mazda MX-5 models covered by this manual were introduced in 1989 and initially were only available with a 1.6 litre petrol engine. Its classic front-engine, rear-wheel-drive, 2-door convertible layout soon became a sales success, due somewhat to its attractive design, but mainly because of the sheer sense of fun derived from driving. In 1994 a 1.8 litre engine was added to the range, whilst a reduced output 1.6 litre model was also introduced.

A redesigned 'Mk 2' model was launched in 1998. All of the body panels were changed, but the most striking difference was the replacement of the iconic 'pop-up' headlights, with fixed units streamlined between the front bumper and bonnet. The interior became a little more luxurious, with a slightly higher level of specification, but overall the car retained its sense of fun that rewarded spirited driving. In 2000 the facelifted 'Mk 2.5' model was released, with subtle changes to the body and interior, a higher level of equipment, and an uprated 1.8 litre engine with variable valve timing.

All engines are of a well-proven double-overhead (DOHC) camshaft design, mounted longitudinally, with the transmission mounted on its rear. Although automatic transmission models were available, they are not covered by this manual.

All models have fully-independent front and rear suspension, with anti-roll bars fitted to the front and rear.

A wide range of standard and optional equipment is available within the Mazda MX-5 range to suit most tastes, including central locking, electric windows, air conditioning, and numerous airbags.

Provided that regular servicing is carried out in accordance with the manufacturer's recommendations, the Mazda MX-5 should prove reliable and economical. The engine compartment is well-designed, and most of the items requiring frequent attention are easily accessible.

Your Mazda MX-5 manual

The aim of this manual is to help you get the best value from your vehicle. It can do so in several ways. It can help you decide what work must be done (even should you choose to get it done by a garage). It will also provide information on routine maintenance and servicing, and give a logical course of action and diagnosis when random faults occur. However, it is hoped that you will use the manual by tackling the work yourself. On simpler jobs it may even be quicker than booking the car into a garage and going there twice, to leave and collect it. Perhaps most important, a lot of money can be saved by avoiding the costs a garage must charge to cover its labour and overheads.

The manual has drawings and descriptions to show the function of the various components so that their layout can be understood. Tasks are described and photographed in a clear step-by-step sequence.

References to the 'left' and 'right' of the vehicle are in the sense of a person in the driver's seat facing forward.

Acknowledgements

Thanks are due to Draper Tools Limited, who provided some of the workshop tools, to MX5 Heaven (mx5heaven.co.uk), and to all those people at Sparkford who helped in the production of this manual.

We take great pride in the accuracy of information given in this manual, but vehicle manufacturers make alterations and design changes during the production run of a particular vehicle of which they do not inform us. No liability can be accepted by the authors or publishers for loss, damage or injury caused by any errors in, or omissions from, the information given.

Working on your car can be dangerous. This page shows just some of the potential risks and hazards, with the aim of creating a safety-conscious attitude.

General hazards

Scalding

• Don't remove the radiator or expansion tank cap while the engine is hot.
• Engine oil, transmission fluid or power steering fluid may also be dangerously hot if the engine has recently been running.

Burning

• Beware of burns from the exhaust system and from any part of the engine. Brake discs and drums can also be extremely hot immediately after use.

Crushing

• When working under or near a raised vehicle, always supplement the jack with axle stands, or use drive-on ramps. *Never venture under a car which is only supported by a jack.*
• Take care if loosening or tightening high-torque nuts when the vehicle is on stands. Initial loosening and final tightening should be done with the wheels on the ground.

Fire

• Fuel is highly flammable; fuel vapour is explosive.
• Don't let fuel spill onto a hot engine.
• Do not smoke or allow naked lights (including pilot lights) anywhere near a vehicle being worked on. Also beware of creating sparks (electrically or by use of tools).
• Fuel vapour is heavier than air, so don't work on the fuel system with the vehicle over an inspection pit.
• Another cause of fire is an electrical overload or short-circuit. Take care when repairing or modifying the vehicle wiring.
• Keep a fire extinguisher handy, of a type suitable for use on fuel and electrical fires.

Electric shock

• Ignition HT and Xenon headlight voltages can be dangerous, especially to people with heart problems or a pacemaker. Don't work on or near these systems with the engine running or the ignition switched on.

• Mains voltage is also dangerous. Make sure that any mains-operated equipment is correctly earthed. Mains power points should be protected by a residual current device (RCD) circuit breaker.

Fume or gas intoxication

• Exhaust fumes are poisonous; they can contain carbon monoxide, which is rapidly fatal if inhaled. Never run the engine in a confined space such as a garage with the doors shut.
• Fuel vapour is also poisonous, as are the vapours from some cleaning solvents and paint thinners.

Poisonous or irritant substances

• Avoid skin contact with battery acid and with any fuel, fluid or lubricant, especially antifreeze, brake hydraulic fluid and Diesel fuel. Don't syphon them by mouth. If such a substance is swallowed or gets into the eyes, seek medical advice.
• Prolonged contact with used engine oil can cause skin cancer. Wear gloves or use a barrier cream if necessary. Change out of oil-soaked clothes and do not keep oily rags in your pocket.
• Air conditioning refrigerant forms a poisonous gas if exposed to a naked flame (including a cigarette). It can also cause skin burns on contact.

Asbestos

• Asbestos dust can cause cancer if inhaled or swallowed. Asbestos may be found in gaskets and in brake and clutch linings. When dealing with such components it is safest to assume that they contain asbestos.

Special hazards

Hydrofluoric acid

• This extremely corrosive acid is formed when certain types of synthetic rubber, found in some O-rings, oil seals, fuel hoses etc, are exposed to temperatures above 4000C. The rubber changes into a charred or sticky substance containing the acid. *Once formed, the acid remains dangerous for years. If it gets onto the skin, it may be necessary to amputate the limb concerned.*
• When dealing with a vehicle which has suffered a fire, or with components salvaged from such a vehicle, wear protective gloves and discard them after use.

The battery

• Batteries contain sulphuric acid, which attacks clothing, eyes and skin. Take care when topping-up or carrying the battery.
• The hydrogen gas given off by the battery is highly explosive. Never cause a spark or allow a naked light nearby. Be careful when connecting and disconnecting battery chargers or jump leads.

Air bags

• Air bags can cause injury if they go off accidentally. Take care when removing the steering wheel and trim panels. Special storage instructions may apply.

Diesel injection equipment

• Diesel injection pumps supply fuel at very high pressure. Take care when working on the fuel injectors and fuel pipes.

Warning: Never expose the hands, face or any other part of the body to injector spray; the fuel can penetrate the skin with potentially fatal results.

Remember...

DO

• Do use eye protection when using power tools, and when working under the vehicle.

• Do wear gloves or use barrier cream to protect your hands when necessary.

• Do get someone to check periodically that all is well when working alone on the vehicle.

• Do keep loose clothing and long hair well out of the way of moving mechanical parts.

• Do remove rings, wristwatch etc, before working on the vehicle – especially the electrical system.

• Do ensure that any lifting or jacking equipment has a safe working load rating adequate for the job.

DON'T

• Don't attempt to lift a heavy component which may be beyond your capability – get assistance.

• Don't rush to finish a job, or take unverified short cuts.

• Don't use ill-fitting tools which may slip and cause injury.

• Don't leave tools or parts lying around where someone can trip over them. Mop up oil and fuel spills at once.

• Don't allow children or pets to play in or near a vehicle being worked on.

The following pages are intended to help in dealing with common roadside emergencies and breakdowns. You will find more detailed fault finding information at the back of the manual, and repair information in the main chapters.

If your car won't start and the starter motor doesn't turn

☐ Open the luggage compartment and make sure that the battery terminals are clean and tight.
☐ Switch on the headlights and try to start the engine. If the headlights go very dim when you're trying to start, the battery is probably flat. Get out of trouble by jump starting using a friend's car.

If your car won't start even though the starter motor turns as normal

☐ Is there fuel in the tank?
☐ Is there moisture on electrical components under the bonnet? Switch off the ignition, then wipe off any obvious dampness with a dry cloth. Spray a water-repellent aerosol product (WD-40 or equivalent) on ignition and fuel system electrical connectors like those shown in the photos.

A Check the security of the throttle body connector.

B Check the airflow meter wiring connector with the ignition switched off.

C Check the security and condition of the battery terminals (located on the right-hand side of the luggage compartment).

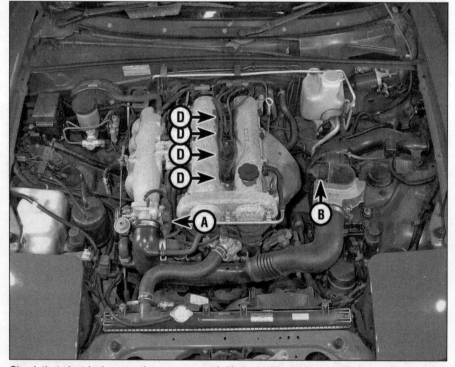

Check that electrical connections are secure (with the ignition switched off) and spray them with a water-dispersant spray like WD-40 if you suspect a problem due to damp.

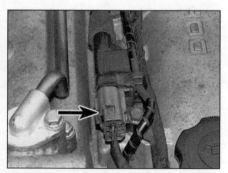

D Check the spark plug HT lead and coil connections.

Jump starting

HAYNES HINT *Jump starting will get you out of trouble, but you must correct whatever made the battery go flat in the first place. There are three possibilities:*

1 *The battery has been drained by repeated attempts to start, or by leaving the lights on.*

2 *The charging system is not working properly (alternator drivebelt slack or broken, alternator wiring fault or alternator itself faulty).*

3 *The battery itself is at fault (electrolyte low, or battery worn out).*

When jump-starting a car, observe the following precautions:

✓ Before connecting the booster battery, make sure that the ignition is switched off.

Caution: Remove the key in case the central locking engages when the jump leads are connected

✓ Ensure that all electrical equipment (lights, heater, wipers, etc) is switched off.
✓ Take note of any special precautions printed on the battery case.
✓ Make sure that the booster battery is the same voltage as the discharged one in the vehicle.

✓ If the battery is being jump-started from the battery in another vehicle, the two vehicles MUST NOT TOUCH each other.

✓ Make sure that the transmission is in neutral (or PARK, in the case of automatic transmission).

HAYNES HINT *Budget jump leads can be a false economy, as they often do not pass enough current to start large capacity or diesel engines. They can also get hot.*

1 Unclip the plastic cover (where fitted) from the positive terminal (+) on battery on the right-hand side of the luggage compartment, and connect the red jump lead to the terminal. On some models, it might be necessary to remove a cover over the battery.

2 Connect the other end of the red lead to the positive (+) terminal of the booster battery.

3 Connect one end of the black jump lead to the negative (-) terminal of the booster battery.

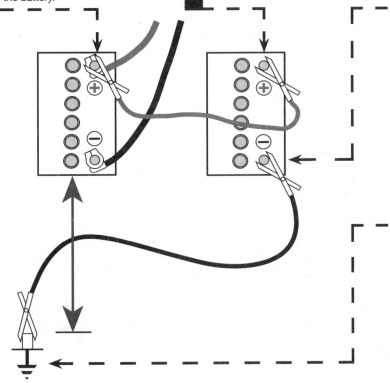

4 Connect the other end of the black jump lead an exposed metallic part (eg, the boot lid lock).

5 Start the engine, then with the engine running at fast idle speed, disconnect the jump leads in the reverse order of connection, ie, negative (black) lead first. Securely refit the plastic cover to the positive terminal.

Wheel changing

⚠️ *Warning: Do not change a wheel in a situation where you risk being hit by other traffic. On busy roads, try to stop in a lay-by or a gateway. Be wary of passing traffic while changing the wheel – it is easy to become distracted by the job in hand.*

Preparation

- ☐ When a puncture occurs, stop as soon as it is safe to do so.
- ☐ Park on firm level ground, if possible, and well out of the way of other traffic.
- ☐ Use hazard warning lights if necessary.

- ☐ If you have one, use a warning triangle to alert other drivers of your presence.
- ☐ Apply the handbrake and engage first or reverse gear.

- ☐ Chock the wheel diagonally opposite the one being removed – a couple of large stones will do for this.
- ☐ If the ground is soft, use a flat piece of wood to spread the load under the jack.

Changing the wheel

1 The spare wheel and tools are stored in the luggage compartment.

2 On Mk 2 models (1998-on) fold back the floor covering and lift up the cover panel.

3 Unscrew the retaining bolts/nuts, and lift out the tools, followed by the spare wheel.

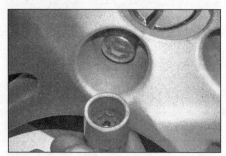

4 Where applicable, prise off the wheel trim or centre cover for access to the wheel nuts. Models with alloy wheels may have special locking nuts – these are removed with a special tool, which should be provided with the wheel brace (or it may be in the glovebox).

5 Slacken each wheel nut by a half turn, using the wheel brace. If the nuts are too tight, DON'T stand on the wheel brace to undo them – call for assistance from one of the motoring organisations.

6 Two jacking points are provided on each side – use the one nearest the punctured wheel. Locate the jack head at the point in the lower sill flange indicated by the indentation in the metal sill (don't jack the vehicle at any other point of the sill, nor on a plastic panel). Turn the jack handle clockwise until the wheel is raised clear of the ground.

7 Unscrew the wheel nuts, and remove the wheel.

8 Fit the spare wheel, and screw on the nuts. Lightly tighten the nuts with the wheel brace, then lower the vehicle to the ground. Securely tighten the wheel nuts, then refit the wheel trim or centre cover, as applicable. Note that the wheel nuts should be slackened and retightened to the specified torque at the earliest possible opportunity.

Finally . . .

- ☐ Remove the wheel chocks and stow the punctured wheel and tools away.
- ☐ Check the tyre pressure on the tyre just fitted. If it is low, or if you don't have a pressure gauge with you, drive slowly to the next garage and inflate the tyre to the correct pressure. In the case of the narrow 'space-saver' spare wheel this pressure is much higher than for a normal tyre.

Note: *Some models are supplied with a special lightweight 'space-saver' spare wheel. This is intended only for temporary use, and **must** be replaced with a standard wheel as soon as possible. Drive with particular care with this wheel fitted, especially through corners and when braking; do not exceed 50 mph.*

Identifying leaks

Puddles on the garage floor or drive, or obvious wetness under the bonnet or underneath the car, suggest a leak that needs investigating. It can sometimes be difficult to decide where the leak is coming from, especially if an engine undershield is fitted. Leaking oil or fluid can also be blown rearwards by the passage of air under the car, giving a false impression of where the problem lies.

Warning: Most automotive oils and fluids are poisonous. Wash them off skin, and change out of contaminated clothing, without delay.

HAYNES HiNT *The smell of a fluid leaking from the car may provide a clue to what's leaking. Some fluids are distinctively coloured. It may help to remove the engine undershield, clean the car carefully and to park it over some clean paper overnight as an aid to locating the source of the leak. Remember that some leaks may only occur while the engine is running.*

Sump oil

Engine oil may leak from the drain plug...

Oil from filter

...or from the base of the oil filter.

Gearbox oil

Gearbox oil can leak from the seals at the inboard ends of the driveshafts.

Antifreeze

Leaking antifreeze often leaves a crystalline deposit like this.

Brake fluid

A leak occurring at a wheel is almost certainly brake fluid.

Power steering fluid

Power steering fluid may leak from the pipe connectors on the steering rack.

Towing

When all else fails, you may find yourself having to get a tow home – or of course you may be helping somebody else. Long-distance recovery should only be done by a garage or breakdown service. For shorter distances, DIY towing using another car is easy enough, but observe the following points:

☐ Use a proper tow-rope – they are not expensive. The vehicle being towed must display an ON TOW sign in its rear window.
☐ Always turn the ignition key to the 'on' position when the vehicle is being towed, so that the steering lock is released, and the direction indicator and brake lights work.

☐ Only attach the tow-rope to the towing eyes provided at the front and rear of the vehicle (see illustration).
☐ Before being towed, release the handbrake and select neutral on the transmission.
☐ Note that greater-than-usual pedal pressure will be required to operate the brakes, since the vacuum servo unit is only operational with the engine running.
☐ On models with power steering, greater-than-usual steering effort will also be required.
☐ The driver of the car being towed must keep the tow-rope taut at all times to avoid snatching.

☐ Make sure that both drivers know the route before setting off.
☐ Only drive at moderate speeds and keep the distance towed to a minimum. Drive smoothly and allow plenty of time for slowing down at junctions.

Introduction

There are some very simple checks which need only take a few minutes to carry out, but which could save you a lot of inconvenience and expense.

These checks require no great skill or special tools, and the small amount of time they take to perform could prove to be very well spent, for example:

☐ Keeping an eye on tyre condition and pressures, will not only help to stop them wearing out prematurely, but could also save your life.

☐ Many breakdowns are caused by electrical problems. Battery-related faults are particularly common, and a quick check on a regular basis will often prevent the majority of these.

☐ If your car develops a brake fluid leak, the first time you might know about it is when your brakes don't work properly. Checking the level regularly will give advance warning of this kind of problem.

☐ If the oil or coolant levels run low, the cost of repairing any engine damage will be far greater than fixing the leak, for example.

Underbonnet check points

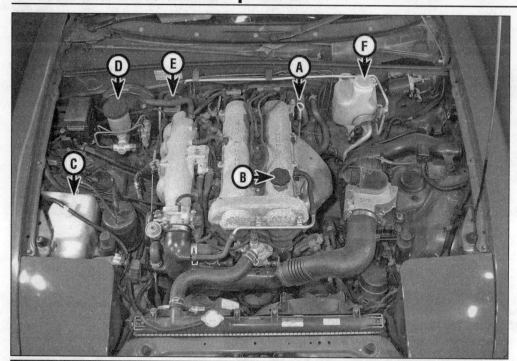

◀ **1.6 litre engine**

A *Engine oil level dipstick*

B *Engine oil filler cap*

C *Coolant expansion tank*

D *Brake fluid reservoir*

E *Clutch fluid reservoir*

F *Screen washer fluid reservoir*

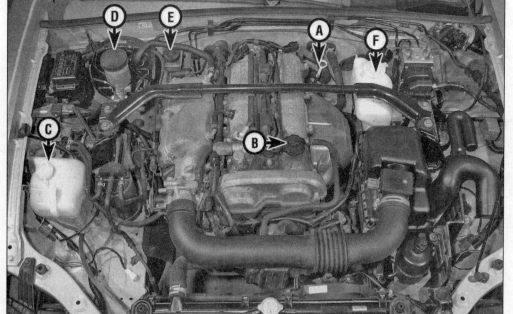

◀ **1.8 litre engine (2000-on shown)**

A *Engine oil level dipstick*

B *Engine oil filler cap*

C *Coolant expansion tank*

D *Brake fluid reservoir*

E *Clutch fluid reservoir*

F *Screen washer fluid reservoir*

Engine oil level

Before you start
✔ Make sure that the car is on level ground.
✔ Check the oil level before the car is driven, or at least 10 minutes after the engine has been switched off.

HAYNES HiNT *If the oil is checked immediately after driving the vehicle, some of the oil will remain in the upper engine components, resulting in an inaccurate reading on the dipstick.*

The correct oil
Modern engines place great demands on their oil. It is very important that the correct oil for your car is used (see *Lubricants and fluids*).

Car care
● If you have to add oil frequently, you should check whether you have any oil leaks. Place some clean paper under the car overnight, and check for stains in the morning. If there are no leaks, then the engine may be burning oil.
● Always maintain the level between the upper and lower dipstick marks. If the level is too low, severe engine damage may occur. Oil seal failure may result if the engine is overfilled by adding too much oil.

1 The dipstick top is sometimes brightly coloured for easy identification (see *Underbonnet check points* for exact location). Withdraw the dipstick.

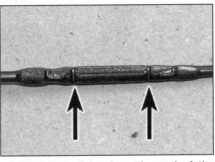

3 Note the oil level on the end of the dipstick, which should be between the upper maximum mark and lower minimum mark. Approximately 0.8 litres of oil will raise the level from the lower mark to the upper mark.

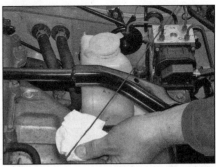

2 Using a clean rag or paper towel remove all oil from the dipstick. Insert the clean dipstick into the tube as far as it will go, then withdraw it again.

4 Oil is added through the filler cap. Unscrew the cap and top-up the level; a funnel may help to reduce spillage. Add the oil slowly, checking the level on the dipstick often. Don't overfill (see *Car care*).

Coolant level

Warning: Do not attempt to remove the expansion tank pressure cap when the engine is hot, as there is a very great risk of scalding. Do not leave open containers of coolant about, as it is poisonous.

Car care
● With a sealed-type cooling system, adding coolant should not be necessary on a regular basis. If frequent topping-up is required, it is likely there is a leak. Check the radiator, all hoses and joint faces for signs of staining or wetness, and rectify as necessary.

● It is important that antifreeze is used in the cooling system all year round, not just during the winter months. Don't top up with water alone, as the antifreeze will become diluted.

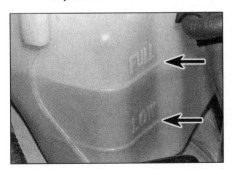

1 The coolant level must be maintained between the FULL and LOW marks on the coolant expansion tank.

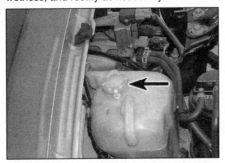

2 If topping-up is necessary, **wait until the engine is cold**. Unclip the expansion tank cap.

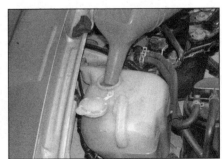

3 Add a mixture of water and antifreeze to the expansion tank until the level of the coolant is just below the FULL mark on the expansion tank. Refit the cap and tighten it until the arrow marks align.

Brake fluid level

Warning:
• **Brake fluid can harm your eyes and damage painted surfaces, so use extreme caution when handling and pouring it.**
• **Do not use fluid that has been standing open for some time, as it absorbs moisture from the air, which can cause a dangerous loss of braking effectiveness.**
• **The fluid level in the reservoir will drop slightly as the brake pads wear down, but the fluid level must never be allowed to drop below the MIN mark.**

Before you start

✔ Make sure that your car is on level ground.

Safety first!

● If the reservoir requires repeated topping-up this is an indication of a fluid leak somewhere in the system, which should be investigated immediately.

● If a leak is suspected, the car should not be driven until the braking system has been checked. Never take any risks where brakes are concerned.

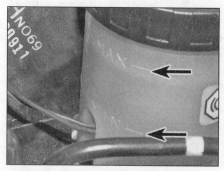

1 The MAX and MIN marks are indicated on the side of the reservoir. The fluid level must be kept between the marks at all times.

2 If topping-up is necessary, first wipe clean the area around the filler cap to prevent dirt entering the hydraulic system.

3 Unscrew the reservoir cap and carefully lift it out of position. Inspect the reservoir, if the fluid is dirty the hydraulic system should be drained and refilled (see Chapter 1, Section 18).

4 Carefully add fluid taking care not to spill it onto the surrounding components. Use only the specified fluid; mixing different types can cause damage to the system. After topping-up to the correct level, securely refit the cap and wipe off any spilt fluid.

Power steering fluid level

✔ Park the vehicle on level ground.

✔ Set the steering wheel straight-ahead.

✔ The engine should be turned off.

 HAYNES HINT *For the check to be accurate, the steering must not be turned while the level is being checked.*

Safety first!

● The need for frequent topping-up indicates a leak, which should be investigated immediately.

1 The reservoir is located near the front of the engine compartment. Wipe clean the area around the reservoir filler neck and unscrew the filler cap/dipstick from the reservoir.

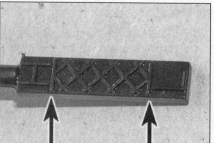

2 Insert the dipstick into the reservoir (without screwing on the cap), then remove it. The fluid level should be between H and L.

3 When topping-up, use the specified type of fluid and do not overfill the reservoir. When the level is correct, securely refit the cap.

Clutch fluid level

Warning:
- *Hydraulic fluid can harm your eyes and damage painted surfaces, so use extreme caution when handling and pouring it.*
- *Do not use fluid that has been standing open for some time, as it absorbs moisture from the air, which can cause a dangerous loss of clutch control.*
- *The fluid level must never be allowed to drop below the MIN mark.*

Before you start

✔ Make sure that your car is on level ground.

Safety first!

● If the reservoir requires repeated topping-up this is an indication of a fluid leak somewhere in the system, which should be investigated immediately.

● If a leak is suspected, the car should not be driven until the clutch hydraulic system has been checked.

1 The MAX and MIN marks are indicated on the side of the reservoir. The fluid level must be kept between the marks at all times.

2 If topping-up is necessary, first wipe clean the area around the filler cap to prevent dirt entering the hydraulic system.

3 Unscrew the reservoir cap and lift it out of position.

4 Carefully add fluid taking care not to spill it onto the surrounding components. Use only the specified fluid; mixing different types can cause damage to the system. After topping-up to the correct level, securely refit the cap and wipe off any spilt fluid.

Screen washer fluid level*

* On models with a headlight washer system, the screenwash is also used to clean the headlights

● Screenwash additives not only keep the windscreen clean during bad weather, they also prevent the washer system freezing in cold weather – which is when you are likely to need it most. Don't top-up using plain water, as the screenwash will become diluted, and will freeze in cold weather.

Warning: On no account use engine coolant antifreeze in the screen washer system – this may damage the paintwork.

1 The screen washer fluid reservoir is located at the left-hand side of the engine compartment.

2 Unclip the cap. When topping-up, add a screenwash additive in the quantities recommended by the manufacturer.

Tyre condition and pressure

It is very important that tyres are in good condition, and at the correct pressure - having a tyre failure at any speed is highly dangerous. Tyre wear is influenced by driving style - harsh braking and acceleration, or fast cornering, will all produce more rapid tyre wear. As a general rule, the front tyres wear out faster than the rears. Interchanging the tyres from front to rear ("rotating" the tyres) may result in more even wear. However, if this is completely effective, you may have the expense of replacing all four tyres at once!

Remove any nails or stones embedded in the tread before they penetrate the tyre to cause deflation. If removal of a nail does reveal that the tyre has been punctured, refit the nail so that its point of penetration is marked. Then immediately change the wheel, and have the tyre repaired by a tyre dealer.

Regularly check the tyres for damage in the form of cuts or bulges, especially in the sidewalls. Periodically remove the wheels, and clean any dirt or mud from the inside and outside surfaces. Examine the wheel rims for signs of rusting, corrosion or other damage. Light alloy wheels are easily damaged by "kerbing" whilst parking; steel wheels may also become dented or buckled. A new wheel is very often the only way to overcome severe damage.

New tyres should be balanced when they are fitted, but it may become necessary to re-balance them as they wear, or if the balance weights fitted to the wheel rim should fall off. Unbalanced tyres will wear more quickly, as will the steering and suspension components. Wheel imbalance is normally signified by vibration, particularly at a certain speed (typically around 50 mph). If this vibration is felt only through the steering, then it is likely that just the front wheels need balancing. If, however, the vibration is felt through the whole car, the rear wheels could be out of balance. Wheel balancing should be carried out by a tyre dealer or garage.

1 *Tread Depth - visual check*
The original tyres have tread wear safety bands (B), which will appear when the tread depth reaches approximately 1.6 mm. The band positions are indicated by a triangular mark on the tyre sidewall (A).

2 *Tread Depth - manual check*
Alternatively, tread wear can be monitored with a simple, inexpensive device known as a tread depth indicator gauge.

3 *Tyre Pressure Check*
Check the tyre pressures regularly with the tyres cold. Do not adjust the tyre pressures immediately after the vehicle has been used, or an inaccurate setting will result.

Tyre tread wear patterns

Shoulder Wear

Underinflation (wear on both sides)
Under-inflation will cause overheating of the tyre, because the tyre will flex too much, and the tread will not sit correctly on the road surface. This will cause a loss of grip and excessive wear, not to mention the danger of sudden tyre failure due to heat build-up.
Check and adjust pressures
Incorrect wheel camber (wear on one side)
Repair or renew suspension parts
Hard cornering
Reduce speed!

Centre Wear

Overinflation
Over-inflation will cause rapid wear of the centre part of the tyre tread, coupled with reduced grip, harsher ride, and the danger of shock damage occurring in the tyre casing.
Check and adjust pressures

If you sometimes have to inflate your car's tyres to the higher pressures specified for maximum load or sustained high speed, don't forget to reduce the pressures to normal afterwards.

Uneven Wear

Front tyres may wear unevenly as a result of wheel misalignment. Most tyre dealers and garages can check and adjust the wheel alignment (or "tracking") for a modest charge.
Incorrect camber or castor
Repair or renew suspension parts
Malfunctioning suspension
Repair or renew suspension parts
Unbalanced wheel
Balance tyres
Incorrect toe setting
Adjust front wheel alignment
Note: *The feathered edge of the tread which typifies toe wear is best checked by feel.*

Wiper blades

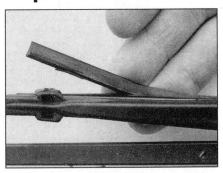

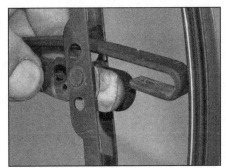

1 Check the condition of the wiper blades; if they are cracked or show any signs of deterioration, or if the glass swept area is smeared, renew them. Wiper blades should be renewed annually.

2 To remove a wiper blade, pull the arm away from the screen, then rotate the blade, compress the retaining clip ...

3 ... and side the blade from the arm.

Battery

Caution: Before carrying out any work on the vehicle battery, read the precautions given in 'Safety first!' at the start of this manual.

✔ Make sure that the battery tray is in good condition, and that the clamp is tight. Corrosion on the tray, retaining clamp and the battery itself can be removed with a solution of water and baking soda. Thoroughly rinse all cleaned areas with water. Any metal parts damaged by corrosion should be covered with a zinc-based primer, then painted.

✔ Periodically (approximately every three months), check the charge condition of the battery, as described in Chapter 5A, Section 3.

✔ If the battery is flat, and you need to jump start your vehicle, see *Roadside repairs*.

1 The battery is located on the right-hand side of the luggage compartment. Lift the carpet and remove the battery cover (where fitted).

2 Check the tightness of battery clamps to ensure good electrical connections ...

HAYNES HiNT *Battery corrosion can be kept to a minimum by applying a layer of petroleum jelly to the clamps and terminals after they are reconnected.*

3 ... you should not be able to move them. Also check each cable for cracks and frayed conductors.

4 If corrosion (white, fluffy deposits) is evident, remove the cables from the battery terminals, clean them with a small wire brush, then refit them. Automotive stores sell a tool for cleaning the battery post ...

5 ... as well as the battery cable clamps.

Electrical systems

✔ Check all external lights and the horn. Refer to Chapter 12 Section 2 for details if any of the circuits are found to be inoperative.

✔ Visually check all accessible wiring connectors, harnesses and retaining clips for security, and for signs of chafing or damage.

 If you need to check your brake lights and indicators unaided, back up to a wall or garage door and operate the lights. The reflected light should show if they are working properly.

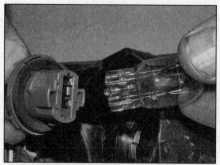

1 If a single indicator light, brake light or headlight has failed, it is likely that a bulb has blown and will need to be renewed. Refer to Chapter 12, Section 5 for details. If both brake lights have failed, it is possible that the switch has failed (see Chapter 9, Section 16).

2 If more than one indicator light or tail light has failed check that a fuse has not blown or that there is a fault in the circuit (see Chapter 12, Section 2). The fuses are located in the fusebox under the driver's side of the facia …

3 … and on the right-hand side of the engine compartment. Details of the circuits protected by the fuses are shown on the fusebox cover.

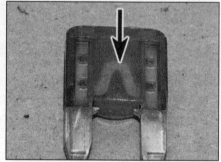

4 To renew a blown fuse, simply pull it out using the tweezers clipped to the fusebox, and fit a new fuse of the correct rating (see Chapter 12, Section 3). Examine the 'bridge' between the fuse terminals. If the fuse blows again, it is important that you find out why – a complete checking procedure is given in Chapter 12, Section 2.

Lubricants and fluids

Engine . . . . 10W/40 multigrade semi-synthetic or synthetic oil
to specification ACEA A3/B4

Cooling system . . . . Ethylene glycol based antifreeze

Manual transmission oil . . . . 75W/90 GL4 or GL5

Final drive unit oil . . . . SAE 90 GL5

Brake and clutch fluid . . . . Hydraulic fluid to DOT 4

Power steering fluid . . . . Dexron II

Tyre pressures

The tyre pressures are given on a label affixed to the rear edge of the driver's door.

Chapter 1
Routine maintenance and servicing

Contents

Degrees of difficulty

| **Easy,** suitable for novice with little experience | **Fairly easy,** suitable for beginner with some experience | **Fairly difficult,** suitable for competent DIY mechanic | **Difficult,** suitable for experienced DIY mechanic | **Very difficult,** suitable for expert DIY or professional |

Lubricants and fluids.................................. Refer to end of *Weekly checks* on page 0•17

Capacities

Engine oil (including filter)
1.6 litre engines .... 3.7 litres
1.8 litre engines .... 3.8 litres

Cooling system
All models) .... 6.0 litres

Manual transmission
5-speed .... 2.0 litres
6-speed .... 1.8 litres

Final drive
1.6 litre engines:
  1993 and earlier models................................ 0.65 litres
  1994-on models .... 1.0 litre
1.8 litre engines .... 1.0 litre

Fuel tank
1997 and earlier models.................................. 45 litres
1998-on models.. 50 litres

Engine

Auxiliary drivebelt deflection:	**New belt**	**Used belt**
1997 and earlier models....................	8.0 to 9.0 mm	9.0 to 10.0 mm
1998-on models:		
Alternator belt....................	5.5 to 7.0 mm	6.0 to 7.5 mm
Power steering/air conditioning compressor	8.0 to 9.0 mm	9.0 to 10.0 mm
Valve clearances 1998-on only (cold):	**Inlet**	**Exhaust**
1.6 litre engines	0.17 to 0.23 mm	0.27 to 0.33 mm
1.8 litre engines	0.18 to 0.24 mm	0.28 to 0.34 mm

Cooling system
Antifreeze mixture (50% antifreeze) .... Protection down to –35ºC
Note: *Refer to antifreeze manufacturer for latest recommendations.*

Ignition system
Ignition timing... 10° ± 1° BTDC @ idle speed
Spark plugs .... Consult your dealer or motor factor
Spark plug gap... 1.0 to 1.1 mm

Remote control
Battery type CR2025

Clutch pedal
Overall pedal height (with carpet)......................... 175 to 185 mm
Freeplay .... 0.6 to 3.1 mm
Disengagement height (with carpet) – minimum .... 68 mm

Brakes
Brake pad minimum thickness:
  Except sports suspension .... 1.0 mm
  Sports suspension .... 2.0 mm

Torque wrench settings

	Nm	lbf ft
Final drive:		
Filler/level plug	44	32
Drain plug......................	44	32
Rear reinforcement frame bolts:		
1998-on	65	48
2000-on	105	77
Roadwheel nuts	110	81
Spark plugs	20	15
Sump drain plug......................	35	26
Transmission oil drain plug:		
5-speed......................	44	32
6-speed......................	35	26
Transmission oil filler/level plug	35	26

The maintenance intervals in this manual are provided with the assumption that you, not the dealer, will be carrying out the work. These are the minimum maintenance intervals recommended by us for vehicles driven daily. If you wish to keep your vehicle in peak condition at all times, you may wish to perform some of these procedures more often. We encourage frequent maintenance, because it enhances the efficiency, performance and resale value of your vehicle.

When the vehicle is new, it should be serviced by a dealer service department (or other workshop recognised by the vehicle manufacturer as providing the same standard of service) in order to preserve the warranty. The vehicle manufacturer may reject warranty claims if you are unable to prove that servicing has been carried out as and when specified, using only original equipment parts or parts certified to be of equivalent quality.

Every 250 miles or weekly
☐ Refer to *Weekly checks*

Every 6000 miles or 6 months – whichever comes first
☐ Renew the engine oil and filter (Section 3).
Note: *Oil and filter changes are good for the engine and we recommend that the oil and filter are renewed frequently, especially if the vehicle is used on a lot of short journeys*
☐ Check and adjust the brake pedal height (Section 4).
☐ Check and adjust the clutch pedal height (Section 5).

Every 12 000 miles or 12 months – whichever comes first
In addition to the items listed above, carry out the following:
☐ Check the condition and tension of the auxiliary drivebelt (Section 6).
☐ Hose and fluid leak check (Section 7).
☐ Check the brake pads for wear (Section 8).
☐ Check the condition of the driveshaft gaiters (Section 9).
☐ Check the steering and suspension components for condition and security (Section 10).
☐ Check the underbody and sealant for damage (Section 11).
☐ Check the condition of the exhaust system and its mountings (Section 12).
☐ Check and if necessary adjust the handbrake (Section 13).
☐ Lubricate all hinges and locks (Section 14).
☐ Carry out a road test (Section 15).

Every 24 000 miles or 2 years – whichever comes first
In addition to the items listed above, carry out the following:
☐ Renew the spark plugs and check the condition of the HT leads (Section 16).
☐ Check the engine management system (Section 17).
☐ Renew the brake fluid (Section 18).
☐ Renew the engine coolant (Section 19).
☐ Renew the air filter element (Section 20).
☐ Check the PCV valve (Section 21).
☐ Check the evaporative loss system (Section 22).
☐ Renew the fuel filter (Section 23).
☐ Check the manual transmission oil level (Section 24).
☐ Renew the final drive fluid (Section 25).

Every 48 000 miles or 4 years – whichever comes first
In addition to the items listed above, carry out the following:
☐ Renew the timing belt (Section 26)*.
☐ Renew manual transmission oil (Section 24).
☐ Renew the remote control battery (Section 27).
☐ Check the valve clearances (Section 28).
* **Note:** *Although the normal interval for timing belt renewal is 54 000 miles, it is strongly recommended that the belt is renewed at 48 000 miles. The actual belt renewal interval is therefore very much up to the individual owner, but bear in mind that severe engine damage will result if the belt breaks.*

Underbonnet view – 1997 and earlier

1 Engine oil level dipstick
2 Engine oil filler cap
3 Air cleaner housing
4 Washer fluid reservoir
5 Carbon canister
6 Coolant expansion tank
7 Brake fluid reservoir
8 Radiator cap
9 Mass airflow sensor
10 Power steering fluid level dipstick
11 Engine compartment fusebox
12 Headlight manual retractor

Underbonnet view – 2000-on shown, 1998 to 2000 similar

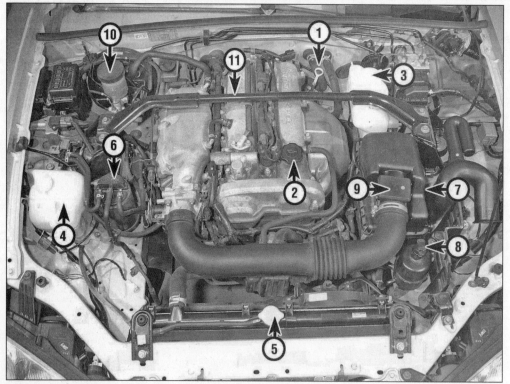

1 Engine oil level dipstick
2 Engine oil filler cap
3 Washer fluid reservoir
4 Coolant expansion tank
5 Radiator cap
6 Carbon canister
7 Air cleaner housing
8 Power steering fluid level dipstick
9 Mass airflow meter
10 Brake fluid reservoir
11 Engine crossbrace

Front underbody view

1 Engine oil drain plug
2 Radiator drain plug
3 Steering rack
4 Suspension lower arm
5 Brake caliper
6 Transmission undershield
7 Anti-roll bar
8 Auxiliary drivebelt(s)

Rear underbody view

1 Final drive fluid drain plug
2 Power plant frame
3 Driveshaft
4 Handbrake cable
5 Reinforcement frame
6 Fuel filter
7 Shock absorber
8 Suspension lower arm

1 Introduction

This Chapter is designed to help the home mechanic maintain his/her vehicle for safety, economy, long life and peak performance.

The Chapter contains a master maintenance schedule, and Sections dealing specifically with each task in the schedule. Visual checks, adjustments, component renewal and other helpful items are included. Refer to the accompanying illustrations of the engine compartment and the underside of the vehicle for the locations of the various components.

Servicing your vehicle in accordance with the mileage/time maintenance schedule and the following Sections will provide a planned maintenance programme, which should result in a long and reliable service life. This is a comprehensive plan, so maintaining some items but not others at the specified service intervals, will not produce the same results.

As you service your vehicle, you will discover that many of the procedures can, and should, be grouped together, because of the particular procedure being performed, or because of the proximity of two otherwise unrelated components to one another. For example, if the vehicle is raised for any reason, the exhaust can be inspected at the same time as the suspension and steering components.

The first step in this maintenance programme is to prepare yourself before the actual work begins. Read through all the Sections relevant to the work to be carried out, then make a list and gather all the parts and tools required. If a problem is encountered, seek advice from a parts specialist, or a dealer service department.

2 Regular maintenance

1 If, from the time the vehicle is new, the routine maintenance schedule is followed closely, and frequent checks are made of fluid levels and high-wear items, as suggested throughout this manual, the engine will be kept in relatively good running condition, and the need for additional work will be minimised.

2 It is possible that there will be times when the engine is running poorly due to the lack of regular maintenance. This is even more likely if a used vehicle, which has not received regular and frequent maintenance checks, is purchased. In such cases, additional work may need to be carried out, outside of the regular maintenance intervals.

3 If engine wear is suspected, a compression test (refer to Chapter 2A, Section 2) will provide valuable information regarding the overall performance of the main internal components. Such a test can be used as a basis to decide on the extent of the work to be carried out. If, for example, a compression test indicates serious internal engine wear, conventional maintenance as described in this Chapter will not greatly improve the performance of the engine, and may prove a waste of time and money, unless extensive overhaul work is carried out first.

4 The following series of operations are those usually required to improve the performance of a generally poor-running engine:

Primary operations

a) Clean, inspect and test the battery (See 'Weekly checks').
b) Check all the engine-related fluids (See 'Weekly checks').
c) Check the condition and tension of the auxiliary drivebelt(s) (Section 6).
d) Check the condition of all hoses, and check for fluid leaks (Section 7).
e) Renew the spark plugs (Section 16).
f) Inspect the ignition HT leads (Section 16).
g) Check the condition of the air filter, and renew if necessary (Section 20).

5 If the above operations do not prove fully effective, carry out the following secondary operations:

Secondary operations

All items listed under *Primary operations*, plus the following:

a) Check the charging system (Chapter 5A, Section 5).
b) Check the ignition system (Chapter 5B, Section 2).
c) Check the fuel system (Chapter 4A, Section 8).
d) Renew the ignition HT leads (Section 16).

Every 6000 miles or 6 months

3 Engine oil and filter renewal

1 Frequent oil and filter changes are the most important preventative maintenance which can be undertaken by the DIY owner. As engine oil ages, it becomes diluted and contaminated, which leads to premature engine wear.

2 Before starting this procedure, gather all the necessary tools and materials. Also make sure that you have plenty of clean rags and newspapers handy to mop-up any spills. Ideally, the engine oil should be warm, as it will drain better, and any impurities suspended in the oil will be removed with it. Take care, however, not to touch the exhaust or any other hot parts of the engine when working under the vehicle. To avoid any possibility of scalding, and to protect yourself from possible skin irritants and other harmful contaminants in used engine oils, it is advisable to wear gloves when carrying out this work. Access to the underside of the vehicle will be greatly improved if it can be raised on a lift, driven onto ramps, or jacked up and supported on axle stands (see *Jacking and vehicle support*). Whichever method is chosen, make sure that the vehicle remains level, or if it is at an angle, that the drain plug is at the lowest point.

3 Slacken the drain plug about half a turn **(see illustrations)**. Position the draining container under the drain plug, then remove the plug completely. Renew the sealing washer.

4 Allow some time for the old oil to drain, noting that it may be necessary to reposition the container as the oil flow slows to a trickle.

5 After all the oil has drained, wipe off the drain plug with a clean rag, then clean the area around the drain plug opening and refit the plug with a new sealing washer. Tighten the plug to the specified torque.

6 Move the container into position under the oil filter, which is located on the right-hand side of the engine.

3.3a Engine oil drain plug (arrowed)

3.3b Renew the drain plug sealing washer (arrowed)

3.7 The oil filter is located on the right-hand side of the engine

3.9 Lubricate the sealing ring with clean engine oil

7 Using an oil filter removal tool if necessary, slacken the filter initially, then unscrew it by hand the rest of the way **(see illustration)**. Empty the oil in the old filter into the container.

8 Use a clean rag to remove all oil, dirt and sludge from the filter sealing area on the engine. Check the old filter to make sure that the rubber sealing ring has not stuck to the engine. If it has, carefully remove it.

9 Apply a light coating of clean engine oil to the sealing ring on the new filter, then screw it into position on the engine **(see illustration)**. Tighten the filter firmly by hand only – **do not** use any tools.

10 Remove the old oil and all tools from under the car then lower it to the ground (if applicable).

11 Withdraw the dipstick, and remove the oil filler cap from the cylinder head cover. Fill the engine, using the correct grade and type of oil (see *Lubricants and fluids*). An oil can spout or funnel may help to reduce spillage. Pour in half the specified quantity of oil first, then wait a few minutes for the oil to run to the sump. Continue adding oil a small quantity at a time until the level is up to the MAX mark on the dipstick. Refit the filler cap.

12 Start the engine and run it for a few minutes; check for leaks around the oil filter seal and the sump drain plug. Note that there may be a delay of a few seconds before the oil pressure warning light goes out when the engine is first started, as the oil circulates through the engine oil galleries and the new oil filter before the pressure builds-up. Where applicable, refit the engine undershield.

13 Switch off the engine, and wait a few minutes for the oil to settle in the sump once more. With the new oil circulated and the filter completely full, recheck the level on the dipstick, and add more oil as necessary.

14 Dispose of the used engine oil and filter safely, referring to *General repair procedures* in the Reference Chapter. Do not discard the old filter with domestic household waste. The facility for waste oil disposal provided by many local council refuse tips generally has a filter receptacle alongside.

4 Brake pedal check and adjustment

1 The brake pedal height checking and adjustment procedure is described in Chapter 9, Section 11.

5 Clutch pedal check and adjustment

1 To check the clutch pedal height, measure the horizontal distance from the centre of the clutch pedal surface to the carpet or pad on the bulkhead **(see illustration)**. The height should be within the limits listed in this Chapter's Specifications. If it isn't, it must be adjusted.

2 To adjust the clutch pedal height, disconnect the clutch switch electrical connector.

3 Loosen the switch locknut **(see illustration 5.1)**.

4 Turn the clutch switch until the pedal height is correct.

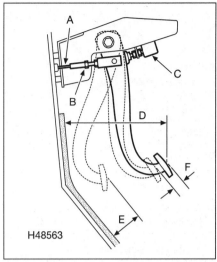

H48563

5.1 Clutch pedal height adjustment details

A Pushrod	E Disengagement
B Locknut	height
C Clutch switch	F Pedal free play
D Pedal height	

5 Tighten the locknut and recheck the pedal height to verify it is correct. **Note:** *Whenever the pedal height is adjusted it will most likely be necessary to adjust the freeplay because increasing or decreasing pedal height will cause a similar change in pedal freeplay.*

6 Check the clutch pedal freeplay by lightly pushing the clutch pedal down and, with a small steel ruler, measure the distance that it moves freely before the clutch resistance is felt **(see illustration 5.1)**. The freeplay should be within the limits listed in this Chapter's Specifications. If it isn't, it must be adjusted.

7 To adjust the clutch pedal freeplay, loosen the locknut on the pedal end of the clutch pushrod **(see illustration 5.1)**.

8 Turn the pushrod until pedal freeplay is correct.

9 Tighten the locknut and recheck the pedal freeplay to verify it is correct.

10 Complete this procedure by checking the disengagement height (from the upper surface of the pedal to the floor carpet). The disengagement height should be equal to or more than the minimum listed in the Specifications.

Every 12 000 miles or 12 months

6 Auxiliary drivebelt(s) – checking, adjustment and renewal

Checking

1 Using a socket on the crankshaft pulley bolt, rotate the crankshaft so that the full length of the drivebelt(s) can be examined.

Look for cracks, splitting and fraying on the surface of the belt(s); check also for signs of glazing (shiny patches) and separation of the belt plies. If damage or wear is visible, the belt should be renewed.

2 If the condition of the belt is satisfactory, check the drivebelt tension as described below.

3 To check the tension of each belt in accordance with factory specifications, apply

moderate pressure (10 kg or 22 pounds) midway between the specified pulleys. Measure the deflection **(see illustration)** and compare your measurement to the specified drivebelt deflection for either a used or new belt. **Note:** *A 'used' belt is defined as any belt which has been operated more than five minutes on the engine; a 'new' belt is one that has been used for less than five minutes.*

6.3 Measure the belt deflection, applying moderate hand pressure

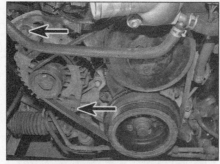

6.4a Slacken the alternator mounting bolts (arrowed)

6.4b Alternator drivebelt adjusting bolt (arrowed)

6.5a The lower steering pump bolt is accessible through the slot in the pulley

6.5b Power steering pump drivebelt adjusting bolt (arrowed)

Adjustment

4 If the alternator/coolant pump belt must be adjusted, slacken the alternator mounting bolts located above and under the alternator. On some models, the lower bolt is inserted from the rear. Tighten the adjusting bolt to push the alternator away from the engine and tighten the belt **(see illustrations)**. Tighten the mounting bolts. Measure the belt deflection in accordance with the above method. Repeat this step until the drivebelt is properly adjusted.

5 Adjust the power steering pump belt by slackening the bolt and two locknuts that secure the pump to the engine. Adjust the belt tension by turning the adjusting bolt **(see illustrations)**. Tighten the adjusting locknut and the pump bolt and nut. Measure the belt deflection in accordance with the above method. Repeat this step until the drivebelt is properly adjusted.

6 Vehicles that do not have power steering but are equipped with air conditioning have an idler pulley installed above the compressor. Loosen the idler pulley locknut and turn the adjusting bolt to tension the drivebelt. Tighten the locknut. Measure the belt deflection in accordance with the above method. Repeat this step until the drivebelt is properly adjusted.

Renewal

7 To renew a belt, follow the above procedures to loosen the drivebelt enough to slip the belt off the crankshaft pulley and remove it. If you are renewing the alternator/coolant pump belt,

you will have to remove the power steering and/or air conditioning belt first because of the way they are arranged on the crankshaft pulley. Because of this and because belts tend to wear out more or less together, it is a good idea to renew both belts at the same time. Mark each belt and its appropriate pulley groove so the new belts can be installed in their proper positions.

8 Take the old belts to the parts store in order to make a direct comparison for length, width and design.

9 After renewing the drivebelt, make sure that it fits properly. When installing a multi-ribbed belt, make sure that it is centred – it must not overlap either edge of the pulley.

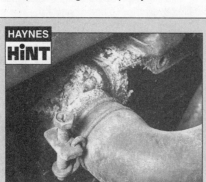

A leak in the cooling system will usually show up as white- or antifreeze-coloured deposits on the area adjoining the leak.

7 Hose and fluid leak check

1 Visually inspect the engine joint faces, gaskets and seals for any signs of water or oil leaks. Pay particular attention to the areas around the camshaft cover, cylinder head, oil filter and sump joint faces. Bear in mind that, over a period of time, some very slight seepage from these areas is to be expected – what you are really looking for is any indication of a serious leak. Should a leak be found, renew the offending gasket or oil seal by referring to the appropriate Chapters in this manual.

2 Also check the security and condition of all the engine-related pipes and hoses. Ensure that all cable-ties or securing clips are in place and in good condition. Clips which are broken or missing can lead to chafing of the hoses, pipes or wiring, which could cause more serious problems in the future.

3 Carefully check the radiator hoses and heater hoses along their entire length. Renew any hose which is cracked, swollen or deteriorated. Cracks will show up better if the hose is squeezed. Pay close attention to the hose clips that secure the hoses to the cooling system components. Hose clips can pinch and puncture hoses, resulting in cooling system leaks.

4 Inspect all the cooling system components (hoses, joint faces etc.) for leaks. A leak in the cooling system will usually show up as white- or antifreeze-coloured deposits on the area adjoining the leak **(see Haynes Hint)**. Where any problems of this nature are found on system components, renew the component or gasket with reference to Chapter 3.

5 With the vehicle raised, inspect the fuel tank and filler neck for punctures, cracks and other damage. The connection between the filler neck and tank is especially critical. Sometimes a rubber filler neck or connecting hose will leak due to loose retaining clamps or deteriorated rubber.

6 Carefully check all rubber hoses and metal fuel lines leading away from the fuel tank. Check for loose connections, deteriorated hoses, crimped lines, and other damage.

Pay particular attention to the vent pipes and hoses, which often loop up around the filler neck and can become blocked or crimped. Follow the lines to the front of the vehicle, carefully inspecting them all the way. Renew damaged sections as necessary.

7 From within the engine compartment, check the security of all fuel hose attachments and pipe unions, and inspect the fuel hoses and vacuum hoses for kinks, chafing and deterioration.

8 Brake pad check

1 Firmly apply the handbrake, then jack up the front or rear of the car and support it securely on axle stands (see *Jacking and vehicle support*). Remove the roadwheels.

2 Using a steel rule, measure the thickness of the friction material of the brake pads on both front brakes. Compare the measurement obtained with that given in the Specifications **(see illustration)**.

3 For a comprehensive check, the brake pads should be removed and cleaned. The operation of the caliper can then also be checked, and the condition of the brake disc itself can be fully examined on both sides. Refer to Chapter 9 for further information.

4 If any pad's friction material is worn to the specified thickness or less, *all four pads must be renewed as a set.* Refer to Chapter 9, Section 4 or 5.

5 On completion refit the roadwheels and lower the car to the ground.

9 Driveshaft gaiter check

1 Raise the rear of the vehicle and support it securely on axle stands (see *Jacking and vehicle support*). Slowly rotate the roadwheel, and inspect the condition of the outer constant velocity (CV) joint rubber gaiters, squeezing the gaiters to open out the folds. Check for signs of cracking, splits or deterioration of the rubber, which may allow the grease to escape, and lead to water and grit entry into the joint. Also check the security and condition of the retaining clips. Repeat these checks on the inner CV joints **(see illustration)**. If any damage or deterioration is found, the gaiters should be renewed (see Chapter 8, Section 5).

2 At the same time, check the general condition of the CV joints themselves by first holding the driveshaft and attempting to rotate the wheel. Repeat this check by holding the inner joint and attempting to rotate the driveshaft. Any appreciable movement indicates wear in the joints, wear in the driveshaft splines, or a loose driveshaft retaining nut.

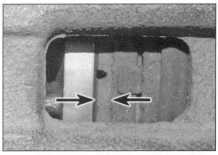

8.2 Measure the thickness of the pad friction material (arrowed) through the aperture in the caliper body

10 Steering and suspension check

Front suspension and steering

1 Firmly apply the handbrake, then jack up the front of the car and support it securely on axle stands (see *Jacking and vehicle support*).

2 Inspect the balljoint dust covers and the steering rack and pinion gaiters for splits, chafing or deterioration **(see illustration)**. Any wear of these will cause loss of lubricant, together with dirt and water entry, resulting in rapid deterioration of the balljoints or steering gear.

3 Grasp the roadwheel at the 12 o'clock and 6 o'clock positions, and try to rock it **(see illustration)**. Very slight free play may be felt, but if the movement is appreciable, further investigation is necessary to determine the source. Continue rocking the wheel while an assistant depresses the footbrake. If the movement is now eliminated or significantly reduced, it is likely that the hub bearings are at fault. If the free play is still evident with the footbrake depressed, then there is wear in the suspension joints or mountings.

4 Now grasp the wheel at the 9 o'clock and 3 o'clock positions, and try to rock it as before. Any movement felt now may again be caused by wear in the hub bearings or the steering track rod balljoints. If the inner or outer balljoint is worn, the visual movement will be obvious.

5 Using a large screwdriver or flat bar, check

10.2 Check the condition of the steering rack rubber gaiters

9.1 Check the condition of the driveshaft CV joint rubber gaiters

for wear in the suspension mounting bushes by levering between the relevant suspension component and its attachment point. Some movement is to be expected as the mountings are made of rubber, but excessive wear should be obvious. Also check the condition of any visible rubber bushes, looking for splits, cracks or contamination of the rubber.

6 With the car standing on its wheels, have an assistant turn the steering wheel back-and-forth about an eighth of a turn each way. There should be very little, if any, lost movement between the steering wheel and roadwheels. If this is not the case, closely observe the joints and mountings previously described, but in addition check the steering column universal joints for wear, and the rack and pinion steering gear itself.

Strut/shock absorber check

7 Check for any signs of fluid leakage around the suspension strut/shock absorber body, or from the rubber gaiter around the piston rod. Should any fluid be noticed, the suspension strut/shock absorber is defective internally, and should be renewed. **Note:** *Suspension struts/shock absorbers should always be renewed in pairs on the same axle.*

8 The efficiency of the suspension strut/shock absorber may be checked by bouncing the vehicle at each corner. Generally speaking, the body will return to its normal position and stop after being depressed. If it rises and returns on a rebound, the suspension strut/shock absorber is probably suspect. Examine also the suspension strut/shock absorber upper and lower mountings for any signs of wear.

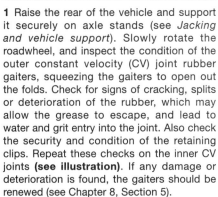

10.3 Check for wear in the hub bearings by grasping the wheel and trying to rock it

12.2 Examine the exhaust rubber mountings for signs of deterioration

11 Underbody sealant check

1 Jack up the front and rear of the car and support it securely on axle stands (see *Jacking and vehicle support*). Alternatively position the car over an inspection pit.
2 Check the underbody, wheel housings and side sills for rust and/or damage to the underbody sealant. If evident, repair as necessary.

12 Exhaust system check

1 With the engine cold (at least an hour after the vehicle has been driven), check the complete exhaust system from the engine to the end of the tailpipe. The exhaust system is most easily checked with the car raised on a hoist, or suitably supported on axle stands (see *Jacking and vehicle support*), so that the exhaust components are readily visible and accessible.
2 Check the exhaust pipes and connections for evidence of leaks, severe corrosion and damage. Make sure that all brackets and mountings are in good condition, and that all relevant nuts and bolts are tight **(see illustration)**. Leakage at any of the joints or in other parts of the system will usually show up as a black sooty stain in the vicinity of the leak.
3 Rattles and other noises can often be traced to the exhaust system, especially the brackets and mountings. Try to move the pipes and silencers. If the components are able to come into contact with the body or suspension parts, secure the system with new mountings. Otherwise separate the joints (if possible) and twist the pipes as necessary to provide additional clearance.

13 Handbrake check and adjustment

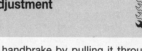

1 Apply the handbrake by pulling it through a maximum of 5 to 7 clicks of the ratchet mechanism and check that this locks the rear wheels, holding the vehicle stationary on an incline. If not, the handbrake mechanism should be adjusted as described in Chapter 9, Section 14.

14 Hinge and lock lubrication

1 Lubricate the hinges of the bonnet, doors and tailgate with a light general-purpose oil. Similarly, lubricate all latches, locks and lock strikers. At the same time, check the security and operation of all the locks, adjusting them if necessary (see Chapter 11).
2 Lightly lubricate the bonnet release mechanism and cable with suitable grease.

15 Road test

Instruments and electrical equipment

1 Check the operation of all instruments and electrical equipment.
2 Make sure that all instruments read correctly, and switch on all electrical equipment in turn, to check that it functions properly.

Steering and suspension

3 Check for any abnormalities in the steering, suspension, handling or road feel.
4 Drive the vehicle, and check that there are no unusual vibrations or noises.
5 Check that the steering feels positive, with no excessive sloppiness, or roughness, and check for any suspension noises when cornering and driving over bumps.

Drivetrain

6 Check the performance of the engine, clutch, transmission and driveshafts.
7 Listen for any unusual noises from the engine, clutch and transmission.
8 Make sure that the engine runs smoothly when idling, and that there is no hesitation when accelerating.
9 Check that, the clutch action is smooth and progressive, that the drive is taken up smoothly, and that the pedal travel is not excessive. Also listen for any noises when the clutch pedal is depressed.
10 Check that all gears can be engaged smoothly without noise, and that the gear lever action is smooth and not abnormally vague or notchy.

Braking system

11 Make sure that the vehicle does not pull to one side when braking, and that the wheels do not lock when braking hard.
12 Check that there is no vibration through the steering when braking.
13 Check that the handbrake operates correctly without excessive movement of the lever, and that it holds the vehicle stationary on a slope.
14 Test the operation of the brake servo unit as follows. With the engine off, depress the footbrake four or five times to exhaust the vacuum. Hold the brake pedal depressed, then start the engine. As the engine starts, there should be a noticeable give in the brake pedal as vacuum builds-up. Allow the engine to run for at least two minutes, and then switch it off. If the brake pedal is depressed now, it should be possible to detect a hiss from the servo as the pedal is depressed. After about four or five applications, no further hissing should be heard, and the pedal should feel considerably harder.

Every 24 000 miles or 2 years

16 Spark plug renewal and ignition system check

Spark plug renewal

1 The correct functioning of the spark plugs is vital for the correct running and efficiency of the engine. It is essential that the plugs fitted are appropriate for the engine. If this type is used and the engine is in good condition, the spark plugs should not need attention between scheduled renewal intervals. Spark plug cleaning is rarely necessary, and should not be attempted unless specialised equipment is available, as damage can easily be caused to the firing ends.

1999 and earlier models

2 To prevent the possibility of mixing up spark plug HT leads, work on one spark plug at a time. Remove the lead and boot from one spark plug. Grasp the boot – not the lead – give it a half twisting motion and pull straight up **(see illustration 16.4)**.

2000-on models

3 Remove the two ignition coils as described in Chapter 5B, Section 3.
4 There are only two spark plug HT leads; the two coils are fitted directly on top of the other two spark plugs. Pull the HT leads and boots

16.4 With a half twisting motion and a straight pull up, disconnect the HT boot/cap from the spark plug – grasp the boot not the lead

16.6 Use a special socket and extension to remove the spark plugs

from the spark plugs, grasping the boot – not the lead **(see illustration)**.

All models

5 If compressed air is available, blow any dirt or foreign material away from the spark plug area before proceeding (a common bicycle pump will also work).

6 Unscrew and remove the spark plug **(see illustration)**.

7 The spark plug electrode gap is of considerable importance as, if it is too large or too small, the size of the spark and its efficiency will be seriously impaired. The gap should be set to the value given in the *Specifications* at the beginning of this Chapter. Note that if the recommended spark plugs are fitted, the electrode gap is pre-set by the manufacturer and should not require adjustment.

8 To set the gap, measure it with a feeler blade and then bend open, or closed, the outer plug electrode until the correct gap is achieved. The centre electrode should never be bent, as this may crack the insulator and cause plug failure, if nothing worse. If using feeler blades, the gap is correct when the appropriate-size blade is a firm sliding fit **(see illustration)**.

9 Special spark plug electrode gap adjusting tools are available from most motor accessory shops, or from some spark plug manufacturers **(see illustration)**.

10 Prior to installation, it's a good idea to coat the spark plug threads with anti-seize compound. Also, it's often difficult to insert spark plugs into their holes without cross-threading them. To avoid this possibility, fit a short piece of 8 mm ID rubber hose over the end of the spark plug **(see illustration)**. The flexible hose acts as a universal joint to help align the plug with the plug hole. Should the plug begin to cross-thread, the hose will slip on the spark plug, preventing thread damage. Tighten the plug to the specified torque.

11 Attach the plug lead/boot to the new spark plug, again using a twisting motion on

16.8 Checking the spark plug gap using feeler gauges

the boot until it is firmly seated on the end of the spark plug.

12 Follow the above procedure for the remaining spark plugs, renewing them one at a time to prevent mixing up the spark plug HT leads.

13 After fitting the spark plugs, refit the HT leads/ignition coils as applicable.

Ignition system check

> ⚠ *Warning: Due to the high voltages produced by the electronic ignition system, extreme care must be taken when working on the system with the ignition switched on. Persons with surgically-implanted cardiac pacemaker devices should keep well clear of the ignition circuits, components and test equipment.*

14 The spark plug (HT) leads should be checked whenever new spark plugs are fitted.

15 Pull the leads from the plugs by gripping the end fitting, not the lead, otherwise the lead connection may be fractured.

16 Check inside the end fitting for signs of corrosion, which will look like a white crusty powder. Push the end fitting back onto the spark plug, ensuring that it is a tight fit on the plug. If not, remove the lead again and use pliers to carefully crimp the metal connector inside the end fitting until it fits securely on the end of the spark plug.

16.9 Special tools are available to adjust the spark plug electrode gap

17 Using a clean rag, wipe the entire length of the lead to remove any built-up dirt and grease. Once the lead is clean, check for burns, cracks and other damage. Do not bend the lead excessively, nor pull the lead lengthways – the conductor inside might break.

18 Disconnect the other end of the lead from the ignition coil. Again, pull only on the end fitting. Check for corrosion and a tight fit in the same manner as the spark plug end. Refit the lead securely on completion.

19 Check the remaining leads one at a time, in the same way.

16.10 Use a length of rubber/plastic hose over the spark plug to start them in the holes, without risk of damage from cross-threading

19.2 The radiator drain plug (arrowed) is accessible through an opening in the engine undershield

20 If new spark plug (HT) leads are required, purchase a set for your specific car and engine.
21 Even with the ignition system in first-class condition, some engines may still occasionally experience poor starting attributable to damp ignition components. To disperse moisture, a water-dispersant aerosol should be liberally applied.

17 Engine management system check

1 This check is part of the manufacturer's maintenance schedule, and involves testing the engine management system using special dedicated test equipment. Such testing will allow the test equipment to read any fault codes stored in the electronic control unit memory.
2 Unless a fault is suspected, this test is not essential, although it should be noted that it is recommended by the manufacturers.
3 If access to suitable test equipment is not possible, make a thorough check of all ignition, fuel and emission control system components, hoses, and wiring, for security and obvious signs of damage. Further details of the fuel system, emission control system and ignition system can be found in the relevant parts of Chapter 4A, 4B and 5B.

18 Brake fluid renewal

⚠️ *Warning: Brake hydraulic fluid can harm your eyes and damage painted surfaces, so use extreme caution when handling and pouring it. Do not use fluid that has been standing open for some time, as it absorbs moisture from the air. Excess moisture can cause a dangerous loss of braking effectiveness.*

1 The procedure is similar to that for the bleeding of the hydraulic system as described in Chapter 9, Section 2, except that the brake fluid reservoir should be emptied by using a clean poultry baster or similar before starting, and allowance should be made for the old

fluid to be expelled when bleeding a section of the circuit.
2 Working as described in Chapter 9, Section 2, open the first bleed screw in the sequence, and pump the brake pedal gently until nearly all the old fluid has been emptied from the master cylinder reservoir.
3 Top-up to the MAX level with new fluid, and continue pumping until only the new fluid remains in the reservoir, and new fluid can be seen emerging from the bleed screw. Tighten the screw, and top the reservoir level up to the MAX level line.
4 Work through all the remaining bleed screws in the sequence until new fluid can be seen at all of them. Be careful to keep the master cylinder reservoir topped-up to above the MIN level at all times, or air may enter the system and greatly increase the length of the task.
5 When the operation is complete, check that all bleed screws are securely tightened, and that their dust caps are refitted. Wash off all traces of spilt fluid, and recheck the master cylinder reservoir fluid level.
6 Check the operation of the brakes before taking the car on the road.

19 Coolant renewal

⚠️ *Warning: Wait until the engine is cold before starting this procedure. Do not allow antifreeze to come in contact with your skin, or with the painted surfaces of the vehicle. Rinse off spills immediately with plenty of water. Never leave antifreeze lying around in an open container, or in a puddle in the driveway or on the garage floor. Children and pets are attracted by its sweet smell, but antifreeze can be fatal if ingested.*

Cooling system draining

1 With the engine completely cold, cover the radiator cap with a wad of rag, and slowly turn the cap anti-clockwise to relieve the pressure in the cooling system (a hissing sound may be heard). Wait until any pressure remaining in the system is released, then continue to turn the cap until it can be removed.
2 Position a suitable container beneath the radiator drain plug, then completely unscrew the drain plug and allow the coolant to drain into the container **(see illustration)**.
3 Once all the coolant has drained, tighten the drain plugs securely.

Radiator flushing

4 Refer to Chapter 3, Section 3.

Cooling system filling

5 Before attempting to fill the cooling system, make sure that all hoses and clips are in good condition, and that the clips are tight. Note that an antifreeze mixture must be used all year round, to prevent corrosion of the engine components (see below).

6 Place the heater controls in the maximum heat position.
7 Remove the radiator cap, and fill the system by slowly pouring the coolant into the radiator to prevent airlocks from forming.
8 If the coolant is being renewed, begin by pouring in a couple of litres of water, followed by the correct quantity of antifreeze, then top-up with more water. Periodically squeeze the radiator top and bottom hoses to help expel any trapped air in the system.
9 Fill the expansion tank to the MIN or LOW mark.
10 Refit the radiator pressure cap, then start the engine and allow it to idle until it reaches normal operating temperature.
Caution: If the temperature gauge indicates an overheating condition, stop the engine and allow it to cool completely, then recheck the coolant level.
11 Once the engine has warmed up, increase the engine speed to 2500 rpm and hold it there for 5 minutes, then increase the engine speed to 3000 rpm for 5 seconds and allow it to return to idle.
12 Repeat the procedure in Paragraph 11 four times, then stop the engine and allow it to cool completely.
13 Top-up the expansion tank if necessary. Note that the system must be cold before an accurate level is indicated.

Antifreeze mixture

14 The antifreeze should always be renewed at the specified intervals. This is necessary not only to maintain the antifreeze properties, but also to prevent corrosion which would otherwise occur as the corrosion inhibitors become progressively less effective.
15 Always use a monoethylene-glycol based antifreeze of the specified type (see *Lubricants and fluids*). The quantity of antifreeze and levels of protection are indicated in the Specifications.
16 Before adding antifreeze, the cooling system should be completely drained, preferably flushed, and all hoses checked for condition and security.
17 After filling with antifreeze, a label should be attached to the expansion tank, stating the type and concentration of antifreeze used, and the date installed. Any subsequent topping-up should be made with the same type and concentration of antifreeze.
Caution: Do not use engine antifreeze in the windscreen washer system, as it will cause damage to the vehicle paintwork. A screenwash additive should be added to the washer system in the quantities stated on the bottle.

20 Air filter renewal

1 The air filter is located inside a housing on the left front corner of the engine compartment.
2 Remove the bolts or release the clips (as

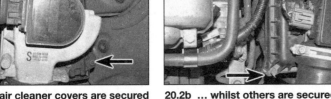

20.2a Some air cleaner covers are secured by bolts (arrowed) ...

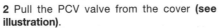

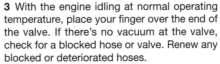

20.2b ... whilst others are secured by clips (arrowed)

20.2c Note the orientation of the filter element

applicable) attaching the air cleaner cover to the housing, then lift the cover up and remove the air filter element **(see illustrations)**.

3 Inspect the outer surface of the filter element. If it is dirty, renew it. If it is only moderately dusty, it can be re-used by blowing it clean from the back to the front surface with compressed air. Because it is a pleated paper type filter, it cannot be washed or oiled. If it cannot be cleaned satisfactorily with compressed air, discard and renew it. While the cover is off, be careful not to drop anything down into the housing.

Caution: Never drive the vehicle with the air cleaner removed. Excessive engine wear could result and backfiring could even cause a fire under the bonnet.

4 Wipe out the inside of the air cleaner housing with a damp cloth.

5 Place the new filter into the air cleaner housing, making sure it seats properly.

6 Refitting of the cover is the reverse of removal.

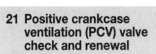

21 Positive crankcase ventilation (PCV) valve check and renewal

1 The PCV valve and hose is located in the cylinder head cover.

2 Pull the PCV valve from the cover **(see illustration)**.

3 With the engine idling at normal operating temperature, place your finger over the end of the valve. If there's no vacuum at the valve, check for a blocked hose or valve. Renew any blocked or deteriorated hoses.

4 Turn off the engine. Remove the PCV valve from the hose. Blow low-pressure air through the valve from the cylinder head cover end. If air will not pass through the valve in this direction, renew it.

22 Evaporative loss system check

1 Refer to Chapter 4B, Section 2, and check that all wiring and hoses are correctly connected to the evaporative loss system components.

23 Fuel filter renewal

1 Disconnect the negative battery cable as described in Chapter 5A, Section 4.

2 Raise the rear of the vehicle and support

21.2 Pull the PCV valve from the cylinder head cover

it securely on axle stands (see *Jacking and vehicle support*). The fuel filter is mounted behind the fuel tank at the right-hand side rear of the vehicle.

3 On models with a rear reinforcement frame, undo the bolts and remove the frame **(see illustration)**.

4 Remove the fuel filter cover **(see illustration)**.

5 Disconnect the fuel hoses from the fuel filter **(see illustrations)**. Be prepared for fuel spillage.

6 Loosen the clamp bolt and remove the old filter from the bracket **(see illustration)**.

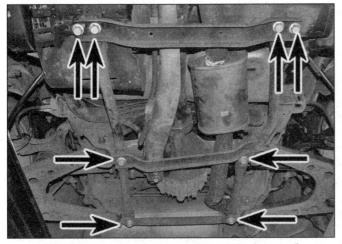

23.3 Reinforcement frame mounting bolts (arrowed)

23.4 Undo the centre screws, prise out the plastic rivets (arrowed) and remove the fuel pump cover

23.5a Disconnect the fuel pipe couplings (arrowed) ...

23.5b ... using a tool which fits into the coupling retainer (arrowed) and spreads apart the clips

23.6 Slacken the fuel filter clamp bolt (arrowed)

7 Note that the inlet and outlet pipes are clearly labelled on their respective ends. Make sure the new filter is installed so that it's facing the proper direction.

8 Installation is the reverse of the removal procedure. Be sure to push the fuel lines all the way onto the fittings, and tighten the reinforcement frame bolts to their specified torque (where applicable).

24 Manual transmission oil level check and renewal

Level check

1 Park the car on a level surface, if possible over an inspection pit or on a ramp. The oil level must be checked before the car is driven, or at least 5 minutes after the engine has been switched off. If the oil is checked immediately after driving the car, some of the oil will remain distributed around the transmission components, resulting in an inaccurate level reading.

2 Wipe clean the area around the filler/level plug, which is situated on the left-hand side of the transmission (see illustration). Unscrew the plug and clean it.

3 The oil level should reach the lower edge of the filler/level hole. A certain amount of oil will have gathered behind the filler/level plug, and will trickle out when it is removed; this does **not**

necessarily indicate that the level is correct. To ensure that a true level is established, wait until the initial trickle has stopped, then add oil as necessary until a trickle of new oil can be seen emerging (see illustration). The level will be correct when the flow ceases; use only good-quality oil of the specified type. Make sure that the vehicle is completely level when checking the level and do not overfill.

4 When the level is correct refit and tighten the plug and wipe away any spilt oil.

Renewal

5 At the specified time intervals, the manual transmission lubricant should be drained and renewed.

6 Before beginning work, purchase the specified lubricant and a new drain plug washer/seal.

7 The oil should be drained immediately after the vehicle has been driven. Hot oil is more effective than cold oil at removing built up sediment. Wear protective gloves.

8 After the vehicle has been driven to warm up the oil, raise the vehicle and support it securely on axle stands (see *Jacking and vehicle support*). Make sure it is safely supported and as level as possible.

9 Place the drain pan under the transmission and slacken the drain plug (see illustration 24.2).

10 Carefully unscrew the drain plug and washer with your fingers. Be careful not to burn yourself on the oil.

11 Allow the oil to drain completely. Clean the drain plug then refit it with a new washer. Tighten the drain plug to the specified torque.

12 With the engine off, add new oil to the transmission through the filler/level plug hole.

13 Refit the filler/level plug and tighten it to the specified torque.

25 Final drive fluid renewal

1 The oil should be drained immediately after the vehicle has been driven. Hot oil is more effective than cold oil at removing built up sediment. Wear protective gloves.

2 After the vehicle has been driven to warm up the oil, raise the vehicle and support it securely on axle stands (see *Jacking and vehicle support*). Make sure it is safely supported and as level as possible.

3 Place the drain pan under the final drive and slacken the drain plug (see illustration).

4 Carefully unscrew the drain plug and washer with your fingers. Be careful not to burn yourself on the oil.

5 Allow the oil to drain completely. Clean the drain plug then refit it with a new washer. Tighten the drain plug to the specified torque.

6 With the engine off, add new oil to the final drive through the filler/level plug hole.

7 Refit the filler/level plug and tighten it to the specified torque.

24.2 Transmission drain and filler/level plugs (arrowed)

24.3 Add oil until it emerges from the filler/level plug hole

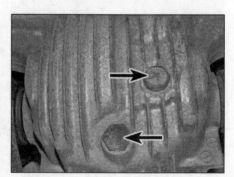

25.3 Final drive oil drain and filler/level plugs (arrowed)

Every 48 000 miles or 4 years

26 Timing belt renewal

Refer to Chapter 2A, Section 6.

27 Remote control battery renewal

1 Using a small flat-bladed screwdriver, prise apart the halves of the key casing **(see illustration)**.
2 Note the orientation of the battery, and remove it from the casing.
3 Insert the new battery into place, with the positive (+) side upwards **(see illustration)**. Avoid touching the battery or the terminals with bare fingers.
4 Snap the 2 halves of the control together, and check for correct operation.

28 Valve clearance check and adjustment

Note: *This procedure only applies to 1998-on models. On models before this date, the valve clearances are automatically maintained by hydraulic adjusters.*
1 The importance of having the valve clearances correctly adjusted cannot be overstressed, as they vitally affect the performance of the engine. The engine must be cold for the check to be accurate. The clearances are checked as follows.
2 Remove all spark plugs as described in Section 16.
3 Remove the cylinder head cover as described in Chapter 2A, Section 4.
4 Each valve clearance must be checked when the high point of the cam lobe is pointing directly upward away from the cam follower.
5 Check the clearances in the firing order 1–3–4–2, No 1 cylinder being at the timing belt end of the engine. This will minimise the amount of crankshaft rotation required.
6 Insert the appropriate feeler blade between the heel of the cam and the cam follower shim of the first valve (see illustration). If necessary alter the thickness of the feeler blade until it is a stiff, sliding fit. Record the thickness, which will, of course, represent the valve clearance for this particular valve.

7 Turn the engine using a socket and bar on the crankshaft pulley centre bolt, then check the second valve clearance and record it.
8 Repeat the operations on all the remaining valves, recording their respective clearances.
9 Remember that the clearance for inlet and exhaust valves differs – see Specifications.
10 Where clearances are incorrect, the particular shim will have to be changed.
11 Remove the camshafts as described in Chapter 2A, Section 8.
12 Carefully remove the relevant shim from the top of the cam follower using a magnet or 'suction' tool.
13 Once the shim is extracted, establish its thickness and change it for a thicker or thinner one to bring the previously recorded clearance within specification. For example, if the measured valve clearance was 1.27 mm too great, a shim thicker by this amount will be required. Conversely, if the clearance was 1.27 mm too small, a shim thinner by this amount will be required.

14 Shims have their thickness (mm) engraved on them; although the engraved side should be fitted so as not to be visible, wear still occurs and often obliterates the number. In this case, measuring their thickness with a metric micrometer is the only method to establish their thickness **(see illustration)**.
15 In practice, if several shims have to be changed, they can often be interchanged, so avoiding the necessity of having to buy more new shims than is necessary, but do not turn the engine with any shims missing.
16 Where no clearance can be measured, even with the thinnest available shim in position, the valve will have to be removed and the end of its stem ground off squarely. This will reduce its overall length by the minimum amount to provide a clearance. This job should be entrusted to an engine reconditioning specialist as it is important to keep the end of the valve stem square.
17 On completion, refit the camshafts as described in Chapter 2A, Section 8, and the spark plugs as described in Section 16.

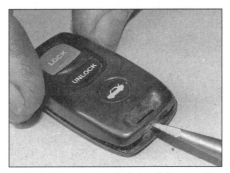

27.1 Prise apart the halves of the remote control

27.3 Insert the new battery with the positive (+) side up

28.6 Insert a feeler gauge between the heel of the camshaft and the follower shim

28.14 Measure the thickness of the shims using a micrometer

BATTERY FOR REMOTE CR2025.

Chapter 2 Part A:
Engine in-car repair procedures

Contents

Degrees of difficulty

Easy, suitable for novice with little experience 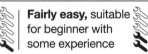	**Fairly easy,** suitable for beginner with some experience	**Fairly difficult,** suitable for competent DIY mechanic	**Difficult,** suitable for experienced DIY mechanic	**Very difficult,** suitable for expert DIY or professional

Specifications

General

Engine code:

1597 cc engine	B6
1840 cc engine	BP

Bore:

1.6 litre	70.0 mm
1.8 litre	83.0 mm

Stroke:

1.6 litre	83.6 mm
1.8 litre	85.0 mm
Direction of engine rotation	Clockwise (viewed from front of vehicle)
No 1 cylinder location	Timing belt end
Firing order	1-3-4-2

Minimum compression pressure:

1.6 litre	9.0 bar

1.8 litre:

Up to 2000 models	8.7 bar
2000-on models	10.0 bar
Maximum compression difference between cylinders	2.0 bar

Compression ratio:

1.6 litre	9.4 : 1
1.6 litre (low power)	9.0 : 1

1.8 litre:

Up to 2000 models	9.0 : 1
2000-on models	10.0 : 1

Valve clearance:

1997 and earlier models	Hydraulic adjusters (maintenance free)
1998-on models	See Chapter 1

Camshafts

Endfloat	0.20 mm max

Hydraulic adjusters:

Adjuster-to-cam lobe clearance:

1997 and earlier models	0.15 mm
1998-on models	See Chapter 1

Lubrication system

Minimum oil pressure:
    Idle speed . . . . 2.0 bar
    3000 rpm . . . . 3.0 bar

Torque wrench settings

	Nm	lbf ft
Big-end bearing cap nuts:		
Stage 1	20	15
Stage 2	52	38
Camshaft bearing cap bolts	14	10
Camshaft sprocket bolts:		
Non-variable valve timing	60	44
Variable valve timing:		
Sprocket bolt	70	52
Blanking cap bolts	5	4
Coolant pump pulley bolts	10	7
Crankshaft rear oil seal housing bolts	11	8
Crankshaft vibration damper/pulley-to-hub/sprocket bolts	15	11
Crankshaft hub/sprocket bolt:*		
1997 and earlier models:		
53 mm overall length	118	87
74 mm overall length	160	118
1998-on models	160	118
Cylinder head bolts	80	59
Cylinder head cover bolts	8	6
Engine mountings nuts	78	58
Engine mounting brackets to cylinder block/sump	50	37
Flywheel bolts	103	76
Intake manifold bracket bolts	50	37
Main bearing cap bolts:		
Stage 1	20	15
Stage 2	59	44
Main bearing support plate bolts	20	15
Oil control valve bolt	10	7
Oil control valve casing bolts	10	7
Oil pick-up pipe	11	8
Oil pressure switch	15	11
Oil pump to cylinder block	25	18
Oil spray nozzle/jet	18	13
Oil supply pipe banjo bolts:		
Upper	40	30
Lower	20	15
Oil supply pipes bracket bolts	10	7
Rear oil seal housing bolts	10	7
Sump	11	8
Sump oil drain plug	35	26
Timing belt cover	10	7
Timing belt idler bolt	50	37
Timing belt tensioner bolt	50	37
Thermostat housing	22	16

* Do not re-use

1 General information

How to use this Chapter

This Chapter describes the repair procedures that can reasonably be carried out on the engine while it remains in the vehicle. If the engine has been removed from the vehicle and is being dismantled as described in Part B, any preliminary dismantling procedures can be ignored.

Note that, while it may be possible physically to overhaul items such as the piston/connecting rod assemblies while the engine is in the car, such tasks are not usually carried out as separate operations. Usually, several additional procedures are required (not to mention the cleaning of components and oilways); for this reason, all such tasks are classed as major overhaul procedures, and are described in Part B of this Chapter.

Part B describes the removal of the engine/transmission from the car, and the full overhaul procedures that can then be carried out.

Engine description

The 4-cylinder engines in this Chapter are of double overhead camshaft 16 valve design, mounted in-line, with the transmission bolted to the rear end. Engine sizes are 1.6 litre or 1.8 litre with various power/torque outputs depending on market/specification. Although different in size, the basic design of the engines is identical, with the exception of 1.8 litre engines from 2000 model year. These engines were equipped with variable intake camshaft timing, where the relationship of the sprocket to the camshaft is varied by hydraulic pressure, controlled by the engine management ECM. The result of this system is improved driveability, with lower emissions.

The two camshafts are driven by a timing belt, itself driven by a sprocket on the front end of the crankshaft. Each camshaft acts directly upon the camshaft followers, which are located directly above their respective valves. On Mk 1 models (1997 and earlier) the cam followers incorporate hydraulic clearance adjusters, whereas after this date, solid followers are fitted with interchangeable shims to adjust the valve clearances.

The crankshaft is supported in five main bearings of the usual shell-type. Endfloat is controlled by thrustwashers fitted each side of No 2 or 5 upper main bearing.

The pistons are selected to be of matching weight, and incorporate fully-floating gudgeon pins retained by circlips, and are cooled by oil jets bolted to the inside of the cylinder block.

The rotor-type oil pump is located at the front of the engine, and is driven directly flats machined in the crankshaft.

Operations with engine in car

The following operations can be carried out without having to remove the engine from the vehicle:

a) Removal and refitting of the cylinder head.
b) Removal and refitting of the belt and sprockets.
c) Removal and refitting of the camshafts.
d) Removal and refitting of the sump.*
e) Removal and refitting of the big-end bearings, connecting rods, and pistons.*
f) Removal and refitting of the oil pump.
g) Renewal of the engine/transmission mountings.
h) Removal and refitting of the flywheel.

* Although in theory it is possible to remove these components with the engine in place, for reasons of access and cleanliness it is recommended that the engine is removed.

2 Compression test – description and interpretation

1 When engine performance is down, or if misfiring occurs which cannot be attributed to the ignition or fuel systems, a compression test can provide diagnostic clues as to the engine's condition. If the test is performed regularly, it can give warning of trouble before any other symptoms become apparent.
2 The engine must be fully warmed-up to normal operating temperature, the battery must be fully charged, and all the spark plugs must be removed (Chapter 1, Section 16). The aid of an assistant will also be required.
3 Disable the ignition system by disconnecting the coil connector, and remove the fuel pump relay (see Chapter 12, Section 3).

4 Fit a compression tester to the No 1 cylinder spark plug hole – the type of tester which screws into the plug thread is to be preferred.
5 Have the assistant fully depress the throttle pedal, and crank the engine on the starter motor. After one or two revolutions, the compression pressure should build up to a maximum figure, and then stabilise. Record the highest reading obtained.
6 Repeat the test on the remaining cylinders, recording the pressure in each.
7 All cylinders should produce very similar pressures; a difference of more than 2 bars between any two cylinders indicates a fault. Note that the compression should build up quickly in a healthy engine; low compression on the first stroke, followed by gradually-increasing pressure on successive strokes, indicates worn piston rings. A low compression reading on the first stroke, which does not build up during successive strokes, indicates leaking valves or a blown head gasket (a cracked head could also be the cause). Deposits on the undersides of the valve heads can also cause low compression.
8 Mazda recommended values for compression pressures are given in the Specifications.
9 If the pressure in any cylinder is low, carry out the following test to isolate the cause. Introduce a teaspoonful of clean oil into that cylinder through its spark plug hole, and repeat the test.
10 If the addition of oil temporarily improves the compression pressure, this indicates that bore or piston wear is responsible for the pressure loss. No improvement suggests that leaking or burnt valves, or a blown head gasket, may be to blame.
11 A low reading from two adjacent cylinders is almost certainly due to the head gasket having blown between them; the presence of coolant in the engine oil will confirm this.
12 If one cylinder is about 20 percent lower than the others and the engine has a slightly rough idle, a worn camshaft lobe could be the cause.
13 If the compression reading is unusually high, the combustion chambers are probably coated with carbon deposits. If this is the case, the cylinder head should be removed and decarbonised.
14 On completion of the test, refit the spark plugs (see Chapter 1, Section 16) and reconnect the ignition coil.

3 Top Dead Centre (TDC) for No 1 piston – locating

Note: *The TDC marks align when No. 1 cylinder is at TDC on its exhaust stroke, as well as when it's on the compression stroke. Piston position must be determined by feeling for compression at the number one spark plug*

hole, then aligning the ignition timing marks as described in Paragraph 6 or 9.

1 Top Dead Centre (TDC) is the highest point in the cylinder that each piston reaches traveling up-and-down as the crankshaft turns. Each piston reaches TDC on the compression stroke and again on the exhaust stroke, but TDC generally refers to piston position on the compression stroke.
2 Positioning the piston(s) at TDC is an essential part of many procedures such as camshaft and timing belt/sprocket removal.
3 Before beginning this procedure, be sure to place the transmission in Neutral and apply the parking brake or block the rear wheels. Also, disable the ignition system by detaching the primary (low voltage) wires from the coil (Chapter 5B, Section 3). Remove the spark plugs (see Chapter 1, Section 16).
4 In order to bring any piston to TDC, the crankshaft must be turned using a socket and ratchet attached to the bolt threaded into the front of the crankshaft. When looking at the front of the engine, normal crankshaft rotation is clockwise.
5 Install a compression gauge in the No. 1 spark plug hole (closest to the front of the vehicle). As the No. 1 piston rises to the top of its compression stroke, compression pressure will be indicated on the gauge.

1999 and earlier models

6 Turn the crankshaft (paragraph 4 above) until the notch in the crankshaft sprocket is aligned with the T on the timing plate (located at the front of the engine) (see illustration).
7 If compression pressure was not indicated on the gauge as the marks were aligning, the number one piston is at TDC on the exhaust stroke.
8 To get the piston to TDC on the compression stroke, turn the crankshaft one complete turn (360-degrees) clockwise. The ignition timing marks should now be aligned, indicating that the number one piston is at TDC on the compression stroke.

2000-on models

9 Remove the timing covers as described in Section 6, then align the notch on the crankshaft sprocket with the mark on the oil pump housing, and the marks on the camshaft

3.6 Align the notch with the T on the plate (arrowed)

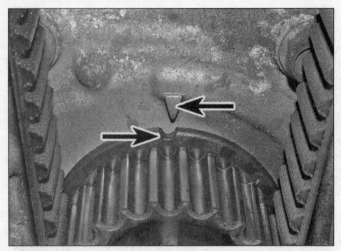

3.9a Align the notch on the crankshaft sprocket with the mark on the oil pump housing (arrowed) ...

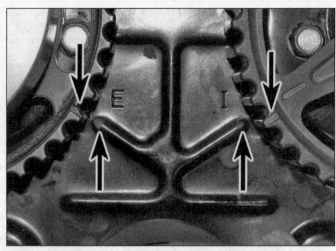

3.9b ... and the marks on the camshaft sprockets with the inner timing belt cover marks (arrowed)

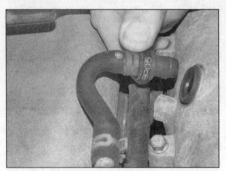

4.2a Pull the PCV valve from the cylinder head cover ...

4.2b ... and disconnect the breather hose

4.4a Undo the banjo bolt at the rear of the cylinder head. Note the copper sealing washers (arrowed)

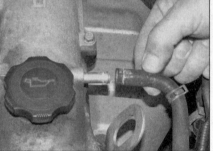

4.4b Oil pipe retaining bolts (arrowed)

4.5 Oil control valve retaining bolts (arrowed)

4.6 Undo the bolts (arrowed) at each end and remove the strut brace

sprockets with the marks on the inner timing belt cover (see illustrations).

All models

10 After the number one piston has been positioned at TDC on the compression stroke, TDC for any of the remaining pistons can be located by turning the crankshaft and following the firing order.

4 Cylinder head cover – removal and refitting

Removal

1 Disconnect the negative cable from the battery as described in Chapter 5A, Section 4.
2 Detach the PCV (Positive Crankcase Ventilation) valve and breather hoses from the cylinder head cover (see illustrations).
3 Remove the ignition coils as described in Chapter 5B, Section 3. On models from 2000, pull the remaining HT caps/leads from the spark plugs.

Models with variable valve timing

4 Slacken the upper and lower banjo bolts, and disconnect the oil supply pipe from the union on the cylinder head, then undo the bolts and remove the pipe on the head (see illustrations). Renew the O-ring seals and sealing washers.
5 Undo the bolts, disconnect the wiring plug, and carefully remove the oil control valve casing assembly from the cylinder head cover (see illustration). Recover the gasket.

All models

6 Undo the bolts and remove the engine compartment strut brace (where fitted) (see illustration).
7 Remove the bolts attaching the cylinder head cover to the cylinder head in the **reverse** order of the tightening sequence (see illustration 4.13).

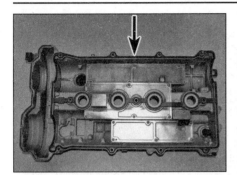

4.10 Ensure the rubber gasket is correctly located in the grooves (arrowed)

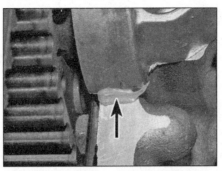

4.11a Apply a little sealant each side of the bearing caps (arrowed) at the front …

4.11b … and rear of the cylinder head

4.13 Cylinder head cover bolts tightening sequence

4.14 Renew the oil control valve gasket

8 Disconnect any tubing or other connected components and move them out of the way, and remove the cylinder head cover. If the cover sticks, knock it loose with a rubber mallet or a hammer and a block of wood. Do not pry between the sealing surfaces.

Refitting

9 The mating surfaces of the housing or cylinder head and cover must be clean when the cover is installed. Carefully use a gasket scraper to remove all traces of sealant and old gasket material – be careful to not gouge the gasket surfaces when cleaning. Then clean the mating surfaces. If there is residue or oil on the mating surfaces when the cover is installed, oil leaks may develop.

10 Examine the cover rubber gasket, and renew it if necessary. Press the gasket into the groove of the cylinder head cover (see illustration).

11 Apply a light coating of silicone sealant to the areas shown (see illustrations).

12 Position the cylinder head cover in place and insert the bolts by hand, starting the threads several turns before using a socket/spanner.

13 Following the recommended sequence (see illustration), tighten the bolts in two or three steps to the torque listed in this Chapter's Specifications.

Models with variable valve timing

14 Using a new gasket, carefully refit the oil control valve casing, ensuring that the O-ring seals on the camshaft cap are not damaged (see illustration). Tighten the retaining bolts to the specified torque evenly.

15 Check that the filter is correctly located within the oil supply pipe where it abuts the control valve casing. The ribs of the filter frame should be located within 15° either side of a line through the pipe mounting flange holes (see illustration).

16 Using new sealing washers, position the oil supply pipes against the cylinder head

cover/cylinder head/cylinder block, but only hand-tighten the retaining bolts at this stage.

17 Starting with the pipe on the cylinder head cover, tighten the retaining bolts to the specified torque, starting at the ends of the pipe, working to the centre.

18 Tighten the lower oil supply pipe banjo bolts to their specified torque in several steps, starting with the lower bolt, then tighten the support bracket bolt (see illustration).

All models

19 The remainder of refitting is a reversal of removal.

20 Run the engine and check for oil leaks.

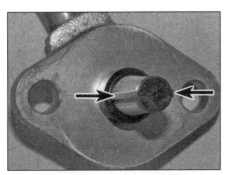

4.15 The filter frame ribs (arrowed) must be in-line with the flange bolt holes

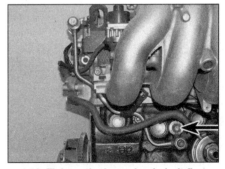

4.18 Tighten the lower banjo bolt first (arrowed)

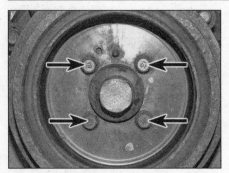

5.2 Crankshaft vibration damper/pulley retaining bolts (arrowed)

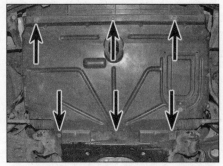

6.3a The engine undershield is retained by screws underneath (arrowed) ...

6.3b ... and each side (arrowed)

5 Crankshaft vibration damper/pulley – removal and refitting

Removal

1 Remove the auxiliary drivebelt(s) as described in Chapter 1, Section 6.

2 Unscrew the 4 securing bolts, and remove the vibration damper/pulley from the hub or sprocket (as applicable). If necessary, counterhold the hub using a socket or spanner on the hub securing bolt **(see illustration)**.

Refitting

3 Refitting is a reversal of removal, applying a little threadlocking compound to the pulley bolts, remembering to tighten all fasteners to the specified torque where given.

6 Timing belt and sprockets – removal, inspection and refitting

Removal

1 Disconnect the battery negative lead as described in Chapter 5A, Section 4.

2 Drain the cooling system as described in Chapter 1, Section 19.

3 Remove the engine undershield (where fitted) **(see illustrations)**.

4 Slacken the clamps, undo the bolt (where applicable) and remove the air intake duct **(see illustrations)**.

5 Disconnect the upper radiator hose and the small coolant hoses from the thermostat housing (see Chapter 3, Section 4).

6 On 1998-on models, remove the crankshaft position sensor as described in Chapter 4A, Section 10.

7 Slacken the coolant pump pulley bolts, and remove the crankshaft pulley as described in Section 5. On some 1.6 litre models (1989 to 1991 with 4 slots in the crankshaft pulley), recover the inner and outer timing belt guide plates **(see illustration)**. On 1998-on models, recover the crankshaft position sensor signal wheel from behind the pulley **(see illustration)**.

8 Remove the coolant pump pulley **(see illustration)**.

9 Remove the cylinder head cover as described in Section 4.

10 Remove the timing belt upper cover, middle cover, and lower cover **(see illustrations)**.

11 Using a socket on the crankshaft sprocket bolt, rotate the crankshaft to align

6.4a Release the clamps (arrowed) and remove the intake ducting

6.4b On some models, the ducting is also retained by a bolt (arrowed)

6.7a Early 1.6 litre models have timing belt guide plates (arrowed) – usually stuck to the crankshaft pulley

6.7b The crankshaft position sensor signal wheel locates over a peg (arrowed) on the rear of the pulley – 1998-on models

6.8 Remove the coolant pump pulley

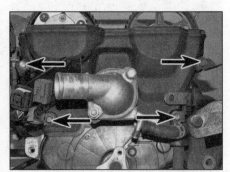

6.10a Timing belt upper cover bolts (arrowed)

the crankshaft and camshaft sprocket timing marks **(see illustrations)**.

12 On all except very early 1.6 litre models with 4 slots in the crankshaft pulley, there are no inner and outer timing belt guide plates fitted. The crankshaft sprocket bolt must be unscrewed, and the hub removed to facilitate belt removal **(see illustrations)**. **Note:** *To prevent the crankshaft from turning, fabricate a holding tool that will bolt to the crankshaft. To improve access to the sprocket bolt, undo the clamp bolts and lower the anti-roll bar (see Chapter 10, Section 7).*

13 If re-using the timing belt (not recommended), paint match marks on the pulley and belt and an arrow indicating direction of travel on the belt.

14 Loosen the timing belt tensioner bolt **(see illustration)**. Cover the thermostat housing with a rag to protect it while prying the tensioner outward with a prybar. Temporarily tighten the tensioner with the spring fully extended.

15 Remove the timing belt.

16 If necessary, remove the crankshaft sprocket using two prybars or screwdrivers placed behind the sprocket to apply even pressure on the sprocket to slide it off the crankshaft. Note the orientation of the key **(see illustration)**.

17 If necessary, remove the camshaft sprocket bolts and remove the sprockets from the camshafts. On models with variable valve timing, undo the 3 screws and remove the blanking cap from the centre of the intake camshaft sprocket actuator. Prevent the

6.10b **Timing belt middle cover bolt (arrowed)**

6.10c **Timing belt lower cover bolts (arrowed)**

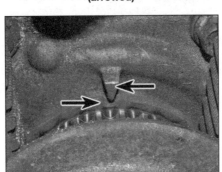

6.11a **Align the notch in the crankshaft sprocket with the lug on the oil pump housing (arrowed)**

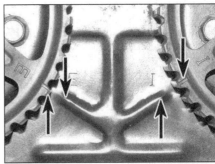

6.11b **Align the notches on the camshaft sprockets rims with the raised sections of the timing belt inner cover (arrowed)**

camshaft from turning by placing a spanner on the hexagon surface on the shaft **(see illustrations)**. **Note:** *On models with variable intake valve timing, in the 'at rest' state, the*

variable pulley mechanism locks itself in its start position. It should not be possible to rotate the sprocket independently of the camshaft.

6.12a **Undo the bolt ...**

6.12b **... and remove the hub**

6.12c **Using a home-made tool to counterhold the pulley hub**

6.14 **Timing belt tensioner bolt (arrowed)**

6.16 **The crankshaft sprocket key must have the tapered end towards the oil pump (arrowed)**

6.17a **Undo the 3 Torx screws (arrowed) ...**

6.17b ... and remove the blanking cap to access the sprocket bolt – variable valve timing models

Inspection

Caution: Do not bend, twist or turn the timing belt inside out. Do not allow it to come in contact with oil, coolant or fuel. Do not use timing belt tension to keep the camshaft or crankshaft from turning when installing the sprocket bolts. Do not turn the crankshaft or camshaft more than a few degrees (necessary for tooth alignment) while the timing belt is removed.

18 Check the tensioner and idler pulley bearings for smooth operation and excessive play. Inspect the tensioner spring for damage. We recommend that the tensioner, idler pulley and spring are renewed regardless of their condition. **Note:** *The spring free length (from the inside of each hook at the ends) must not exceed 58.8 mm (1997 and earlier) or 59.2 mm (1998-on). If it does, renew it.*

6.25a Fit the idler pulley

6.27a The intake sprocket has the I mark at the top (arrowed) – non-variable timing models ...

6.17c Use a spanner (arrowed) on the hexagonal section of the camshaft to prevent rotation

19 If the timing belt was broken during engine operation, the belt may have been fouled by debris or may have been damaged by a defective component in the area of the timing belt; check for belt material in the teeth of the sprockets. Any defective parts or debris in the sprockets must be cleaned out of all the sprockets before installing the new belt or the belt will not mesh properly when installed.

20 If the belt teeth are cracked or pulled off, the oil pump or camshaft(s) may have seized.

21 If there is noticeable wear or cracks in the belt, check to see if there are nicks or burrs on the sprockets.

22 If there is wear or damage on only one side of the belt, check the belt guide and the alignment of all sprockets. Also check the oil seals at the front of the engine and renew them if they are leaking.

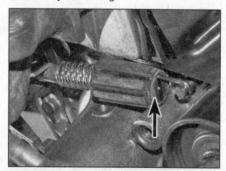

6.25b The closed end of the spring/cover must be uppermost (arrowed)

6.27b ... and the exhaust sprocket has E at the top (arrowed)

23 Renew the timing belt if obvious wear or damage is noted or if it is the least bit questionable. Correct any problems which contributed to belt failure prior to belt installation. **Note:** *We recommend renewing the belt whenever it is removed, since belt failure can lead to expensive engine damage.*

Refitting

24 Remove all dirt and oil from the timing belt area at the front of the engine.

25 Fit the new tensioner, spring and idler pulley. Note that the closed end of the spring cover must be uppermost **(see illustrations)**. The tensioner pulley should be pulled back against spring tension with the spring fully extended and the tensioner bolt temporarily tightened.

26 If they were removed, refit the camshaft and crankshaft sprockets. Make sure the crankshaft sprocket key is installed with the tapered end toward the oil pump body. Tighten the camshaft sprocket bolts to the specified torque, referring to paragraph 17 above.

27 Align the camshaft sprocket and crankshaft sprocket timing marks **(see illustrations 6.11a and 6.11b)**. The notch on the rear flange of the crankshaft sprocket is aligned with the mark on the oil pump body. The marks on the camshaft sprockets are aligned with the E and I marks on the rear timing belt cover, and on models without variable valve timing, the second set of E and I marks are at approximately 12 o'clock **(see illustrations)**. **Note:** *If necessary, rotate the crankshaft and camshaft sprockets slightly to achieve proper alignment.*

28 Slip the timing belt over the crankshaft sprocket, camshaft sprockets, idler pulley and tensioner, then position the belt so it's tight on the side opposite the tensioner pulley and between the camshaft sprockets. If the original belt is being reinstalled, align the marks made during removal with the marks on the sprockets, and be sure to install the timing belt so that it will rotate in the same direction as removed (the direction of rotation was marked during removal). If a new belt is fitted, observe the direction of rotation arrows (where given) on the belt **(see illustrations)**.

29 Install the crankshaft pulley hub and new crankshaft sprocket bolt (where applicable), then slacken the tensioner bolt, allow the spring to tension the belt, and temporarily tighten the bolt again.

30 Rotate the crankshaft 1 5/6 turns clockwise and align the crankshaft sprocket timing mark (notch) with the tension set mark on the oil pump body **(see illustration)**.

Caution: If you feel resistance while rotating the engine by hand, do not continue. The valves may be contacting the pistons due to incorrect valve timing. Recheck the camshaft and crankshaft sprockets to be sure they are correctly aligned with their marks.

6.28a Timing belt routing

6.28b Observe the direction of rotation arrows on the new belt

31 Loosen the tensioner pulley bolt and allow the tensioner spring to apply tension to the timing belt. **Note:** *The tensioner pulley spring applies the proper tension to the belt.*

32 Tighten the tensioner pulley bolt to the specified torque.

33 Turn the crankshaft 2 1/6 turns clockwise and verify that the crankshaft sprocket timing mark and the camshaft sprocket timing marks are correctly aligned **(see illustrations 6.11a and 6.11b)**. If the timing marks do not align, remove the timing belt and repeat the installation procedure.

34 Check the timing belt tension by applying moderate force by hand midway between the camshaft sprockets and measure the belt deflection **(see illustration)**. Belt deflection should be 9.0 to 11.5 mm.

35 If the belt deflection is not correct, repeat the installation procedure. If the proper tension is still not obtained, renew the tensioner spring with a new spring and reset belt tension as described above.

36 Tighten the crankshaft sprocket bolt to the specified torque. Note that there are two torque settings for the bolt, depending on its length.

37 Refit the remaining parts in the reverse order of removal. Run the engine and check for proper operation.

---

7 Variable valve timing – description and component renewal

Description

1 1.8 litre engines 2000-on were equipped with a mechanism which varied the relationship between the intake camshaft and its drive sprocket. This is achieved by supplying engine oil under pressure to 'advance' or 'retard' chambers within the sprocket's variable timing actuator, bolted to the end of the camshaft. The flow of oil is controlled by

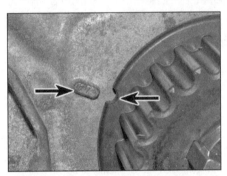

6.30 Align the notch with the 'tension set' mark on the oil pump housing (arrowed) – belt removed for clarity

6.34 Using moderate hand pressure, the deflection should be 9.0 to 11.5 mm

an electrically operated solenoid valve, itself controlled by the engine management ECM. At low engine speed the camshaft is set in the retarded position to enhance torque output, and as the speed increases, the camshaft timing is advanced to enhance power output. The overall result is increased engine output, efficiency and driveability, with lower emissions.

Component renewal

Variable valve timing actuator

2 The actuator is integral with the intake

7.5 Renew the oil control valve O-ring seal (arrowed)

camshaft sprocket. Removal of the sprocket is described in Section 6.

3 The actuator is designed to return to the fully retarded position as the engine stops, under spring pressure. In this position 2 'stopper pins' are intended to engage, locking the sprocket to the camshaft. With the timing belt removed, hold the camshaft stationary using its hexagonal section, then attempt to rotate the actuator by hand. If it's possible to rotate the actuator, it has failed and may need renewing.

Oil control valve

4 The oil control valve is located on cylinder head cover, over the intake camshaft.

5 Disconnect the wiring plug, then undo the retaining bolt and pull the valve from the cylinder head cover **(see illustration)**. Renew the O-ring seal.

6 With the valve removed, connect an ohmmeter across the valve terminals and check its resistance. The correct specification is 6.9 to 7.9 ohms. If the reading differs from this, the valve may be defective.

7 With no voltage applied to the valve, it should be in the 'fully retarded' position **(see illustration)**. Apply battery voltage to the valve and check that the spool valve within moved

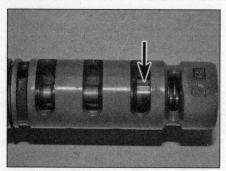

7.7 The spool valve in the fully retarded position (arrowed)

to the 'fully advanced' position, then returns to the original position once the voltage is removed.

8 Refitting is a reversal of removal, tightening the retaining bolt to the specified torque.

8 Camshafts and followers – removal and refitting

Removal

1 Disconnect the battery negative lead as described in Chapter 5A, Section 4.

2 Remove the cylinder head cover (see Section 4).

3 Remove the camshaft position sensor (see Chapter 4A, Section 10).

4 On Mk 1 models (1997 and earlier) turn the engine over with a socket bar on the crankshaft pulley centre bolt to position

the base of each camshaft lobe against the hydraulic adjusters. Measure the clearance between the cam lobe base and adjuster with a feeler gauge. If it's more than the limit listed in this Chapter's Specifications, the adjuster probably needs cleaning or renewal. Write down the locations of any adjusters that need cleaning or renewal, then continue measuring until all adjusters have been checked.

5 Remove the timing belt covers, timing belt, and camshaft sprockets (see Section 6).

6 Measure the thrust clearance (endplay) of the camshaft with a dial test indicator **(see illustration)**. If the clearance is greater than the value listed in this Chapter's Specifications, renew the camshaft, cylinder head or both, whichever is worn.

7 Remove the rear timing belt cover **(see illustration)**.

8 Working from the ends of the camshaft inwards, slacken the camshaft bearing cap bolts gradually, in five or six steps. Remove the camshaft bearing caps, marking or packaging to record their locations for correct refitting later. To further ensure correct refitting, take note of the factory camshaft cap stamped numbers and direction arrows (where applicable) **(see illustration)**.

9 Make note how far into the bearing cap the old oil seal is located and use this as a guide for fitting depth later.

10 Mark the camshafts to ensure proper refitting later. Remove the camshafts. Remove the oil seals from the camshafts.

11 Using a magnet, lift out each camshaft follower and set them in numbered boxes,

plastic bags or other containers so they can be refitted in the same position during reassembly **(see illustration)**. If you're planning to store the hydraulic adjusters for some time, keep them upside down in a container of engine oil, but be sure to keep them in their original order.

Inspection

12 Examine all parts, looking for signs of pitting, scoring or scuffing.

13 Inspect each camshaft follower for scuffing and scoring marks.

14 Visually examine the camshaft lobes and bearing journals for scoring marks, pitting, galling and evidence of overheating (blue, discoloured areas). Look for flaking away of the hardened surface of each lobe. If in doubt as to the condition of the camshafts, have them examined by an automotive engineering specialist.

Refitting

15 Apply engine assembly lubricant or clean engine oil to the camshaft followers and refit them in the cylinder head bores, in their original locations. Check that the followers travel smoothly in their bores.

16 Apply camshaft assembly lubricant or clean engine oil to the camshaft lobes and bearing journals. Install the camshafts with the locating pins on the ends at the 12 o'clock position **(see illustration)**. Make sure the exhaust camshaft is refitted on the exhaust manifold side of the engine, and the intake camshaft is refitted on the intake manifold side of the engine.

17 Apply silicone sealant to the portions of the bearing cap surfaces that surround the camshaft seals **(see illustration)**. Don't put any sealant on the portion of the cap that surrounds the camshaft journal.

18 Refit the camshaft bearing caps in the proper order as marked when removed, in the stamped numerical order with the arrows pointing (where applicable) as removed. Then working from the centre outwards, tighten the cap bolts in two or three steps to the specified torque.

19 Apply clean engine oil to the lips of the new camshaft oil seals and fit the oil seals (see Section 12).

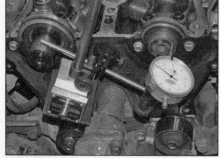

8.6 Use a DTI gauge to measure camshaft endplay

8.7 Rear timing belt cover bolts (arrowed)

8.8 Take note of the camshaft bearing cap stamped numbers (arrowed). E for exhaust, I for intake, No. 1 at the timing belt end

8.11 Use a magnet to remove the cam followers

8.16 Position the pins at the 12 o'clock location (arrowed)

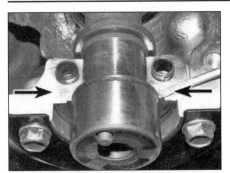

8.17 Apply sealant around the seal area, not the journal (arrowed)

9.3a Reinforcement frame bolts (arrowed)

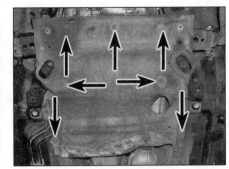

9.3b Transmission undershield bolts (arrowed)

20 Refit the camshaft sprockets as described in Section 6.

21 Fit the timing belt as described in Section 6.

22 On models with solid cam followers (1998-on), check and if necessary, adjust the valve clearances as described in Chapter 1, Section 28.

23 On 1997 and earlier models, before refitting the camshaft position sensor, install a new O-ring. Apply grease to the O-ring and apply grease or engine assembly lubricant to the camshaft position sensor drive lugs. Refer to Chapter 4A, Section 10 and refit the sensor.

24 The remainder of refitting is a reversal of removal. Check the engine for proper operation, and where applicable check the ignition timing as described in Chapter 5B, Section 4.

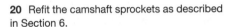

9 Cylinder head –
removal and refitting

Caution: The engine must be completely cool before beginning this procedure.

Removal

1 Disconnect the negative cable from the battery as described in Chapter 5A, Section 4.

2 Drain the coolant as described in Chapter 1, Section 19.

3 Undo the bolts and remove the front reinforcement frame and transmission undershield (where fitted) **(see illustrations)**.

4 Drain the engine oil and remove the oil filter as described in Chapter 1, Section 3.

5 Remove the air intake duct assembly.

6 Disconnect the throttle cable from the

throttle body and support bracket (see Chapter 4A, Section 4).

7 Disconnect the brake servo vacuum hose, fuel supply hose, the purge control vacuum hose, cruise control vacuum hose (as applicable), and the heater hoses **(see illustrations)**. Mark the hoses for later refitting.

8 Disconnect all electrical connectors/wiring harness connections to the cylinder head. Mark the connectors for later reconnection.

9 Remove the air cleaner assembly as described in Chapter 4A, Section 2, then on 2000-on models, undo the bolts and move the washer reservoir to one side.

10 Undo the retaining bolts, remove the exhaust manifold heat shield, disconnect the front exhaust pipe from the manifold, then undo the bolts securing the front exhaust pipe support bracket **(see illustrations)**. Discard the gasket – a new one must be fitted.

9.7a Servo vacuum hose (arrowed)

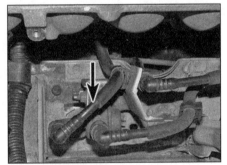

9.7b Fuel supply hose (arrowed)

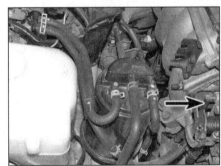

9.7c Purge valve hose (arrowed)

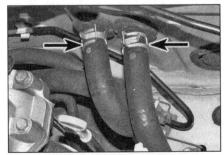

9.7d Release the clamps (arrowed) and disconnect the heater hoses from the bulkhead

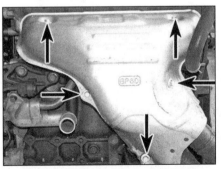

9.10a Exhaust manifold heat shield retaining bolts (arrowed)

9.10b Exhaust pipe support bracket bolts (arrowed)

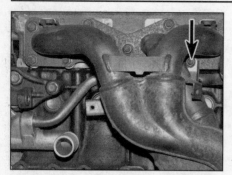

9.11a Water bypass tube retaining nut (arrowed)

9.11b Pull the pipe out and renew the O-ring seal (arrowed)

9.14 Remove the EGR pipe (arrowed) – engine removed for clarity

9.16 Intake manifold support bracket bolts (arrowed)

11 Remove water bypass tubing bolts/nuts (where applicable, the bypass tubing is mounted on the cylinder head) **(see illustrations)**. As the seal at the front of the pipe has been disturbed, we recommend pulling the pipe from the housing and renewing the seal.

12 Slacken the coolant pump pulley retaining bolts, then remove the auxiliary drivebelt(s) as described in Chapter 1, Section 6.

13 Remove timing belt as described in Section 6.

Models with variable valve timing

14 Remove the EGR pipe by undoing the 2 nuts at the intake manifold end, the union at the exhaust manifold end, and the support bracket bolt in the middle **(see illustration)**.

Recover the gasket at the intake manifold end.

15 Undo the bolt securing the oil supply pipe support bracket to the underside of the intake manifold **(see illustration 4.18)**. Access is limited.

All models

16 Undo the bolts and remove the support bracket from the underside of the intake manifold **(see illustration)**.

17 Label and detach any remaining components that would interfere with cylinder head removal. Including the coolant hose from the rear of the cylinder head to the oil cooler (where applicable).

18 Working is the **reverse** of the tightening sequence **(see illustration 9.27)**, slacken the cylinder head bolts in 1/4-turn increments, until they can be removed by hand, complete with washers.

19 With the help of an assistant, lift the cylinder head off the engine block. If it is stuck, very carefully pry up at the transmission end, away from the head gasket surface.

20 If required, remove the intake and exhaust manifolds from the cylinder head as described in Chapter 4A, Section 11.

Refitting

21 The mating surfaces of the cylinder head and block must be perfectly clean when the head is installed. Use a gasket scraper to remove all traces of carbon and old gasket material, then clean the mating surfaces with lacquer thinner or acetone. If any oil residue is on the mating surfaces when the head is fitted, the gasket may not seal correctly and leaks could develop. When working on the block, fill the cylinders with clean shop rags to prevent the entry of debris. Use a vacuum cleaner to remove material that falls into the cylinders.

Caution: Be careful not to gouge the soft aluminium of the cylinder head.

22 Inspect the threads of the cylinder head bolts for wear, stretching or damage. Although the bolts can be re-used, it may be prudent to renew them as a set as a precaution.

23 Refit the intake and exhaust manifolds (as applicable) as described in Chapter 4A, Section 11.

24 Position the new gasket over the locating dowels in the block gasket surface, then carefully position the cylinder head on the block without disturbing the gasket **(see illustration)**.

25 Before installing the head bolts, apply a small amount of clean engine oil to the threads and the underside of the heads.

26 Install the bolts and washers, then tighten them finger-tight.

27 Tighten the bolts following the recommended sequence in several steps to the specified torque **(see illustration)**.

9.24 Gasket locating dowels (arrowed)

9.27 Cylinder head bolt tightening sequence

10.2 Unbolt the engine mounting plate each side

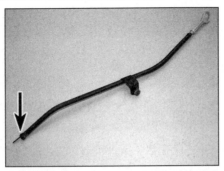

10.3 Renew the O-ring seal at the base of the dipstick guide tube (arrowed)

10.4 The long sump bolts are at the rear (arrowed)

28 The remainder of refitting is a reversal of removal, remembering the following points:
a) *Refill the cooling system as described in Chapter 1, Section 19.*
b) *Renew the engine oil and filter as described in Chapter 1, Section 3.*
c) *Start the engine and check for leaks/ correct operation.*
d) *Where applicable, check the ignition timing as described in Chapter 5B, Section 4.*
e) *Tighten all fasteners to their specified torque where given.*

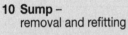

10 Sump –
removal and refitting

Removal

1 Given the extremely limited access within the engine compartment, and the close proximity of the front subframe, we recommend that the easiest method of sump removal is with the engine removed. Consequently, begin by removing the engine as described in Chapter 2B, Section 4.
2 Undo the bolts and remove the engine mounting plates each side **(see illustration)**.
3 Remove engine oil dipstick, undo the retaining nut and pull the guide tube upwards from the sump. Discard the O-ring seal – a new one must be fitted **(see illustration)**.
4 Remove the oil sump-to-engine bolts **(see illustration)**. Oil sump bolts may be of varying sizes. Mark, tag, or store each oil sump bolt/ nut with the location removed from the oil sump for correct refitting later.
5 Remove the oil sump. If the oil sump is stuck, pry it loose very carefully by inserting a screwdriver or putty knife at the engine block ears. **Note:** *Do not insert the screwdriver or prying tool between the oil baffle/support plate and the engine block. Be very careful not to scratch, bend, or otherwise damage the mating surfaces of the oil sump, baffle plate, and block or oil leaks could develop.*
6 Unbolt the oil pick up pipe from the oil pump and plate **(see illustration)**. Renew the gasket.

1.6 and 1.8 litre models up to 1999

7 Remove the baffle plate, prying as

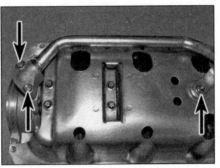

10.6 Oil pick up pipe fasteners (arrowed)

necessary against the main bearing journal or at the corners of the baffle.

1.8 litre models 2000-on

8 Remove the rubber gasket at the oil pump end and rear cover end.
9 Undo the retaining bolts, then carefully prise the main bearing support plate from the base of the cylinder block, using a flat-bladed tool. Take great care not to damage the sealing surfaces **(see illustration)**.

Refitting

10 Use a scraper to remove all traces of old gasket material and sealant from the block, baffle/support plate, oil sump and pick-up pipe. Clean the mating surfaces with gasket cleaner or equivalent solvent, available at automotive parts stores. Be very careful not to scratch, bend, or otherwise damage the mating surfaces of the sump and block or oil leaks could develop.

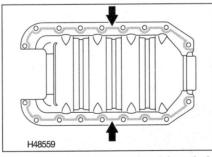

10.13 Apply a bead of sealant inboard of the bolts holes (arrowed) – 1999 and earlier models ...

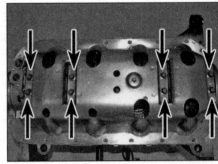

10.9 Undo the bolts and remove the main bearing support plate (arrowed)

11 Make sure the threaded bolt holes in the block are clean. Visually check the condition of the oil strainer.
12 Check the oil sump flange for cracks or distortion, particularly at the bolting flange.

1.6 and 1.8 litre models up to 1999

13 Apply a continuous bead of silicone sealant to the bolting flange (lip) of the baffle plate inside the bolt holes **(see illustration)**. Install the baffle plate. **Note:** *Install the component within 5 minutes after applying the sealant.*

1.8 litre models 2000-on

14 Apply a continuous 2.5mm thick bead of sealant (No. SH780 or TB1207B from Mazda dealers) to the main bearing support plate sealing surfaces, ensuring the bead is inboard of the bolt holes, and install the support plate and tighten the bolts to the specified torque **(see illustration)**.

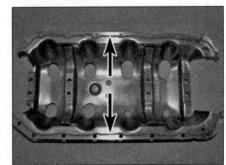

10.14 ... 2000-on models (arrowed)

10.16a Apply a bead of the sealant to the grooves in the rear cover (arrowed) ...

10.16b ... and oil pump body (arrowed) ...

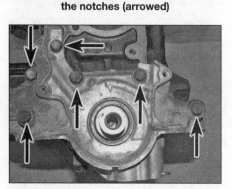

10.16c ... then press the rubber seals into place, ensuring the projections align with the notches (arrowed)

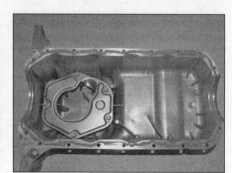

10.17 Apply sealant inboard of the sump bolt holes

11.3 Oil pump retaining bolts (arrowed)

All models

15 Refit the oil pick-up pipe with a new gasket and tighten the bolts to the specified torque.

16 Apply silicone sealant to grooves in the oil pump body and rear cover. Install the new gaskets on the oil pump body and rear cover on the engine block, inserting the projections on the gaskets into the notches **(see illustrations)**.

17 Apply a continuous bead of silicone sealant around the perimeter of the oil sump flange, inboard of the bolt holes **(see illustration)**.

18 Carefully position the oil sump on the

engine block and refit the bolts/nuts. Working from the centre outwards, tighten the bolts to the specified torque in three or four steps.

19 The remainder refitting is the reverse of removal, bearing in mind the following points:

a) *Renew the engine oil and filter as described in Chapter 1, Section 3.*

b) *Tighten all fasteners to their specified torque where given.*

c) *Start the engine and check for leaks.*

11 Oil pump –
removal, inspection
and refitting

Removal

1 Remove the timing belt and crankshaft sprocket as described in Section 6.

2 Remove the oil sump, pick-up tube, and baffle plate/support plate (as applicable) as described in Section 10.

3 Remove the retaining bolts/nuts and separate the oil pump from the engine block **(see illustration)**. You may have to lever carefully between the front main bearing cap and the pump housing with a screwdriver.

Inspection

4 Place the oil pump on a workbench. Note how far the oil seal is seated in the bore. Using a seal removal tool or a screwdriver taped or wrapped with a rag to protect the pump bore, remove the oil seal from the housing **(see illustration)**. Take care not to damage the housing bore.

5 Remove the screws retaining the oil pump cover to the housing and remove the cover **(see illustration)**. Inspect the oil pump cover for distortion or damage.

6 Remove the oil pressure relief valve. Note or mark the direction of the components as installed, then remove the oil pump inner and outer rotors from the housing **(see illustrations)**. Thoroughly clean all of the components in clean solvent.

7 Check the pump components for signs

11.4 Note the fitted depth of the oil seal

11.5 Oil pump cover Torx screws (arrowed)

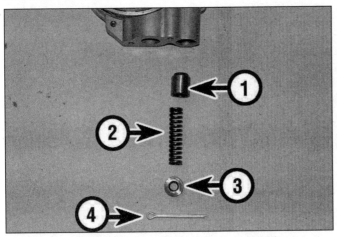

11.6a Oil pressure relief valve components

1 Plunger   2 Spring   3 Washer   4 Split pin

11.6b The indents on the rotors (arrowed) must face inwards towards the cylinder block

of wear or damage. If in any doubt as to the pump's condition, renew it.

8 Ensure the surfaces of the pump housing are clean and dry before reassembly.

9 Lightly coat the outer edge of a new oil seal with engine assembly lubricant or clean engine oil. Using a socket with an outside diameter slightly smaller than the outside diameter of the seal, carefully drive the new seal into place with a hammer. Make sure it's installed squarely and driven in to the same depth as the original. If a socket is not available, a short section of large diameter pipe will also work. Apply engine assembly lubricant to the seal lip surface that contacts the crankshaft.

10 Lubricate the oil pressure relief valve piston with clean engine oil and refit the valve components into the pump case.

11 Lubricate the rotor set with clean engine oil. Refit the rotors.

12 Pack the pump cavities with petroleum jelly (this will prime the pump and ensure good suction when the engine is started).

13 Refit the cover, apply thread-locking compound to the screw threads and tighten the screws securely.

14 Inspect the screen at the end of the oil pick-up tube for any debris that might clog it. Either clean the tube and screen completely or renew it with a new one at this time.

Refitting

15 Use a scraper to remove all traces of gasket (where applicable) and sealant from the cover and engine block, then clean the mating surfaces with lacquer thinner or acetone.

16 Install a new gasket (where applicable) with a thin coat of silicone sealant on the oil pump sealing surface. Refit the oil pump to the engine block, aligning the flats on the crankshaft with the flats on the pump drive gear. Where no gasket is fitted, simply apply a thin coating of silicone sealant to the surfaces, and fit a new O-ring seal **(see illustrations)**. Ensure the sealant doesn't plug or cover any oil passages.

17 Refit the bolts and tighten them to the specified torque.

11.16a Apply sealant to the sealing surface, and renew the O-ring seal (arrowed)

18 Using a sharp knife, trim the oil pump gasket (where applicable) flush with the oil sump sealing surface.

19 The remainder of refitting is the reverse of the removal procedure.

12 Oil seals – renewal

Camshaft oil seals

1 Remove the camshaft sprockets as described in Section 6.

2 Punch or drill a small hole in the oil seal.

12.2a Drill a small hole ...

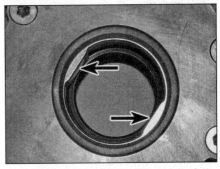

11.16b Align the flats in the pump rotor (arrowed) with the flats on the crankshaft

Screw a self-tapping screw into the hole, and pull on the screw with pliers to extract the seal **(see illustrations)**.

3 Clean the seal housing, and polish off any burrs or raised edges, which may have caused the seal to fail in the first place.

4 Lubricate the lips of the new seal with clean engine oil, and drive it into position until the outer edge of the seal is flush with the end of the camshaft bearing cap **(see illustration)**. Use a suitable tubular drift, such as a socket, which bears only on the hard outer edge of the seal. Take care not to damage the seal lips during fitting. Note that the seal lips should face inwards.

12.2b ... insert a self-tapping screw, and pull out the oil seal

12.4 The outer edge of the seal must be flush with the bearing cap

12.7 Using a shaft knife, cut around the oil seal lip ...

12.8 ... then prise the seal out. Note the tape around the screwdriver head

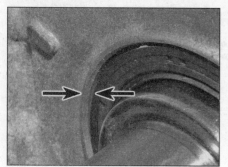

12.10 Depending on model, the seal should be flush, or just underflush with the oil pump body face (arrowed)

12.15 Prise the rear oil seal from place

12.16 The seal should be flush with the edge of the rear cover

5 Refit the camshaft sprockets and timing belt as described in Section 6.

Crankshaft front oil seal

6 Remove the crankshaft sprocket as described in Section 6.

7 Cut completely around the front oil seal lip with a sharp knife, be careful not to damage the crankshaft sealing surface **(see illustration)**.

8 Note how far the seal is seated in the bore and the direction the oil seal lip faces. Remove the front oil seal with a screwdriver taped or wrapped with a rag to protect the crankshaft surface and engine block **(see illustration)**.

9 Clean the bore in the engine block and clean the crankshaft surface. Apply engine assembly lubricant or clean engine oil to the seal lip.

10 Press the oil seal in slightly by hand, with

the oil seal lip facing the same direction as removed. Using a seal driver or a socket with an outside diameter slightly smaller than the outside diameter of the front oil seal, carefully tap the new seal into place with a hammer **(see illustration)**. On 1997 and earlier models, the oil seal is flush with the face of the oil pump body, and on models after this date, the seal should be 0.5 to 1.0 mm underflush with the face of the oil pump body. Make sure the oil seal is installed squarely.

11 Reinstall the crankshaft sprocket and timing belt (see Section 6).

12 Run the engine and check for oil leaks at the front oil seal.

Crankshaft rear oil seal

13 Remove the flywheel as described in Section 13.

14 Cut completely around the rear main oil

seal lip with a sharp knife, be careful not to damage the crankshaft sealing surface **(see illustration 12.7)**.

15 Prise out the old seal with a screwdriver taped or wrapped in a rag, or use a seal removal tool **(see illustration)**.

16 Apply engine oil to the crankshaft seal journal and to the lip of the new seal. Carefully push the new seal part way into place by hand. Carefully tap into place using a flat punch, wooden block, large socket, or a suitable short pipe or tubing of the correct diameter until the oil seal is flush with the edge of the rear cover **(see illustration)**.

17 Refit the flywheel as described in Section 13.

13 Flywheel – removal and refitting

Removal

1 Remove the clutch as described in Chapter 6, Section 2.

2 Use paint to make alignment marks on the flywheel and crankshaft to ensure correct refitting alignment later **(see illustration)**.

3 Undo the retaining bolts and remove the flywheel. If the crankshaft turns, wedge a screwdriver in the ring gear teeth to jam the flywheel, or use a home-made locking tool **(see illustrations)**.

4 Remove the flywheel from the crankshaft. Note that the flywheel is heavy – support it while removing the last bolt.

13.2 Make alignment marks (arrowed) between the flywheel and the crankshaft

13.3a Home-made flywheel locking tool

13.3b Flywheel retaining bolts

15.1 Oil pressure switch location (arrowed)

15.2 Unscrew the oil pressure switch (arrowed)

5 Clean the flywheel to remove grease and oil. Inspect the surface for cracks, rivet grooves, burned areas and score marks. Light scoring can be removed with emery cloth. Check for cracked and broken ring gear teeth. Lay the flywheel on a flat surface and use a straight-edge to check for warpage. If necessary, take the flywheel to an automotive engineering workshop to have it resurfaced.
6 Clean and inspect the mating surfaces of the flywheel and the crankshaft. If the crankshaft rear seal is leaking, renew it before refitting the flywheel (see Section 12).
7 Check and if necessary, renew the pilot bearing as described in Chapter 6, Section 7.

Refitting

8 Remove any thread-locking compound from the crankshaft flywheel bolt holes and bolts.
Caution: If all the thread-locking compound cannot be removed from a bolt, renew that bolt. Do not apply new thread-locking compound when installing a new bolt.
9 Position the flywheel at the crankshaft. Be sure to align the marks made during removal. Before installing the bolts, apply thread-locking compound to the threads of any re-used bolts, but not to new bolts.
10 Tighten the bolts to the specified torque, working is a diagonal pattern.
11 The remainder of refitting is a reversal of removal.

14 Engine mountings – inspection and renewal

1 Engine mountings seldom require attention, but broken or deteriorated mountings should be renewed immediately or the added strain placed on the driveline components may cause damage or wear.

Inspection

2 During the inspection, the engine must be raised slightly to remove the weight from the mountings.
3 Raise the vehicle and support it securely on axle stands, then position a jack with a block of wood under the engine oil sump or use an engine support fixture from above. Carefully raise the engine just enough to take the weight off the mountings. Support the engine just enough to take the weight off the engine mountings but without lifting the weight of the car from the axle stands.

 Warning: DO NOT place any part of your body under the engine when it's supported only by a jack!

4 Check the mountings to see if the rubber is cracked, hardened or separated from the metal portion. Occasionally, the rubber will split down the centre.
5 Check for relative movement between the mountings and the engine or chassis, using a large screwdriver or prybar to attempt to move the mountings. If movement is noted, lower the engine and tighten the mounting fasteners.

Renewal

6 Raise the vehicle and support it securely on axle stands (if not already done). Support the engine as described in Paragraph 3.
7 Renew the engine mountings as follows:
 a) Remove the engine mounting stud nuts to detach from the rubber mounting from the mounting bracket.
 b) Unbolt the engine mountings from the engine block.
 c) Reinstall the engine mountings by reversing the removal steps.
 d) Tighten all bolts/nuts to the specified torque.

15 Oil pressure switch – removal and refitting

1 The oil pressure switch is located on the right-hand side of the engine block between the oil filter and the starter motor **(see illustration)**.
2 Disconnect the wiring plug, and unscrew the switch from the engine block **(see illustration)**. Be prepared for oil spillage.
3 Refitting is a reversal of removal, tightening the switch to the specified torque.

Notes

Chapter 2 Part B:
Engine removal and overhaul procedures

Contents

Degrees of difficulty

| Easy, suitable for novice with little experience | 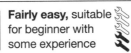 | Fairly easy, suitable for beginner with some experience | | Fairly difficult, suitable for competent DIY mechanic | | Difficult, suitable for experienced DIY mechanic | | Very difficult, suitable for expert DIY or professional | |

Specifications

Cylinder head

Maximum gasket face distortion:
   1.6 litre . . . . 0.15 mm
   1.8 litre . . . . 0.10 mm
Refacing limit:
   1.6 litre . . . . 0.20 mm
   1.8 litre . . . . 0.10 mm

Valves and related components

Valve stem diameter:
   Intake . . . . 5.970 to 5.985 mm
   Exhaust. . . . . 5.965 to 5.950 mm
Valve stem-to-guide clearance:
   Intake:
      Standard. . . . . 0.025 to 0.060 mm
      Service limit . . . . 0.20 mm
   Exhaust:
      Standard. . . . . 0.030 to 0.065 mm
      Service limit . . . . 0.20 mm
Valve spring:
   Out-of-square limit:
      1.6 litre:
         Intake . . . . 1.68 mm
         Exhaust. . . . . 1.69 mm
      1.8 litre:
         Intake and exhaust . . . . 1.62 mm
   Minimum free length:
      1.6 litre:
         Intake . . . . 47.0 mm
         Exhaust. . . . . 47.3 mm
      1.8 litre:
         Intake and exhaust . . . . 46.26 mm

Crankshaft and connecting rods

Connecting rod journal diameter . . . . 44.940 to 44.956 mm (nominal)
Main bearing journal diameter . . . . 49.938 to 49.956 mm (nominal)
Main bearing oil clearance:
  Standard . . . . 0.018 to 0.036 mm
  Limit . . . . 0.10 mm
Crankshaft endfloat:
  Standard . . . . 0.080 to 0.282 mm
  Service limit . . . . 0.30 mm
  Thrustwasher thickness . . . . 2.50 to 2.55 mm (nominal)

Engine block

Gasket surface distortion . . . . 0.15 mm max
Cylinder bore diameter:
  1.6 litre . . . . 78.006 to 78.013 mm (nominal)
  1.8 litre . . . . 83.000 to 83.019 mm (nominal)

Pistons and rings

Piston diameter:
  1.6 litre . . . . 77.954 to 77.974 mm (nominal)
  1.8 litre . . . . 82.954 to 82.974 mm (nominal)
Piston ring end gap:
  No. 1 (top) compression ring:
    Standard . . . . 0.15 to 0.30 mm
    Service limit . . . . 1.0 mm
  No. 2 (middle) compression ring:
    Standard . . . . 0.15 to 0.30 mm
    Service limit . . . . 1.0 mm
  Oil control ring:
    Standard . . . . 0.20 to 0.70 mm
    Service limit . . . . 1.0 mm

Torque wrench settings

Refer to Chapter 2A, Specifications

1 General information

Included in this Chapter are details of removing the engine from the car and general overhaul procedures for the cylinder head, cylinder block/crankcase and all other engine internal components.

The information given ranges from advice concerning preparation for an overhaul and the purchase of parts, to detailed step-by-step procedures covering removal, inspection, renovation and refitting of engine internal components.

After Section 5, all instructions are based on the assumption that the engine has been removed from the car. For information concerning in-car engine repair, as well as the removal and refitting of those external components necessary for full overhaul, refer to Part A of this Chapter and to Section 5. Ignore any preliminary dismantling operations described in Part A that are no longer relevant once the engine has been removed from the car.

Apart from torque wrench settings, which are given at the beginning of Part A, all specifications relating to engine overhaul are at the beginning of this Chapter.

2 Engine overhaul – general information

It is not always easy to determine when, or if, an engine should be completely overhauled, as a number of factors must be considered.

High mileage is not necessarily an indication that an overhaul is needed, while low mileage does not preclude the need for an overhaul. Frequency of servicing is probably the most important consideration. An engine which has had regular and frequent oil and filter changes, as well as other required maintenance, should give many thousands of miles of reliable service. Conversely, a neglected engine may require an overhaul very early in its life.

Excessive oil consumption is an indication that piston rings, valve seals and/or valve guides are in need of attention. Make sure that oil leaks are not responsible before deciding that the rings and/or guides are worn. Perform a compression test, as described in Chapter 2A, Section 2, to determine the likely cause of the problem.

Check the oil pressure with a gauge fitted in place of the oil pressure switch, and compare it with that specified. If it is extremely low, the main and big-end bearings, and/or the oil pump, are probably worn out.

Loss of power, rough running, knocking or metallic engine noises, excessive valve gear noise, and high fuel consumption may also point to the need for an overhaul, especially if they are all present at the same time. If a complete service does not cure the situation, major mechanical work is the only solution.

A full engine overhaul involves restoring all internal parts to the specification of a new engine. During a complete overhaul, the pistons and the piston rings are renewed, and the cylinder bores are reconditioned. New main and big-end bearings are generally fitted; if necessary, the crankshaft may be reground, to compensate for wear in the journals. The valves are also serviced as well, since they are usually in less-than-perfect condition at this point. Always pay careful attention to the condition of the oil pump when overhauling the engine, and renew it if there is any doubt as to its serviceability. The end result should be an as-new engine that will give many trouble-free miles.

Critical cooling system components such as the hoses, thermostat and coolant pump should be renewed when an engine is overhauled. The radiator should also be checked carefully, to ensure that it is not clogged or leaking.

Before beginning the engine overhaul, read through the entire procedure, to familiarise yourself with the scope and requirements of the job. Check on the availability of parts and make sure that any necessary special tools and equipment are obtained in advance. Most work can be done with typical hand tools, although a number of precision measuring tools are required for inspecting parts to determine if they must be renewed.

The services provided by an engineering machine shop or engine reconditioning specialist will almost certainly be required, particularly if major repairs such as crankshaft regrinding or cylinder reboring are necessary. Apart from carrying out machining operations, these establishments will normally handle the inspection of parts, offer advice concerning reconditioning or renewal and supply new components such as pistons, piston rings and bearing shells. It is recommended that the establishment used is a member of the Federation of Engine Re-Manufacturers, or a similar society.

Always wait until the engine has been completely dismantled, and until all components (especially the cylinder block/crankcase and the crankshaft) have been inspected, before deciding what service and repair operations must be performed by an engineering works. The condition of these components will be the major factor to consider when determining whether to overhaul the original engine, or to buy a reconditioned unit. Do not, therefore, purchase parts or have overhaul work done on other components until they have been thoroughly inspected. As a general rule, time is the primary cost of an overhaul, so it does not pay to fit worn or sub-standard parts.

As a final note, to ensure maximum life and minimum trouble from a reconditioned engine, everything must be assembled with care, in a spotlessly-clean environment.

3 Engine removal – methods and precautions

Although Mazda recommend that the engine and transmission are removed as an assembly, from our experience we found it quite possible to remove the engine upwards from the body, leaving the transmission in place.

If you have decided that the engine must be removed for overhaul or major repair work, several preliminary steps should be taken.

Locating a suitable place to work is extremely important. Adequate work space, along with storage space for the car, will be needed. If a workshop or garage is not available, at the very least, a flat, level, clean work surface is required.

Cleaning the engine compartment and engine before beginning the removal procedure will help keep tools clean and organised.

An engine hoist will also be necessary. Make sure the equipment is rated in excess of the weight of the engine. Auxiliary workshop jacks/axle stands will be required to support the transmission, once the engine has been removed. Safety is of primary importance, considering the potential hazards involved in removing the engine from the car.

The help of an assistant is essential. Apart from the safety aspects involved, there are many instances when one person cannot

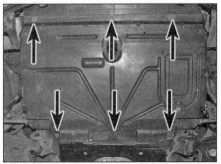

4.7a The engine undershield is retained by fasteners underneath (arrowed) ...

simultaneously perform all of the operations required during engine removal.

Plan the operation ahead of time. Before starting work, arrange for the hire of or obtain all of the tools and equipment you will need. Some of the equipment necessary to perform engine removal and installation safely (in addition to an engine hoist) is as follows: a heavy duty trolley jack, complete sets of spanners and sockets as described in the rear of this manual, wooden blocks, and plenty of rags and cleaning solvent for mopping-up spilled oil, coolant and fuel. If the hoist must be hired, make sure that you arrange for it in advance, and perform all of the operations possible without it beforehand. This will save you money and time.

Plan for the car to be out of use for quite a while. An engineering machine shop or engine reconditioning specialist will be required to perform some of the work which cannot be accomplished without special equipment. These places often have a busy schedule, so it would be a good idea to consult them before removing the engine, in order to accurately estimate the amount of time required to rebuild or repair components that may need work.

During the engine removal procedure, it is advisable to make notes of the locations of all brackets, cable-ties, earthing points, etc, as well as how the wiring harnesses, hoses and electrical connections are attached and routed around the engine and engine compartment. An effective way of doing this is to take a series of photographs of the various components before they are disconnected or removed; the resulting photographs will prove invaluable when the engine is refitted.

4.7c Where fitted, undo the reinforcement plate bolts (arrowed) ...

4.7b ... and each side (arrowed)

Always be extremely careful when removing and refitting the engine. Serious injury can result from careless actions. Plan ahead and take your time, and a job of this nature, although major, can be accomplished successfully.

4 Engine – removal and refitting

Note: *Such is the complexity of the power unit arrangement on these vehicles, and the variations that may be encountered according to model and optional equipment fitted, that the following should be regarded as a guide to the work involved, rather than a step-by-step procedure. Where differences are encountered, or additional component disconnection or removal is necessary, make notes of the work involved as an aid to refitting.*

Removal

1 Relieve the fuel system pressure (see Chapter 4A, Section 6).
2 Disconnect the negative cable from the battery as described in Chapter 5A, Section 4.
3 Place protective covers on the front wings.
4 Remove the air cleaner housing assembly and the resonance chamber (see Chapter 4A, Section 2).
5 Disconnect the accelerator cable (see Chapter 4A, Section 4).
6 Disconnect the cruise control cable, if equipped, from the throttle body.
7 Undo the fasteners and remove the engine undershields **(see illustrations)**.

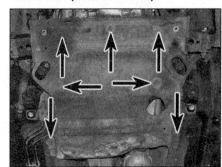

4.7d ... and undo the transmission undershield fasteners (arrowed)

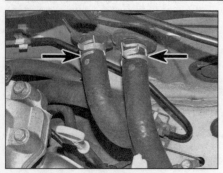

4.18 Release the clamps (arrowed) and disconnect the heater hoses at the engine compartment bulkhead

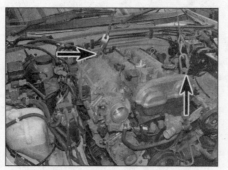

4.22 Attach a lifting sling/chain to the transport eyes (arrowed)

8 Remove the auxiliary drivebelt(s) as described in Chapter 1, Section 6.

9 On power steering-equipped vehicles, unbolt the power steering pump. If clearance allows, tie the pump aside without disconnecting the hoses. If necessary, remove the pump (see Chapter 10, Section 18).

10 Remove the alternator (see Chapter 5A, Section 7), coolant pump pulley (see Chapter 3, Section 7) and crankshaft pulley (see Chapter 2A, Section 5).

11 Remove the bonnet as described in Chapter 11, Section 8.

12 Raise the vehicle and support it securely on axle stands (see *Jacking and vehicle support*).

13 Remove the starter motor (see Chapter 5A, Section 10).

14 On air conditioned models, unbolt the compressor and set it aside. Do not disconnect the refrigerant hoses. **Note:** *Tie the compressor out of the way with a wire/ string/cable-ties, etc; don't let the compressor hang on the hoses.*

15 Disconnect the exhaust pipe from the exhaust manifold.

16 Drain the cooling system and engine oil (see Chapter 1, Section 19 and 3).

17 Lower the vehicle.

18 Disconnect the heater hoses **(see illustration)**.

19 Remove the cooling fan(s), the radiator hoses and the radiator as described in Chapter 3, Section 3 and 5.

20 Detach the fuel feed and return lines

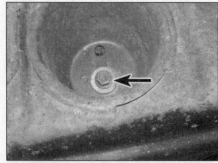

4.24 The engine mounting nuts are accessible each side of the subframe from underneath (arrowed)

(where applicable) from the fuel rail. Plug or cap all open fittings.

21 Clearly label, then disconnect all vacuum lines, coolant and emissions hoses, wiring harness connectors, earth straps and fuel lines. Masking tape and/or a touch-up paint applicator work well for marking items. Take photos or sketch the locations of components and brackets.

22 Attach a lifting sling/chain to the engine. Position a hoist and connect the sling/chain to it. Take up the slack until there is slight tension on the hoist **(see illustration)**.

23 Recheck to be sure nothing except the mountings are still connecting the engine to the vehicle or to the transmission. Disconnect and label anything still remaining.

24 Support the front of the transmission with a workshop/trolley jack. Place a block of wood on the jack head to prevent damage to the transmission. Remove the transmission-to-engine bolts, then disconnect the engine mountings **(see illustration)**.

25 Lift the engine up slightly, then move it forward to separate it from the transmission. If it does not move forward easily, check to ensure all transmission-to-engine bolts are removed. It may help to prise the engine loose from the transmission with a lever. Also, it will be necessary to tilt the engine up at the front to provide enough clearance. When the engine is separated from the transmission, lift the engine straight up, out of the vehicle.

26 Move the engine away from the vehicle and carefully lower the hoist until the engine can be set on the floor; or remove the flywheel and mount the engine on an engine stand.

Refitting

27 Check the engine/transmission mountings. If they're worn or damaged, renew them.

28 Inspect the clutch components and renew as necessary. Given the amount of work involved, it would be prudent to renew the clutch at this stage, regardless of condition, as described in Chapter 6, Section 2.

29 Attach the hoist to the engine and carefully lower the engine assembly into the engine compartment.

30 Carefully guide the engine into place against the transmission, then align the engine mountings with the brackets. **Note:** *It*

will be necessary to guide the transmission input shaft into the clutch, which requires precise angling and alignment. Repositioning the transmission with the jack may help. Do not use the bolts to force the engine and transmission into alignment. It may crack or damage major components.

31 Refit the engine-to-transmission bolts and tighten them to the torque listed in Chapter 7, Specifications.

32 Refit the engine mounting bolts and tighten them to the specified torque.

33 The reminder of refitting is a reversal of removal, noting the following points:

a) *Tighten all fasteners to their specified torque where given.*

b) *Fill the engine with fresh oil as described in Chapter 1, Section 3.*

c) *Replenish the coolant as described in Chapter 1, Section 19.*

d) *Check for leaks before venturing out onto the road.*

5 Engine overhaul – dismantling sequence

1 It is much easier to dismantle and work on the engine if it is mounted on a portable engine stand. These stands can often be hired from a tool hire shop. Before the engine is mounted on a stand, the flywheel should be removed, so that the stand bolts can be tightened into the end of the cylinder block/crankcase.

2 If a stand is not available, it is possible to dismantle the engine with it blocked up on a sturdy workbench, or on the floor. Be extra careful not to tip or drop the engine when working without a stand.

3 If you are going to obtain a reconditioned engine, all the external components must be removed first, to be transferred to the new engine (just as they will if you are doing a complete engine overhaul yourself). These components include the following:

a) *Engine wiring harness and supports.*

b) *Alternator and air conditioning compressor mounting brackets (as applicable).*

c) *Coolant pump (where applicable) and inlet/outlet housings.*

d) *Dipstick tube.*

e) *Fuel system components.*

f) *All electrical switches and sensors.*

g) *Intake and exhaust manifolds.*

h) *Flywheel.*

Note: *When removing the external components from the engine, pay close attention to details that may be helpful or important during refitting. Note the fitted position of gaskets, seals, spacers, pins, washers, bolts, and other small items.*

4 If you are obtaining a 'short' engine (which consists of the engine cylinder block/ crankcase, crankshaft, pistons and connecting rods all assembled), then the cylinder head, sump, oil pump, and timing belt will have to be removed also.

5 Before beginning the dismantling and overhaul procedures, make sure that you have all of the correct tools necessary. See *Tools and working facilities* for further information.

6 If you are planning a complete overhaul, the engine can be dismantled, and the internal components removed, in the order given below.

a) *Intake and exhaust manifolds (see Chapter 4A, Section 11).*
b) *Coolant pump (see Chapter 3, Section 7).*
c) *Cylinder head (see Chapter 2A, Section 9).*
d) *Flywheel (see Chapter 2A, Section 13).*
e) *Sump (see Chapter 2A, Section 10).*
f) *Oil pump (see Chapter 2A, Section 11).*
g) *Timing belt and sprockets (see Chapter 2A, Section 6).*
h) *Pistons/connecting rod assemblies (see Section 9).*
i) *Crankshaft (see Section 10).*

6 Cylinder head – dismantling

Note: *New and reconditioned cylinder heads maybe available from the manufacturer, and from engine overhaul specialists. Due to the fact that some specialist tools are required for the dismantling and inspection procedures, and that new components may not be readily available, it may be more practical and economical for the home mechanic to purchase a reconditioned head rather than to dismantle, inspect and recondition the original head. A valve spring compressor tool will be required for this operation.*

1 With the cylinder head removed as described in Chapter 2A, Section 9, clean away all external dirt, and remove the following components as applicable, if not already done:

a) *Manifolds (see Chapter 4A, Section 11).*
b) *Spark plugs (see Chapter 1, Section 16).*
c) *Camshafts and followers (see Chapter 2A, Section 8).*
d) *Engine lifting brackets.*

2 To remove a valve, fit a valve spring compressor tool. Ensure that the arms of the compressor tool are securely positioned on the head of the valve and the spring cap **(see illustration).**

6.2 Ensure the valve spring compressor is securely positioned

3 Compress the valve spring to relieve the pressure of the spring cap acting on the collets.

4 Extract the two split collets by hooking them out using a small screwdriver, then slowly release the compressor tool **(see illustration).**

5 Remove the valve cap, spring and seat, then withdraw the valve through the combustion chamber. Remove the valve stem oil seal (using long-nosed pliers if necessary) **(see illustrations).**

6 Repeat the procedure for the remaining valves, keeping all components in strict order so that they can be refitted in their original positions, unless all the components are to be renewed. If the components are to be kept and used again, place each valve assembly in a labelled polythene bag or a similar small container. Note that, as with cylinder numbering, the valves are normally numbered from the timing belt end of the engine. Make

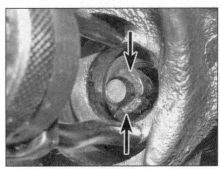

6.4 Extract the 2 collets (arrowed)

sure that the valve components are identified as intake and exhaust, as well as numbered.

7 Cylinder head and valve components – cleaning and inspection

1 Thorough cleaning of the cylinder head and valve components, followed by a detailed inspection, will enable a decision to be made on whether further work is necessary before reassembling the components.

Cleaning

2 Scrape away all traces of old gasket material and sealing compound from the cylinder head surfaces. Take care not to damage the cylinder head surfaces, as the head is made of light alloy.

3 Scrape away the carbon from the combustion chambers and ports, then wash

6.5a Remove the valve cap ...

6.5b ... spring ...

6.5c ... seat ...

6.5d ... and valve

6.5e Use long-nosed pliers to extract the valve stem oil seal

7.6 Use a straight-edge to check for surface distortion

the cylinder head thoroughly with paraffin or a suitable solvent.

4 Scrape off any heavy carbon deposits that may have formed on the valves, then use a power-operated wire brush to remove deposits from the valve heads and stems.

Inspection

Note: *Be sure to perform all the following inspection procedures before concluding that the services of a machine shop or engine overhaul specialist are required. Make a list of all items that require attention.*

Cylinder head

5 Inspect the head very carefully for cracks, evidence of coolant leakage, and other damage. If cracks are found, a new cylinder head should be obtained.

6 Use a straight-edge and feeler blades to check that the cylinder head surface is not distorted **(see illustration)**. If the specified distortion limit is exceeded, it may be possible to have the cylinder head resurfaced.

7 Examine the valve seats in each of the combustion chambers. If the seats are severely pitted, cracked or burned, then they will need to be recut or renewed by an engine overhaul specialist. If only slight pitting is evident, this can be removed by grinding the valve heads and seats together with coarse, then fine, grinding paste, as described later in this Section.

8 If the valve guides are worn, indicated by a side-to-side motion of the valve, oversize valve guides maybe available, and valves with oversize stems can be fitted. This work is best

8.5a Press the oil seal down using a suitable deep socket ...

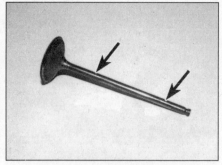

7.10 Measure the valve stem diameter at several points

carried out by an engine overhaul specialist. A dial gauge may be used to determine whether the amount of side play of a valve exceeds the specified maximum.

9 Check the follower bores in the cylinder head for wear. If excessive wear is evident, the cylinder head must be renewed. Also check the follower oil holes in the cylinder head for obstructions.

Valves

10 Examine the head of each valve for pitting, burning, cracks and general wear, and check the valve stem for scoring and wear ridges. Rotate the valve, and check for any obvious indication that it is bent. Look for pitting and excessive wear on the end of each valve stem. If the valve appears satisfactory at this stage, measure the valve stem diameter at several points using a micrometer **(see illustration)**. Any significant difference in the readings obtained indicates wear of the valve stem. Should any of these conditions be apparent, the valve(s) must be renewed. If the valves are in satisfactory condition, they should be ground (lapped) onto their respective seats to ensure a smooth gas-tight seal.

11 Valve grinding is carried out as follows. Place the cylinder head upside-down on a bench, with a block of wood at each end to give clearance for the valve stems.

12 Smear a trace of coarse carborundum paste on the seat face in the cylinder head, and press a suction grinding tool onto the relevant valve head. With a semi-rotary action, grind the valve head to its seat, lifting the valve occasionally to redistribute the grinding

8.5b ... until it's fully engaged with the valve guide

paste. When a dull, matt, even surface is produced on the faces of both the valve seat and the valve, wipe off the paste and repeat the process with fine carborundum paste. When a smooth unbroken ring of light grey matt finish is produced on both the valve and seat faces, the grinding operation is complete. Carefully clean away every trace of grinding paste, taking great care to leave none in the ports or in the valve guides. Clean the valves and valve seats with a paraffin-soaked rag, then with a clean rag, and finally, if an airline is available, blow the valves, valve guides and cylinder head ports clean.

Valve springs

13 Check that all the valve springs are intact. If any one is broken, all should be renewed.

14 If possible, check the free height of the springs against new ones, then stand each spring on a flat surface and check it for squareness. If a spring is found to be too short, or damaged in any way, renew all the springs as a set. Springs suffer from fatigue, and it is a good idea to renew them even if they look serviceable.

Followers

15 Inspect the tappets for obvious signs of wear on the contact faces, and check the oil holes for obstructions, particularly for oil sludge. If excessive wear is evident, or if any tappet has been noisy in operation, all the tappets must be renewed as a set.

8 Cylinder head – reassembly

Note: *New valve stem oil seals should be used on reassembly. A valve spring compressor tool will be required for this operation.*

1 With all the components cleaned, starting at one end of the cylinder head, fit the valve components as follows.

2 Insert the appropriate valve into its guide (if new valves are being fitted, insert each valve into the location to which it has been ground), ensuring that the valve stem is well-lubricated with clean engine oil. If the original components are being refitted, all components must be refitted in their original positions.

3 Fit the spring seat.

4 New valve stem oil seals may be supplied with a fitting sleeve, which fits over the collet groove in the valve stem, to prevent damage to the oil seal as it is slid down the valve stem. If no sleeve is supplied, wind a short length of tape round the top of the valve stem to cover the collet groove.

5 Lubricate the valve stem oil seal with clean engine oil, then push the oil seal down the valve stem using a suitable tube or socket, until the seal is fully engaged with the valve guide **(see illustrations)**. Remove the fitting sleeve or the tape, as applicable, from the valve stem.

6 Fit the valve spring and the spring cap.

7 Fit the spring compressor tool, and compress the valve spring until the spring cap passes beyond the collet groove in the valve stem.

8 Refit the split collets to the groove in the valve stem, with the narrow ends nearest the spring **(see illustration)**.

9 Slowly release the compressor tool, ensuring that the collets are not dislodged from the groove. When the compressor is fully released, give the top of the valve assembly a tap with a soft-faced mallet to settle the components.

10 Repeat the procedure for the remaining valves, ensuring that if the original components are being used, they are all refitted in their original positions.

11 Refit the components removed in Section 6, paragraph 1.

9 Piston/connecting rod assemblies – removal

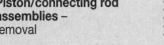

1 Remove the sump (including oil pick up tube and baffle/support plate) and cylinder head as described in Chapter 2A.

2 If there is a pronounced wear ridge at the top of any bore, it may be necessary to remove it with a scraper or ridge reamer, to avoid piston damage during removal. Such a ridge indicates excess bore wear.

3 Check to see if the big-end caps and connecting rods are numbered **(see illustration)**. If no numbers are visible, use quick-drying paint, or similar, to mark each connecting rod and big-end cap with its respective cylinder number on the flat machined surface provided. Note that No. 1 cylinder is at the timing belt end of the engine.

4 Turn the crankshaft to bring pistons 1 and 4 to BDC (bottom dead centre).

5 Unscrew the nuts from No. 1 piston big-end bearing cap, and remove the big-end cap and bearing shell. If the bearing shells are to be re-used, tape the cap and the shell together.

6 Using a hammer handle, push the piston up through the bore, and remove it from the top of the cylinder block. Recover the bearing shell, and tape it to the connecting rod for safe-keeping.

7 Loosely refit the big-end cap to the connecting rod, and secure with the bolts – this will help to keep the components in their correct order.

8 Remove No. 4 assembly in the same way.

9 Turn the crankshaft through 180° to bring pistons 2 and 3 to BDC (bottom dead centre), and remove them in the same way.

10 Crankshaft – removal

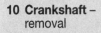

1 Remove the flywheel and oil pump as described in Chapter 2A, Section 13 and 11.

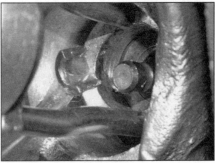

8.8 Use a little grease to hold the collet in place

2 Undo the bolts and remove the rear oil seal housing **(see illustration)**.

3 Remove the pistons and connecting rods, as described in Section 9.

4 Invert the engine so that the crankshaft is uppermost.

5 Before removing the crankshaft, check the endfloat using a dial gauge in contact with the end of the crankshaft. Push the crankshaft fully one way, and then zero the gauge. Push the crankshaft fully the other way, and check the endfloat **(see illustration)**. The result should be compared with the specified limit, and will give an indication as to the size of the main bearing thrustwasher which will be required for reassembly.

6 If a dial gauge is not available, a feeler gauge can be used to measure crankshaft endfloat. Push the crankshaft fully towards one end of the crankcase, and insert a feeler gauge between the thrust flange of the main bearing shell and the machined surface of the crankshaft web. Before measuring, ensure that the crankshaft is fully forced towards one end of the crankcase, to give the widest possible gap at the measuring location. **Note:** *Measure at the bearing with the thrustwasher (see Section 17).*

7 Check the main bearing caps to see if they're marked to indicate their locations. They should be numbered consecutively from the front of the engine to the rear. If they aren't, mark them with paint or a centre punch. Main bearing caps generally have a cast-in arrow, which points to the front of the engine. Loosen the main bearing cap bolts 1/4-turn at a time each, in the **reverse** order of

10.2 Rear oil seal housing bolts (arrowed)

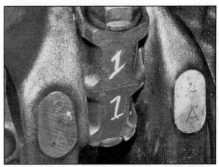

9.3 Mark the connecting rod and bearing cap with the cylinder number

the recommended tightening sequence **(see illustration 17.10)**, until they can be removed by hand.

8 Gently tap the caps with a soft-face hammer, then separate them from the engine block. If necessary, use the bolts as levers to remove the caps. Try not to drop the bearing shells if they come out with the caps.

9 Carefully lift the crankshaft out of the engine. It may be a good idea to have an assistant available, since the crankshaft is quite heavy. With the bearing shells in place in the engine block and main bearing caps or cap assembly, return the caps to their respective locations on the engine block and tighten the bolts finger-tight.

11 Cylinder block – cleaning and inspection

Cleaning

1 For complete cleaning, remove all external components (senders, sensors, brackets, oil pipes, coolant pipes, etc) from the cylinder block.

2 Scrape all traces of gasket and/or sealant from the cylinder block and cylinder block baseplate, taking particular care not to damage the cylinder head and sump mating faces.

3 Remove all oil gallery plugs, where fitted. The plugs are usually very tight – they may have to be drilled out and the holes retapped. Use new plugs when the engine is

10.5 Use a DTI gauge to measure the crankshaft endfloat

11.3a Piston oil spray nozzles (arrowed)

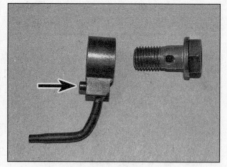

11.3b Note the nozzle locating pin (arrowed)

reassembled. Undo the retaining bolts and remove the piston oil spray nozzles from inside the cylinder block **(see illustrations)**.

4 If the block is extremely dirty, they should be steam-cleaned.

5 If the components have been steam-cleaned, clean all oil holes and oil galleries one more time on completion. Flush all internal passages with warm water until the water runs clear. Dry the block thoroughly and wipe all machined surfaces with a light oil. If you have access to compressed air, use it to speed-up the drying process, and to blow out all the oil holes and galleries.

 Warning: Wear eye protection when using compressed air.

6 If the block is relatively clean, an adequate cleaning job can be achieved with hot soapy water and a stiff brush. Take plenty of time, and do a thorough job. Regardless of the cleaning method used, be sure to clean all oil holes and galleries very thoroughly, dry everything completely, and coat all cast-iron machined surfaces with light oil.

7 The threaded holes in the cylinder block must be clean, to ensure accurate torque readings when tightening fixings during reassembly. Run the correct-size tap (which can be determined from the size of the relevant bolt) into each of the holes to remove rust, corrosion, thread sealant or other contamination, and to restore damaged threads. If possible, use compressed air to clear the holes of debris produced by this operation. Do not forget to clean the threads of all bolts and nuts which are to be re-used, as well.

12.2 Use and old feeler gauge to stop the rings dropping into the grooves

8 Where applicable, apply suitable sealant to the new oil gallery plugs, and insert them into the relevant holes in the cylinder block. Tighten the plugs securely. Refit the oil spray nozzles into the block and secure with the retaining bolts tightened to their specified torque.

9 If the engine is to be left dismantled for some time, cover the cylinder block with a large plastic bag to keep it clean and prevent corrosion. Where applicable, refit the baseplate and tighten the bolts finger-tight.

Inspection

10 Visually check the block for cracks, rust and corrosion. Look for stripped threads in the threaded holes. It's also a good idea to have the block checked for hidden cracks by an engine reconditioning specialist that has the equipment to do this type of work, especially if the vehicle had a history of overheating or using coolant. If defects are found, have the block repaired, if possible, or renewed.

11 If in any doubt as to the condition of the cylinder block, have it inspected and measured by an engine reconditioning specialist. If the bores are worn or damaged, they will be able to carry out any necessary reboring (where possible), and supply appropriate oversized pistons, etc.

12 Piston/connecting rod assemblies – inspection

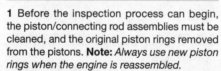

1 Before the inspection process can begin, the piston/connecting rod assemblies must be cleaned, and the original piston rings removed from the pistons. **Note:** *Always use new piston rings when the engine is reassembled.*

2 Carefully expand the old rings over the top of the pistons. The use of two or three old feeler gauges will be helpful in preventing the rings dropping into empty grooves **(see illustration)**. Take care, however, as piston rings are sharp.

3 Scrape away all traces of carbon from the top of the piston. A hand-held wire brush, or a piece of fine emery cloth, can be used once the majority of the deposits have been scraped away.

4 Remove the carbon from the ring grooves

in the piston, using an old ring. Break the ring in half to do this (be careful not to cut your fingers – piston rings are sharp). Be very careful to remove only the carbon deposits – do not remove any metal, and do not nick or scratch the sides of the ring grooves.

5 Once the deposits have been removed, clean the piston/connecting rod assembly with paraffin or a suitable solvent, and dry thoroughly. Make sure that the oil return holes in the ring grooves are clear.

6 If the pistons and cylinder bores are not damaged or worn excessively, and if the cylinder block does not need to be rebored, the original pistons can be refitted. Normal piston wear shows up as even vertical wear on the piston thrust surfaces, and slight looseness of the top ring in its groove.

7 Carefully inspect each piston for cracks around the skirt, at the gudgeon pin bosses, and at the piston ring lands (between the ring grooves).

8 Look for scoring and scuffing on the thrust faces of the piston skirt, holes in the piston crown, and burned areas at the edge of the crown. If the skirt is scored or scuffed, the engine may have been suffering from overheating, and/or abnormal combustion ('pinking') which caused excessively-high operating temperatures. The cooling and lubrication systems should be checked thoroughly. A hole in the piston crown, or burned areas at the edge of the piston crown indicates that abnormal combustion (pre-ignition, 'pinking', knocking or detonation) has been occurring. If any of the above problems exist, the causes must be investigated and corrected, or the damage will occur again.

9 Corrosion of the piston, in the form of pitting, indicates that coolant has been leaking into the combustion chamber and/or the crankcase. Again, the cause must be corrected, or the problem may persist in the rebuilt engine.

10 If in any doubt as to the condition of the pistons and connecting rods, have them inspected and measured by an engine reconditioning specialist. If new parts are required, they will be able to supply and fit appropriate-sized pistons/rings, and rebore (where possible) or hone the cylinder block.

13 Crankshaft – inspection

1 Clean the crankshaft using paraffin or a suitable solvent, and dry it, preferably with compressed air if available. Be sure to clean the oil holes with a pipe cleaner or similar probe, to ensure that they are not obstructed.

 Warning: Wear eye protection when using compressed air.

2 Check the main and big-end bearing journals for uneven wear, scoring, pitting and cracking.

3 Big-end bearing wear is accompanied by distinct metallic knocking when the engine is running (particularly noticeable when the engine is pulling from low revs), and some loss of oil pressure.

4 Main bearing wear is accompanied by severe engine vibration and rumble – getting progressively worse as engine revs increase – and again by loss of oil pressure.

5 Check the bearing journal for roughness by running a finger lightly over the bearing surface. Any roughness (which will be accompanied by obvious bearing wear) indicates that the crankshaft requires regrinding.

6 If the crankshaft has been reground, check for burrs around the crankshaft oil holes (the holes are usually chamfered, so burrs should not be a problem unless regrinding has been carried out carelessly). Remove any burrs with a fine file or scraper, and thoroughly clean the oil holes as described previously.

7 Have the crankshaft journals measured by an engine reconditioning specialist. If the crankshaft is worn or damaged, they may be able to regrind the journals and supply suitable undersize bearing shells. If no undersize shells are available and the crankshaft has worn beyond the specified limits, it will have to be renewed. Consult your Mazda dealer or engine reconditioning specialist for further information on parts availability.

14 Main and big-end bearings – inspection

1 Even though the main and big-end bearings should be renewed during the engine overhaul, the old bearings should be retained for close examination, as they may reveal valuable information about the condition of the engine.

2 Bearing failure occurs because of lack of lubrication, the presence of dirt or other foreign particles, overloading the engine, or corrosion **(see illustration)**. If a bearing fails, the cause must be found and eliminated before the engine is reassembled, to prevent the failure from happening again.

3 To examine the bearing shells, remove them from the cylinder block, the cylinder block baseplate, the connecting rods and the big-end bearing caps, and lay them out on a clean surface in the same order as they were fitted to the engine. This will enable any bearing problems to be matched with the corresponding crankshaft journal.

4 Dirt and other foreign particles can enter the engine in a variety of ways. Contamination may be left in the engine during assembly, or it may pass through filters or the crankcase ventilation system. Normal engine wear produces small particles of metal, which can eventually cause problems. If particles find their way into the lubrication system, it is likely that they will eventually be carried to the bearings. Whatever the source, these foreign particles often end up embedded in the soft

bearing material, and are easily recognised. Large particles will not embed in the bearing, and will score or gouge the bearing and journal. To prevent possible contamination, clean all parts thoroughly, and keep everything spotlessly-clean during engine assembly. Once the engine has been installed in the vehicle, ensure that engine oil and filter changes are carried out at the recommended intervals.

5 Lack of lubrication (or lubrication breakdown) has a number of interrelated causes. Excessive heat (which thins the oil), overloading (which squeezes the oil from the bearing face), and oil leakage (from excessive bearing clearances, worn oil pump or high engine speeds) all contribute to lubrication breakdown. Blocked oil passages, which may be the result of misaligned oil holes in a bearing shell, will also starve a bearing of oil and destroy it. When lack of lubrication is the cause of bearing failure, the bearing material is wiped or extruded from the steel backing of the bearing. Temperatures may increase to the point where the steel backing turns blue from overheating.

6 Driving habits can have a definite effect on bearing life. Full-throttle, low-speed operation (labouring the engine) puts very high loads on bearings, which tends to squeeze out the oil film. These loads cause the bearings to flex, which produces fine cracks in the bearing face (fatigue failure). Eventually the bearing material will loosen in places, and tear away from the steel backing. Regular short journeys can lead to corrosion of bearings, because insufficient engine heat is produced to drive off the condensed water and corrosive gases which form inside the engine. These products collect in the engine oil, forming acid and sludge. As the oil is carried to the bearings, the acid attacks and corrodes the bearing material.

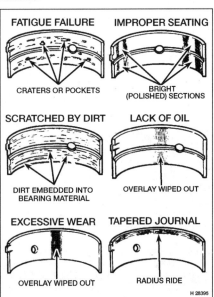

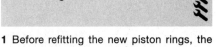

14.2 Main bearing failures

7 Incorrect bearing installation during engine assembly will also lead to bearing failure. Tight-fitting bearings leave insufficient bearing lubrication clearance, and will result in oil starvation. Dirt or foreign particles trapped behind a bearing shell results in high spots on the bearing which can lead to failure.

8 *Do not* touch any shell's bearing surface with your fingers during reassembly; there is a risk of scratching the delicate surface, or of depositing particles of dirt on it.

9 As mentioned at the beginning of this Section, the bearing shells should be renewed as a matter of course during engine overhaul; to do otherwise is false economy.

15 Engine overhaul – reassembly sequence

1 Before reassembly begins, ensure that all necessary new parts have been obtained (particularly gaskets, and various bolts which must be renewed), and that all the tools required are available. Read through the entire procedure to familiarise yourself with the work involved, and to ensure that all items necessary for reassembly of the engine are to hand. In addition to all normal tools and materials, a thread-locking compound will be required. A tube of suitable sealant will be required to seal certain joint faces which are not fitted with gaskets.

2 At this stage, all engine components should be absolutely clean and dry, with all faults repaired. The components should be laid out (or in individual containers) on a completely clean work surface.

3 In order to save time and avoid problems, engine reassembly can be carried out in the following order:
 a) *Piston rings (see Section 16).*
 b) *Crankshaft (see Section 17).*
 c) *Piston/connecting rod assemblies (see Section 18).*
 d) *Oil pump (see Chapter 2A, Section 11).*
 e) *Sump (see Chapter 2A, Section 10).*
 f) *Flywheel (see Chapter 2A, Section 13).*
 g) *Cylinder head (see Chapter 2A, Section 9).*
 h) *Coolant pump (see Chapter 3, Section 7).*
 i) *Timing belt and sprockets (see Chapter 2A, Section 6).*
 j) *Intake and exhaust manifolds (see Chapter 4A, Section 11).*

16 Piston rings – refitting

1 Before refitting the new piston rings, the ring end gaps must be checked as follows.

2 Lay out the piston/connecting rod assemblies and the new piston ring sets, so that the ring sets will be matched with the same piston and cylinder during the end gap measurement and subsequent engine reassembly.

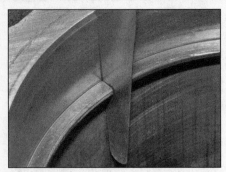

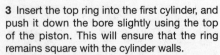

16.4 Measure the ring end gap with feeler gauges

16.9 Oil control ring assembly

16.10 Fit the compression rings, using a feeler gauge

3 Insert the top ring into the first cylinder, and push it down the bore slightly using the top of the piston. This will ensure that the ring remains square with the cylinder walls.

4 Measure the end gap using feeler gauges, and compare the measurements with the figures given in the Specifications **(see illustration)**.

5 If the gap is too small (unlikely if genuine Mazda parts are used), it must be enlarged or the ring ends may contact each other during engine operation, causing serious damage. Ideally, new piston rings providing the correct end gap should be fitted, but as a last resort, the end gap can be increased by filing the ring ends very carefully with a fine file. Mount the file in a vice equipped with soft jaws, slip the ring over the file with the ends contacting the file face, and slowly move the ring to remove material from the ends – take care, as piston rings are sharp, and are easily broken.

6 With new piston rings, it is unlikely that the end gap will be too large. If they are too large, check that you have the correct rings for your engine and for the particular cylinder bore size.

7 Repeat the checking procedure for each ring in the first cylinder, and then for the rings in the remaining cylinders. Remember to keep rings, pistons and cylinders matched up.

8 Once the ring end gaps have been checked and if necessary corrected, the rings can be fitted to the pistons.

9 The oil control ring (lowest one on the piston) is composed of three sections and should be installed first. Fit the lower steel ring, then the spreader ring, followed by the upper steel ring **(see illustration)**.

10 With the oil control ring components installed, the second (middle) ring can be fitted. It is usually stamped with a mark which must face up, towards the top of the piston. **Note:** *Always follow the instructions supplied with the new piston ring sets – different manufacturers may specify different procedures. Do not mix up the top and middle rings, as they have different cross-sections.* Using two or three old feeler blades, as for removal of the old rings, carefully slip the ring into place in the middle groove **(see illustration)**.

11 Fit the top ring in the same manner, ensuring that, where applicable, the mark on the ring is facing up.

12 Repeat the procedure for the remaining pistons and rings.

17 Crankshaft – refitting

1 Refitting the crankshaft is the first step in the engine reassembly procedure. It is assumed at this point that the cylinder block and crankshaft have been cleaned, inspected and repaired or reconditioned as necessary.

2 Clean the bearing shells and the bearing recesses in both the cylinder block and the main bearing caps.

3 If new shells are being fitted, ensure that all traces of the protective grease are cleaned off using paraffin. Wipe the shells dry with a clean lint-free cloth.

4 Note that the crankshaft endfloat is controlled by thrustwashers located either side of the No. 4 main bearing shell in the cylinder block.

5 If the original bearing shells are being re-used, they must be refitted to their original locations in the block and bearing caps.

6 Fit the upper main bearing shells and thrustwashers in place in the cylinder block **(see illustrations)**.

7 Liberally lubricate each bearing shell in the cylinder block, and lower the crankshaft into position **(see illustrations)**.

8 If necessary, seat the crankshaft using light taps from a soft-faced mallet on the crankshaft balance webs.

9 Clean the faces of the bearings in the caps, then apply lubricant to them. Install the caps in their respective positions with the arrows pointing toward the front of the engine **(see illustration)**.

10 Apply a light coat of oil to the bolt threads and the undersides of the bolt heads, then install them. Tighten all main bearing cap bolts to the specified torque, following the recommended sequence **(see illustration)**.

11 Rotate the crankshaft a number of times by hand to check for any obvious binding.

12 Check the crankshaft endfloat with a feeler gauge or a dial indicator as described in Section 10. The endfloat should be correct if the

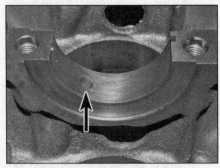

17.6a The oil hole in the saddle (arrowed) ...

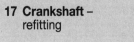

17.6b ... must align with the hole in the bearing shell. Note that the shells in the block have an oil groove (arrowed)

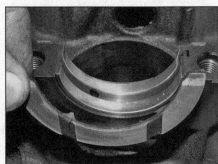

17.6c Fit the thrustwashers, oil groove outwards to the No. 4 main bearing location in the block

crankshaft thrust faces aren't worn or damaged and new thrustwashers have been installed.

13 Refit the rear oil seal housing and the new oil seal (see Chapter 2A, Section 12).

14 Refit the pistons and connecting rods as described in Section 18.

15 Refit the flywheel and oil pump as described in Chapter 2A, Section 13 and 11.

18 Pistons/connecting rods – refitting

1 Clean the backs of the big-end bearing shells and the recesses in the connecting rods and big-end caps. If new shells are being fitted, ensure that all traces of the protective grease are cleaned off using paraffin. Wipe the shells, caps and connecting rods dry with a lint-free cloth.

2 Press the bearing shells into the connecting rods and caps in their correct positions. **Note:** *Ensure that the mating faces of the connecting rods and big-end bearing caps are clean before refitting (refer to Section 9).*

3 Lubricate No. 1 piston and piston rings, and check that the ring gaps are correctly positioned. The gaps in the upper and lower steel rings of the oil control ring should be offset by 30° to the right and left of the spreader ring gap. The two upper compression ring gaps should be offset by 60° to each other.

4 Liberally lubricate the cylinder bore with clean engine oil.

5 Slip a section of plastic or rubber hose over each connecting rod cap bolt.

6 Fit a ring compressor to No. 1 piston, then with the dimple on the top of piston facing the front of the engine, insert the piston and connecting rod into the cylinder bore so that the base of the compressor stands on the block. With the crankshaft big-end bearing journal positioned at its lowest point, tap the piston carefully into the cylinder bore with the wooden handle of a hammer, and at the same time guide the connecting rod onto the bearing journal **(see illustrations)**.

7 Remove the plastic/rubber hose from the connecting rod studs.

8 Fit the bearing shells to the bearing caps.

9 Liberally lubricate the bearing journals and

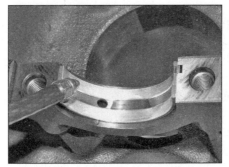

17.7a Liberally lubricate the bearing shells ...

17.9 The arrow on the bearing caps (arrowed) must point to the front of the engine

bearing shells, and fit the bearing cap in its original location. Tighten the bearing cap nuts to the specified torque **(see illustration)**.

10 After refitting each piston/connecting rod assembly, rotate the crankshaft, and check that it turns freely, with no signs of binding or tight spots.

19 Engine – initial start-up after overhaul

1 With the engine refitted in the vehicle, double-check the engine oil and coolant levels. Make a final check that everything has been reconnected, and that there are no tools or rags left in the engine compartment.

2 Start the engine, noting that this may take a little longer than usual. Make sure that the oil pressure warning light goes out.

17.7b ... and lower the crankshaft into place

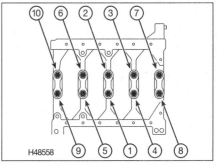

17.10 Main bearing bolts tightening sequence

3 While the engine is idling, check for fuel, water and oil leaks. Don't be alarmed if there are some odd smells and smoke from parts getting hot and burning off oil deposits.

4 Assuming all is well, keep the engine idling until hot water is felt circulating through the top hose, then switch off the engine.

5 After a few minutes, recheck the oil and coolant levels as described in *Weekly checks*, and top-up as necessary.

6 Note that there is no need to retighten the cylinder head bolts once the engine has first run after reassembly.

7 If new pistons, rings or crankshaft bearings have been fitted, the engine must be treated as new, and run-in for the first 600 miles. Do not operate the engine at full-throttle, or allow it to labour at low engine speeds in any gear. It is recommended that the oil and filter be changed at the end of this period.

18.6a Gently tap the piston/rod assembly into the bore

18.6b The dimple on the top of the piston (arrowed) must face the front of the engine

18.9 Ensure the previously-made marks (arrowed) align

Chapter 3
Cooling, heating and ventilation systems

Contents

Degrees of difficulty

Easy, suitable for novice with little experience	Fairly easy, suitable for beginner with some experience	Fairly difficult, suitable for competent DIY mechanic	Difficult, suitable for experienced DIY mechanic	Very difficult, suitable for expert DIY or professional

Specifications

General

Radiator cap.. 0.75 to 1.25 bar

Coolant temperature sensor

Resistance:
1993 and earlier @ 80°C.................................	290 to 350 Ω
1994 to 2000 @ 60°C...................................	560 to 640 Ω
2000-on @ 80°C......................................	290 to 340 Ω

Thermostat

Opening temperature:
1.6 litre engines	80.5 to 83.5°C
1.8 litre engines	83.5 to 86.5°C

Torque wrench settings	Nm	lbf ft
Coolant inlet pipe bolts	22	16
Coolant pump bolts	20	15
Coolant temperature sensor..............................	25	17
Thermostat housing cover bolts...........................	22	16

1 General information and precautions

The cooling system is of pressurised type, comprising a pump driven by the auxiliary drivebelt, an aluminium crossflow radiator, electric cooling fan, and a thermostat. The system functions as follows. Cold coolant from the radiator passes through the hose to the coolant pump, where it is pumped around the cylinder block and head passages. After cooling the cylinder bores, combustion surfaces and valve seats, the coolant reaches the underside of the thermostat, which is initially closed. The coolant passes through the heater, and is returned to the coolant pump.

When the engine is cold, the coolant circulates only through the cylinder block, cylinder head and heater. When the coolant reaches a predetermined temperature, the thermostat opens and the coolant passes through to the radiator. As the coolant circulates through the radiator, it is cooled by the inrush of air when the car is in forward motion. Airflow is supplemented by the action of the electric cooling fan when necessary. Once the coolant has passed through the radiator, and has cooled, the cycle is repeated.

The electric cooling fan, mounted on the rear of the radiator, is controlled by a thermostatic switch/sensor. At a predetermined coolant temperature, the fan is actuated.

An expansion tank is fitted into the engine compartment to accommodate expansion of the coolant when it gets hot. The expansion tank is connected to the top of the radiator by a small bore rubber hose.

⚠️ *Warning: Do not attempt to remove the expansion tank filler cap, or disturb any part of the cooling system, while the engine is hot; there is a high risk of scalding. If the expansion tank filler cap must be removed before the engine and radiator have fully cooled (even though* this is not recommended) the pressure in the cooling system must first be relieved. Cover the cap with a thick layer of cloth, to avoid scalding, and slowly unscrew the filler cap until a hissing sound can be heard. When the hissing has stopped, indicating that the pressure has reduced, slowly unscrew the filler cap until it can be removed; if more hissing sounds are heard, wait until they have stopped before unscrewing the cap completely. At all times, keep well away from the filler cap opening.*

• *Do not allow antifreeze to come into contact with skin, or with the painted surfaces of the vehicle. Rinse off spills immediately, with plenty of water. Never leave antifreeze lying around in an open container, or in a puddle on the driveway or garage floor. Children and pets are attracted by its sweet smell, but antifreeze can be fatal if ingested.*

• *If the engine is hot, the electric cooling fan may start rotating even if the engine is not running; be careful to keep hands, hair and loose clothing well clear when working in the engine compartment.*

• *Refer to Section 10 for precautions to be observed when working on models equipped with air conditioning.*

2 Cooling system hoses – disconnection and renewal

Note: *Refer to the warnings given in Section 1 of this Chapter before proceeding. Do not attempt to disconnect any hose while the system is still hot.*

1 If the checks described in Chapter 1, Section 7 reveal a faulty hose, it must be renewed as follows.

2 First drain the cooling system (see Chapter 1, Section 19). If the coolant is not due for renewal, it may be re-used if it is collected in a clean container.

3 Before disconnecting a hose, first note its routing in the engine compartment, and whether it is secured by any additional retaining clips or cable-ties. Use a pair of pliers to release the clamp-type clips, or a screwdriver to slacken the screw-type clips, then move the clips along the hose, clear of the relevant inlet/outlet union. Carefully work the hose free.

4 Note that the radiator inlet and outlet unions are fragile; do not use excessive force when attempting to remove the hoses. If a hose proves to be difficult to remove, try to release it by rotating the hose ends before attempting to free it.

5 When fitting a hose, first slide the clips onto the hose, then work the hose into position. If clamp-type clips were originally fitted, it is a good idea to use screw-type clips when refitting the hose. If the hose is stiff, use a little soapy water (washing-up liquid is ideal) as a lubricant, or soften the hose by soaking it in hot water.

6 Work the hose into position, checking that it is correctly routed and secured. Slide each clip along the hose until it passes over the flared end of the relevant inlet/outlet union, before tightening the clips securely.

7 Refill the cooling system with reference to Chapter 1, Section 19.

8 Check thoroughly for leaks as soon as possible after disturbing any part of the cooling system.

3 Radiator – removal, inspection and refitting

Removal

1 Drain the engine coolant as described in Chapter 1, Section 19.

2 Remove the cooling fan(s) as described in Section 5.

3 Disconnect the reservoir hose from the filler neck, loosen the clamps and disconnect the upper and lower radiator hoses **(see illustrations)**.

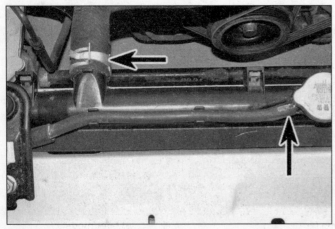

3.3a Disconnect the reservoir hose, then release the clamps and disconnect the radiator upper hose (arrowed) …   **3.3b … and lower hose (arrowed)**

4 Remove the radiator mounting bolts. On 1997 and earlier models, there are two bolts, one at each upper corner of the radiator. On some earlier models, there are also mounting pins at the lower left and right edges of the radiator (**see illustrations**). The radiator on models from 1998 is secured by two mounting brackets, one near each upper corner, which are secured by nuts. Lift the radiator out from above.

Inspection

5 With the radiator removed, it can be inspected for leaks, damage and internal blockage. If in need of repairs, have a professional radiator repairer perform the work as special techniques are required.
6 Insects and dirt can be cleaned from the radiator with compressed air and a soft brush. Don't bend the cooling fins as this is done.

 Warning: Wear eye protection when using compressed air.

Radiator flushing

7 Disconnect the top and bottom hoses and any other relevant hoses from the radiator.
8 Insert a garden hose into the radiator top inlet. Direct a flow of clean water through the radiator, and continue flushing until clean water emerges from the radiator bottom outlet.
9 If after a reasonable period, the water still does not run clear, the radiator can be flushed with a good proprietary cleaning agent. It is important that their manufacturer's instructions are followed carefully. If the contamination is particularly bad, insert the hose in the radiator bottom outlet, and reverse-flush the radiator.

Refitting

10 Refitting is a reversal of removal, bearing in mind the following points:
   a) *Ensure that all hoses are correctly reconnected, and their retaining clips securely tightened.*
   b) *On completion, refill the cooling system as described in Chapter 1, Section 19.*

---

4   Thermostat –
    testing, removal and refitting

Removal

1 Before assuming the thermostat is responsible for a cooling system problem, check the coolant level (*Weekly checks*), drivebelt tension (Chapter 1, Section 6) and temperature gauge (or light) operation.
2 If the engine takes a long time to warm up (as indicated by the temperature gauge or heater operation), the thermostat is probably stuck open. Renew the thermostat.
3 If the engine runs hot, use your hand to check the temperature of the upper radiator hose. If the hose is not hot, but the engine is, the thermostat is probably stuck in the closed

3.4a On early models, the radiator is secured by a bolt (arrowed) at the top each side ...

3.4b ... and rests on mounting pins (arrowed)

3.4c On later models, the radiator retaining bracket at the top each side is secured by a nut (arrowed)

3.4d The radiator is removed upwards from the engine compartment

position, preventing the coolant inside the engine from traveling through the radiator. Renew the thermostat.
4 If the lower radiator hose is hot, it means that the coolant is flowing and the thermostat is open. Consult the *Fault finding* Section at the end of this manual for further diagnosis.

Removal

5 On 1993 or earlier models, disconnect the negative cable from the battery as described in Chapter 5A, Section 4.
6 Drain the coolant from the radiator (see Chapter 1, Section 19).
7 If you're working on a 1993 or earlier model, disconnect the thermoswitch electrical connector from the thermostat cover located at the front of the cylinder head.

8 Loosen the clamp (do this with pliers on original-equipment spring-type clamps) and disconnect the radiator hose from the thermostat cover (**see illustrations**). **Note:** *The radiator hose can be left attached to the thermostat cover, unless the thermostat cover itself is to be renewed.*
9 Detach the thermostat cover from the engine (**see illustrations**). Be prepared for some coolant spillage as the gasket seal is broken.
10 Remove the thermostat, noting the direction in which it was installed in the block.
11 Remove the gasket and thoroughly clean the sealing surfaces.

Refitting

12 Fit the thermostat with the spring end down (1993 and earlier) or toward the engine

4.8a Slacken the clamp (arrowed) and disconnect the radiator hose from the thermostat cover – early models ...

4.8b ... and later models

4.9a Thermostat cover bolts (arrowed) – early models ...

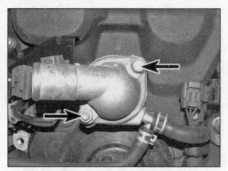

4.9b ... and later models

4.12a Fit the thermostat with the spring side down – early models ...

4.12b ... or towards the engine with the bleed hole (arrowed) at the top – later models

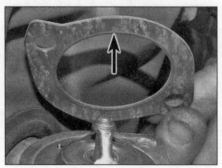

4.13 Fit the gasket with the sealant (arrowed) facing the thermostat

with the bleed hole at the top (1994 and later) **(see illustrations).**
13 Fit a new gasket, aligning the gasket with the bolt holes in the block.

a) *On 1993 and earlier models, if fitting a genuine Mazda gasket, fit the gasket with the sealant side facing down (toward the thermostat)* **(see illustration).**

b) *On 1994 and later models, fit the gasket with the tab facing the thermostat cover.*
14 Refitting is a reversal of removal, bearing in mind the following points:
   a) *Fit the new sealing rings to all applicable mating faces.*
   b) *Tighten the thermostat cover bolts to the specified torque.*
   c) *On completion, refill the cooling system as described in Chapter 1, Section 19.*

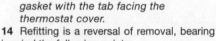

5 Electric cooling fan – removal and refitting

⚠ **Warning: If the engine is hot, the cooling fan may start up at any time. Take extra precautions when working in the vicinity of the fan.**

Removal

1 Disconnect the negative battery cable as described in Chapter 5A, Section 4.
2 Remove the air intake duct **(see illustration).**
3 Disconnect the wiring connector at the fan motor.
4 Unbolt the left-hand fan shroud and lift the fan assembly from the engine compartment, then unbolt and remove the right-hand fan assembly (where fitted) **(see illustrations).** Note that on later models, the lower edge of the shroud locates in rubber mountings.
5 While holding the fan blades, remove the fan retaining nut **(see illustration).** Remove the fan from the fan motor.
6 Remove the fan motor from the fan shroud.

Refitting

7 Refitting is a reversal of removal, bearing in mind the following points:
   a) *Ensure that the shroud is correctly located on the radiator.*
   b) *Use new cable-ties to secure all disturbed wiring harnesses.*
   c) *On completion, start the engine and run it until it reaches normal operating temperature; continue to run the engine, and check that the cooling fan cuts in and functions correctly.*

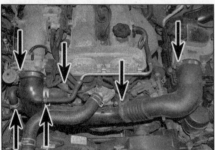

5.2 Depending on the model, the intake ducting may be secured by various clamps, bolts and hoses (arrowed)

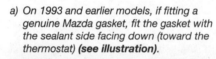

5.4a Undo the bolts at the top of the fan shroud (arrowed)

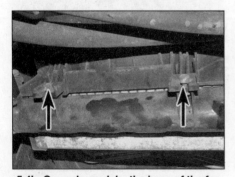

5.4b On early models, the base of the fan shroud is also retained by bolts (arrowed)

5.5 Undo the fan retaining nut

6 Cooling system switches and sensors – testing, removal and refitting

Coolant temperature sensor

Testing

1 If the coolant temperature gauge is inoperative, check the fuses first (see Chapter 12, Section 3).

2 If the temperature gauge indicates excessive temperature after running a while, see the *Fault finding* Section at the end of the manual.

3 If the temperature gauge indicates HOT as soon as the engine is started cold, disconnect the electrical connector at the coolant sensor, located at rear of the engine **(see illustration)**. If the gauge reading drops, renew the sensor. If the reading remains high, the wire to the gauge may be shorted to earth or the gauge is faulty.

4 If the coolant temperature gauge fails to show any indication after the engine has been warmed up, (approximately 10 minutes) and the fuses are good, shut off the engine. Disconnect the electrical connector at the sending unit and, using a jumper wire, connect the wire to a clean earth on the engine. Briefly turn on the ignition without starting the engine. If the gauge now indicates HOT, renew the sending unit.

5 Additionally, the sending unit may be checked for resistance using an ohmmeter; with the engine coolant hot, compare the resistance measured with the Specifications.

6 If the gauge fails to respond, the circuit may be open or the temperature gauge may be faulty.

Removal

7 Drain the coolant (see Chapter 1, Section 19).

8 Disconnect the wiring connector from the sensor.

9 Using a deep socket or a spaner, remove the sensor.

Refitting

10 Install the new sensor, and tighten it to the specified torque. Do not use thread sealer as it may electrically insulate the sending unit. Connect the electrical connector.

11 Refill the cooling system and check for coolant leakage and proper gauge operation.

Cooling fan thermoswitch

Note: *Only fitted to 1993 and earlier models*

Removal

12 Drain the cooling system (see Chapter 1, Section 19).

13 To renew the fan thermoswitch, disconnect the electrical connector and unscrew the switch from the thermostat housing **(see illustration)**.

14 Install the new switch with a new O-ring and tighten it securely. Connect the electrical connector.

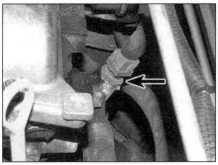

6.3 The coolant temperature sensor is located at the rear of the cylinder head (arrowed)

Refitting

15 Refitting is a reversal of removal, bearing in mind the following points:

 a) *Where applicable fit a new sealing O-ring to the switch.*

 b) *On completion, top-up/refill the cooling system as described in Chapter 1, Section 19.*

7 Coolant pump – testing, removal and refitting

Testing

1 A failure in the coolant pump can cause serious engine damage due to overheating. If the pump is defective, it should be renewed or rebuilt unit fitted.

2 Remove the timing belt cover(s) (see Chapter 2A, Section 6).

3 Coolant pumps are equipped with weep or vent holes. If a failure occurs in the pump seal, coolant will leak from the hole. In most cases you'll need an electric torch to find the hole on the coolant pump from underneath to check for leaks. Any coolant coming from this hole is vented to the outside of the timing belt cover on the rear in order to not damage the timing belt.

4 Check the coolant pump shaft bearing for wear by grasping the pump hub and gently rocking the hub and shaft from side to side. If

6.13 The thermoswitch is located on the top of the thermostat housing (arrowed)

any looseness is apparent, excessive coolant pump shaft/bearing wear is possible.

5 If the coolant pump shaft bearings fail there may be a howling sound at the drivebelt end of the engine while it's running. Don't mistake drivebelt slippage, which causes a squealing sound, for coolant pump bearing failure. If a squealing sound is heard, check belt condition and belt tension.

Removal

6 Remove the timing belt as described in Chapter 2A, Section 6. If the pump is to be renewed, remove the timing belt tensioner and idler pulleys – also as described in Chapter 2A, Section 6.

7 Undo the bolts securing the coolant inlet pipe to the coolant pump **(see illustration)**. Recover the gasket.

8 Undo the mounting bolts **(see illustration)** and detach the coolant pump from the engine. If the coolant pump is stuck, gently tap it with a soft-faced hammer to break the seal.

Refitting

9 Clean the bolt threads and the threaded holes in the engine to remove corrosion and sealant.

10 Remove all traces of old gasket material from the sealing surfaces.

11 Fit the new gasket and position the coolant pump on the engine **(see illustration)**.

12 Refit the mounting bolts and tighten them to the specified torque.

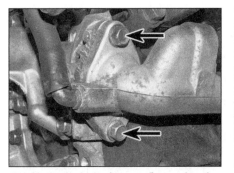

7.7 Undo the bolts (arrowed) securing the coolant inlet pipe to the pump

7.8 Coolant pump bolts (arrowed)

7.11 Renew the coolant pump gasket

7.13 Don't forget to refit the sealing strip at the top of the pump

9 Heater/ventilation system components – removal and refitting

13 The remainder of refitting is a reversal of removal **(see illustration)**.

14 Refill the cooling system (see Chapter 1, Section 19), then start the engine and check for leaks.

8 Heater/ventilation system – general information

The heater/ventilation system consists of a four-speed blower, face-level vents in the facia, and air ducts to the footwells and windscreen.

The controls operate flap valves to deflect and mix the air flowing through the various parts of the heater/ventilation system. The flap valves are contained in the air distribution housing, which acts as a central distribution unit, passing air to the various ducts and vents.

Cold air enters the system through the grille at the rear of the engine compartment. A pollen filter is fitted to the ventilation intake, to filter out dust, soot, pollen and spores from the air entering the vehicle.

The air (boosted by the blower fan if required) then flows through the various ducts, according to the settings of the controls. Stale air is expelled through ducts behind the doors. If warm air is required, the cold air is passed through the heater matrix, which is heated by the engine coolant.

A recirculation lever enables the outside air supply to be closed off, while the air inside the vehicle is recirculated. This can be useful to prevent unpleasant odours entering from outside the vehicle, but should only be used briefly, as the recirculated air inside the vehicle will soon deteriorate.

Heater controls – removal and refitting

1 Disconnect the battery negative terminal as described in Chapter 5A, Section 4.

1997 and earlier models

2 Remove the centre console and glovebox as described in Chapter 11, Section 27 and 26.

3 Carefully prise out the air ducts from the facia centre panel **(see illustration)**.

4 Undo the screw in the top of each duct aperture and the screw at the base of the panel. Manoeuvre the panel rearwards, disconnecting the wiring pugs as the panel is withdrawn **(see illustrations)**.

5 Disconnect the temperature blend, airflow mode and recirculation cables from the side of the heater distribution housing **(see illustrations)**. To improve access, remove the glovebox (Chapter 11, Section 26), then undo the screws and remove the trim panel above the pedals.

6 Undo the screws and pull the control assembly from the facia **(see illustration)**. Disconnect the wiring plugs as the assembly is withdrawn.

1998-on models

7 Disconnect the temperature blend, airflow mode and recirculation cables from the side of the heater distribution housing **(see**

9.3 Prise out the air ducts from the centre panel ...

9.4a Undo the screw at the top of each air vent aperture ...

9.4b ... and the screw at the base (arrowed) ...

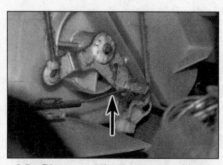

9.4c ... then gently pull the panel rearwards

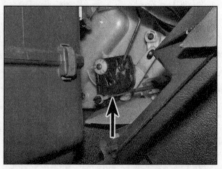

9.5a Disconnect the temperature blend cable (arrowed) on the right-hand side of the heater housing ...

9.5b ... the airflow mode cable (arrowed) on the left-hand side ...

9.5c ... and the recirculation cable (arrowed) adjacent to the blower motor housing

9.6 Heater control panel retaining screws (arrowed)

9.8a Carefully prise the trim pieces from each side of the control panel

illustrations 9.5a to 9.5c). To improve access, remove the glovebox (Chapter 11, Section 26), then undo the screws and remove the trim panel above the pedals.

8 Carefully prise away the small trim pieces each side of the control panel, then insert Mazda special tools No. SST 49 D066 801A (or equivalent) into the holes and pull the panel from place (see illustrations). Disconnect the wiring plugs as the panel is withdrawn. Note that these tools are identical to the commonly used audio unit removal tools.

All models

9 Refitting is a reversal of removal, carrying out the adjustment procedure described below, prior to refitting the centre panel and console.

Heater controls – adjustment

10 Set the temperature blend control lever to the maximum heat position, move the lever on the housing to the maximum heat position, reconnect the cable and press the outer cable into the clamp (see illustration 9.5a). Check the control lever moves to its full stroke.

11 Set the airflow mode control lever to the facia vent position, move the lever on the housing to facia vent position, then reconnect the cable and press the outer cable into the clamp (see illustration 9.5b). Check the control lever moves to its full stroke.

12 Set the recirculation control lever to the Fresh air position, move the lever on the housing to the Fresh position, then reconnect the cable and press the outer cable into the clamp (see illustration 9.5c). Check the control lever moves to its full stroke.

Heater control assembly cables

Removal

13 Remove the control panel as described earlier in this Section.

14 Note the orientation of the control cables, then release the outer cable retaining clips and disconnect the inner cable ends from the control levers (see illustrations).

Refitting

15 Refitting is a reversal of removal.

9.8b Insert the special tools into the holes each (arrowed)

Heater matrix

Removal

16 Remove the air distribution housing as described later in this Section.

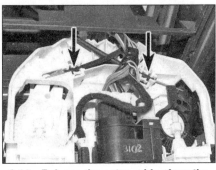

9.14a Release the outer cables from the retaining clips (arrowed) – later models ...

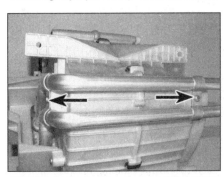

9.17 Undo the screws (arrowed) securing the pipe clamps

9.8c The special tools simply force the retaining clips (arrowed) inwards

17 Undo the screws securing the matrix pipe clamps (see illustration).

18 Unclip the control rod over the matrix cover (see illustrations).

19 Undo the screws securing the cover,

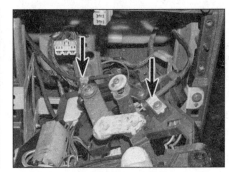

9.14b ... and early models (arrowed)

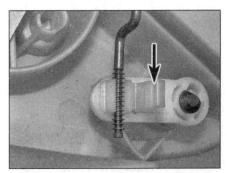

9.18a Prise open the clip (arrowed) ...

9.18b ... and unclip the control rod over the cover (arrowed)

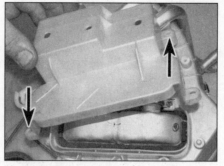

9.19a Undo the screws (arrowed), remove the cover ...

9.19b ... then pull the matrix from the housing

then pull the matrix from the housing **(see illustrations)**. Check the condition of the foam seal around the matrix. If required, slacken the clamps and disconnect the pipes from the matrix. Discard the pipe seals – new ones must be fitted.

Refitting

20 Refitting is a reversal of the removal procedure.

Heater blower motor

Removal

21 Disconnect the battery negative terminal as described in Chapter 5A, Section 4.
22 Remove the passenger's side glovebox as described in Chapter 11, Section 26.
23 Reach under the passenger's side of the facia, trace the loom back and disconnect the blower motor wiring plug **(see illustration)**.
24 Undo the retaining screws, and lower the

blower motor from the air distribution housing **(see illustration)**.

Refitting

25 Refitting is a reversal of the removal procedure.

Heater blower motor resistor

Removal

26 Disconnect the battery negative terminal as described in Chapter 5A, Section 4.
27 Remove the passenger's side glovebox as described in Chapter 11, Section 26.
28 Trace the wiring loom back and disconnect the resistor wiring plug **(see illustration 9.23)**.
29 Undo the retaining screw and remove the resistor from the blower motor housing **(see illustration)**.

Refitting

30 Refitting is the reverse of removal.

Air distribution housing

Note: *On models with air conditioning, it is not possible to remove the air distribution housing without opening the refrigerant circuit (see Sections 10 and 11). Have the refrigerant discharged at a dealer service department or an automotive air conditioning repair facility before proceeding.*

Removal

31 Remove the complete facia assembly as described in Chapter 11, Section 28.
32 Drain the cooling system as described in Chapter 1, Section 19, then disconnect the air conditioning refrigerant pipes at the bulkhead (where applicable) **(see illustration)**. Renew the pipes O-ring seals.
33 Working in the engine compartment, release the retaining clips, and disconnect both hoses from the heater matrix unions **(see illustration)**. Be prepared for coolant spillage.

9.23 Blower motor and resistor wiring plugs (arrowed)

9.24 Blower motor retaining screws (arrowed)

9.29 Blower motor resistor retaining screws (arrowed)

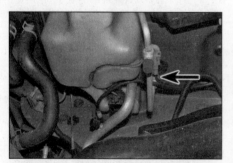

9.32 The refrigerant pipe connections (arrowed) are on the left-hand side of the engine compartment bulkhead

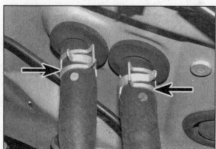

9.33 Release the clamps (arrowed) and disconnect the heater hoses at the engine compartment bulkhead

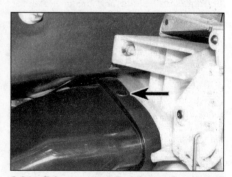

9.34a Prise out the clip (arrowed) securing the air duct ...

9.34b ... or release the clamp (arrowed) as applicable

9.36a Undo the retaining nuts (arrowed) ...

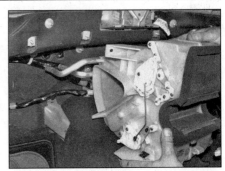

9.36b ... and manoeuvre the housing from place

34 Prise out the clip/release the clamp securing the housing/duct on the left-hand side of the distribution housing (see illustrations).
35 Unclip the wiring harness plug from the right-hand side of the distribution housing (where applicable).
36 Undo the 3 retaining nuts and manoeuvre the distribution housing rearwards from place (see illustrations). Be prepared for coolant spillage.

Refitting

37 Refitting is the reverse of removal. On completion, refill the cooling system as described in Chapter 1, Section 19. On models with air conditioning, have the system evacuated, charged and leak-tested by the specialist who discharged it.

10 Air conditioning system – general information and precautions

General information

1 Air conditioning is available on certain models. It enables the temperature of incoming air to be lowered, and also dehumidifies the air, which makes for rapid demisting and increased comfort.
2 The cooling side of the system works in the same way as a domestic refrigerator. Refrigerant gas is drawn into a belt-driven compressor, and passes into a condenser mounted in front of the radiator, where it loses heat and becomes liquid. The liquid passes through an expansion valve to an evaporator, where it changes from liquid under high pressure to gas under low pressure. This change is accompanied by a drop in temperature, which cools the evaporator. The refrigerant returns to the compressor, and the cycle begins again.
3 Air blown through the evaporator passes to the air distribution unit, where it is mixed with hot air blown through the heater matrix, to achieve the desired temperature in the passenger compartment.
4 The heating side of the system works in the same way as on models without air conditioning (see Section 8).
5 The operation of the system is controlled

electronically. Any problems with the system should be referred to a Mazda dealer or air conditioning specialist.

Air conditioning service ports

6 The low-pressure and high-pressure service ports are located on the left-hand side of the engine compartment (see illustration).

Precautions

7 It is necessary to observe special precautions whenever dealing with any part of the system, its associated components, and any items which necessitate disconnection of the system.

⚠ *Warning: The refrigeration circuit contains a liquid refrigerant. This refrigerant is potentially dangerous, and should only be handled by qualified persons. If it is splashed onto the skin, it can cause frostbite. It is not itself poisonous, but in the presence of a naked flame it forms a poisonous gas; inhalation of the vapour through a lighted cigarette could prove fatal. Uncontrolled discharging of the refrigerant is dangerous, and potentially damaging to the environment. It is therefore dangerous to disconnect any part of the system without specialised knowledge and equipment. If for any reason the system must be disconnected, entrust this task to your Mazda dealer or air conditioning specialist.*
Caution: Do not operate the air conditioning system if it is known to be short of refrigerant, as this may damage the compressor.

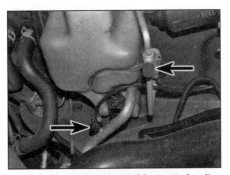

10.6 Air conditioning refrigerant circuit service ports (arrowed)

11 Air conditioning system components – removal and refitting

⚠ *Warning: The air conditioning system is under high pressure. Do not loosen any fittings or remove any components until after the system has been discharged. Air conditioning refrigerant should be properly discharged into an approved type of container at a dealer service department or an automotive air conditioning repair facility capable of handling R134a refrigerant. Cap or plug the pipe lines as soon as they are disconnected, to prevent the entry of moisture. Always wear eye protection when disconnecting air conditioning system fittings.*

Note: *This Section refers to the components of the air conditioning system itself – refer to Section 9 for details of components common to the heating/ventilation system.*

Condenser

1 Remove the receiver/drier as described later in this Section.
2 With the system discharged, working under the front of the vehicle, undo the retaining nuts and disconnect the refrigerant pipe connector blocks. Discard the O-ring seals – new ones must be used when refitting. Suitably cap the open fittings immediately to keep moisture and contamination out of the system.
3 Undo the mounting nuts and lift the condenser out from under the vehicle and store it upright, to prevent fluid loss. Take care not to damage the condenser or radiator fins.
4 Refitting is the reverse of removal. Renew the O-rings and lubricate with refrigerant oil.
5 Have the system evacuated, charged and leak-tested by the specialist who discharged it.

Evaporator and expansion valve

6 Have the refrigerant discharged at a dealer service department or a suitably-equipped repairer.
7 Disconnect the air conditioning pipes at the engine compartment bulkhead (see illustration 9.32). Plug/cover the open fittings after disassembly to prevent the entry of air or dirt.

11.9 The thermoswitch is located on the evaporator housing (arrowed)

11.10 Unlatch the seal clamp (arrowed) each side of the evaporator housing

11.11 Evaporator housing mounting nut (arrowed)

8 Remove the glovebox (see Chapter 11, Section 26). Remove the glovebox cover inside the dash.
9 Disconnect the thermoswitch electrical connector, located on the upper housing of the cooling unit **(see illustration)**.

11.12 Disconnect the condensation drain hose (arrowed) from the base of the evaporator housing

10 Unlatch the seal clamps on each side of the evaporator housing **(see illustration)**.
11 Remove the evaporator housing nut from the mounting stud at the bulkhead **(see illustration)**.
12 Disconnect the drain hose, and remove the evaporator housing **(see illustration)**.

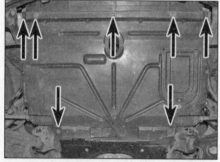

11.24a Undershield fasteners beneath (arrowed) ...

11.24b ... and each side (arrowed)

11.25 The compressor (arrowed) is located beneath the power steering pump

11.31 The receiver/drier (arrowed) is located behind the front bumper

13 Separate the lower and upper evaporator housings.
14 Remove the evaporator.
15 Disconnect the expansion valve fittings and remove the expansion valve from the evaporator. Immediately plug/cover the open fittings to keep moisture and contamination out of the system.
16 If necessary, remove the air conditioning thermoswitch from the upper evaporator housing.
17 Check the evaporator core and fittings for cracks or any other damage. Renew the evaporator if necessary.
18 Refit the expansion valve, renewing the gaskets on the expansion valve. Tighten the expansion valve inlet and outlet fittings securely.
19 Evaporator housing refitting is the reverse of removal. Renew any O-rings with new ones and lubricate them with refrigerant oil prior to installation.
20 Have the system evacuated, charged and leak-tested by the specialist who discharged it.

Compressor

21 Have the refrigerant discharged at a dealer service department or a suitably-equipped repairer.
22 Disconnect the battery negative terminal as described in Chapter 5A, Section 4.
23 Remove the auxiliary drivebelt as described in Chapter 1, Section 6.
24 Block the rear wheels so the vehicle can't roll. Raise up the front of the vehicle at least 300 mm and place it securely on axle stands. Remove the engine undershield **(see illustrations)**.
25 Disconnect the refrigerant pipes and compressor electrical connector **(see illustration)**. Unbolt the compressor and lower it from the vehicle.
26 If a new or rebuilt compressor is being fitted, follow the directions supplied with the compressor regarding the proper level of refrigerant oil prior to installation.
27 Refit the compressor in the reverse order of removal; renew all seals disturbed.
28 Have the system evacuated, charged and leak-tested by the specialist that discharged it.

Receiver/drier

29 Have the refrigerant discharged at a dealer service department or a suitably-equipped repairer.
30 Remove the front bumper as described in Chapter 11, Section 6.
31 Disconnect the refrigerant pipes from the receiver/drier **(see illustration)**. Plug/cover the open fittings immediately to prevent entry of moisture.
32 Remove the bolt from the receiver/drier clamping band and remove the receiver/drier.
33 Refitting is the reverse of removal. Renew any O-rings as necessary, lubricating them with refrigerant oil prior to reassembly.
34 Have the system evacuated, charged and leak-tested by the specialist that discharged it.

Chapter 4 Part A:
Fuel and exhaust systems

Contents

Degrees of difficulty

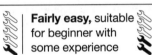

| **Easy,** suitable for novice with little experience | **Fairly easy,** suitable for beginner with some experience | **Fairly difficult,** suitable for competent DIY mechanic | **Difficult,** suitable for experienced DIY mechanic | **Very difficult,** suitable for expert DIY or professional |

Specifications

System type
All models . . . .   Indirect multi-point injection with electronic engine management

Fuel system data
Fuel pump type . . . .   Electric, immersed in tank
Fuel pump output pressure . . . .   4.5 to 6.0 bar
Fuel pressure regulator rating . . . .   2.7 to 3.2 bar
Injector resistance . . . .   12 to 16 Ω
Idle air control valve resistance:
    Up to 1993 . . . .   11 to 13 Ω
    1994-on . . . .   10.7 to 12.3 Ω
Idle speed . . . .   800 to 900 rpm
Throttle cable freeplay . . . .   1 to 3 mm

Torque wrench settings

	Nm	lbf ft
Air intake chamber to manifold	22	16
Camshaft position sensor bolt	10	7
Crankshaft position sensor bolt	10	7
Exhaust manifold nuts/bolts	42	31
Fuel rail	22	16
Intake manifold	22	16
Throttle body	22	16

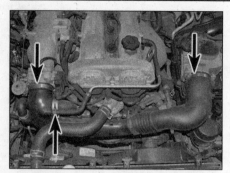

2.1a Slacken the air duct clamps, and disconnect the breather hose (arrowed)

2.1b Some models have an air hose at the right-hand end of the duct (arrowed) ...

2.1c ... and are also secured by a bolt (arrowed)

2.1d Resonance tube retaining bolt (arrowed)

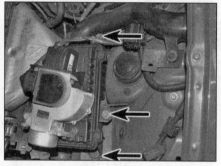

2.5a Air cleaner mounting bolts (arrowed) – early models ...

2.5b ... and later models (arrowed)

1 General information and precautions

The fuel supply system consists of a fuel tank (which is mounted under the rear of the vehicle, with an electric fuel pump immersed in it), a fuel filter, and fuel supply pipe. The fuel pump supplies fuel to the fuel rail, which acts as a reservoir for the fuel injectors which inject fuel into the intake tracts. A fuel filter and pressure regulator are incorporated into the fuel supply circuit.

⚠️ **Warning: Many of the procedures in this Chapter required the disconnection of fuel lines and connections, which may result in some fuel spillage. Before carrying out any operation on the fuel system, refer to the precautions given in 'Safety first!', and follow then implicitly. Petrol is a highly dangerous and volatile liquid, and the precautions necessary when handling it cannot be overstressed.**

⚠️ **Warning: Residual pressure will remain in the fuel lines long after the vehicle was last used. When disconnecting any fuel line, first depressurise the fuel system as described in Section 6.**

2 Air cleaner assembly – removal and refitting

1 Unbolt the intake and outlet ducts and slacken their clamps **(see illustrations)**, then disconnect the resonance tubes from the air cleaner housing.

2 Disconnect the mass airflow sensor electrical connector from the top of the air cleaner.

3 On 1998-on models, disconnect the intake air temperature sensor wiring plug from the left-hand side of the air cleaner assembly.

4 On models with a brace fitted between the strut towers, undo the bolts and remove the strut brace to improve access.

5 Remove the retaining bolt(s)/nut **(see illustrations)** and remove the air cleaner assembly from the engine compartment.

6 Refitting is the reverse of removal.

3 Fuel tank – removal and refitting

Removal

1 Disconnect the battery negative lead as described in Chapter 5A, Section 4.

2 Before removing the fuel tank, all fuel should be drained from the tank. Since a fuel tank drain plug is not provided, it is preferable to carry out the removal operation when the tank is nearly empty.

3 Remove the fuel filler cap to relieve fuel tank pressure. Relieve the fuel system pressure (see Section 6)

4 Raise the vehicle and place it securely on axle stands (see *Jacking and vehicle support*).

5 Remove the parcel shelf as described in Chapter 11, Section 26, remove the access panel, then disconnect the fuel pump hoses and electrical connectors **(see illustrations 7.4a and 7.4b)**.

6 Remove the power plant frame (see Chapter 7, Section 6), and the propeller shaft and differential (see Chapter 8, Section 6 and 2). At this point, the entire rear suspension/crossmember assembly must be supported with a transmission jack, unbolted from the body and removed from under the vehicle. This will also necessitate disconnecting the brake pipes at the crossmember and detaching the handbrake cables from the calipers (see Chapter 9, Section 15).

7 Support the fuel tank with a trolley jack. Place a sturdy plank between the jack head and the fuel tank to protect the tank. Remove the tank protector.

8 Remove the access panel **(see illustration)**.

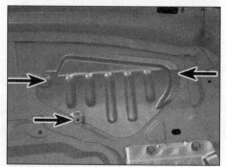

3.8 Undo the screws, remove the access panel (arrowed) ...

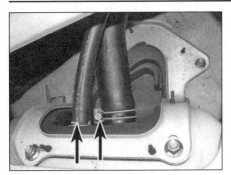

3.9 ... then release the clamps (arrowed) and disconnect the hoses

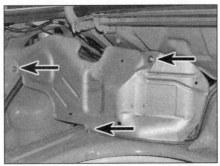

3.10 Undo the screws (arrowed) and remove the luggage compartment access panel

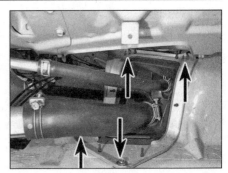

3.11 Seal retaining frame nuts (arrowed – one hidden)

9 Detach the hoses at the tank **(see illustration)**. **Note:** *Plug the hoses to prevent leakage and contamination of the fuel system.*

10 Undo the screws and remove the access panel in the luggage compartment **(see illustration)**.

11 Undo the nuts and remove the seal retaining frame around the filler pipe in the luggage compartment **(see illustration)**.

12 Remove the bolts from the fuel tank retaining brackets.

13 Remove the tank from the vehicle.

Refitting

14 Refitting is the reverse of removal. Bleed the brakes as described in Chapter 9, Section 2.

4 Throttle cable – removal, refitting and adjustment

Removal

1 Loosen the locknut on the threaded portion of the throttle cable at the plenum chamber **(see illustration)**.

2 Rotate the throttle quadrant and slip the throttle cable end out of the slot in the quadrant **(see illustration)**.

3 Detach the throttle cable from the accelerator pedal and release the cable guide attached to the bulkhead **(see illustration)**.

4 From the engine compartment side, pull the cable through the bulkhead, releasing any retaining clips as the cable is withdrawn.

Refitting and adjustment

5 Refitting is the reverse of removal. Make sure the cable casing grommet seats properly in the bulkhead.

6 To adjust the cable, fully depress the accelerator pedal and check that the throttle is fully opened.

7 Measure the play in the accelerator and compare your measurement to that listed (see Specifications).

8 If the throttle is not fully opened and/or if the play is incorrect, loosen the locknuts and adjust the cable accordingly.

9 Tighten the locknuts and recheck the adjustment. Make sure the throttle closes fully when the pedal is released.

10 Press the pedal to the floor and make sure the throttle opens fully. If it doesn't, loosen the pedal adjuster locknut, adjust pedal position with the bolt, then tighten the locknut **(see illustration)**.

5 Fuel injection system – general information

The fuel system consists of a fuel tank, an electric fuel pump (located in the fuel tank), an EFI/fuel pump relay, fuel injectors, a fuel pressure regulator, an air cleaner assembly and a throttle body unit. All models covered by this manual are equipped with a multi point fuel injection (MPFI) system.

Fuel injection system

Multi-point fuel injection (MPFI) uses

4.1 Slacken the locknut (arrowed)

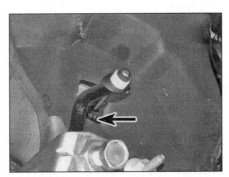

4.3 Release the clip (arrowed) securing the cable guide

timed impulses to sequentially inject the fuel directly into the intake port of each cylinder. The injectors are controlled by the electronic control module (ECM). The ECM monitors various engine parameters and delivers the exact amount of fuel, in the correct sequence, into the intake ports. The throttle body serves only to control the amount of air passing into the system. Because each cylinder is equipped with an injector mounted immediately adjacent to the intake valve, much better control of the fuel/air mixture ratio is possible.

Fuel pump and pipes

Fuel is circulated from the fuel tank to the fuel injection system, and back to the fuel tank, through a pair of metal pipes running along the underside of the vehicle. An electric fuel pump is attached to the fuel level sending unit inside the fuel tank. On 1999 and earlier models, all excess fuel is routed back to the

4.2 Rotate the quadrant and disconnect the cable

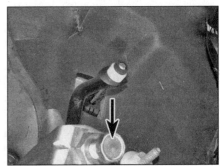

4.10 Pedal adjuster bolt and locknut

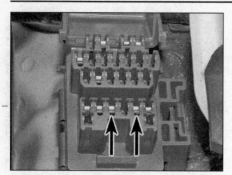

6.8 Connect the earth and fuel pump terminals (arrowed) together

fuel tank through a separate return pipe. After this date, a 'return-less' system is used, whereby a pressure regulator incorporated into the pump assembly returns excess fuel straight back into the reservoir of fuel.

The fuel pump will operate as long as the engine is cranking or running, and the ECM is receiving ignition reference pulses from the electronic ignition system (see Chapter 5B, Section 1). If there are no reference pulses, the fuel pump will shut off after 2 or 3 seconds.

Exhaust system

The exhaust system includes an exhaust manifold, a catalytic converter, an exhaust pipe, and a silencer.

The catalytic converter is an emission control device added to the exhaust system to reduce pollutants. A single-bed converter is used in combination with a three-way (reduction) catalyst.

6 Fuel injection system – depressurisation and priming

Depressurisation

1 Before servicing any fuel system component, you must relieve the fuel pressure to minimise the risk of fire or injury.
2 Remove the fuel filler cap – this will relieve any pressure built up in the tank.
3 Undo the 2 screws and remove the trim panel from beneath the steering column and locate the connector for the circuit opening relay (1993 and earlier models) or fuel pump relay (1994 and later models).
 a) *The circuit opening relay connector (1993 and earlier models) has six terminals, one of which is unused. The other five terminals wire colours are violet, white/red, blue/red, light green and black.*
 b) *The fuel pump relay connector (1994 and later models) has six terminals, two of which are unused. The other four terminals wire colours are white/red, white/red, blue/red and light green.*
4 Unplug the circuit opening relay or fuel pump relay connector.
5 Start the engine, wait for it to stall, then turn the ignition key to Off.
6 The fuel system is now depressurised. **Note:** *Place a rag around the fuel pipe before removing any hose clamp or fitting to prevent any residual fuel from spilling onto the engine.*
7 Connect the circuit opening relay electrical connector and refit the trim panel.

Priming

8 Whenever fuel system pressure has been relieved, the fuel system should be primed before the vehicle is placed back in operation to prevent excessive cranking of the starter, as follows:
 a) *Locate the diagnostic connector in the engine compartment.*
 b) *Connect the earth and fuel pump terminals together with a short jumper wire* **(see illustration).**
 c) *Turn the key to On for approximately 10 seconds (but don't operate the starter), then turn the key off. Remove the jumper wire from the diagnostic connector.*
 d) *Check for any fuel leaks before operating the vehicle.*

7 Fuel pump and level sensor – removal and refitting

Fuel pump

1 Depressurise the fuel system as described in Section 6.
2 Disconnect the battery negative lead as described in Chapter 5A, Section 4.
3 Remove the parcel shelf trim behind the seats as described in Chapter 11, Section 26.
4 Remove the fuel pump access cover **(see illustrations).**
5 Disconnect the wiring plug from the top of the fuel pump **(see illustration).**
6 Disconnect the fuel supply and return hoses (where applicable) from the pump **(see illustrations).**

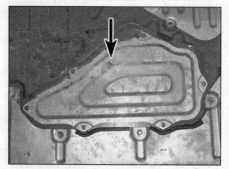

7.4a Remove the access cover (arrowed) – early models ...

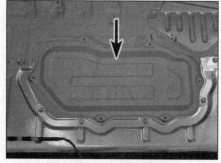

7.4b ... and later models

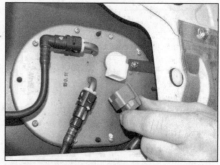

7.5 Disconnect the pump wiring plug

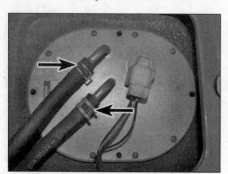

7.6a Release the clamps (arrowed) and disconnect the hoses – early models

7.6b On later models, use a screwdriver (or similar) to spread apart the internal clips ...

7.6c ... and pull the hoses from the ports

7.7a Undo the pump retaining screws

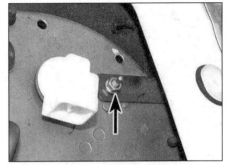

7.7b On some models, undo the nut (arrowed) and move the bracket to one side

7.8 Manoeuvre the pump assembly from the tank, taking care not to damage the float arm

7.9a Disconnect the pump wiring plug (arrowed) ...

7.9b ... and move the clamp upwards (arrowed)

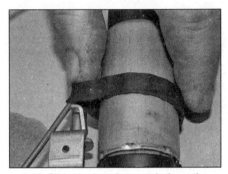

7.10 Slide the band upwards from the bracket

7 Remove the fuel pump retaining screws **(see illustrations)**.

8 Carefully lift the fuel pump assembly out of the fuel tank **(see illustration)**.

9 Disconnect the electrical connector and move the hose clamp (where fitted) clear of the pump fitting **(see illustrations)**.

10 Remove the band (where fitted) securing the pump to the bracket **(see illustration)**.

11 Remove the bracket at the bottom of the pump with the rubber mount **(see illustrations)**.

12 Remove the fuel pump.

13 Remove the filter from the bottom of the pump and inspect it for contamination. If it is dirty, renew it.

14 Refitting is the reverse of removal. Install a new O-ring set (O-ring, cap and spacer) at the hose connection where applicable **(see illustration)** and a new tank seal during installation. **Note:** *After installing the fuel pump to the bracket, pull the pump down so it is seated tightly against the pad on the bottom of the bracket, then position the hose clamps (later models only).*

Level sensor

Testing

15 The fuel level sensor is part of the fuel pump assembly mounted in the fuel tank.

16 Remove the fuel pump assembly from the fuel tank as previously described in this Section.

17 Using an ohmmeter, check the resistance of the sensor with the float arm completely down (tank empty) and with the arm up (tank full) **(see illustration)**. The resistance should change steadily from approximately 110 ohms to 3 ohms.

7.11a Undo the screw (arrowed) ...

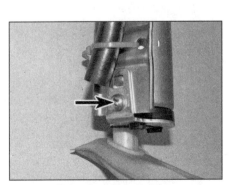

7.11c Pump bracket retaining screw (arrowed) – later models

18 If the readings are incorrect, the sensor may need renewing.

Renewal

19 Remove the fuel pump assembly from

7.11b ... and remove the bottom bracket – early models

7.14 Renew the O-ring, cap and spacer (arrowed) – early models only

7.17 Check the resistance of the level sensor with the arm up and down

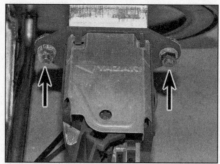

7.21 Fuel level sensor retaining nuts (arrowed)

8.9a The service diagnostic connector (arrowed) is located on the left-hand side of the engine compartment – up to 2000 ...

the fuel tank as previously described in this Section.

20 Disconnect the electrical connection to the fuel level sensor.

21 Remove the nuts securing the sensor to the bracket and separate the sensor from the assembly **(see illustration)**.

22 Refitting is the reverse of removal.

8 Fuel injection system – testing and adjustment

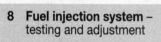

Testing

1 Check the earth wire connections for tightness. Check all wiring and electrical connectors that are related to the system. Loose electrical connectors and poor earths can cause many problems that resemble more serious malfunctions.

9.4 Label and disconnect the coolant hoses (arrowed) from the throttle body

8.9b ... or under the right-hand side of the facia (arrowed) – 2000-on

2 Check to see that the battery is fully charged, as the control unit and sensors depend on an accurate supply voltage in order to properly meter the fuel.

3 Check the air filter element – a dirty or partially blocked filter will severely impede performance and economy (see Chapter 1, Section 20).

4 If a blown fuse is found, renew it and see if it blows again. If it does, search for an earthed wire in the harness related to the system.

5 Check the air intake duct from the air cleaner housing to the intake manifold for leaks, which will result in an excessively lean mixture. Also check the condition of the vacuum hoses connected to the intake manifold.

6 Remove the air intake duct from the throttle body and check for carbon and residue build-up. If it's dirty, clean it with aerosol carburettor cleaner (make sure the can says it's safe for use with oxygen sensors and catalytic converters) and a toothbrush.

9.6 Throttle body nuts/bolts (arrowed)

Caution: Be sure not to remove the thin sealing film from the edge of the throttle plate and the area where it seats inside the throttle body.

7 With the engine running, place a stethoscope against each injector, one at a time, and listen for a clicking sound, indicating operation. If you don't have an automotive stethoscope you can use a long screwdriver; just place the tip of the screwdriver against the injector body and press your ear against the handle.

8 With the engine Off and the fuel injector electrical connectors disconnected, measure the resistance of each injector. Compare the measured resistance to the values listed (see Specifications). Out of range injectors are probably faulty.

9 The remainder of the system checks should be left to a dealer service department or other qualified repairer, as there is a chance that the control unit may be damaged if not performed properly. For information, the service diagnostic connector is located in the engine compartment on 1999 and earlier models, and under the right-hand side of the facia on 2000-on models **(see illustrations)**.

Adjustment

10 Experienced home mechanics with a considerable amount of skill and equipment (including a tachometer and an accurately calibrated exhaust gas analyser) may be able to check the exhaust CO level and the idle speed. However, if these are found to be in need of adjustment, the car should be taken to a Mazda dealer or suitably-equipped specialist for further testing.

9 Throttle body – removal and refitting

Removal

1 Remove the air intake duct as described in Section 2.

2 Detach the throttle cable from the throttle quadrant as described in Section 4.

3 Clearly label, then disconnect any vacuum hoses from the throttle body.

4 Clearly label, then disconnect all coolant hoses from the throttle body **(see illustration)**. Plug the coolant hoses to prevent coolant loss.

5 Disconnect the electrical connectors from the throttle position sensor (TPS) and idle air control (IAC) valve attached to the throttle body.

6 Remove the 4 throttle body mounting nuts/ bolts **(see illustration)**.

7 Detach the throttle body and gasket from the intake manifold.

8 Using a soft brush and carburettor cleaner, thoroughly clean the throttle body casting, then blow out all passages with compressed air.

Caution: Do not clean the throttle position

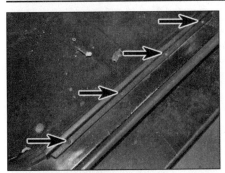

10.2a Undo the screws (arrowed) and pull up the sill trim panel

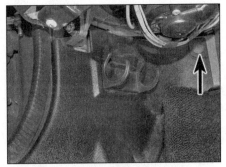

10.2b Prise out the clip (arrowed) and remove the kick panel

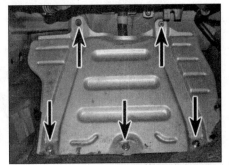

10.3 Undo the nuts/bolt (arrowed) and remove the ECM cover

10.4 Disconnect the plugs, unclip the harness and lift the ECM

10.6a Pull the up the sill trim panel

10.6b Prise up the centre pin, and remove the clip (arrowed)

sensor with anything. Just wipe it off carefully with a clean, soft cloth.

Refitting

9 Refitting of the throttle body is the reverse of removal. Tighten all fasteners to their specified torque where given.

10 Fuel injection system components – removal and refitting

Electronic control module (ECM)

1 Disconnect the battery negative lead, as described in Chapter 5A, Section 4. **Note:** *It is recommended that the fault code memory of the module is interrogated using special test equipment prior to battery disconnection. Entrust this task to a Mazda dealer or suitably-equipped specialist.*

1997 and earlier models

2 the ECM is located under the passenger's side front carpet. Undo the screws, pull up the door sill trim panel, unclip the rubber weatherstrip from the pillar, then prise out the clip at the front edge and remove the lower kickpanel **(see illustrations)**.
3 Fold back the carpet, then undo the nuts/bolt and remove the ECM protective cover **(see illustration)**. If improved access is required, remove the glovebox as described in Chapter 11, Section 26.
4 Lift the ECM from place, disconnect the wiring plugs, and unclip the wiring harness **(see illustration)**. If required, undo the screws and detach the mounting brackets from the ECM.
5 Refitting is a reversal of removal.

1998-on models

6 The ECM is located under the passenger's

side of the facia. Pull up the door sill trim panel, unclip the rubber weatherstrip from the pillar, then prise out the clip and remove the lower kickpanel **(see illustrations)**.
7 Pull back the carpet, then undo the nuts/bolt, drill out the heads of the shear bolts, and remove the metal cover over the ECM **(see illustrations)**.
8 Lift the ECM from place and disconnect the wiring plugs **(see illustration)**. If required, undo the screws and separate the ECM from the mounting bracket.
9 Refitting is a reversal of removal, using new shear bolts.

Fuel rail and injectors

⚠ **Warning: Refer to the warning notes in Section 1 before proceeding.**

10 Disconnect the battery negative lead as described in Chapter 5A, Section 4.

10.7a Drill out the shear bolts ...

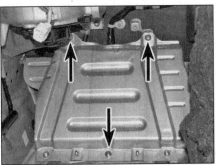

10.7b ... undo the nuts (arrowed) and remove the ECM cover

10.8 Lift the ECM and disconnect the wiring plugs

10.13 Detach the air valve from the side of the intake plenum

10.14 Depress the lock lever (arrowed) and disconnect the injector wiring plugs

10.15 Disconnect the vacuum hose (arrowed)

10.17 Fuel rail mounting bolts (arrowed)

14 Carefully mark each injector and its electrical connector with a felt pen or paint, then remove the connectors from each injector and set the wire harness aside (see illustration). Note: Use a small flat-blade screwdriver to release each connectors lock lever while gently pulling the connector.

15 On 1997 and earlier models, disconnect the vacuum hose from the fuel pressure regulator (see illustration).

16 Disconnect the fuel pipes from the fuel pressure regulator and the fuel rail.

17 Remove the fuel rail mounting bolts and pull the fuel rail off the injectors (see illustration).

18 Remove the mounting insulators, lift out the fuel rail and pressure regulator, then pull the injectors out of their bores.

1998-on models

19 Remove the throttle body as described in Section 9.

20 Undo the bolts, and remove the air intake chamber support bracket (see illustration).

21 Note their fitted positions, then disconnect the various hoses from the air intake chamber.

22 Undo the bolts/nuts and remove the air intake chamber (see illustration). Discard the gasket – a new one must be fitted. **Note:** When fitting the new gasket, the convex side must face the intake manifold surface (see illustration).

23 Disconnect the fuel supply hose from the front end of the fuel rail. Be prepared for fuel spillage.

24 Unclip the wiring harness tray, then undo the fuel rail retaining bolts (see illustration).

25 Pull the fuel rail upwards and remove it complete with injectors (see illustrations).

26 Pull the injectors from the fuel rail.

All models

27 Set the fuel injectors aside in a clearly-labelled storage container so they can be returned to the same bores if reused.

28 If you intend to re-use the same injectors, renew the insulators, grommets and O-rings (see illustration).

29 Refitting of the fuel injectors is the reverse of removal. Apply a thin coating of clean engine oil to the injector O-ring prior to fitting. Tighten the fuel rail mounting bolts to the specified torque.

11 Relieve the fuel pressure as described in Section 6.

1997 and earlier models

12 Remove the PCV hose from the valve cover and intake manifold.

13 On 1993 and earlier models, remove the hose clamps and hoses from the air valve, then unbolt and remove the air valve from the engine side of the air intake plenum (see illustration).

10.20 Undo the bolts and remove the support bracket from the underside of the chamber

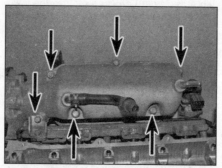

10.22a Air intake chamber retaining bolts/nuts (arrowed)

10.22b The convex side of the gasket must face the intake manifold

10.24a Unclip the wiring harness tray ...

10.24b ... then undo the fuel rail mounting bolts (arrowed)

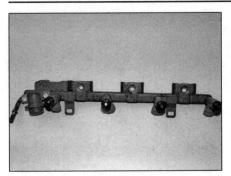

10.25a Remove the fuel rail, complete with injectors

10.25b Recover the mounting spacers from the cylinder head

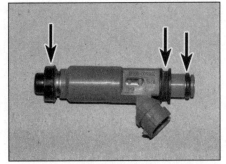

10.28 Renew the insulator, grommet and O-ring (arrowed)

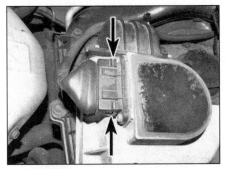

10.30 Prise out the clip each side (arrowed) and disconnect the mass airflow sensor wiring plug

10.32a The mass airflow sensor is secured by nuts at the rear (arrowed) ...

10.32b ... and a bolt at the front (arrowed)

Mass airflow/ intake air temperature sensor

1993 and earlier models

30 Disconnect the sensor wiring plug **(see illustration)**.
31 Slacken the clamp and remove the air intake duct.
32 Undo the retaining nuts/bolt and remove the sensor assembly **(see illustrations)**.
33 Refitting is a reversal of removal.

1994 to 1997 models

34 Slacken the clamp and remove the air intake duct.
35 Disconnect the wiring plug and remove the sensor from the filter housing.
36 Refitting is a reversal of removal.

Mass airflow sensor – 1998-on models

Note: On these models, the mass airflow

sensor and intake air temperature sensors are separate.
37 Slacken the clamp and remove the air intake duct, then disconnect the sensor wiring plug **(see illustration)**.
38 Undo the bolts and remove the sensor from the filter housing **(see illustration)**.
39 Refitting is a reversal of removal.

Intake air temperature sensor – 1998-on models

Note: On these models, the mass airflow sensor and intake air temperature sensors are separate.
40 The sensor is located in the upper section of the air cleaner housing. Disconnect the sensor wiring plug.
41 Pull the sensor from the air cleaner housing **(see illustration)**.
42 Refitting is a reversal of removal.

Throttle position sensor – renewal

Note: The throttle position sensor, which is located on the throttle body, is used on all models. The sensor is replaceable separately from the throttle body, but on 1996-on models there is no way to adjust the sensor without special factory tools. Therefore, we don't recommend removing the sensor on these models at home.
43 Disconnect the wiring plug from the sensor **(see illustration)**.
44 Undo the retaining screws and remove the sensor.
45 Refitting is a removal of refitting, then carry out the adjustment procedure as follows.

Throttle position sensor – adjustment

46 Disconnect the wiring plug from the

10.37 Depress the catch (arrowed) and disconnect the sensor wiring plug

10.38 Mass airflow sensor retaining bolts (arrowed)

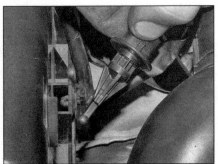

10.41 Pull the intake air temperature sensor from the side of the air cleaner housing

10.43 Lift the wire clip and disconnect the throttle position sensor wiring plug

10.47 Connect an ohmmeter to the sensor terminals (see text)

10.49 Insert a feeler gauge between the stop screw and lever

sensor, and check the throttle valve is in the closed position.

47 Connect an ohmmeter between the sensor lower terminals (1993 and earlier models) or terminals C and D (1994 and 1995 models) **(see illustration)**.

48 Slacken the 2 sensor retaining screws.

1993 and earlier models

49 Insert a 0.4 mm feeler gauge between the throttle stop screw and the stop lever **(see illustration)**.

50 Rotate the sensor clockwise approximately 30°, then rotate it back until there is continuity across the terminals.

51 Replace the feeler gauge with a 0.7 mm one, and check that there is no continuity.

52 If there is continuity, repeat the procedure in paragraphs 49 to 51.

53 Without moving the sensor, tighten the retaining screws securely.

1994 and 1995 models

54 Position the sensor so there is continuity between the sensor terminals when a 0.3 mm feeler gauge is inserted between the throttle stop screw and stop lever, and no continuity when a 0.4 mm feeler gauge is inserted.

55 Without moving the sensor, tighten the retaining screws securely.

Coolant temperature sensor

56 Removal of the sensor is described in Chapter 3, Section 6.

Crankshaft position sensor

Note: *Only fitted to models from 1998.*

57 Trace the wiring harness from the sensor to its wiring plug and disconnect it, releasing and harness clips.

58 Remove the retaining bolt and withdraw the sensor from the bracket **(see illustration)**.

59 When refitting, position the sensor so that the gap between the sensor tip and one of the teeth of the timing signal wheel is 0.5 to 1.5 mm, then tighten the retaining bolt to the specified torque **(see illustration)**.

60 Reconnect the wiring plug.

Camshaft position sensor/ crank angle sensor

Note: *On 1997 and earlier models, Mazda refer to this sensor as a 'crank angle sensor'.*

1997 and earlier models

61 The sensor is located on the left rear corner of the cylinder head. Disconnect the sensor wiring plug.

62 Make alignment marks between the sensor body and the cylinder head, then undo the retaining bolt and withdraw the sensor from place **(see illustrations)**. Renew the O-ring seal.

63 Upon refitting, align the sensor drive lugs with the slot in the end of the camshaft and insert it into place **(see illustration)**. Note that the sensor will only fit one-way round.

64 Temporarily tighten the sensor retaining bolt, then check and if necessary, adjust the ignition timing as described in Chapter 5B, Section 4.

1.6 and 1.8 litre models 1998 to 2000

65 The sensor is located on the upper right-hand front corner of the timing belt cover. Disconnect the sensor wiring plug.

66 Undo the retaining bolt and remove the sensor **(see illustration)**.

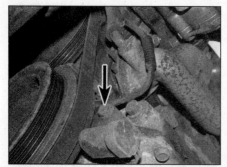

10.58 Crankshaft position sensor retaining bolt (see illustration)

10.59 Insert a feeler gauge between the timing signal wheel teeth and the sensor tip

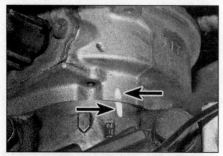

10.62a Make alignment marks between the camshaft position sensor and the cylinder head (arrowed)

10.62b Camshaft position sensor retaining bolt (arrowed)

10.62c Renew the sensor O-ring seal (arrowed)

67 Before refitting, ensure the sensor is free from any metallic particles or shavings.
68 Refitting is a reversal of removal.

1.8 litre models 2000-on

69 The sensor is located on the rear of the cylinder head cover. Disconnect the sensor wiring plug.
70 Undo the retaining bolt and pull the sensor from the cylinder head cover **(see illustration)**.
71 Refitting is a reversal of removal.

Oxygen sensor

72 Refer to Chapter 4B, Section 2.

Fuel pressure regulator

1997 and earlier models

73 Depressurise the fuel system as described in Section 6.
74 Disconnect the vacuum hose from the regulator, located on the fuel rail **(see illustration)**.
75 Release the clamp and disconnect the fuel return hose from the regulator **(see illustration)**. Be prepared for fuel spillage.
76 Undo the retaining bolts and detach the regulator from the fuel rail. Discard the O-ring seal – a new one must be fitted.
77 Refitting is a reversal of removal.

1998-on models

78 The fuel pressure regulator is integral with the fuel pump assembly in the fuel tank. Remove the fuel pump assembly as described in Section 7.

---

11 Manifolds – removal and refitting

Intake manifold

Removal

1 Depressurise the fuel system as described in Section 6.
2 Disconnect the battery negative lead as described in Chapter 5A, Section 4.
3 Drain the cooling system as described in Chapter 1, Section 19.
4 Remove the throttle body as described in Section 9.

11.7 Remove the intake manifold bracket (arrowed)

10.63 Align the drive lugs (arrowed) with the slot in the camshaft

10.70 Camshaft position sensor location (2000-on)

5 Label and detach all wire harness, control cables and hoses connected to the intake manifold.
6 Remove the fuel rail, injectors and injector wiring harness as described in Section 10.
7 Under the intake manifold, remove the intake manifold bracket **(see illustration)**.
8 Remove the intake manifold mounting bolts/nuts, while supporting the intake manifold from above the engine, and manoeuvre it from place **(see illustration)**.

Refitting

9 Carefully use a gasket scraper to remove all traces of old gasket material and any sealant from the manifold and cylinder head, then clean the mating surfaces with gasket cleaner or solvent – be careful to not gouge the gasket surfaces when cleaning. If the gasket was leaking, have the manifold checked for warpage at an automotive engineering workshop and resurfaced if necessary.

11.8 Intake manifold upper retaining nuts (arrowed)

10.66 Camshaft position sensor location (1998 to 2000)

10.74 Fuel pressure regulator (arrowed)

10 Using a new gasket, position the manifold on the head and refit the nuts/bolts.
11 Tighten the nuts/bolts evenly to the specified torque.
12 The remainder of refitting is a reversal of removal.

Exhaust manifold

Removal

13 Disconnect the battery negative lead as described in Chapter 5A, Section 4.
14 Trace the oxygen sensor (located on the exhaust manifold) wiring harness back to the wiring plug and disconnect it. If the manifold is being renewed, remove the sensor as described in Chapter 4B, Section 2.
15 Remove the heat shield bolts and remove the heat shield from the manifold **(see illustration)**.
16 Undo the nut securing the EGR pipe to the manifold (where fitted).

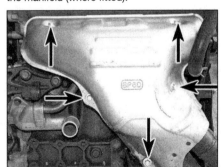

11.15 Exhaust manifold heat shield bolts (arrowed)

11.20 Undo the nuts and remove the exhaust manifold

17 Apply penetrating oil to the exhaust manifold mounting bolts/nuts and to the exhaust pipe nuts.

18 Raise the vehicle and support it securely on axle stands (see *Jacking and vehicle support*).

19 Disconnect the exhaust pipe from the exhaust manifold. Discard the gasket – a new one must be used.

20 Remove the manifold bolts/nuts and detach the manifold from the cylinder head **(see illustration). Note:** *If any bolts/nuts are difficult to remove, reapply penetrating oil to the bolts/ nuts and let them soak for at least 15 minutes. If any bolts or studs break during removal, you may be able to use a vice-grip pliers after the manifold is removed to unscrew the broken bolt/stud. If unable to remove the broken bolt/ stud, see your automotive parts store for stud removal tools. Renew any damaged parts with factory parts, or parts specifically designed for exhaust system application.*

Refitting

21 Use a scraper to remove all traces of old gasket material and carbon deposits from the manifold and cylinder head mating surfaces. *Caution: When scraping, be very careful not to gouge or scratch the delicate aluminium cylinder head manifold mounting surface.*

12.1 Check the condition of the exhaust rubber hangers

22 Position a new exhaust manifold gasket over the studs on the cylinder head.

23 Refit the manifold, then evenly tighten the nuts/bolts to the specified torque.

24 The remainder of refitting is a reversal of removal.

12 Exhaust system – removal and refitting

Note: *New exhaust front section-to-rear section securing nuts may be required on refitting.*

1 The exhaust system consists of the exhaust manifold, catalytic converter, the silencer, the tailpipe and all connecting pipes, brackets, hangers and clamps. The exhaust system is attached to the body with mounting brackets and rubber hangers **(see illustration)**. If any of these parts are damaged or deteriorated, excessive noise and vibration will be transmitted to the body.

2 Conducting regular inspections of the exhaust system will keep it safe and quiet. Look for any damaged or bent parts, open seams, holes, loose connections, excessive corrosion or other defects which could allow exhaust fumes to enter the vehicle.

Deteriorated exhaust system components should not be repaired – they should be renewed.

3 If the exhaust system components are extremely corroded or rusted together, they will probably have to be cut from the exhaust system. The convenient way to accomplish this is to have an exhaust specialist remove the corroded sections with a cutting torch. If, however, you want to save money by doing it yourself and you don't have an oxygen/ acetylene welding outfit with a cutting torch, simply cut off the old components with a hacksaw. If you have compressed air, special pneumatic cutting chisels can also be used. If you do decide to tackle the job at home, be sure to wear eye protection to guard your eyes from metal chips and work gloves to protect your hands.

4 Here are some simple guidelines to apply when repairing the exhaust system:

 a) *Work from the back to the front when removing exhaust system components.*

 b) *Apply penetrating oil to the exhaust system component fasteners to make them easier to remove.*

 c) *Use new gaskets, hangers and clamps when installing exhaust system components.*

 d) *Apply anti-seize compound to the threads of all exhaust system fasteners during reassembly.*

5 Be sure to allow sufficient clearance between newly installed parts and all points on the underbody to avoid overheating the floor pan and possibly damaging the interior carpet and insulation. Pay particularly close attention to the catalytic converter and its heat shield.

⚠ *Warning: The catalytic converter operates at very high temperatures and takes a long time to cool. Wait until it's completely cool before attempting to remove the converter. Failure to do so could result in serious burns.*

Chapter 4 Part B:
Emission control systems

Contents

Degrees of difficulty

Easy, suitable for novice with little experience	Fairly easy, suitable for beginner with some experience	Fairly difficult, suitable for competent DIY mechanic	Difficult, suitable for experienced DIY mechanic	Very difficult, suitable for expert DIY or professional

Specifications

Torque wrench settings	Nm	lbf ft
Exhaust gas recirculation (EGR) valve/pipe bolts:		
M6 bolts	10	7
M8 bolts	25	18
Oxygen sensors	45	33

1 General information

All models use unleaded petrol and also have various other features built into the fuel system to help minimise harmful emissions. All models are equipped with a crankcase emission control system, a catalytic converter and an evaporative emission control system to keep fuel vapour/exhaust gas emissions down to a minimum.

Some models are also fitted with an exhaust gas recirculation (EGR) system to further reduce exhaust emissions.

The emission control systems function as follows.

Crankcase emission control

To reduce the emission of unburned hydrocarbons from the crankcase into the atmosphere, the engine is sealed and the blow-by gases and oil vapour are drawn from inside the crankcase, through a wire mesh oil separator, into the intake tract to be burned by the engine during normal combustion.

Under conditions of high manifold depression (idling, deceleration) the gases will be sucked positively out of the crankcase through a small diameter pipe and into the intake tract 'downstream' of the throttle valve. A larger diameter pipe, 'upstream' of the throttle valve, allows fresh air to be drawn back into the crankcase, and mix with the crankcase gases. Under conditions of low manifold depression (acceleration, full-throttle running) the gases are forced out of the crankcase by the (relatively) higher crankcase pressure; and drawn through both pipes 'upstream and downstream' of the throttle valve.

Exhaust emission control

To minimise the amount of pollutants which escape into the atmosphere, all models are fitted with a catalytic converter in the exhaust system. The system is of the closed-loop type, in which an oxygen sensor(s) in the exhaust system supplies a voltage signal to the engine management system ECM, enabling the ECM to adjust the mixture to provide the best possible conditions for the converter to operate. One or two oxygen sensors are fitted depending on model. One fitted to the exhaust manifold or front exhaust pipe (pre-catalyst sensor), and on models with 2 sensors, the 2nd one is fitted 'downstream' of the catalytic converter (post-catalyst sensor). Some oxygen sensor(s) have a built-in heating element which is controlled by the ECM; the heating element is used to warm the sensor when the engine is cold to bring it quickly up to an efficient operating temperature.

The oxygen sensor's tip is sensitive to oxygen and sends the ECM a varying voltage depending on the amount of oxygen in the exhaust gases; the leaner the air/fuel mixture, the higher the oxygen content, and the lower the voltage from the sensor(s). If the intake air/fuel mixture is too rich, the exhaust gases are low in oxygen so the sensor sends a higher-voltage signal. Peak conversion efficiency of all major pollutants occurs if the intake air/fuel mixture is maintained at the chemically-correct ratio for the complete combustion of petrol of 14.7 parts (by weight) of air to 1 part of fuel (the 'stoichiometric' ratio). The sensor output voltage alters in a large step at this point, the ECM using the signal change as a reference point and correcting the intake air/fuel mixture accordingly by altering the fuel injector pulse width.

Evaporative emission control

To minimise the escape into the atmosphere of unburned hydrocarbons, an evaporative emissions control system is also fitted to all models. The fuel tank filler cap is sealed and a charcoal canister is mounted in the engine compartment. The canister collects the petrol vapours generated in the tank when the car is parked and stores them until they can be cleared from the canister (under the control of the engine management system ECM) via the purge valve into the intake tract to be burned by the engine during normal combustion.

To ensure that the engine runs correctly when it is cold and/or idling and to protect the catalytic converter from the effects of an over-rich mixture, the purge control valve is not opened by the ECM until the engine has warmed up, and the engine is under load; the valve solenoid is then modulated on and off to allow the stored vapour to pass into the intake tract.

Exhaust gas recirculation (EGR)

On models from 1994, this system is designed to recirculate small quantities of exhaust gas into the intake tract, and therefore into the combustion process. This process reduces the level of unburnt hydrocarbons present in the exhaust gas before it reaches the catalytic converter. The system is controlled by the engine management system ECM, using the information from its various sensors, via the EGR valve connecting the intake and exhaust manifolds.

2.7 Pull the PCV valve from the cylinder head cover

2.14 Label and disconnect the hoses from the charcoal canister

2.17 The purge valve is located on the right-hand side of the engine compartment

2 Engine emission control systems – testing and component renewal

Crankcase emission control

General information

1 The positive crankcase ventilation (PCV) system reduces hydrocarbon emissions by scavenging crankcase vapours. It does this by circulating fresh air from the air cleaner through the crankcase, where it mixes with blow-by gases and is then rerouted through a PCV valve to the intake manifold.

2 The main components of the PCV system are the PCV valve, a fresh air intake and the vacuum hoses connecting these components to the engine.

3 To maintain idle quality, the PCV valve restricts the flow when the intake manifold vacuum is high. If abnormal operating conditions (such as piston ring problems) arise, the system is designed to allow excessive amounts of blow-by gases to flow back through the crankcase vent tube into the air cleaner to be consumed by normal combustion.

4 This system directs the blow-by into the throttle body which, over time, can cause an oily residue build up in the area near the throttle plate. Consequently, it is a good idea to periodically clean this residue from the throttle body. Refer to Chapter 4A, Section 9 for this cleaning procedure.

Check

5 To check the valve, first pull it out of the grommet in the valve cover and shake the valve. It should rattle, indicating that it's not clogged with deposits. If the valve does not rattle, renew it.

6 Start the engine and allow it to idle, then place your finger over the valve opening. If vacuum is felt, the PCV valve is working properly. If no vacuum is felt, the PCV valve may be bad or the hose may be plugged. Also, check for vacuum leaks at the valve, engine oil filler cap and all the hoses.

Renewal

7 Pull straight up on the valve to remove it **(see illustration)**. Check the rubber grommet

for cracks and distortion. If it's damaged, renew it.

8 If the valve is clogged, the hose is probably also plugged. Remove the hose and clean it with solvent.

9 After cleaning the hose, inspect it for damage, wear and deterioration. Make sure it fits snugly on the fittings.

10 If necessary, fit a new PCV valve.

11 Fit the clean PCV hose. Make sure that the PCV valve and hose are secure.

Evaporative emission control

Testing

12 If the system is thought to be faulty, disconnect the hoses from the charcoal canister and purge control valve and check that they are clear by blowing through them. Full testing of the system can only be carried out using specialist electronic equipment which is connected to the engine management system diagnostic wiring connector (see Chapter 4A, Section 8). If the purge control valve or charcoal canister is thought to be faulty, they must be renewed.

Charcoal canister renewal

13 The canister is located on the right-hand side of the engine compartment.

14 Note the fitted locations of the pipes. Disconnect the tank air and purge pipes from the canister **(see illustration)**.

15 Remove the canister.

16 Refitting is a reverse of the removal procedure, ensuring the hoses are correctly and securely reconnected.

2.24 Catalytic converter location (arrowed)

Purge valve renewal

17 The valve is located on a bracket on the right-hand side of the engine compartment **(see illustration)**.

18 Ensure the ignition is switched off, and disconnect the wiring plug from the valve.

19 Note their fitted locations and disconnect the hoses from the valve.

20 Release the clip and slide the valve from the bracket.

21 Refitting is a reversal of removal. Ensure the valve and hose are securely held by the retaining clips.

Exhaust emission control

Testing

22 The performance of the catalytic converter can be checked only by measuring the exhaust gases using a good-quality, carefully-calibrated exhaust gas analyser.

23 If the CO level at the tailpipe is too high, the vehicle should be taken to a Mazda dealer or specialist so that the complete fuel injection and ignition systems, including the oxygen sensor, can be thoroughly checked using the special diagnostic equipment. Once these have been checked and are known to be free from faults, the fault must be in the catalytic converter, which may need to be renewed.

Catalytic converter renewal

24 On 1999 and earlier models, the catalytic converter is bolted between the front and rear sections of the exhaust system. On models after this date, the catalytic converter is integral with the front section of the exhaust system **(see illustration)**.

25 Where applicable, trace the oxygen sensor wiring back to the connector, and disconnect it. If the catalytic converter is being removed, it will be necessary to unscrew the sensor. Use a special oxygen sensor removal socket for this task, and use plenty of penetrating/releasing fluid.

26 Undo the bolts/nuts securing the catalytic converter to the rest of the exhaust system and manoeuvre it from place. Renew any gaskets as necessary.

27 Refitting is a reversal of removal, but apply a little high-temperature anti-seize grease to the oxygen sensor threads prior to refitting.

Oxygen sensor(s) renewal

Note: *The oxygen sensor is delicate and will not work if it is dropped or knocked, if its power supply is disrupted, or if any cleaning materials are used on it.*

28 Ensure the ignition is switched off then trace the wiring back from the oxygen sensor(s). Free the connector(s) from its retaining clip and disconnect the two halves of the connector.

29 Unscrew the sensor and remove it from the manifold or exhaust pipe as applicable. Note that the use of a special deep, split socket is recommended **(see illustration)**.

30 Refitting is a reverse of the removal procedure. Apply a little high-temperature anti-seize compound (Copperslip) to the threads, then tighten the sensor to the specified torque and ensure that the wiring is correctly routed and in no danger of contacting either the exhaust manifold or the engine.

Exhaust gas recirculation (EGR)

Testing

31 Comprehensive testing of the system can only be carried out using specialist electronic equipment which is connected to the injection system diagnostic wiring connector (see Chapter 4A, Section 8). If the EGR valve or solenoid valve are thought to be faulty, they must be renewed as follows.

EGR valve renewal

32 The EGR valve is located on the right-hand side of the engine, behind the intake manifold (1.8 litre engines) or in front of the intake manifold (1.6 litre engines) **(see illustration)**.

33 Disconnect the wiring plug and vacuum pipe (where applicable) from the EGR valve.

34 Undo the retaining bolts and remove the valve. Renew the gasket.

35 Refitting is a reversal of removal.

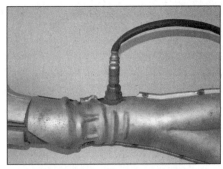

2.29 Unscrew the oxygen sensor using a special deep socket slotted to accommodate the wiring lead

3 Catalytic converter – general information and precautions

1 The catalytic converter is a reliable and simple device which needs no maintenance in itself, but there are some facts which an owner should be aware if the converter is to function properly for its full service life.

a) *DO NOT use leaded petrol in a car equipped with a catalytic converter – the lead will coat the precious metals, reducing their converting efficiency and will eventually destroy the converter.*

b) *Always keep the ignition and fuel systems well-maintained in accordance with the manufacturer's schedule.*

c) *If the engine develops a misfire, do not drive the car at all (or at least as little as possible) until the fault is cured.*

d) *DO NOT push- or tow-start the car – this will soak the catalytic converter in unburned fuel, causing it to overheat when the engine does start.*

e) *DO NOT switch off the ignition at high engine speeds.*

2.32 EGR valve – 1.8 litre engines shown

f) *DO NOT use fuel or engine oil additives – these may contain substances harmful to the catalytic converter.*

g) *DO NOT continue to use the car if the engine burns oil to the extent of leaving a visible trail of blue smoke.*

h) *Remember that the catalytic converter operates at very high temperatures. DO NOT, therefore, park the car in dry undergrowth, over long grass or piles of dead leaves after a long run.*

i) *Remember that the catalytic converter is FRAGILE – do not strike it with tools during servicing work.*

j) *In some cases a sulphurous smell (like that of rotten eggs) may be noticed from the exhaust. This is common to many catalytic converter-equipped cars and once the car has covered a few thousand miles the problem should disappear.*

k) *The catalytic converter, used on a well-maintained and well-driven car, should last for between 50 000 and 100 000 miles – if the converter is no longer effective it must be renewed.*

Chapter 5 Part A:
Starting and charging systems

Contents

Degrees of difficulty

Easy, suitable for novice with little experience	**Fairly easy,** suitable for beginner with some experience	**Fairly difficult,** suitable for competent DIY mechanic	**Difficult,** suitable for experienced DIY mechanic	**Very difficult,** suitable for expert DIY or professional

Specifications

System type	12 volt negative earth

Alternator

Regulated voltage:
  1997 and earlier:

1.6 litre	14.1 to 14.7 volts
1.8 litre	14.3 to 14.9 volts
1998-on	13.0 to 15.0 volts

Output:
  1999 and earlier:

1.6 litre	60 A
1.8 litre	65 A
2000-on	80 A

Brush length:
  New:
    1997 and earlier:

1.6 litre	21.5 mm
1.8 litre	18.5 mm
1998-on	22.0 mm

  Minimum:
    1997 and earlier:

1.6 litre	8.0 mm
1.8 litre	11.5 mm
1998-on	6.0 mm

Starter

Brush length:
  New:

1997 and earlier	17.0 mm
1998-on	12.3 mm

  Minimum:

1997 and earlier	11.5 mm
1998-on	7.0 mm

Torque wrench settings	Nm	lbf ft
Alternator:		
Upper mounting bolt	22	16
Lower mounting bolt	45	33
Intake manifold support bracket bolts	50	37
Starter motor mounting bolts	45	33

1 General information and precautions

The engine electrical system consists mainly of the charging and starting systems. Because of their engine-related functions, these components are covered separately from the body electrical devices such as the lights, instruments, etc (which are covered in Chapter 12). For information on the ignition system refer to Chapter 5B.

The electrical system is of the 12 volt negative earth type.

The battery is charged by the alternator, which is belt-driven from the crankshaft pulley.

The starter motor is of the pre-engaged type incorporating an integral solenoid. On starting, the solenoid moves the drive pinion into engagement with the flywheel ring gear before the starter motor is energised. Once the engine has started, a one-way clutch prevents the motor armature being driven by the engine until the pinion disengages from the flywheel.

Precautions

Further details of the various systems are given in the relevant Sections of this Chapter. While some repair procedures are given, the usual course of action is to renew the component concerned. The owner whose interest extends beyond mere component renewal should obtain a copy of the *Automobile Electrical and Electronic Systems Manual*, available from the publishers of this manual.

It is necessary to take extra care when working on the electrical system to avoid damage to semi-conductor devices (diodes and transistors), and to avoid the risk of personal injury. In addition to the precautions given in *Safety first!* at the beginning of this manual, observe the following when working on the system:

• Always remove rings, watches, etc, before working on the electrical system. Even with the battery disconnected, capacitive discharge could occur if a component's live terminal is earthed through a metal object. This could cause a shock or nasty burn.

• Do not reverse the battery connections. Components such as the alternator, electronic control modules/units, or any other components having semi-conductor circuitry could be irreparably damaged.

• Never disconnect the battery terminals, the alternator, any electrical wiring or any test instruments when the engine is running.

• Do not allow the engine to turn the alternator when the alternator is not connected.

• Never 'test' for alternator output by 'flashing' the output lead to earth.

• Never use an ohmmeter of the type incorporating a hand-cranked generator for circuit or continuity testing.

• Always ensure that the battery negative lead is disconnected when working on the electrical system.

• Before using electric-arc welding equipment on the car, disconnect the battery, alternator and components such as the fuel injection/ignition electronic control unit to protect them from the risk of damage.

If an audio unit with a built-in security code is fitted, note the following precautions. If the power source to the unit is cut, the anti-theft system will activate. Even if the power source is immediately reconnected, the audio unit will not function until the correct security code has been entered. Therefore, if you do not know the correct security code for the audio unit do not disconnect the battery negative terminal of the battery or remove the audio unit from the vehicle.

2 Electrical fault finding – general information

Refer to Chapter 12, Section 2.

3 Battery – testing and charging

Note: *The following is intended as a guide only. Always refer to the manufacturer's recommendations (often printed on a label attached to the battery) before charging a battery.*

1 All models may be fitted with a maintenance-free battery in production, which should require no maintenance under normal operating conditions.

2 If the condition of the battery is suspect, remove the battery as described in Section 4, and check that the electrolyte level in each cell is up to the MAX mark on the outside of the battery case (about 5.0 mm above the tops of the plates in the cells). If necessary, the electrolyte level can be topped-up by removing the cell plugs from the top of the battery and adding distilled water (**not** acid).

3 An approximate check on battery condition can be made by checking the specific gravity of the electrolyte, using the following as a guide.

4 Use a hydrometer to make the check and compare the results with the following table. The temperatures quoted are ambient (air) temperatures. Note that the specific gravity readings assume an electrolyte temperature of 15°C; for every 10°C below 15°C subtract 0.007. For every 10°C above 15°C add 0.007.

	Above 25°C	Below 25°C
Fully-charged	1.210 to 1.230	1.270 to 1.290
70% charged	1.170 to 1.190	1.230 to 1.250
Discharged	1.050 to 1.070	1.110 to 1.130

5 If the battery condition is suspect, first check the specific gravity of electrolyte in each cell. A variation of 0.040 or more between any cells indicates loss of electrolyte or deterioration of the internal plates.

6 If the specific gravity variation is 0.040 or more, the battery should be renewed. If the cell variation is satisfactory but the battery is discharged, it should be charged in accordance with the manufacturer's instructions.

7 In cases where a 'sealed for life' maintenance-free battery is fitted, topping-up and testing of the electrolyte in each cell is not possible. The condition of the battery can therefore only be tested using a battery condition indicator or a voltmeter.

8 Models may be fitted with a battery with a built-in charge condition indicator. The indicator is located in the top of the battery casing, and indicates the condition of the battery from its colour. If the indicator shows green, then the battery is in a good state of charge. If the indicator turns darker, eventually to black, then the battery requires charging. If the indicator shows clear/yellow, then the electrolyte level in the battery is too low to allow further use, and the battery should be renewed. **Do not** attempt to charge, load or jump start a battery when the indicator shows clear/yellow.

9 If testing the battery using a voltmeter, connect the voltmeter across the battery. A fully-charged battery should give a reading of 12.5 volts or higher. The test is only accurate if the battery has not been subjected to any kind of charge for the previous six hours. If this is not the case, switch on the headlights for 30 seconds, then wait four to five minutes before testing the battery after switching off the headlights. All other electrical circuits must be switched off, so check that the doors and boot lid are fully shut when making the test.

10 Generally speaking, if the voltage reading is less than 12.2 volts, then the battery is discharged, whilst a reading of 12.2 to 12.4 volts indicates a partially-discharged condition.

4 Battery – disconnection, removal and refitting

Note: *When the battery is disconnected, any fault codes stored in the engine management ECM memory will be erased. If any faults are suspected, do not disconnect the battery until the fault codes have been read by a Mazda dealer or specialist. If the vehicle is fitted with a code-protected audio unit, refer to the Owners handbook before disconnecting the battery.*

Disconnection

1 The battery is located in the luggage compartment.

2 Remove the battery cover (where fitted) **(see illustration)**.

3 Slacken the nut and disconnect the battery negative lead **(see illustrations)**.

4 Upon reconnection, ensure the battery terminal and lead clamp are clean, then reconnect the negative lead and tighten the retaining nut securely.

4.2 Fold back the carpet and lift out the battery cover

4.3a Disconnect the battery negative lead (arrowed) – early models ...

4.3b ... and later models

4.6 Lift the plastic cover and slacken the positive clamp nut

4.7a Battery hold-down clamp nut (arrowed)

4.7b Battery hold-down clamp bolt (arrowed)

Removal

5 Disconnect the battery negative lead as described previously.
6 Prise up the plastic cover and slacken the nut securing the positive lead to the battery (see illustration).
7 Undo the nut or bolt (as applicable) and remove the battery hold-down clamp (see illustrations).
8 Disconnect the vent hose(s) and lift the battery from place. Take care as the battery is heavy!

Refitting

9 Refitting is a reversal of removal. Always reconnect the positive lead first, and the negative lead last. Tighten the clamp bolts securely.

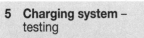

5 Charging system – testing

Note: Refer to the warnings given in 'Safety first!' and in Section 1 of this Chapter before starting work.
1 If the ignition warning light fails to illuminate when the ignition is switched on, first check the alternator wiring connections for security. If satisfactory, check that the warning light bulb has not blown, and that the bulbholder is secure in its location in the instrument panel. If the light still fails to illuminate, check the continuity of the warning light feed wire from the alternator to the bulbholder. If all is satisfactory, the alternator is at fault and

should be renewed or taken to an auto-electrician for testing and repair.
2 If the ignition warning light illuminates when the engine is running, stop the engine and check that the drivebelt is correctly tensioned (see Chapter 1, Section 6) and that the alternator connections are secure. If all is so far satisfactory, have the alternator checked by an auto-electrician for testing and repair. See the note in the previous paragraph.
3 If the alternator output is suspect even though the warning light functions correctly, the regulated voltage may be checked as follows.
4 Connect a voltmeter across the battery terminals and start the engine.
5 Increase the engine speed until the voltmeter reading remains steady; the reading should be approximately 12 to 13 volts, and no more than 15.0 volts.

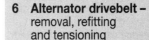

7.4 Undo the bolts (arrowed) and remove the manifold support bracket – engine removed for clarity

6 Switch on as many electrical accessories (eg, the headlights, heated rear window and heater blower) as possible, and check that the alternator maintains the regulated voltage at around 13 to 14 volts.
7 If the regulated voltage is not as stated, the fault may be due to worn alternator brushes, weak brush springs, a faulty voltage regulator, a faulty diode, a severed phase winding or worn or damaged slip-rings. The alternator should be renewed or taken to an auto-electrician for testing and repair.

6 Alternator drivebelt – removal, refitting and tensioning

Refer to the procedure given for the auxiliary drivebelt(s) in Chapter 1, Section 6.

7 Alternator – removal and refitting

Removal

1 Disconnect the battery negative lead (see Section 4).
2 Remove the alternator drivebelt as described in Chapter 1, Section 6.
3 Slacken the clamps, undo the bolt and remove the intake air duct (Chapter 4A, Section 2).
4 On 1998-on models, undo the bolts and remove the intake manifold support bracket (see illustration).

7.5 Release the clip, prise up the cap, and disconnect the wiring from the alternator (arrowed)

5 Disconnect the wiring connections from the rear of the alternator **(see illustration)**.
6 Undo the alternator mounting bolts and manoeuvre it from position **(see illustrations)**. On early models, the lower mounting bolt is removed from the front of the alternator, whilst on later models, the bolt is removed from the rear – necessitating the manifold bracket removal.

Refitting

7 Refitting is a reversal of removal, tightening all fasteners to the specified torque where given.

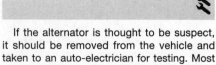

8 Alternator – testing and overhaul

If the alternator is thought to be suspect, it should be removed from the vehicle and taken to an auto-electrician for testing. Most auto-electricians will be able to supply and fit brushes at a reasonable cost. However, check on the cost of repairs before proceeding as it may prove more economical to obtain a new or exchange alternator.

9 Starting system – testing

Note: *Refer to the precautions given in 'Safety first!' and in Section 1 of this Chapter before starting work.*

1 If the starter motor fails to operate when the ignition key is turned to the appropriate position, the following possible causes may be to blame.

10.4 Undo the nut, and pull off the wiring plug – starter connections

7.6 Alternator mounting bolts (arrowed)

a) *The battery is faulty.*
b) *The electrical connections between the switch, solenoid, battery and starter motor are somewhere failing to pass the necessary current from the battery through the starter to earth.*
c) *The solenoid is faulty.*
d) *The starter motor is mechanically or electrically defective.*

2 To check the battery, switch on the headlights. If they dim after a few seconds, this indicates that the battery is discharged – recharge or renew the battery. If the headlights glow brightly, operate the ignition switch and observe the lights. If they dim, then this indicates that current is reaching the starter motor, therefore the fault must lie in the starter motor. If the lights continue to glow brightly (and no clicking sound can be heard from the starter motor solenoid), this indicates that there is a fault in the circuit or solenoid – see following paragraphs. If the starter motor turns slowly when operated, but the battery is in good condition, then this indicates that either the starter motor is faulty, or there is considerable resistance somewhere in the circuit.
3 If a fault in the circuit is suspected, disconnect the battery leads (including the earth connection to the body), the starter/solenoid wiring and the engine/transmission earth strap. Thoroughly clean the connections, and reconnect the leads and wiring, then use a voltmeter or test lamp to check that full battery voltage is available at the battery positive lead connection to the solenoid, and that the earth is sound. Smear petroleum jelly around the battery terminals to prevent corrosion – corroded connections are amongst the most frequent causes of electrical system faults.

10.5 Starter motor mounting bolts/nut (arrowed – engine removed for clarity

4 If the battery and all connections are in good condition, check the circuit by disconnecting the wire from the solenoid blade terminal. Connect a voltmeter or test lamp between the wire end and a good earth (such as the battery negative terminal), and check that the wire is live when the ignition switch is turned to the 'start' position. If it is, then the circuit is sound – if not the circuit wiring can be checked as described in Chapter 12, Section 2.
5 The solenoid contacts can be checked by connecting a voltmeter or test lamp between the battery positive feed connection on the starter side of the solenoid, and earth. When the ignition switch is turned to the 'start' position, there should be a reading or lighted bulb, as applicable. If there is no reading or lighted bulb, the solenoid is faulty and should be renewed.
6 If the circuit and solenoid are proved sound, the fault must lie in the starter motor. In this event, it may be possible to have the starter motor overhauled by a specialist, but check on the cost of spares before proceeding, as it may prove more economical to obtain a new or exchange motor.

10 Starter motor – removal and refitting

Removal

1 Disconnect the battery negative lead (see Section 4).
2 On 1998-on models, undo the bolts and remove the intake manifold support bracket **(see illustration 7.4)**. If improved access is required, remove the intake manifold as described in Chapter 4A, Section 11.
3 On 1997 and earlier models, undo the bolts and remove the support bracket from the front of the starter motor.
4 On all models, note their fitted positions, then undo the nut and disconnect the leads from the starter solenoid **(see illustration)**.
5 Undo the 3 bolts and remove the starter motor **(see illustration)**. Note that access is extremely limited.

Refitting

6 Refitting is a reversal of removal. Tighten the starter motor mounting bolts to the specified torque.

11 Starter motor – testing and overhaul

If the starter motor is thought to be suspect, it should be removed from the vehicle and taken to an auto-electrician for testing. Most auto-electricians will be able to supply and fit brushes at a reasonable cost. However, check on the cost of repairs before proceeding, as it may prove more economical to obtain a new or exchange motor.

Chapter 5 Part B:
Ignition system

Contents

Degrees of difficulty

Easy, suitable for novice with little experience	Fairly easy, suitable for beginner with some experience	Fairly difficult, suitable for competent DIY mechanic	Difficult, suitable for experienced DIY mechanic	Very difficult, suitable for expert DIY or professional

Specifications

General

System type . . . .   Electronic distributorless ignition system controlled by engine management system (electronic control module)
Firing order   1-3-4-2
Location of No 1 cylinder . . . .   Timing belt end

Ignition system data

Ignition timing (see text):
  1997 and earlier . . . .   9° to 11° BTDC @ 850 rpm
  1998 to 1999. . . . .   9° to 11° BTDC @ 800 rpm
  2000-on . . . .   Not adjustable – ECM controlled
Ignition coil resistances:
  Primary windings:
    1.6 litre:
      1997 and earlier . . . .   0.78 to 0.94 Ω
      1998-on. . . . .   Not available
    1.8 litre . . . .   Not available
  Secondary windings:
    1997 and earlier:
      1.6 litre . . . .   11.2 to 15.2 kΩ
      1.8 litre . . . .   8.7 to 12.9 kΩ
    1998 to 1999. . . . .   8.24 to 12.36 kΩ
    2000-on . . . .   7.0 to 11.0 kΩ

Torque wrench settings

	Nm	lbf ft
Ignition coil:		
1999 and earlier	22	16
2000-on	10	7
Knock sensor	27	20

3.4 Use an ohmmeter to measure the ignition coil's secondary resistance – 1993 and earlier ...

1 Ignition system – general information and precautions

1 The electronic ignition system includes the ignition switch, the battery, the igniter (1993 and earlier models), the ignition coil assembly and the spark plugs. The ignition coil assembly contains two ignition coils, one for terminals 1 and 4 and the other for terminals 2 and 3. The ignition system is controlled by the engine management electronic control module (ECM). Using data provided by information sensors which monitor various engine functions (such as rpm, intake air volume, engine temperature, etc), the ECM ensures a perfectly timed spark under all conditions. **Note:** *On 1994 and later models the igniter function is handled by the ECM.*

2 When diagnosing the electronic ignition system, be sure to make all the necessary ignition system checks before renewing any components.

3 The information contained in this Chapter concentrates on the ignition-related components of the engine management system. Information covering the fuel, exhaust and emission control components can be found in Chapter 4A and 4B.

Precautions

4 When working on the ignition system, take the following precautions:

a) *Do not keep the ignition switch on for more than 10 seconds if the engine will not start.*

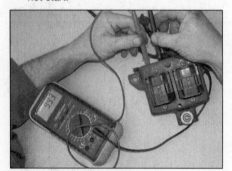

3.6 ... 1994 to 1999 models ...

b) *Always connect a tachometer in accordance with the manufacturer's instructions. Some tachometers may be incompatible with this ignition system.*
c) *Some timing lights that work on No. 1 and No. 3 cylinders may not light when connected to No. 2 and No. 4 cylinders, even if the ignition system is working properly.*
d) *Never allow the ignition coil terminals to touch earth. Earthing the coil could result in damage to the igniter and/or the ignition coil.*
e) *Do not disconnect the battery when the engine is running.*
f) *On 1993 and earlier models, make sure the igniter is properly earthed.*

⚠️ **Warning: Voltages produced by an electronic ignition system are considerably higher than those produced by conventional ignition systems. Extreme care must be taken when working on the system with the ignition switched on. Persons with surgically-implanted cardiac pacemaker devices should keep well clear of the ignition circuits, components and test equipment.**

2 Ignition system – testing

General

1 The components of the ignition system are normally very reliable; most faults are far more likely to be due to loose or dirty connections, or to tracking of HT voltage due to dirt, dampness or damaged insulation, than to the failure of any of the system's components. **Always** check all wiring thoroughly before condemning an electrical component, and work methodically to eliminate all other possibilities before deciding that a particular component is faulty.

2 The old practice of checking for a spark by holding the live end of an HT cap a short distance away from the engine is **not** recommended; not only is there a high risk of a powerful electric shock, but the ECM, igniter or HT coil may be damaged. Similarly, **never** try to diagnose misfires by pulling off one HT coil at a time.

3 The following tests should be carried out when an obvious fault such as non-starting or a clearly detectable misfire exists. Some faults, however, are more obscure and are often disguised by the fact that the ECM will adopt an emergency program (limp-home) mode to maintain as much driveability as possible. Faults of this nature usually appear in the form of excessive fuel consumption, poor idling characteristics, lack of performance, knocking or pinking noises from the engine under certain conditions, or a combination of these conditions. Where problems such as this are experienced, the best course is to refer the car

to a suitably-equipped garage for diagnostic testing using dedicated test equipment.

Engine will not start

Note: *Remember that a fault with the anti-theft alarm or immobiliser will give rise to apparent starting problems. Make sure that the alarm or immobiliser has been deactivated, referring to the vehicle handbook for details.*

4 If the engine either will not turn over at all, or only turns very slowly, check the battery and starter motor. Connect a voltmeter across the battery terminals (meter positive probe to battery positive terminal) then note the voltage reading obtained while turning the engine over on the starter for (no more than) ten seconds. If the reading obtained is less than approximately 9.5 volts, first check the battery, starter motor and charging system as described in Chapter 5A.

Engine misfires

5 An irregular misfire is probably due to a loose connection to one of the ignition coils or system sensors.

6 With the ignition switched off, check carefully through the system, ensuring that all connections are clean and securely fastened.

7 Regular misfiring indicates a problem with one of the ignition coils or spark plugs. As no resistance values are available, testing the coils is best left to a Mazda dealer or suitable-equipped specialist.

8 Any further checking of the system components should be carried out after first checking the ECM for fault codes.

3 Electronic ignition HT coil(s) – testing and renewal

Testing

1 Perform the ignition system checks as described in Section 2.

2 Crank the engine and verify that a strong blue spark is visible at the coil wire or spark plug wire.

1993 and earlier models

3 Use an ohmmeter to measure the resistance of the primary coil winding. If not within the values listed in this Chapter's Specifications, renew the coil.

4 Use an ohmmeter to measure the resistance of the secondary coil winding **(see illustration)**. If not within the values listed (see Specifications), renew the coil.

1994 to 1999 models

5 Perform the ignition system checks as described in Section 6.

6 Use an ohmmeter to measure the resistance of the secondary coil winding **(see illustration)**. If not within the range listed (see Specifications), renew the coil. Primary winding resistance is not tested on 1994 and later models.

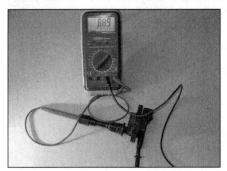

3.8 ... and 2000-on models

3.10 Depress the clip and disconnect the ignition coil's wiring plug (arrowed)

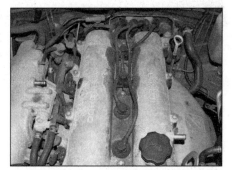

3.11 Pull the HT lead caps from the spark plugs

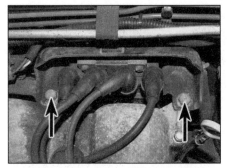

3.12a The ignition coil assembly is secured by a bolt each side (arrowed) ...

3.12b ... and a bolt in the centre underneath (arrowed)

3.14 Depress the clip (arrowed) and disconnect the wiring plugs from the coils

2000-on models

7 Perform the ignition system checks as described in Section 6.

8 Remove the coil as described later in this Section, then using an ohmmeter, measure the secondary resistance between the two high tension terminals **(see illustration)**, and compare the results with those specified. If not within the range specified, renew the coil. Primary winding resistance is not tested on these models.

Renewal

9 Disconnect the battery negative lead as described in Chapter 5A, Section 4.

1999 and earlier models

10 Disconnect the wiring plugs from the coil **(see illustration)**.

11 Label and disconnect the HT leads from the spark plugs **(see illustration)**.

12 Undo the retaining bolts and remove the coil assembly **(see illustrations)**. If necessary, separate the coil from the mounting bracket.

13 Refitting is a reversal of removal. Ensure the HT leads are connected to their original locations.

2000-on models

14 Disconnect the wiring plugs from the ignition coils **(see illustration)**.

15 Disconnect the HT leads from the ignition coils. Note that the HT lead from cylinder No. 4 spark plug is connected to the ignition coil above cylinder No. 1 spark plug, and the HT lead from cylinder No. 2 spark plug is connected to the ignition coil above cylinder No. 3 spark plug **(see illustration)**.

16 Undo the mounting bolts and pull the relevant coil (complete with spark plug cap) upwards from place **(see illustrations)**. **Note:** As damage to the connection can result, only

separate the coil from the spark plug cap if either component is to be renewed.

17 Refitting is a reversal of removal. Tighten the fasteners to their specified torque.

| 4 | Ignition timing – checking and adjustment | |

Note: The following ignition timing procedure applies to 1997 and earlier models. However, if the procedure specified on the VECI label of your vehicle differs from this one, use the procedure found on the VECI label. Ignition timing adjustment on 1998-on models requires a special tester and should be performed by a dealer service department or other suitably equipped repairer.

1 Connect a tachometer according to the manufacturer's specifications. External

3.15 Note the routing of the HT leads

3.16a Undo the mounting bolts (arrowed) ...

3.16b ... and pull the ignition coils upwards from the spark plugs

4.1 12V DC connector in the front, left-hand corner of the engine compartment (arrowed)

4.2a Unclip the diagnostic connector cover (arrowed) …

4.2b … bridge between TEN and GND terminals (arrowed)

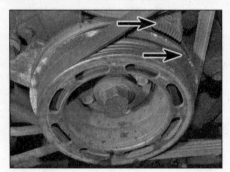

4.4 Ignition timing index plate and timing notch on the crankshaft pulley (arrowed)

4.5 Camshaft position sensor retaining bolt (arrowed)

slowly rotate the camshaft position sensor until the timing marks align **(see illustration)**. Tighten the bolt and recheck the timing.
6 Remove the jumper wire from the diagnostic connector. Operate the throttle to increase engine speed and confirm that the ignition timing advances.
7 Turn the engine off and remove the tachometer and the timing light.

5 Igniter (1993 and earlier models) – renewal

1 Disconnect the battery negative lead as described in Chapter 5A, Section 4.
2 The igniter is located on the right-hand side of the engine compartment. Disconnect the igniter wiring plug **(see illustration)**.
3 Undo the retaining bolts and remove the igniter.
4 Refitting is a reversal of removal.

6 Knock sensor (1998-on) – removal and refitting

5.2 The igniter is located on the right-hand side inner wing (arrowed)

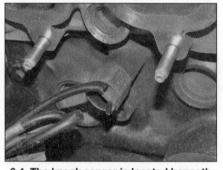

6.4 The knock sensor is located beneath the intake manifold

DC power for the tachometer should be obtained by connecting to the single-pin connector on the blue wire in the left-hand front corner of the engine compartment **(see illustration)**.
2 Locate the diagnostic connector, unclip the cover and insert a jumper wire between terminals TEN and GND **(see illustrations)**.
3 With the ignition switch off, connect a timing light according to the tool manufacturer's instructions. Most timing lights are powered by the battery. Also, an inductive style pick-up

is connected to the number one cylinder spark plug wire.
4 Locate the timing marks on the pointer index and the crankshaft pulley **(see illustration)**.
5 Start the engine and allow it to warm up to normal operating temperature (upper radiator hose hot). Verify that the engine idle is as listed in this Chapter's Specifications. Aim the timing light at the index pointer. The mark on the crankshaft pulley should line up with the timing indicator. If necessary, loosen the camshaft position sensor retaining bolt and

1 Disconnect the battery negative lead as described in Chapter 5A, Section 4.
2 The knock sensor(s) is located on the right-hand side of the cylinder block under the intake manifold. Remove the intake manifold as described in Chapter 4A, Section 11.
3 Trace the wiring back from the sensor to the connector, then disconnect the wiring plug.
4 Note its fitted position, then unscrew the sensor from the cylinder block **(see illustration)**.
5 Refitting is a reversal of removal. Note that tightening the knock sensor to the specified torque is absolutely essential. Failure to do so could impair the performance of the sensor, causing engine damage.

Chapter 6
Clutch

Contents

Degrees of difficulty

Easy, suitable for novice with little experience	Fairly easy, suitable for beginner with some experience	Fairly difficult, suitable for competent DIY mechanic	Difficult, suitable for experienced DIY mechanic	Very difficult, suitable for expert DIY or professional

Specifications

Type	Single dry plate with diaphragm spring, hydraulically-operated

Friction disc

Minimum lining thickness above rivet head	0.3 mm	
Diameter:		
1.6 litre	200 mm	
1.8 litre	215 mm	

Torque wrench setting	Nm	lbf ft
Clutch cover-to-flywheel bolts	22	16

1 General information

All models are fitted with a single dry plate clutch, which consists of five main components; friction disc, pressure plate, diaphragm spring, cover and release bearing.

The friction disc is free to slide along the splines of the gearbox input shaft, and is held in position between the flywheel and the pressure plate by the pressure exerted on the pressure plate by the diaphragm spring. Friction lining material is riveted to both sides of the friction disc.

The diaphragm spring is mounted on pins, and is held in place in the cover by annular fulcrum rings.

The release bearing is located on a guide sleeve at the front of the gearbox, and the bearing is free to slide on the sleeve, under the action of the release arm which pivots inside the clutch bellhousing.

The release mechanism is operated by the clutch pedal, using hydraulic pressure. The pedal acts on the hydraulic master cylinder pushrod, and a slave cylinder, mounted on the gearbox bellhousing, operates the clutch release lever via a pushrod.

When the clutch pedal is depressed, the release arm pushes the release bearing forwards, to bear against the centre of the diaphragm spring, thus pushing the centre of the diaphragm spring inwards. The diaphragm spring acts against the fulcrum rings in the cover, and so as the centre of the spring is pushed in, the outside of the spring is pushed out, so allowing the pressure plate to move backwards away from the friction disc.

When the clutch pedal is released, the diaphragm spring forces the pressure plate into contact with the friction linings on the friction disc, and simultaneously pushes the friction disc forwards on its splines, forcing it against the flywheel. The friction disc is now firmly sandwiched between the pressure plate and the flywheel, and drive is taken up.

2 Clutch assembly – removal, inspection and refitting

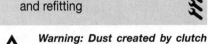

Warning: Dust created by clutch wear and deposited on the clutch components may contain asbestos, which is a health hazard. DO NOT blow it out with compressed air, or inhale any of it. DO NOT use petrol (or petroleum-based solvents) to clean off the dust. Brake system cleaner or methylated spirit should be used to flush the dust into a suitable receptacle.

After the clutch components are wiped clean with rags, dispose of the contaminated rags and cleaner in a sealed, marked container.

Removal

1 Remove the gearbox, as described in Chapter 7, Section 7.

2 If the original clutch is to be refitted, make alignment marks between the clutch cover and the flywheel, so that the clutch can be refitted in its original position.

3 Progressively unscrew the bolts securing the clutch cover/pressure plate assembly to the flywheel, and where applicable recover the washers.

4 Withdraw the clutch cover from the flywheel. Be prepared to catch the clutch friction disc, which may drop out of the cover as it is withdrawn, and note which way round the friction disc is fitted – the two sides of the disc are often marked 'Engine side' and 'Transmission side'. The greater projecting side of the hub faces away from the flywheel.

Inspection

5 With the clutch assembly removed, clean off all traces of dust using a dry cloth. Although most friction discs now have asbestos-free linings, some do not, and it is wise to take suitable precautions; *asbestos dust is harmful, and must not be inhaled.*

2.12 Using an aligning tool, centre the friction disc on the flywheel

2.13 Ensure the clutch cover locates over the dowels (arrowed)

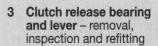

3 Clutch release bearing and lever – removal, inspection and refitting

⚠ **Warning: Dust created by clutch wear and deposited on the clutch components may contain asbestos, which is a health hazard. DO NOT blow it out with compressed air, or inhale any of it. DO NOT use petrol (or petroleum-based solvents) to clean off the dust. Brake system cleaner or methylated spirit should be used to flush the dust into a suitable receptacle. After the clutch components are wiped clean with rags, dispose of the contaminated rags and cleaner in a sealed, marked container.**

6 Examine the linings of the friction disc for wear and loose rivets, and the disc for distortion, cracks, and worn splines. The surface of the friction linings may be highly glazed, but, as long as the friction material pattern can be clearly seen, this is satisfactory. If there is any sign of oil contamination, indicated by a continuous, or patchy, shiny black discolouration, the disc must be renewed. The source of the contamination must be traced and rectified before fitting new clutch components; typically, a leaking crankshaft rear oil seal or gearbox input shaft oil seal – or both – will be to blame (renewal procedures are given in Chapter 2, Section 12 and Chapter 7, Section 3 respectively). The disc must also be renewed if the lining thickness has worn down to, or just above, the level of the rivet heads. Note that Mazda specify a minimum friction material thickness above the heads of the rivets (see Specifications).

7 Check the machined faces of the flywheel and pressure plate. If either is grooved, or heavily scored, renewal is necessary. The pressure plate must also be renewed if any cracks are apparent, or if the diaphragm spring is damaged or its pressure suspect.

8 With the clutch removed, it is advisable to check the condition of the release bearing, as described in Section 3.

9 Check the pilot bearing in the flywheel. Make sure that it turns smoothly and quietly. If the gearbox input shaft contact face on the

bearing is worn or damaged, fit a new bearing, as described in Section 7.

Refitting

10 If new clutch components are to be fitted, where applicable, ensure that all anti-corrosion preservative is cleaned from the friction material on the disc, and the contact surfaces of the pressure plate.

11 It is important to ensure that no oil or grease gets onto the friction disc linings, or the pressure plate and flywheel faces. It is advisable to refit the clutch assembly with clean hands, and to wipe down the pressure plate and flywheel faces with a clean rag before assembly begins.

12 Offer the disc to the flywheel, with the greater projecting side of the hub facing away from the flywheel (most friction discs will have an 'Engine side' or Transmission side' marking which should face the flywheel or gearbox as applicable). Using a suitable Mazda tool or a suitable alternative manufactured by an automotive tool specialist, centre the friction disc in the flywheel **(see illustration)**.

13 Fit the clutch cover assembly, where applicable aligning the marks on the flywheel and clutch cover. Ensure that the clutch cover locates over the dowels on the flywheel **(see illustration)**. Insert the securing bolts and washers, and tighten them to the specified torque.

14 Refit the gearbox as described in Chapter 7, Section 7.

Removal

1 Remove the gearbox as described in Chapter 7, Section 7.

2 Remove the clutch release lever from the ball stud, then remove the bearing from the lever **(see illustration)**.

Inspection

3 Hold the bearing by the outer race and rotate the inner race while applying pressure. If the bearing doesn't turn smoothly or if it's noisy, renew the bearing/hub assembly. Wipe the bearing with a clean rag and inspect it for damage, wear and cracks. Don't immerse the bearing in solvent – it's sealed for life and soaking or dipping in solvent would ruin it. Also check the release lever for cracks and bends.

4 Check the release lever boot for cracks or deterioration **(see illustration)**. If there are problems, pull it out of the hole and renew it.

Installation

5 Fill the inner groove of the release bearing with high-temperature molybdenum grease. Also apply a light coat of the same grease to the transmission input shaft splines and the ball stud **(see illustrations)**.

6 Lubricate the release lever ball socket and lever ends with high-temperature molybdenum grease **(see illustrations)**.

7 Attach the release bearing to the release lever.

8 Slide the release bearing onto the transmission input shaft front bearing retainer while passing

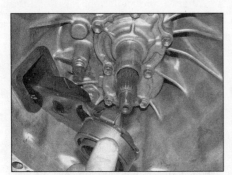

3.2 Pull the lever from the ball stud and slide the bearing out

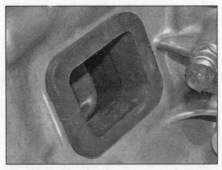

3.4 Check the condition of the rubber boot

3.5a Apply a thin layer of high-temperature moly grease to release bearing inner groove (arrowed) ...

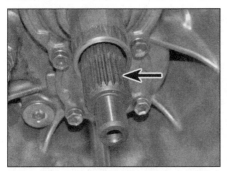

3.5b ... the input shaft splines (arrowed) ...

3.5c ... the ball stud (arrowed) ...

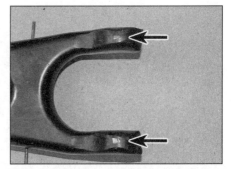

3.6a ... the release lever ends (arrowed) ...

the end of the release lever through the opening in the clutch housing. Push the clutch release lever onto the ball stud until it's firmly seated **(see illustration)**.

9 The remainder of refitting is the reverse of the removal procedure.

4 Hydraulic slave cylinder – removal, inspection and refitting

⚠ *Warning: Hydraulic fluid is poisonous; wash off immediately and thoroughly in the case of skin contact, and seek immediate medical advice if any fluid is swallowed or gets into the eyes. Certain types of hydraulic fluid are inflammable, and may ignite when allowed into contact with hot components; when servicing any hydraulic system, it is safest to assume that the fluid is inflammable, and to take precautions against the risk of fire as though it is petrol that is being handled. Hydraulic fluid is also an effective paint stripper, and will attack plastics; if any is spilt, it should be washed off immediately, using copious quantities of fresh water. Finally, it is hygroscopic (it absorbs moisture from the air) – old fluid may be contaminated and unfit for further use. When topping-up or renewing the fluid, always use the recommended type, and ensure that it comes from a freshly-opened sealed container.*

Note: *Before beginning this procedure, contact local parts stores and dealer service departments concerning the purchase of a rebuild kit or a new slave cylinder. Availability and cost of the necessary parts may dictate whether the cylinder is rebuilt or renewed. If it's decided to rebuild the cylinder, inspect the bore as described in paragraph 7 before purchasing parts.*

Removal

1 Raise the vehicle and support it securely on axle stands (see *Jacking and vehicle support*). Remove the transmission undershields/frame **(see illustrations)**. Remove the right-hand front roadwheel.

2 Working through the wheel arch aperture, disconnect the hydraulic pipe at the slave

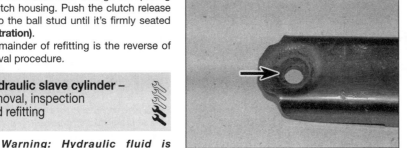

3.6b ... and the lever ball socket (arrowed)

cylinder **(see illustration)**. If available, use a flare-nut spanner on the fitting, which will prevent the fitting from being rounded off. Have a container and rags handy, as some fluid will be spilled as the pipe is disconnected. Plug the pipe to prevent contamination.

4.1a Front reinforcement frame retaining bolts (arrowed)

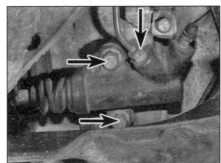

4.2 Slave cylinder pipe union and retaining bolts (arrowed)

3.8 Firmly press the release lever onto the ball stud

3 Remove the slave cylinder mounting bolts and remove it **(see illustration 4.2)**.

Overhaul

4 Remove the pushrod and the boot **(see illustration)**.

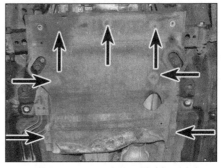

4.1b Transmission undershield retaining bolts (arrowed)

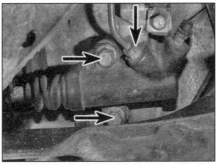

4.4 Remove the pushrod and rubber boot

4.5 Use low-pressure air to force the piston out – note the block of wood to 'catch' the piston

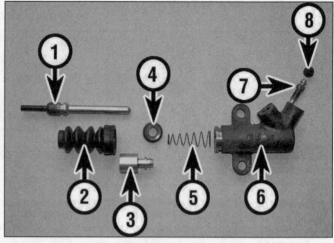

4.6 Slave cylinder components

1 Pushrod	4 Seal	7 Bleed screw
2 Rubber boot	5 Spring	8 Dust cap
3 Piston	6 Cylinder body	

5 Tap the cylinder on a block of wood to eject the piston and seal. If the piston won't come out easily, blow low-pressure air into the fluid pipe fitting **(see illustration)**.

⚠ *Warning: The piston can shoot out forcefully enough to cause injury. Don't use any more air pressure than necessary. Be sure to point the open end of the cylinder at a block of wood. Keep your fingers out of the way.*

6 Remove the spring from inside the cylinder **(see illustration)**.

7 Carefully inspect the bore of the cylinder. Check for deep scratches, score marks and ridges. The bore must be smooth to the touch. If any imperfections are found, the slave cylinder must be renewed.

8 Using the new parts in the rebuild kit, assemble the components using plenty of fresh brake fluid for lubrication **(see illustration)**. Note the installed direction of the spring and the seal.

Refitting

9 Refit the slave cylinder on the clutch housing. Make sure the pushrod is seated in the release fork pocket.

10 Connect the hydraulic pipe to the slave cylinder. Tighten the connection.

11 Fill the clutch master cylinder with brake fluid.

12 Bleed the system (see Section 6).

13 Lower the vehicle.

5 Hydraulic master cylinder – removal, inspection and refitting

⚠ *Warning: Hydraulic fluid is poisonous; wash off immediately and thoroughly in the case of skin contact, and seek immediate medical advice if any fluid is swallowed or gets into the eyes. Certain types of hydraulic fluid are inflammable, and may ignite when allowed into contact with hot components; when servicing any hydraulic system, it is safest to assume that the fluid is inflammable, and to take precautions against the risk of fire as though it is petrol that is being handled. Hydraulic fluid is also an effective paint stripper, and will attack plastics; if any is spilt, it should be washed off immediately, using copious quantities of fresh water. Finally, it is hygroscopic (it absorbs moisture from the air) – old fluid may be contaminated and unfit for further use. When topping-up or renewing the fluid, always use the recommended type, and ensure that it comes from a freshly-opened sealed container.*

Note: Before beginning this procedure, contact local parts stores and dealer service departments concerning the purchase of a rebuild kit or a new master cylinder. Availability and cost of the necessary parts may dictate whether the cylinder is rebuilt or renewed. If you decide to rebuild the cylinder, inspect the bore as described in paragraph 8 before purchasing parts.

Removal

1 Open the bonnet and place rags beneath the clutch master cylinder.

2 Disconnect the hydraulic pipe at the clutch master cylinder **(see illustration)**. If available, use a flare-nut spanner on the fitting, to protect the fitting from being rounded off.

3 Undo the retaining nuts and remove the master cylinder from the engine compartment bulkhead, again being careful not to spill fluid from the master cylinder **(see illustration)**. *Note: On some models, one of the master cylinder retaining nuts is accessed from beneath the facia (see illustrations).*

4.8 Ensure the seal is fitted correctly to the piston

5.2 Clutch fluid pipe union (arrowed)

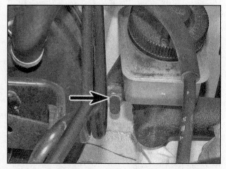

5.3a Undo the retaining nut (arrowed) in the engine compartment

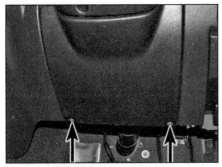

5.3b Undo the screws (arrowed), and remove the panel ...

5.3c ... to access the remaining retaining nut (arrowed)

5.5 Remove the circlip to release the piston

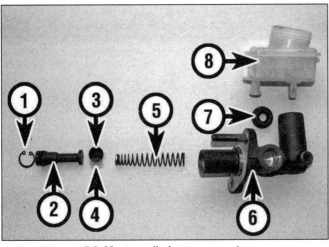

5.6 Master cylinder components

1	Circlip	4	Spacer	7	Sealing
2	Piston and seal	5	Spring		grommet
3	Primary cup	6	Cylinder body	8	Reservoir

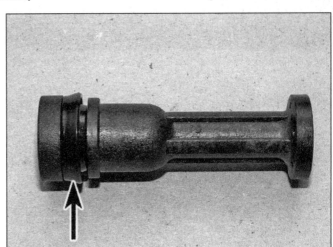

5.10 Ensure the seal (arrowed) is fitted correctly

Overhaul

4 Turn the master cylinder over and allow the trapped fluid to drain from the fluid pipe opening into a container.

5 Place the cylinder in a vice with the piston end up. Push the piston down with a screwdriver and remove the circlip with circlip pliers **(see illustration)**. **Note:** *Do not damage the pushrod contact surface of the piston.*

6 Tap the master cylinder on a block of wood to eject the piston, spacer, primary cup and spring from inside the bore **(see illustration)**.

Note: *If the rebuild kit supplies a complete piston assembly, ignore the paragraphs which don't apply.*

7 Carefully remove the seal from the piston.

8 Inspect the bore of the master cylinder for deep scratches, score marks and ridges. The surface must be smooth to the touch. If the bore isn't perfectly smooth, the master cylinder must be renewed or a reconditioned unit used.

9 If the cylinder will be rebuilt, use the new parts contained in the rebuild kit and follow any specific instructions which may have

accompanied the rebuild kit. Wash all parts to be re-used with brake cleaner, denatured alcohol or clean brake fluid. DO NOT use petroleum-based solvents.

10 Attach a new seal to the piston. The seal lips must face away from the pushrod end of the piston **(see illustration)**.

11 Lubricate the bore of the cylinder, the spring, primary cup, spacer and piston with plenty of fresh brake fluid.

12 Carefully guide the spring, primary cup, spacer and piston into the cylinder bore **(see illustrations)**.

5.12a Fit the primary cup ...

5.12b ... spacer ...

5.12c ... and piston

13 Again place the cylinder in a vice with the piston end up. Push the piston down with a screwdriver and fit a new circlip.

Refitting

14 Apply a small amount of grease on the end of the pushrod. Position the master cylinder on the pushrod and against the bulkhead, the refit the retaining nuts finger-tight.

15 Connect the hydraulic pipe to the master cylinder, moving the cylinder slightly as necessary to thread the fitting properly into the bore. Don't cross-thread the fitting as it's fitted.

16 Tighten the retaining nuts and the hydraulic pipe fitting securely.

17 Fill the clutch fluid reservoir with brake fluid and bleed the clutch system (see Section 6).

18 Check the clutch pedal height and freeplay (see Chapter 1, Section 5).

---

6   Hydraulic system – bleeding

⚠️ *Warning: Hydraulic fluid is poisonous; wash off immediately and thoroughly in the case of skin contact, and seek immediate medical advice if any fluid is swallowed or gets into the eyes. Certain types of hydraulic fluid are inflammable, and may ignite when allowed into contact with hot components; when servicing any hydraulic system, it is safest to assume that the fluid is inflammable, and to take precautions against the risk of fire as though it is petrol that is being handled. Hydraulic fluid is also an effective paint stripper, and will attack plastics; if any is spilt, it should be washed off immediately, using copious quantities of fresh water. Finally, it is hygroscopic (it absorbs moisture from the air) – old fluid may be contaminated and unfit for further use. When topping-up or renewing the fluid, always use the recommended type, and ensure that it comes from a freshly-opened sealed container.*

General

1 The correct operation of any hydraulic system is only possible after removing all

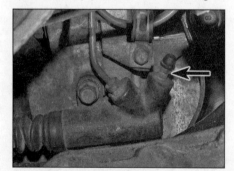

6.6 Slave cylinder bleed screw (arrowed) – viewed through the wheel arch aperture

air from the components and circuit; this is achieved by bleeding the system.

2 During the bleeding procedure, add only clean, unused hydraulic fluid of the recommended type; never re-use fluid that has already been bled from the system. Ensure that sufficient fluid is available before starting work.

3 If there is any possibility of incorrect fluid being already in the system, the clutch components and circuit must be flushed completely with uncontaminated, correct fluid, and new seals should be fitted to the various components.

4 If hydraulic fluid has been lost from the system, or air has entered because of a leak, ensure that the fault is cured before proceeding further.

5 To improve access, apply the handbrake, then jack up the front of the vehicle, and support it securely on axle stands (see *Jacking and vehicle support*). Remove the front, right-hand roadwheel.

6 Check that the clutch hydraulic pipe(s) and hose(s) are secure, that the unions are tight, and that the bleed screw on the rear of the clutch slave cylinder (mounted under the vehicle on the lower left-hand side of the gearbox bellhousing) is closed. Clean any dirt from around the bleed screw **(see illustration)**.

7 Unscrew the clutch fluid reservoir cap, and top the fluid up to the MAX level line; refit the cap loosely, and remember to maintain the fluid level at least above the MIN level line throughout the procedure, or there is a risk of further air entering the system.

8 It is recommended that pressure-bleeding equipment is used to bleed the system. Alternatively, there are a number of one-man, do-it-yourself brake bleeding kits currently available from motor accessory shops. These kits greatly simplify the bleeding operation, and also reduce the risk of expelled air and fluid being drawn back into the system. If such a kit is not available, the basic (two-man) method must be used, which is described in detail below.

9 If pressure-bleeding equipment or a one-man kit is to be used, prepare the vehicle as described previously, and follow the equipment/kit manufacturer's instructions, as the procedure may vary slightly according to the type being used; generally, they are as outlined below in the relevant sub-section.

10 Whichever method is used, the same basic process must be followed to ensure that the removal of all air from the system.

Bleeding

Basic (two-man) method

11 Collect a clean glass jar, a suitable length of plastic or rubber tubing which is a tight fit over the bleed screw, and a ring spanner to fit the screw. The help of an assistant will also be required.

12 Where applicable, remove the dust cap from the bleed screw. Fit the spanner and

tube to the screw, place the other end of the tube in the jar, and pour in sufficient fluid to cover the end of the tube.

13 Ensure that the reservoir fluid level is maintained at least above the MIN level line throughout the procedure.

14 Have the assistant fully depress the clutch pedal several times to build-up pressure, then maintain it on the final downstroke.

15 While pedal pressure is maintained, unscrew the bleed screw (approximately one turn) and allow the compressed fluid and air to flow into the jar. The assistant should maintain pedal pressure, following it down to the floor if necessary, and should not release it until instructed to do so. When the flow stops, tighten the bleed screw again, have the assistant release the pedal slowly, and recheck the reservoir fluid level.

16 Repeat the steps given in paragraphs 14 and 15 until the fluid emerging from the bleed screw is free from air bubbles.

17 When no more air bubbles appear, tighten the bleed screw securely. Do not overtighten the bleed screw.

18 Remove the tube and spanner, and refit the dust cap to the bleed screw.

19 Refit the slave cylinder to the bellhousing, and tighten the securing nuts securely.

Using a one-way valve kit

20 As their name implies, these kits consist of a length of tubing with a one-way valve fitted, to prevent expelled air and fluid being drawn back into the system; some kits include a translucent container, which can be positioned so that the air bubbles can be more easily seen flowing from the end of the tube.

21 The kit is connected to the bleed screw, which is then opened. The user returns to the driver's seat, depresses the clutch pedal with a smooth, steady stroke, and slowly releases it; this is repeated until the expelled fluid is clear of air bubbles.

22 Note that these kits simplify work so much that it is easy to forget the reservoir fluid level; ensure that this is maintained at least above the MIN level line at all times.

Using a pressure-bleeding kit

23 These kits are usually operated by the reservoir of pressurised air contained in the spare tyre. However, note that it will probably be necessary to reduce the pressure to a lower level than normal; refer to the instructions supplied with the kit.

24 By connecting a pressurised, fluid-filled container to the fluid reservoir, bleeding can be carried out simply by opening the bleed screw, and allowing the fluid to flow out until no more air bubbles can be seen in the expelled fluid.

25 This method has the advantage that the large reservoir of fluid provides an additional safeguard against air being drawn into the system during bleeding.

All methods

26 If after following the instructions given, it

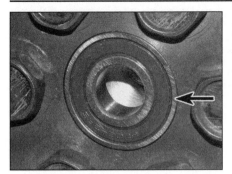

7.1 Flywheel pilot bearing (arrowed)

7.5 Extracting the pilot bearing using a slide hammer with an adjustable tip hooks behind the bearing

8.4 Clutch pedal switch wiring plug (arrowed)

is suspected that air is still present in hydraulic system, remove the slave cylinder (Section 4) without disconnecting the hydraulic pipes, push the cylinder piston all the way in, and holding the cylinder with the bleed screw uppermost, bleed the system again. **Note:** *Steps must be taken to ensure that the slave cylinder piston is prevented from extending during the bleeding procedure. If necessary, use a metal strip and two threaded bars to fabricate a tool to hold the piston in.*

27 When bleeding is complete, and firm pedal feel is restored, wash off any spilt fluid, check that the bleed screw is tightened securely, and refit the dust cap.

28 Check the hydraulic fluid level in the reservoir, and top-up if necessary (see *Weekly checks*).

29 Discard any hydraulic fluid that has been bled from the system; it will not be fit for re-use.

30 Check the feel of the clutch pedal. If it feels at all spongy, air must still be present in the system, and further bleeding is required. Failure to bleed satisfactorily after a reasonable repetition of the bleeding procedure may be due to worn master or slave cylinder seals.

31 On completion, lower the vehicle to the ground.

7 Pilot bearing – renewal

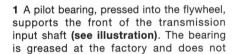

1 A pilot bearing, pressed into the flywheel, supports the front of the transmission input shaft **(see illustration)**. The bearing is greased at the factory and does not

require additional lubrication. The pilot bearing should be inspected whenever the clutch components are removed. Due to its inaccessibility, if you are in doubt as to its condition, renew it.

2 Remove the transmission as described in Chapter 7, Section 7.

3 Remove the clutch components as described in Section 2.

4 Inspect the bearing for excessive wear, scoring, lack of grease, dryness or obvious damage. If any of these conditions are noted, the bearing should be renewed.

5 The bearing must be pulled from its hole in the flywheel, gripping the bearing at the rear. Special tools are available, but you may be able to get by with an alternative or fabricated tool. One method that works well is to use a slide-hammer with a small tip that has two adjustable hooks, 180-degrees apart **(see illustration)**. Such tips are commonly available for slide-hammers, and are often included with better-quality slide-hammer kits.

6 To fit the new bearing, lightly lubricate the outside surface with multipurpose grease, then drive it into the recess with a hammer and a suitable tubular spacer which bears only on the outer race of the bearing. Make sure that the bearing seal faces toward the transmission. Ensure the bearing is driven in squarely. Tap it into place until it's flush with the edge of the bearing bore.

7 Lubricate the pilot bearing with high-temperature grease.

8 Refit the clutch components as described in Section 2.

9 Refit the transmission as described in Chapter 7, Section 7.

8 Clutch switch – testing and renewal

Testing

1 Check the clutch pedal height and freeplay as described in Chapter 1, Section 5.

2 Verify that the engine will not start when the clutch pedal is released. Verify that the engine will start when the clutch pedal is depressed all the way.

3 If the clutch switch doesn't perform as described, renew it. Begin by removing the panel beneath the steering column **(see illustration 5.3b)**.

4 Locate the switch on the clutch pedal assembly and unplug the electrical connector **(see illustration)**.

5 Connect an ohmmeter between the terminals of the switch. Verify that there is continuity between the switch terminals when the switch is On (pedal depressed).

6 Verify that no continuity exists between the switch terminals when the switch is Off (pedal released).

7 If the switch fails either of the tests, renew it.

Renewal

8 Unplug the electrical connector. Loosen the locknuts and remove the switch.

9 Refitting is the reverse of removal.

10 Adjust the pedal height (see Chapter 1, Section 5)

11 Verify again that the engine doesn't start when the clutch pedal is released, and does start when the pedal is depressed.

Chapter 7
Manual gearbox

Contents

Degrees of difficulty

Easy, suitable for novice with little experience	Fairly easy, suitable for beginner with some experience	Fairly difficult, suitable for competent DIY mechanic	Difficult, suitable for experienced DIY mechanic	Very difficult, suitable for expert DIY or professional

Specifications

Type

1.6 litre	M type
1.8 litre 5-speed	M15M-D
6-speed	Y16M-D

Torque wrench settings	Nm	lbf ft
Front crossbar retaining bolts	105	77
Front crossmember reinforcement plate:		
Bolts	105	77
Nuts	35	26
Gearbox-to-engine bolts	71	52
Gearchange lever retaining bolts	42	31
Power plant frame:		
Final drive mounting spacer	45	33
Frame-to-transmission bolts	112	83
Frame-to-final drive bolts	112	83
Bracket to frame	112	83
Bracket to transmission	45	33
Rear reinforcement crossbar bolts	35	26
Rear reinforcement frame bolts:		
1998-on models	65	48
2000-on models	105	77
Reversing light switch	21	15

1 General information

The gearbox is a 5- or 6-speed unit, and is contained in a cast-alloy casing bolted to the rear of the engine.

Drive is transmitted from the crankshaft via the clutch to the input shaft, which has a splined extension to accept the clutch friction disc. The output shaft transmits the drive via the propeller shaft to the rear differential.

The input shaft runs in line with the output shaft. The input shaft and output shaft gears are in constant mesh with the layshaft gear cluster. Selection of gears is by sliding synchromesh hubs, which lock the appropriate output shaft gears to the output shaft.

Gear selection is via a floor-mounted lever and selector. The selector mechanism causes the appropriate selector fork to move its respective synchro-sleeve along the shaft, to lock the gear pinion to the synchro-hub. Since the synchro-hubs are splined to the output shaft, this locks the pinion to the shaft, so that drive can be transmitted.

To ensure that gearchanging can be made quickly and quietly, a synchromesh system is fitted to all forward gears, consisting of baulk rings and spring-loaded fingers, as well as the gear pinions and synchro-hubs. The synchromesh cones are formed on the mating faces of the baulk rings and gear pinions.

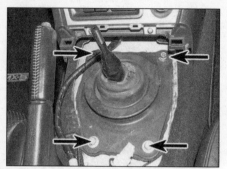

2.2 Gearchange lever plate retaining bolts (arrowed)

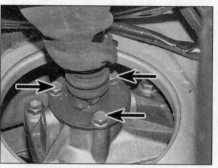

2.3 Undo the bolts (arrowed) and pull the gearchange lever upwards

2.4 Add 85 cc of transmission oil to the extension housing

2 Gearchange lever – removal and refitting

1 Remove the centre console as described in Chapter 11, Section 27.
2 Place the gearchange lever in Neutral and unbolt the gearchange lever plate (see illustration).
3 Remove the three retaining bolts and lift the gearchange lever straight up and out of the transmission (see illustration).
4 If the extension housing has been removed, refill it with 85 cc of the specified lubricant (see *Lubricants and fluids*) before refitting the gearchange lever (see illustration).
5 Coat both sides of a new gasket with sealant, place it in position, lubricate the gearchange lever base and lower it into the transmission.

6 Refit the retaining bolts and tighten them to the specified torque.
7 Refit the centre console as described in Chapter 11, Section 27.

3 Oil seals – renewal

Extension housing oil seal

1 Oil leaks frequently occur due to wear of the extension housing oil seal and/or the speedometer drive gear O-ring. Renewal of these seals is relatively easy, since the repairs can usually be performed without removing the transmission from the vehicle.
2 The extension housing oil seal is located at the extreme rear of the transmission, where the propeller is attached. If leakage

at the seal is suspected, raise the vehicle and support it securely on axle stands (see *Jacking and vehicle support*). If the seal is leaking, transmission lubricant will be built up on the front of the propeller shaft and may be dripping from the rear of the transmission.
3 Refer to Chapter 8, Section 6 and remove the propeller shaft.
4 Using a screwdriver or pry bar, carefully pry the oil seal out of the rear of the transmission (see illustration). Do not damage the splines on the transmission output shaft.
5 If the oil seal cannot be removed with a screwdriver or pry bar, a special oil seal removal tool (available at automotive parts retailers/tool specialists) will be required.
6 Using a large section of pipe or a very large deep socket as a drift, fit the new oil seal. Drive it into the bore squarely and make sure it's completely seated.
7 Lubricate the splines of the transmission output shaft and the outside of the driveshaft sleeve yoke with lightweight grease, then refit the propeller shaft as described in Chapter 8, Section 6. Be careful not to damage the lip of the new seal.

Speedometer cable drive O-ring

8 The speedometer cable and drive gear housing is located on the side of the extension housing. Look for transmission oil around the cable housing to determine if the O-ring is leaking.
9 Disconnect the speedometer cable (see illustration).
10 Undo the retaining bolt and pull the cable gear housing from place (see illustration).
11 Fit a new O-ring in the drive gear housing, then refit the drive gear housing and cable on the extension housing.

Vehicle speed sensor O-ring

12 The vehicle speed sensor is located on the side of the extension housing. Look for transmission oil around the sensor to determine if the O-ring is leaking.
13 Disconnect the sensor wiring plug.
14 Undo the retaining bolt and pull the sensor from place (see illustration).
15 Fit a new O-ring to the sensor, and refit it.

3.4 Carefully prise the oil seal from the extension housing

3.9 Unscrew the speedometer cable collar (arrowed)

3.10 Undo the bolt (arrowed) and pull out the speedometer gear housing

3.14 Vehicle speed sensor retaining bolt (arrowed)

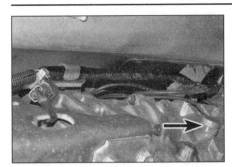

4.4a The neutral switch (arrowed) is on the right-hand side of the transmission casing ...

4.4b ... whilst the reversing light switch is on the left-hand side – 6-speed gearbox ...

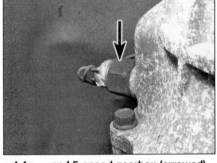

4.4c ... and 5-speed gearbox (arrowed)

4 Reversing light and neutral switches – testing, removal and refitting

Testing

1 The reversing light circuit is controlled by a plunger-type switch screwed into the right-hand side of the gearbox casing. If a fault develops in the circuit, first ensure that the circuit fuse has not blown.

2 To test the switch, disconnect the wiring connector, and use a multimeter (set to the resistance function) or a battery-and-bulb test circuit to check that there is continuity between the switch terminals only when reverse gear is selected. If this is not the case, and there are no obvious breaks or other damage to the wires, the switch is faulty, and must be renewed.

Removal

3 Jack up the vehicle and support securely on axle stands (see *Jacking and vehicle support*).
4 Disconnect the wiring connector, then unscrew the switch from the gearbox casing **(see illustrations)**. Renew the sealing washer.

Refitting

5 Refit the switch back into position in the gearbox housing and tighten it securely.
6 The remainder of refitting is a reversal of removal.

5 Speedometer cable (1997 and earlier models) – renewal

1 Disconnect the battery negative lead as described in Chapter 5A, Section 4.
2 Inside the passenger compartment, remove the instrument cluster and pull it back for access (see Chapter 12, Section 9). Reach behind the cluster, disconnect the speedometer cable by pressing the retaining lever and detaching it from the cluster **(see illustration)**.
3 Push the cable through the bulkhead into the engine compartment.
4 Raise the vehicle and support it securely on axle stands (see *Jacking and vehicle support*).
5 Under the vehicle, unscrew the speedometer

cable collar and pull the cable from the drive gear housing **(see illustration 3.9)**.
6 Detach the cable from the retaining straps and remove it from the vehicle.
7 To refit, push the cable through the bulkhead into the passenger compartment and seat the bulkhead grommet securely. Insert the cable into the instrument cluster housing until it clicks in place. Refit the cluster.
8 Insert the cable end into the drive gear in the transmission, refit the retaining collar and tighten it securely. Secure the cable with the retaining straps.

6 Power plant frame – removal and refitting

Removal

1 The power plant frame is a brace installed

5.2 Press the lever on the side of the collar (arrowed)

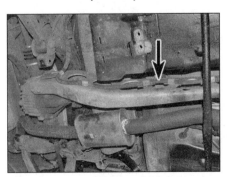

6.3b ... and unclip the wiring harness (arrowed)

along the right side of the transmission. It connects the transmission to the final drive.
2 Raise the vehicle and support it securely on axle stands (see *Jacking and vehicle support*), then remove the rear section of the exhaust system as described in Chapter 4A, Section 12.
3 Detach the wiring harness and earth wire from the power plant frame **(see illustrations)**.
4 On early models, undo the collar and disconnect the speedometer cable **(see illustration 3.9)**.
5 On later models, remove the crossbar from under the vehicle **(see illustration)**.
6 Support the transmission with a jack.
7 Remove the bracket that connects the power plant frame to the transmission **(see illustration)**.
8 Remove the bolts at the rear end of the power plant frame, then prise out the spacer

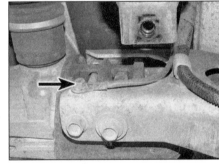

6.3a Detach the earth lead (arrowed) from the frame ...

6.5 Crossbar retaining bolts (arrowed)

6.7 Remove the bracket between the transmission and power plant frame

6.8a Undo the 2 bolts at the rear of the frame (arrowed) ...

6.8b ... and prise out the spacer

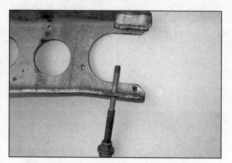

6.8c The reamer bolt (with the large diameter shank) locates in the forward hole in the frame

pull to free the sleeve. Once the sleeve is free, you'll need to get the M14 x 1.5 bolt out of the sleeve. To do this, thread an M6 x 1 bolt through the hole in the side of the block and tighten it against the side of the sleeve. Unscrew the M14 x 1.5 bolt, then unscrew the M6 x 1 bolt and remove the sleeve. On models after this date, it should be possible to release the sleeve with a tap from the a soft-faced hammer, then prise the sleeve down a little using a pair of levers/screwdrivers (see illustrations).

10 Slacken the power plant frame front mounting bolts a little, then slide the power plant frame to the side a little, undo the bolt(s) and remove the final drive mounting spacer (see illustration).

11 Unbolt the front end of the power plant frame from the transmission, then remove it from the vehicle (see illustration).

Refitting

12 Refitting is the reverse of the removal procedure, with the following additions:
  a) Refit the reamer bolt in the forward hole at the rear of the power plant frame.
  b) Tighten the bolts at the rear end of the power plant frame, then the bolts at the front end. Be sure to tighten the nuts/bolts to their specified torque.
  c) On 1998-on models, measure the distance from the front, lower edge of the frame to the lower edge of the chassis rails. The correct distance is 60.0 to 72.0 mm. If the distance is not as specified, slacken the frame-to-gearbox bolts and reposition the frame (see illustration).

(see illustrations). Note that the two bolts are different; the reamer bolt goes in the forward hole.

Caution: Don't remove the spacers from the upper side of the power plant frame. This will degrade the performance of the **torque arm and the entire assembly will have to be renewed.**

9 To remove the sleeve that the reamer bolt passes through on 1997 and earlier models, thread an M14 x 1.5 bolt into the bottom of the sleeve, then using it as a handle, twist and

6.9a Screw an M14 x 1.5 bolt into the base of the sleeve and pull it down

6.9b Use an M6 bolt to trap the sleeve and remove the M14 bolt

6.9c Tap the sleeve (arrowed) and prise it downwards – frame removed for clarity

6.10 Spacer retaining bolts (arrowed)

6.11 Remove the bolts (arrowed) at the front of the frame

6.12 With the straight-edge touching the underside of the chassis rails, measure the distance to the lower edge of the frame

7.5a Reinforcement frame retaining bolts (arrowed)

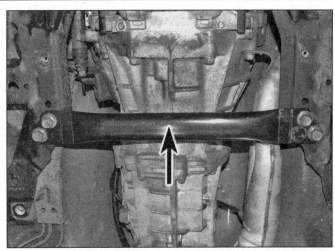

7.5b Undo the bolts and remove the crossbar (arrowed)

7 Manual gearbox –
removal and refitting

Note: *This is an involved operation. Read through the procedure thoroughly before starting work, and ensure that adequate lifting tackle and/or jacking/support equipment is available.*

Removal

1 Disconnect the battery negative lead as described in Section 5A, Section 4.
2 Remove the gearchange lever as described in Section 2.
3 Remove the propeller shaft as described in Chapter 8, Section 6. Use a plastic bag to cover the end of the transmission to prevent fluid loss and contamination.
4 Remove the engine/transmission undershields (where fitted).
5 On late models (2000-on) with sports suspension, undo the bolts/nuts and remove the front reinforcement frame and crossbar **(see illustrations)**.
6 Remove the front section of the exhaust system as described in Chapter 4A, Section 12.
7 Remove the starter motor as described in Chapter 5A, Section 10.
8 Remove the clutch slave cylinder as described in Chapter 6, Section 4.
9 Disconnect the speedometer cable (where applicable) and wiring harness connectors from the transmission **(see illustration 3.9)**.
10 Support the transmission securely on a workshop jack, then remove the power plant frame as described in Section 6.
11 Remove the bolts securing the transmission to the engine.
12 Make a final check that all wires and hoses have been disconnected from the

transmission and then move the transmission and jack toward the rear of the vehicle until the transmission input shaft is clear of the clutch friction disc. Keep the transmission level as this is done. Take care, the transmission is heavy!
Caution: Don't shake the transmission up and down or from side to side in an effort to make it slide out. This may damage the camshaft position sensor on rear of the engine.
13 Once the input shaft is clear, lower the transmission and remove it from under the vehicle.
14 The clutch components can be inspected at this time (see Chapter 6, Section 2). In most cases, new clutch components should be routinely fitted if the transmission is removed.

Refitting

15 If removed, fit the clutch components as described in Chapter 6, Section 2.
16 With the transmission securely supported, raise it into position behind the engine and then carefully slide it forward, engaging the input shaft with the clutch plate hub. Do not use excessive force to install the transmission – if the input shaft does not slide into place, readjust the angle of the transmission so it's level and/or turn the input shaft so the splines engage properly with the clutch.
17 Refit the transmission-to-engine bolts. Tighten the bolts to the specified torque.
18 Refit the power plant frame as described in Section 6.
19 Remove the jack supporting the transmission.
20 The remainder of refitting is a reversal of removal. Tighten all fasteners to their specified torque where given.

8 Manual gearbox overhaul –
general information

Overhauling a manual gearbox is a difficult and involved job for the DIY home mechanic. In addition to dismantling and reassembling many small parts, clearances must be precisely measured and, if necessary, changed by selecting shims and spacers. Internal gearbox components are also often difficult to obtain, and in many instances, extremely expensive. Because of this, if the gearbox develops a fault or becomes noisy, the best course of action is to have the unit overhauled by a specialist repairer, or to obtain an exchange reconditioned unit. Be aware that some gearbox repairs can be carried out with the gearbox in the car.

Nevertheless, it is not impossible for the more experienced mechanic to overhaul the gearbox, provided the special tools are available, and the job is done in a deliberate step-by-step manner, so that nothing is overlooked.

The tools necessary for an overhaul include internal and external circlip pliers, bearing pullers, a slide hammer, a set of pin punches, a dial test indicator, and possibly a hydraulic press. In addition, a large, sturdy workbench and a vice will be required.

During dismantling of the gearbox, make careful notes of how each component is fitted, to make reassembly easier and more accurate.

Before dismantling the gearbox, it will help if you have some idea what area is malfunctioning. Certain problems can be closely related to specific areas in the gearbox, which can make component examination and renewal easier. Refer to the *Fault finding* Section at the end of this manual for more information.

Chapter 8
Final drive, driveshafts and propeller shaft

Contents

Degrees of difficulty

Easy, suitable for novice with little experience 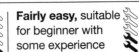	Fairly easy, suitable for beginner with some experience	Fairly difficult, suitable for competent DIY mechanic	Difficult, suitable for experienced DIY mechanic	Very difficult, suitable for expert DIY or professional

Specifications

Final drive

Type	Unsprung, attached to rear suspension crossmember
Capacity	Refer to Chapter 1 Specifications

Driveshaft

Type	Steel shafts with ball-and-cage type constant velocity joints at each end
Constant velocity joint grease capacity:	
Differential side.	75 to 95g in each joint
Hub side	55 to 75g in each joint
Standard length:	
1999 and earlier	659 to 669 mm
2000-on	772 to 782 mm

Propeller shaft

Type	One-piece with front and rear universal joints

Torque wrench settings

	Nm	lbf ft
Final drive unit		
Mounting nuts	90	66
Support frame bolts:		
Large.	70	52
Small.	22	16
Pinion nut (see text):*		
Minimum.	117	86
Maximum	177	131
Driveshaft		
Driveshaft nut:*		
1997 and earlier	255	188
1998-on	275	203
Shaft-to-final drive flange nuts.	60	44
Propeller shaft		
Shaft to final drive:		
1993 and earlier models.	30	22
1994-on models	55	41
Roadwheels		
Wheel nuts	110	81

* Do not re-use

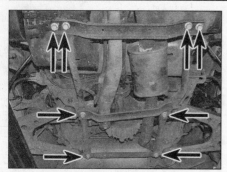

2.7 Undo the bolts (arrowed) and remove the support frame

1 General information

Power is transmitted from the transmission to the rear axle by a one-piece propeller shaft. On all models, the rear end of the shaft is attached to the final drive pinion by bolts and nuts, whilst the front end is a sliding fit on the transmission output shaft. Universal joints are fitted to the front and rear of the shaft.

The final drive assembly includes the drive pinion, the ring gear, and the differential. The drive pinion, which drives the ring gear, is also known as the differential input shaft and is connected to the propeller shaft via an input flange. The differential is bolted to the ring gear and drives the rear wheels through a pair of output flanges bolted to driveshafts (models up to 1998) with constant velocity (CV) joints at either end. The differential allows the wheels to turn at different speeds when cornering. Note that some models are equipped with a Limited Slip Differential (LSD).

The driveshafts deliver power from the final drive unit to the rear wheels. The driveshafts are equipped with constant velocity (CV) joints at each end. The inner CV joints are bolted to the differential flanges (models up to 1998) or are splined to engage with the differential, and the outer CV joints engage the splines of the wheel hubs, and are secured by a large nut.

Major repair work on the differential assembly components (drive pinion, ring-and-pinion, and differential) requires many special tools and a high degree of expertise,

and therefore should not be attempted by the home mechanic. If major repairs become necessary, we recommend that they be performed by a Mazda service department or other suitably-equipped automotive engineer.

2 Final drive unit – removal and refitting

Removal

1 Jack up the rear end of the vehicle and support it securely on axle stands (see *Jacking and vehicle support*). Remove the rear wheels.
2 Remove the exhaust system (see Chapter 4A, Section 12).
3 Remove the propeller shaft (see Section 6).
4 Disconnect the speedometer cable (where fitted) and remove the power plant frame (see Chapter 7, Section 6).
Caution: Once the power plant frame has been removed, the transmission must be supported by a jack at all times, otherwise the transmission will drop down.
5 If you're working on an early model, remove the nuts and washers that attach the inner ends of the driveshafts to the differential output shafts **(see illustration 4.8)**. To gain clearance to separate the driveshafts from the output shafts, you may need to remove the pivot bolt that attaches the upper wishbone/control arm to the rear hub carrier and pull the carrier outward (see Chapter 10, Section 12). Support the driveshafts with wire once they're detached, so they don't hang by the CV joints.
6 If you're working on a later model with driveshafts that fit directly into the differential, remove the driveshafts completely as described in Section 4.
7 Remove the final drive support frame (if equipped) **(see illustration)**.
8 Support the final drive with a jack. Remove the mounting nuts from the upper mount on each side of the final drive. Move the final drive forward and lower it clear of the vehicle.

Refitting

9 Refitting is the reverse of the removal steps. Tighten all fasteners to their specified torques where given.

10 Check the final oil level and top it up if necessary as described in Chapter 1, Section 25.
11 We recommend the rear wheel alignment is checked at the earliest opportunity.

3 Final drive unit oil seals – renewal

Propeller shaft flange oil seal

Note: A new flange nut retaining plate will be required.

1 Raise the rear of the vehicle and place it securely on axle stands (see *Jacking and vehicle support*). Remove the rear wheels and brake calipers as described in Chapter 9, Section 9. There is no need to disconnect the fluid pipes from the calipers.
2 Remove the rear section of the exhaust system (see Chapter 4A, Section 12).
3 Mark the propeller shaft and pinion flange for ease of realignment during assembly, then remove the propeller shaft as described in Section 6.
4 Remove the drain plug from the differential housing and allow the differential lubricant to drain into a container as described in Chapter 1, Section 25. When the draining is complete, refit the drain plug.
5 Using a suitable torque wrench, slowly turn the pinion shaft nut and measure the amount of torque necessary to start the pinion shaft turning **(see illustration)**. Write down this figure.
6 Mark the relationship of the pinion nut and flange **(see illustration)**. Using a suitable tool, counterhold the flange and remove the pinion nut **(see illustration)**. Remove the flange, using a puller if necessary.
7 After noting the orientation of the oil seal, carefully prise it out of the differential with a screwdriver or lever bar. Be careful not to damage the splines on the pinion shaft or disturb the position of the shaft.
8 Clean the oil seal mounting surface, then tap the new seal into place, taking care to insert it squarely.
9 Inspect the splines on the pinion shaft for burrs and nicks. Remove any rough areas with a crocus cloth. Wipe the splines clean.
10 Install the companion flange, aligning it with the marks made during removal. Gently tap the

3.5 Use a deflection-type torque wrench to measure the pinion turning torque

3.6a Make alignment marks between the pinion, nut and flange (arrowed)

3.6b Counterhold the pinion flange, and undo the nut

3.16 Lever the output shaft from the final drive unit

3.17 Carefully prise the driveshaft oil seal from the housing

3.18 Drive the new oil seal squarely into place using a suitably-sized socket

flange on with a soft-faced hammer until you can start the pinion nut on the pinion shaft.

11 Using a suitable tool, hold the companion flange while tightening the pinion nut to the minimum torque listed (see Specifications). Continue tightening, taking frequent rotational torque measurements, using the torque wrench, until the measurement recorded in paragraph 5 is reached. Increase the nut torque in small increments and check the preload after each increase.

Caution: Under no circumstances should the pinion nut be backed off to reduce pinion bearing preload.

12 Refit the propeller shaft, brake calipers and wheels.

13 Refill the final drive as described in Chapter 1, Section 25.

14 Lower the vehicle and test drive it to check for leaks.

Driveshaft oil seal

15 Remove the driveshafts as described in Section 4.

16 On early models, gently prise out the differential output shaft with two levers **(see illustration)**. Note: *Be ready to catch the output shaft as it comes out.*

17 Prise out the seal with a removal tool or screwdriver **(see illustration)**.

18 Use a hammer and a seal driver, large socket or section of pipe to install the new seal **(see illustration)**.

19 Fit a new circlip on the splined end of the output shaft or driveshaft.

20 Apply a film of clean oil to the lips of the seal, then refit the output shaft (early models) and the driveshaft.

21 Fill the differential with oil (see Chapter 1, Section 25).

4 Driveshaft – removal and refitting

Note: *A new driveshaft retaining nut and bolts will be required on refitting.*

Removal

1 If the design of the vehicle's wheels allows access to the driveshaft nuts without removing the wheels, loosen the rear wheel nuts 1/4

turn. Using a hammer and punch, unstake the driveshaft nut and loosen it 1/4 turn. Raise the vehicle and support it securely on axle stands. Remove the wheels.

2 If the wheels must be removed for access to the nut, loosen the rear wheel nuts 1/4 turn. Raise the vehicle and support it securely on axle stands (see *Jacking and vehicle support*). Remove the wheels, then unstake the nut **(see illustration)**.

3 Remove the driveshaft nut. To prevent the hub from turning, attach two lengths of steel to two of the wheel studs and allow the bar to rest against the ground **(see illustration)**.

4 Remove the pivot bolt that secures the upper end of the rear hub carrier (see Chapter 10, Section 11). This will allow the hub carrier to swing out far enough to provide removal clearance for the driveshaft.

5 Loosen the driveshaft from the hub splines with a puller that will attach to the wheel studs

4.2 Use a small punch to 'unstake' the driveshaft nut

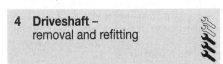

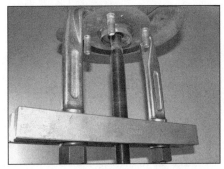

4.5 Use a suitable puller to release the driveshaft from the hub splines

(see illustration). If the driveshaft is reluctant to release (quite likely), remove the hub carrier (Chapter 10, Section 11) complete with the driveshaft, and use a press to release the driveshaft.

Caution: Applying force to the end of the driveshaft, beyond just breaking it loose from the hub, can damage the driveshaft or differential.

6 Pull the top end of the hub carrier outward and detach the driveshaft from the hub **(see illustration)**. Don't let the driveshaft hang by the inner CV joint after the outer end has been detached from the hub carrier, as the inner joint could become damaged. Support the outer end of the driveshaft with a piece of wire, if necessary.

7 Place a container underneath the differential to catch any lubricant that may spill out when the driveshafts are removed.

8 On early models, where the driveshaft is

4.3 Attach two lengths of steel to counterhold the hub flange whilst slackening the driveshaft nut

4.6 Pull the top of the hub carrier outwards and manoeuvre the end of the driveshaft

4.8 Undo the nuts (arrowed) securing the driveshaft to the output shaft

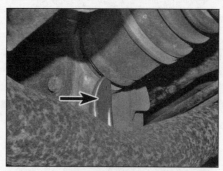

4.9 Use a lever (arrowed) to carefully prise the inner CV joint from the differential

4.11a Fit a new circlip to the end of the shaft

4.11b Use a small punch to 'stake' the new driveshaft nut into the groove in the driveshaft

attached with nuts to the differential output shaft, mark the relationship of the inner CV joint and output shaft, then remove the nuts and washers **(see illustration)**.

9 On later models, where the driveshaft

fits directly into the differential, mark the relationship of the inner CV joint and differential. Gently prise the inner CV joint out of the differential, being careful not to damage the dust cover or oil seal **(see illustration)**.

10 Refer to Section 3 for the driveshaft oil seal renewal procedure.

Refitting

11 Refitting is the reverse of the removal procedure, but note the following additional points:

  a) *On early models, fit the inner driveshaft end over the studs on the differential output shaft, then install the washers and nuts and tighten them to the torque listed in this Chapter's Specifications.*

  b) *On later models, install a new circlip on the end of the driveshaft inner CV joint **(see illustration)**, apply molybdenum based grease to the splines and wipe the differential oil seal with differential oil. With the end gap of the circlip facing up, push the driveshaft sharply in to seat the clip on the inner CV joint in the groove of the differential side gear.*

Caution: The sharp edges of the driveshaft circlip can slice or puncture the oil seal.

  c) *Install a new driveshaft nut, tighten it to the specified torque and stake the nut with a punch **(see illustration)**.*

  d) *Install the wheel and nuts, lower the vehicle and tighten the nuts to the specified torque.*

  e) *Check the final drive fluid level, and if necessary, top it up as described in Chapter 1, Section 25.*

5 Driveshaft gaiters renewal and CV joint inspection

1 Remove the driveshaft as described in Section 4.

Inner CV joint and gaiter

Disassembly

2 Mount the driveshaft in a vice with soft jaws (to prevent damage to the driveshaft). Check the CV joint for excessive play in the radial direction, which indicates worn parts. Check for smooth operation throughout the full range of motion for each CV joint. If a gaiter is torn or damaged, disassemble the joint, clean the components and inspect for damage due to loss of lubrication and possible contamination by foreign matter.

3 Prise the gaiter clamp retaining tabs up with a small screwdriver and slide the clamps off the gaiter **(see illustration)**. If necessary, cut the clamp from the gaiter with a hacksaw.

4 Slide the gaiter back on the driveshaft and prise the wire ring ball retainer from the outer race **(see illustration)**.

5 Mark the relationship of the outer race to the driveshaft and pull the outer race off the inner bearing assembly **(see illustration)**. Note that the balls may fall from the cage as the outer race is removed.

6 Mark the inner race, cage and driveshaft end to ensure that they are reassembled in the same relative positions **(see illustration)**.

5.3 Prise up the tabs and release the gaiter clamps

5.4 Use a small screwdriver to prise out the wire retaining clip

5.5 Make alignment marks between the outer race and shaft (arrowed). The balls will fall out as the outer race is removed!

5.6 Make further alignment marks between the cage, inner race and shaft (arrowed)

5.7 Remove the circlip from the end of the shaft

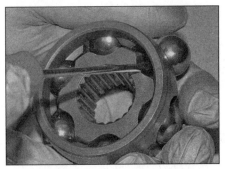

5.9 Prise the balls from the cage

5.10a Align the lands of the inner race with the window of the cage ...

5.10b ... then remove the inner race from the cage

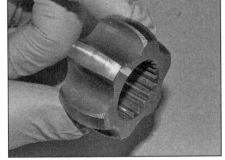

5.11a Check the inner race lands and grooves for pitting and score marks

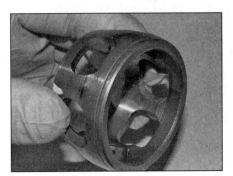

5.11b Check the cage for cracks, pitting and score marks

7 Remove the circlip from the groove in the driveshaft with a pair of circlip pliers **(see illustration)**.

8 Slide the inner bearing assembly off the driveshaft.

9 If necessary, using a small screwdriver or piece of wood, prise the balls from the cage **(see illustration)**. Be careful not to scratch the inner race, the balls or the cage.

Inspection

10 Align the inner race lands with the windows and pull the race out of the cage **(see illustrations)**.

11 Clean the components with solvent to remove all traces of grease. Inspect the cage and races for pitting, score marks, cracks and other signs of wear and damage. Shiny, polished spots are normal and will not adversely affect CV joint performance **(see illustrations)**.

Reassembly

12 Insert the inner race into the cage and align the matchmarks.

13 Press the balls into the cage windows with your thumbs **(see illustration)**.

14 Wrap the driveshaft splines with tape to avoid damaging the gaiter. Slide the small gaiter clamp and gaiter onto the driveshaft, then remove the tape.

15 Install the inner race and cage assembly on the driveshaft with the larger diameter or bulge of the cage (and the previously applied marks) facing the driveshaft end.

16 Install the circlip in the groove. Make sure it's completely seated by pushing on the inner race and cage assembly.

17 Fill the outer race and gaiter with the specified type and quantity of CV joint grease (normally included with the new joint

gaiter kit). Pack the inner race and cage assembly with grease, by hand, until grease is worked completely into the assembly **(see illustration)**.

18 Slide the outer race down onto the inner race, aligning the matchmarks, and install the wire ring retainer.

19 Wipe any excess grease from the driveshaft gaiter groove on the outer race. Seat the small diameter of the gaiter in the recessed area on the driveshaft. Push the other end of the gaiter onto the outer race and move the race in or out to adjust the driveshaft to the length specified **(see illustration)**.

20 With the driveshaft set to the proper length, equalise the pressure in the gaiter by inserting a dull screwdriver between the gaiter and outer race **(see illustration)**. Don't damage the gaiter with the tool.

5.13 Press the balls into the cage using thumb pressure only

5.17 Pack the inner race with the grease supplied in the gaiter kit

5.19 Adjust the driveshaft to the specified length (on early models, measure from the outer end to the inner flange)

5.20 Lift the outer edge a little to equalise the air pressure in the gaiter

5.21a Position the gaiter clamps with the open ends pointing opposite to the normal (forward) direction of rotation (arrowed)

5.21b Use special pliers to crush ...

5.21c ... the gaiter clamps

5.26 Inspect the outer CV joint through its full range of motion

5.27 Pack the outer CV joint with the grease supplied

21 Install the gaiter clamps **(see illustrations)**.
22 Install the driveshaft as described in Section 4.

Outer CV joint and gaiter

Disassembly

23 Following paragraphs 1 to 8, remove the inner CV joint from the driveshaft and disassemble it.
24 Remove the outer CV joint gaiter clamps, using the technique described in paragraph 3. Slide the gaiter off the driveshaft.

Inspection

25 Thoroughly wash the inner and outer CV joints in clean solvent and blow them dry with compressed air, if available. **Note:** *Because the outer CV joint cannot be disassembled, it's difficult to wash away all the old grease and rid the bearing of solvent once it's clean.*

6.2 Make alignment marks between the propeller shaft and the pinion flange (arrowed)

26 Bend the outer CV joint housing at an angle to the driveshaft to expose the bearings, inner race and cage **(see illustration)**. Inspect the bearing surfaces for signs of wear. If the bearings are damaged or worn, renew the driveshaft.

Reassembly

27 Slide the new outer gaiter onto the driveshaft. It's a good idea to wrap vinyl tape around the splines of the shaft to prevent damage to the gaiter **(see illustration)**. When the gaiter is in position, add the specified amount of grease (included in the gaiter renewal kit) to the outer joint and the gaiter (pack the joint with as much grease as it will hold and squeeze the rest into the gaiter). Slide the gaiter on the rest of the way and install the new clamps **(see illustrations 5.21a to 5.21c)**.
28 Clean and reassemble the inner CV joint by following paragraphs 12 to 21, then refit the driveshaft as described in Section 4.

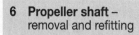

6 Propeller shaft –
removal and refitting

1 Chock the front wheels. Jack up the rear of the vehicle and support it on axle stands (see *Jacking and vehicle support*).
2 Mark the relationship of the propeller shaft to the differential input pinion flange **(see illustration)**.
3 Undo the bolts and remove the rear reinforcement frame assembly (where fitted) **(see illustration 2.7)**.

4 Remove the bolts and separate the propeller from the pinion flange. Pull the propeller shaft toward the rear to remove it.
5 Wrap a plastic bag tightly around the extension housing of the transmission to prevent fluid loss.
6 Refitting is the reverse of removal. Be sure to align the reference marks made during removal.

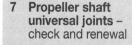

7 Propeller shaft universal joints –
check and renewal

Check

1 Wear in the universal joints is characterised by vibration in the transmission, noise during acceleration, and metallic squeaking and grating sounds as the bearings disintegrate. The joints can be checked with the propeller shaft still fitted.
2 Check for any oil leakage at the front and rear of the propeller shaft. Leakage where the propeller shaft enters the transmission indicates a defective transmission rear seal. Leakage where the propeller shaft enters the differential indicates a defective pinion seal.
3 While under the vehicle, have an assistant turn the rear wheel so the driveshaft will rotate. As it does, make sure the universal joints are operating properly without binding, noise or looseness.
4 The universal joints can also be checked with the propeller motionless, by gripping

your hands on either side of the joint and attempting to twist the joint. Any movement at all in the joint is a sign of considerable wear. Lifting up on the propeller shaft will also indicate movement in the universal joints.

5 Finally, check the propeller mounting bolts at the ends to make sure they are tight.

Renewal

6 At the time of writing, no spare parts were available to enable renewal of the universal joints to be carried out. Therefore, if any joint shows signs of damage or wear the complete propeller shaft assembly must be renewed. Consult your Mazda dealer for latest information on parts availability.

7 If renewal of the propeller shaft is necessary, it may be worthwhile seeking the advice of an automotive engineering specialist. They may be able to repair the original assembly or supply a reconditioned shaft on an exchange basis.

Chapter 9
Braking system

Contents

Degrees of difficulty

Easy, suitable for novice with little experience	Fairly easy, suitable for beginner with some experience	Fairly difficult, suitable for competent DIY mechanic	Difficult, suitable for experienced DIY mechanic	Very difficult, suitable for expert DIY or professional

Specifications

General

ABS sensor resistance	1.1 kΩ ± 0.1 kΩ
Brake pedal height:	
Released (with carpet)	171 to 181 mm
Reserve (depressed, without carpet)	95 mm
Brake pedal freeplay.	4.0 to 7.0 mm
Servo unit pushrod-to-master cylinder piston clearance:	
Non-ABS models	0.1 to 0.4 mm
ABS models	See Section 12

Front brakes

Disc diameter:	
1993 and earlier	235 mm
Non-ABS.	235 mm
ABS.	255 mm
Sports suspension	270 mm
Disc minimum thickness:	
1993 and earlier	16.0 mm
Non-ABS.	16.0 mm
ABS.	18.0 mm
Sports suspension	20.0 mm
Maximum disc run-out	0.1 mm
Brake pad friction material minimum thickness:	
Except sports suspension	1.0 mm
Sports suspension	2.0 mm

Rear disc brakes

Disc diameter:	
1993 and earlier	231 mm
1994-on	231 or 251 mm (depending on spec.)
Sports suspension	276 mm
Disc minimum thickness:	
1993 and earlier	7.0 mm
1994-on	8.0 mm
Maximum disc run-out.	0.1 mm
Brake pad friction material minimum thickness:	
Except sports suspension	1.0 mm
Sports suspension	2.0 mm

Torque wrench settings

	Nm	lbf ft
ABS wheel sensor retaining bolts	20	15
Brake pedal pivot bolt/nut	30	22
Front brake caliper:		
Guide pin bolts:		
All except 270 mm diameter discs	50	37
270 mm diameter discs	26	19
Mounting bracket bolts	65	48
Master cylinder mounting nuts	15	11
Rear brake caliper:		
Guide pin bolts	50	37
Mounting bracket bolts	50	37
Roadwheel nuts	110	81
Servo mounting nuts	22	16

1 General information

The braking system is of the servo-assisted, dual-circuit hydraulic type. Under normal circumstances, both circuits operate in unison. However, if there is hydraulic failure in one circuit, full braking force will still be available at two wheels.

All models are fitted with front and rear disc brakes. ABS is fitted as standard to some models (refer to Section 17 for further information on ABS operation).

The front disc brakes are actuated by single-piston sliding type calipers, which ensure that equal pressure is applied to each disc pad.

All models are fitted with rear disc brakes, actuated by single-piston sliding calipers, incorporating the handbrake actuation mechanism.

Note: *When servicing any part of the system, work carefully and methodically; also observe scrupulous cleanliness when overhauling any part of the hydraulic system. Always renew components (in axle sets, where applicable) if in doubt about their condition, and use only genuine Mazda parts, or at least those of known good quality. Note the warnings given in 'Safety first!' and at relevant points in this Chapter concerning the dangers of asbestos dust and hydraulic fluid.*

2 Hydraulic system – bleeding

⚠ *Warning: Hydraulic fluid is poisonous; wash off immediately and thoroughly in the case of skin contact, and seek immediate medical advice if any fluid is swallowed or gets into the eyes. Certain types of hydraulic fluid are flammable, and may ignite when allowed into contact with hot components; when servicing any hydraulic system, it is safest to assume that the fluid is flammable, and to take precautions against the risk of fire as though it is petrol that is being handled. Hydraulic fluid is also an* *effective paint stripper, and will attack plastics; if any is spilt, it should be washed off immediately, using copious quantities of fresh water. Finally, it is hygroscopic (it absorbs moisture from the air) – old fluid may be contaminated and unfit for further use. When topping-up or renewing the fluid, always use the recommended type, and ensure that it comes from a freshly-opened sealed container.*

⚠ *Warning: Under no circumstances should the hydraulic pipes/ hoses linking the master cylinder, hydraulic unit and the accumulator be disturbed. If these unions are disturbed and air enters the high-pressure hydraulic system, bleeding of the system can only be safely carried out by a Mazda dealer or suitably-equipped specialist using the special service tester.*

General

1 The correct operation of any hydraulic system is only possible after removing all air from the components and circuit; this is achieved by bleeding the system.

2 During the bleeding procedure, add only clean, unused hydraulic fluid of the recommended type; never re-use fluid that has already been bled from the system. Ensure that sufficient fluid is available before starting work.

3 If there is any possibility of incorrect fluid being already in the system, the brake components and circuit must be flushed completely with uncontaminated, correct fluid, and new seals should be fitted to the various components.

4 If hydraulic fluid has been lost from the system, or air has entered because of a leak, ensure that the fault is cured before continuing further.

5 Park the vehicle on level ground, switch off the engine and select first or reverse gear, then chock the wheels and release the handbrake.

6 Check that all pipes and hoses are secure, unions tight and bleed screws closed. Clean any dirt from around the bleed screws.

7 Unscrew the master cylinder reservoir cap, and top the master cylinder reservoir up to the MAX level line; refit the cap loosely, and remember to maintain the fluid level at least above the MIN level line throughout the procedure, or there is a risk of further air entering the system.

8 There are a number of one-man, do-it-yourself brake bleeding kits currently available from motor accessory shops. It is recommended that one of these kits is used whenever possible, as they greatly simplify the bleeding operation, and reduce the risk of expelled air and fluid being drawn back into the system. If such a kit is not available, the basic (two-man) method must be used, which is described in detail below.

9 If a kit is to be used, prepare the vehicle as described previously, and follow the kit manufacturer's instructions, as the procedure may vary slightly according to the type being used; generally, they are as outlined below in the relevant sub-section.

10 Whichever method is used, the same sequence must be followed (paragraphs 11 and 12) to ensure the removal of all air from the system.

Bleeding

Sequence

11 If the system has been only partially disconnected, and suitable precautions were taken to minimise fluid loss, it should be necessary only to bleed that part of the system.

12 If the complete system is to be bled, then it should be done working on the caliper furthest from the master cylinder first.

Basic (two-man) method

13 Collect a clean glass jar, a suitable length of plastic or rubber tubing which is a tight fit over the bleed screw, and a ring spanner to fit the screw. The help of an assistant will also be required.

14 Remove the dust cap from the first screw in the sequence. Fit the spanner and tube to the screw, place the other end of the tube in the jar, and pour in sufficient fluid to cover the end of the tube.

15 Ensure that the master cylinder reservoir fluid level is maintained at least above the MIN level line throughout the procedure.

16 Have the assistant fully depress the brake pedal several times to build-up pressure, then maintain it on the final downstroke.

17 While pedal pressure is maintained,

unscrew the bleed screw (approximately one turn) and allow the compressed fluid and air to flow into the jar. The assistant should maintain pedal pressure, following it down to the floor if necessary, and should not release it until instructed to do so. When the flow stops, tighten the bleed screw again, have the assistant release the pedal slowly, and recheck the reservoir fluid level.

18 Repeat the steps in paragraphs 16 and 17 until the fluid emerging from the bleed screw is free from air bubbles. If the master cylinder has been drained and refilled, and air is being bled from the first screw in the sequence, allow about 5 seconds between cycles for the master cylinder passages to refill.

19 When no more air bubbles appear, tighten the bleed screw securely, remove the tube and spanner, and refit the dust cap. Do not overtighten the bleed screw.

20 Repeat the procedure on the remaining screws in the sequence, until all air is removed from the system and the brake pedal feels firm again.

Using a one-way valve kit

21 As their name implies, these kits consist of a length of tubing with a one-way valve fitted, to prevent expelled air and fluid being drawn back into the system; some kits include a translucent container, which can be positioned so that the air bubbles can be more easily seen flowing from the end of the tube **(see illustration)**.

22 The kit is connected to the bleed screw, which is then opened. The user returns to the driver's seat, depresses the brake pedal with a smooth, steady stroke, and slowly releases it; this is repeated until the expelled fluid is clear of air bubbles.

23 Note that these kits simplify work so much that it is easy to forget the master cylinder reservoir fluid level; ensure that this is maintained at least above the MIN level line at all times.

Using a pressure-bleeding kit

24 These kits are usually operated by the reservoir of pressurised air contained in the spare tyre. However, note that it will probably be necessary to reduce the pressure to a lower level than normal; refer to the instructions supplied with the kit. **Note:** *Mazda specify that a pressure of 2 bar (29 psi) should not be exceeded.*

25 By connecting a pressurised, fluid-filled container to the master cylinder reservoir, bleeding can be carried out simply by opening each screw in turn (in the specified sequence), and allowing the fluid to flow out until no more air bubbles can be seen in the expelled fluid.

26 This method has the advantage that the large reservoir of fluid provides an additional safeguard against air being drawn into the system during bleeding.

27 Pressure-bleeding is particularly effective when bleeding 'difficult' systems, or when bleeding the complete system at the time of routine fluid renewal.

All methods

28 When bleeding is complete, and firm pedal feel is restored, wash off any spilt fluid, tighten the bleed screws securely, and refit their dust caps.

29 Check the hydraulic fluid level in the master cylinder reservoir, and top-up if necessary (Weekly checks).

30 Discard any hydraulic fluid that has been bled from the system; it will not be fit for re-use.

31 Check the feel of the brake pedal. If it feels at all spongy, air must still be present in the system, and further bleeding is required. Failure to bleed satisfactorily after a reasonable repetition of the bleeding procedure may be due to worn master cylinder seals.

3 Hydraulic pipes and hoses – renewal

⚠️ *Warning: Under no circumstances should the hydraulic pipes/hoses linking the master cylinder, hydraulic unit and the accumulator be disturbed. If these unions are disturbed and air enters the high-pressure hydraulic system, bleeding of the system can only be safely carried out by a Mazda dealer or suitably-equipped specialist using the special service tester.*

Note: *Before starting work, refer to the warnings at the beginning of Section 2.*

1 If any pipe or hose is to be renewed, minimise fluid loss by first removing the master cylinder reservoir cap, then tightening it down onto a piece of polythene to obtain an airtight seal. Alternatively, flexible hoses can be sealed, if required, using a proprietary brake hose clamp; metal brake pipe unions can be plugged (if care is taken not to allow dirt into the system) or capped immediately they are disconnected. Place a wad of rag under any union that is to be disconnected, to catch any spilt fluid.

2 If a flexible hose is to be disconnected, unscrew the brake pipe union nut before removing the spring clip which secures the hose to its mounting bracket.

3 To unscrew the union nuts, it is preferable to obtain a brake pipe spanner of the correct size; these are available from most large motor accessory shops. Failing this, a close-fitting open-ended spanner will be required, though if the nuts are tight or corroded, their flats may be rounded-off if the spanner slips. In such a case, using self-locking pliers is often the only way to unscrew a stubborn union, but it follows that the pipe and the damaged nuts must be renewed on reassembly. Always clean a union and surrounding area before disconnecting it. If disconnecting a component with more than one union, make a careful note of the connections before disturbing any of them.

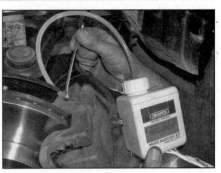

2.21 Attach the kit to the bleed screw on the caliper

4 If a brake pipe is to be renewed, it can be obtained, cut to length and with the union nuts and end flares in place, from Mazda dealers. All that is then necessary is to bend it to shape, following the line of the original, before fitting it to the car. Alternatively, most motor accessory shops can make up brake pipes from kits, but this requires very careful measurement of the original, to ensure that the new one is of the correct length. The safest answer is usually to take the original to the shop as a pattern.

5 On refitting, do not overtighten the union nuts. It is not necessary to exercise brute force to obtain a sound joint.

6 Ensure that the pipes and hoses are correctly routed, with no kinks, and that they are secured in the clips or brackets provided. After fitting, remove the polythene from the reservoir, and bleed the hydraulic system as described in Section 2. Wash off any spilt fluid, and check carefully for fluid leaks.

4 Front brake pads – renewal

⚠️ *Warning: Renew both sets of front brake pads at the same time – never renew the pads on only one wheel, as uneven braking may result. Note that the dust created by wear of the pads may contain asbestos, which is a health hazard. Never blow it out with compressed air, and do not inhale any of it. An approved filtering mask should be worn when working on the brakes. DO NOT use petrol or petroleum-based solvents to clean brake parts; use brake cleaner or methylated spirit only.*

1 Apply the handbrake, then loosen the front roadwheel nuts. Jack up the front of the vehicle and support it securely on axle stands (see *Jacking and vehicle support*). Remove both front roadwheels.

2 Follow the accompanying photos **(illustrations 4.2a to 4.2y)** for the pad renewal procedure. Be sure to stay in order and read the caption under each illustration.

3 Depress the brake pedal repeatedly, until

the pads are pressed into firm contact with the brake disc, and normal (non-assisted) pedal pressure is restored.

4 Repeat the above procedure on the remaining front brake caliper.

5 Refit the roadwheels, then lower the vehicle to the ground and tighten the roadwheel nuts to the specified torque.

6 Check the hydraulic fluid level as described in *Weekly checks*.

Caution: New pads will not give full braking efficiency until they have bedded-in. Be prepared for this, and avoid hard braking as far as possible for the first hundred miles or so after pad renewal.

4.2a Some models are fitted with wire springs between the pads …

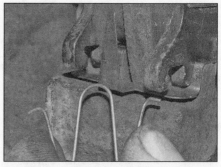

4.2b … squeeze the sides and remove them

4.2c If there's a wear lip on the edge of the disc, you may need to lever between the disc and caliper body to force the piston back into the caliper a little

4.2d Undo the lower guide pin bolt (arrowed) …

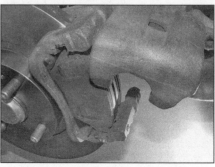

4.2e … pivot the caliper upwards …

4.2f … and secure it to the spring to prevent straining the fluid hose

4.2g Remove the outer pad …

4.2h … followed by the inner pad

4.2i Remove the lower shims …

4.2j … and the upper shims

4.2k On models with wire springs, remove the upper shim …

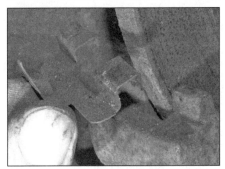

4.2l ... and lower shim

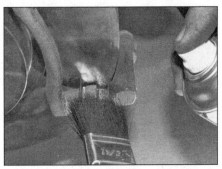

4.2m Clean the pad mounting surfaces using aerosol brake cleaner and a soft brush

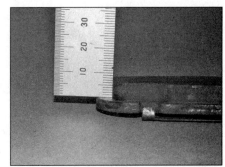

4.2n Measure the thickness of the pad friction material – renew all 4 pads if it's less than the dimension given in Specifications at the start of the Chapter

4.2o Apply a thin smear of high-temperature anti-seize grease (Copperslip) to the pad backplate where it contact the caliper mounting bracket

4.2p Fit the anti-rattle plate to the new pad backing plate

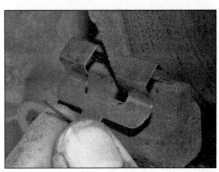

4.2q Refit the lower shim (wire spring type shown) ...

4.2r ... and upper shim

4.2s Fit the outer pad – ensure the friction material is against the disc ...

4.2t ... followed by the inner pad

4.2u If new pads have been fitted, push the piston back into the caliper using a retraction tool. Keep an eye on the fluid level in the reservoir

4.2v Lower the caliper into place and refit the lower guide pin bolt ...

4.2w ... and tighten it to the specified torque

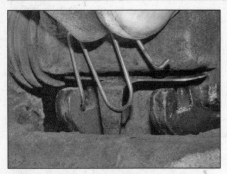

4.2x Refit the upper wire spring (where applicable) ...

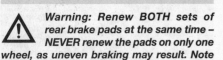

5 Rear brake pads –
renewal

⚠️ **Warning: Renew BOTH sets of rear brake pads at the same time – NEVER renew the pads on only one wheel, as uneven braking may result. Note**

4.2y ... and the lower wire spring

that the dust created by wear of the pads may contain asbestos, which is a health hazard. Never blow it out with compressed air, and don't inhale any of it. An approved filtering mask should be worn when working on the brakes. DO NOT use petroleum-based solvents to clean brake parts – use brake cleaner or methylated spirit only.

1 Apply the handbrake, then loosen the rear

roadwheel nuts. Jack up the rear of the vehicle and support it securely on axle stands (see *Jacking and vehicle support*). Remove both rear roadwheels.

2 Follow the accompanying photos **(illustrations 5.2a to 5.2v)** for the pad renewal procedure. Be sure to stay in order and read the caption under each illustration.

3 Depress the brake pedal repeatedly, until the pads are pressed into firm contact with the brake disc, and normal (non-assisted) pedal pressure is restored.

4 Repeat the above procedure on the remaining rear brake caliper.

5 Refit the roadwheels, then lower the vehicle to the ground and tighten the roadwheel nuts to the specified torque.

6 Check the hydraulic fluid level as described in *Weekly checks*.

Caution: New pads will not give full braking efficiency until they have bedded-in. Be prepared for this, and avoid hard braking as far as possible for the first hundred miles or so after pad renewal.

5.2a Undo the adjustment gear cap (arrowed) on the inside face of the caliper ...

5.2b ... and use an Allen key to rotate the adjustment gear fully anti-clockwise to retract the piston into the caliper body

5.2c Pull off the rubber cap (arrowed) ...

5.2d ... and use an Allen key to unscrew the lower guide pin

5.2e Pivot the caliper upwards and secure it to the suspension spring using wire/ string, etc

5.2f Remove the outer pad ...

5.2g ... followed by the inner pad

5.2h Remove the upper shim ...

5.2i ... and lower shim

5.2j Clean the pad contact surfaces on the mounting bracket using aerosol brake cleaner and a soft brush

5.2k Refit the lower shim ...

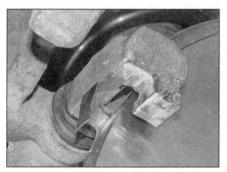

5.2l ... and upper shim

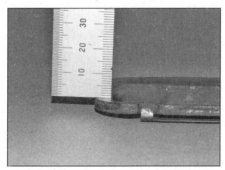

5.2m Measure the thickness of the pad friction material – renew all 4 pads if it's less than the dimension given in Specifications at the start of the Chapter

5.2n Apply a thin smear of high-temperature anti-seize grease (Copperslip) to the pad backplate where it contact the caliper mounting bracket

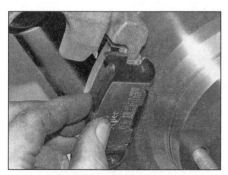

5.2o Fit the outer pad – ensure the friction material is against the disc ...

5.2p ... followed by the inner pad

5.2q Lower the caliper into position over the pads ...

5.2r ... refit the lower guide pin ...

5.2s ... tighten it to the specified torque ...

5.2t ... and refit the plastic cap

5.2u Using an Allen key, rotate the adjusting gear clockwise until the pad contacts the disc, then 1/3rd of a turn anti-clockwise ...

5.2v ... and refit the cap

6 Front brake disc – inspection, removal and refitting

Note: *Before starting work, refer to the note at the beginning of Section 4 concerning the dangers of asbestos dust.*
Note: *If either disc requires renewal, BOTH should be renewed at the same time, to ensure even and consistent braking. New brake pads should also be fitted.*

Inspection

1 Apply the handbrake, then jack up the front of the car and support it on axle stands (see *Jacking and vehicle support*. Remove the appropriate front roadwheel.
2 Slowly rotate the brake disc so that the full

6.3 Measure the thickness of the disc using a micrometer

area of both sides can be checked; remove the brake pads if better access is required to the inboard surface (see Section 4). Light scoring is normal in the area swept by the brake pads, but if heavy scoring or cracks are found, the disc must be renewed.
3 It is normal to find a lip of rust and brake dust around the disc's perimeter; this can be scraped off if required. If, however, a lip has formed due to excessive wear of the brake pad swept area, then the disc's thickness must be measured using a micrometer **(see illustration)**. Take measurements at several places around the disc, at the inside and outside of the pad swept area; if the disc has worn at any point to the specified minimum thickness or less, the disc must be renewed.
4 If the disc is thought to be warped, it can be checked for run-out. Either use a dial gauge mounted on any convenient fixed point, while the disc is slowly rotated, or use feeler blades to measure (at several points all around the disc) the clearance between the disc and a fixed point, such as the caliper mounting bracket. If the measurements obtained are at the specified maximum or beyond, the disc is excessively warped, and must be renewed; however, it is worth checking first that the hub bearing is in good condition (Chapter 10, Section 3). If the run-out is excessive, the disc must be renewed.
5 Check the disc for cracks, especially around the wheel bolt holes, and any other wear or damage, and renew if necessary.

Removal

6 Unscrew the two bolts securing the brake caliper mounting bracket to the hub carrier, then slide the caliper assembly off the disc. Using a piece of wire or string, tie the caliper to the front suspension coil spring, to avoid placing any strain on the hydraulic brake hose.
7 Use chalk or paint to mark the relationship of the disc to the hub, then remove the disc. If the disc is tight, lightly tap its rear face with a hide or plastic mallet.

Refitting

8 Refitting is the reverse of the removal procedure, noting the following points:
  a) *Ensure that the mating surfaces of the disc and hub are clean and flat.*
  b) *Align (if applicable) the marks made on removal.*
  c) *If a new disc has been fitted, use a suitable solvent to wipe any preservative coating from the disc, before refitting the caliper.*
  d) *Slide the caliper and bracket into position over the disc, making sure the pads pass either side of the disc. Tighten the caliper mounting bracket bolts to the specified torque setting.*
  e) *Refit the roadwheel, then lower the vehicle to the ground and tighten the roadwheel nuts to the specified torque. On completion, repeatedly depress the brake pedal until normal (non-assisted) pedal pressure returns.*

7 Rear brake disc – inspection, removal and refitting

Note: *Before starting work, refer to the note at the beginning of Section 5 concerning the dangers of asbestos dust.*
Note: *If either disc requires renewal, BOTH should be renewed at the same time, to ensure even and consistent braking. New brake pads should also be fitted.*

Inspection

1 Firmly chock the front wheels, then jack up the rear of the car and support it on axle stands (see *Jacking and vehicle support*).

Remove the appropriate rear roadwheel. Release the handbrake.

2 Inspect the disc as described in Section 6.

Removal

3 Undo the cap then pull the piston into the caliper by rotating the manual adjustment gear anti-clockwise with an Allen key **(see illustrations 5.2a and 5.2b)**.

4 Unscrew the two bolts securing the brake caliper mounting bracket in position, then slide the caliper assembly off the disc. Using a piece of wire or string, tie the caliper to the rear suspension coil spring, to avoid placing any strain on the hydraulic brake hose **(see illustration)**. If necessary unclip the rubber brake hose from the lower mounting bracket to provide enough slack to manoeuvre the caliper and bracket.

5 It should now be possible to withdraw the brake disc from the hub by hand. If it is tight, lightly tap its rear face with a hide or plastic mallet.

Refitting

6 If a new disc is been fitted, use a suitable solvent to wipe any preservative coating from the disc.

7 Slide the caliper into position over the disc, making sure the pads pass either side of the disc. Tighten the caliper bracket mounting bolts to the specified torque setting.

8 Use an Allen key to rotate the manual adjustment gear clockwise until the pads contact the disc, then 1/3rd of a turn anti-clockwise.

9 Refit the roadwheel, then lower the car to the ground, and tighten the roadwheel nuts to the specified torque. On completion, repeatedly depress the brake pedal until normal (non-assisted) pedal pressure returns. Check the handbrake adjustment.

---

8 Front brake caliper –
removal, overhaul and refitting

Note: *Before starting work, refer to the note at the beginning of Section 2 concerning the dangers of hydraulic fluid, and to the warning at the beginning of Section 4 concerning the dangers of asbestos dust.*

Removal

1 Apply the handbrake, then jack up the front of the vehicle and support it on axle stands (see *Jacking and vehicle support*). Remove the appropriate roadwheel.

2 Minimise fluid loss by using a brake hose clamp, a G-clamp or a similar tool to clamp the flexible hose.

3 Clean the area around the union, then undo the brake hose union bolt. Recover the copper sealing washers **(see illustrations)**. **Note:** *Don't disconnect the hose if you are only removing the caliper for access to other components.*

4 Remove the brake pads (see Section 4).

5 Unscrew the remaining caliper guide pin bolt, remove it from the vehicle.

Overhaul

6 With the caliper on the bench, wipe away all traces of dust and dirt, but *avoid inhaling the dust, as it is a health hazard.*

7 Withdraw the partially-ejected piston from the caliper body, and remove the dust seal **(see illustration)**. **Note:** *If the piston cannot be withdrawn by hand, it can be pushed out by applying compressed air to the brake hose union hole. Only low pressure should be required, such as is generated by a foot pump. As the piston is expelled, take great care not to trap your fingers between the piston and caliper.*

8 Using a small screwdriver, extract the piston hydraulic seal, taking great care not to damage the caliper bore **(see illustration)**.

9 Thoroughly clean all components, using only

7.4 Caliper mounting bracket bolts (arrowed) – caliper removed for clarity

methylated spirit, isopropyl alcohol or clean hydraulic fluid as a cleaning medium. Never use mineral-based solvents such as petrol or paraffin, as they will attack the hydraulic system's rubber components. Dry the components immediately, using compressed air or a clean, lint-free cloth. Use compressed air to blow clear the fluid passages.

10 Check all components, and renew any that are worn or damaged. Check particularly the cylinder bore and piston; these should be renewed (note that this means the renewal of the complete body assembly) if they are scratched, worn or corroded in any way. Similarly check the condition of the guide pins and their bushes; both pins should be undamaged and (when cleaned) a reasonably tight sliding fit in the bushes **(see illustration)**. If there is any doubt about the condition of any component, renew it.

8.3a Unscrew the brake hose union bolt (arrowed)

8.3b Recover the sealing washers (arrowed)

8.7 Place a wooden block to 'catch' the piston if it's ejected using compressed air

8.8 Carefully extract the hydraulic seal (arrowed) from the caliper bore

8.10 Check the condition of the guide pin and rubber sleeve

8.15a Fit the new seal to the inner end of the piston ...

8.15b ... locate the lip of the seal into the recess in the caliper body ...

8.15c ... then push/twist the piston into the caliper body ...

8.15d ... ensuring the inner lip of the seal locates in the piston recess

11 If the assembly is fit for further use, obtain the appropriate repair kit; the components are available from Mazda dealers in various combinations. All rubber seals should be renewed as a matter of course; these should never be re-used.

12 On reassembly, ensure that all components are clean and dry.

13 Soak the piston and the new piston (fluid) seal in clean hydraulic fluid. Smear clean fluid on the cylinder bore surface.

14 Fit the new piston (fluid) seal, using only your fingers (no tools) to manipulate it into the cylinder bore groove.

15 Fit the new dust seal to the piston. Locate the rear of the seal in the recess in the caliper body, and refit the piston to the cylinder bore using a twisting motion. Ensure that the piston enters squarely

into the bore, and press it fully home **(see illustrations)**.

Refitting

16 Refit the brake pads (see Section 4).

17 Reconnect the brake pipe using new copper sealing washers, and tighten the union bolt securely.

18 Remove the brake hose clamp or polythene, as applicable, and bleed the hydraulic system as described in Section 2. Note that, providing the precautions described were taken to minimise brake fluid loss, it should only be necessary to bleed the relevant front brake.

19 Refit the roadwheel, then lower the vehicle to the ground and tighten the roadwheel nuts to the specified torque. On completion, check the hydraulic fluid level as described in *Weekly checks*.

9 Rear brake caliper – removal, overhaul and refitting

Note: *Before starting work, refer to the note at the beginning of Section 2 concerning the dangers of hydraulic fluid, and to the warning at the beginning of Section 5 concerning the dangers of asbestos dust.*

Removal

1 Chock the front wheels, then jack up the rear of the vehicle and support on axle stands (see *Jacking and vehicle support*). Remove the relevant rear wheel.

2 Minimise fluid loss by using a brake hose clamp, a G-clamp or a similar tool to clamp the flexible hose.

3 Clean the area around the union, undo the hose union banjo bolt.

4 Remove the brake pads as described in Section 5.

5 Slide the caliper from the remaining guide pin **(see illustration)**.

Overhaul

6 Due to the complexity of the rear calipers, we do not recommend dismantling them. Renewing them will provide better service for less cost.

Refitting

7 Screw the caliper fully onto the flexible hose union.

8 Refit the brake pads (refer to Section 5).

9 Securely tighten the brake pipe union nut.

10 Remove the brake hose clamp or polythene, as applicable, and bleed the hydraulic system as described in Section 2. Note that, providing the precautions described were taken to minimise brake fluid loss, it should only be necessary to bleed the relevant rear brake.

11 Refit the roadwheel, then lower the vehicle to the ground and tighten the roadwheel nuts to the specified torque. On completion, check the hydraulic fluid level as described in *Weekly checks*.

10 Master cylinder – removal, overhaul and refitting

Removal

1 Follow the wiring harness from the master cylinder to the electrical connector for the fluid level warning switch **(see illustration)**. Unplug the connector. Check continuity with an ohmmeter at the level sensor terminals; no continuity should be measured when the fluid level is above MIN.

2 Carefully remove the brake fluid reservoir cap and remove as much fluid as possible from the reservoir with a syringe. Check continuity of the level sensor; continuity

9.5 Slide the caliper from the guide pin

10.1 Disconnect the fluid level warning switch wiring plug (arrowed)

should be measured when fluid level is below the MIN level.

3 Place rags under the fittings and prepare caps or plastic bags to cover the ends of the pipes once they are disconnected. Loosen the fittings at the ends of the brake pipes where they enter the master cylinder **(see illustration)**. To prevent rounding off the flats, use a flare-nut spanner, which wraps around the fitting union.

4 Remove the nuts and washers attaching the master cylinder to the brake servo unit **(see illustration)**.

5 Pull the brake pipes away from the master cylinder and plug the ends to prevent contamination. Slide the proportioning valve mounting bracket off the studs.

6 Pull the master cylinder off the studs to remove it. Again, be careful not to spill the fluid as this is done.

Overhaul

7 It would appear that master cylinder overhaul kits are no longer available. Consequently, should a fault develop, renewal of the complete assembly may be the only option.

Refitting

8 Refit the master cylinder and proportioning valve bracket over the studs on the servo unit, refit the washers, and tighten the nuts only finger-tight at this time.

9 Thread the brake pipe union nuts into the master cylinder. Since the master cylinder is still loose, it can be moved slightly so the union nuts thread in easily by hand. Be careful not to strip the threads as the fittings are tightened.

10 Connect the remaining brake pipe to the master cylinder with the union bolt, using a new sealing washer on each side of the fitting.

11 Tighten the master cylinder mounting nuts and union bolt to the specified torque. Tighten the brake pipe union nuts securely using a flare-nut spanner.

12 Fill the master cylinder reservoir with fluid,

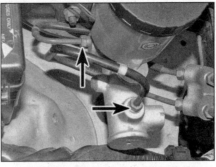

10.3 Slacken the brake pipe unions (arrowed) where they enter the master cylinder

then bleed the master cylinder and the brake system (see Section 2). Check the operation of the brake system carefully before driving the vehicle.

11 Brake pedal – check and adjustment

Pedal height

1 Measure the pedal height **(see illustration)** and compare your measurement to the pedal height listed (see Specifications).

2 If the pedal height is incorrect, adjust it as follows:

3 Unplug the electrical connector from the brake light switch.

4 Loosen the brake light switch locknut and turn the brake switch until it does not contact the pedal.

5 Loosen the pushrod locknut.

6 Adjust the pedal height by turning the pedal pushrod.

7 Tighten the pushrod locknut.

8 Turn the brake light switch until it lightly contacts the pedal stopper, then turn the brake light switch an additional 1/2 turn.

9 Tighten the brake light switch locknut.

10 Plug in the brake light switch electrical connector.

11 Check that brake lights come on when the brake pedal is depressed, and go off when the brake pedal is released.

12 Check the pedal freeplay (see below).

Pedal freeplay

13 Stop the engine if it's running, and depress the brake pedal several times until there's no more vacuum left in the servo unit.

14 Gently press the pedal by hand until you feel some resistance, then measure the distance between the fully released pedal and the point at which you feel resistance **(see illustration 11.1)**. Compare your measurement with the pedal freeplay (see Specifications). If the pedal freeplay is incorrect, adjust it as follows:

15 Adjust the brake pedal pushrod to obtain the specified pedal freeplay, then adjust the brake light switch as described.

Pedal reserve

16 Start the engine, depress the brake pedal a few times, then press down hard and hold it.

17 Pedal reserve travel is measured from the floor to the top of the pedal while it is held depressed. Compare your measurement to the pedal reserve listed (see Specifications).

18 If the pedal reserve is less than specified, check the adjustment of the servo unit pushrod-to-master cylinder piston clearance (see Section 12).

19 If the brake pedal feels spongy, bleed the brake system (see Section 2).

12 Vacuum servo unit – testing, removal and refitting

Testing

1 To test the operation of the servo unit, depress the footbrake several times to

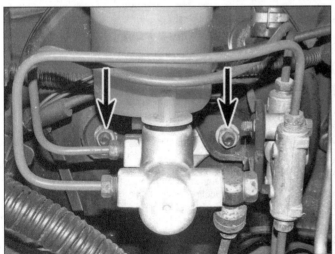

10.4 Master cylinder retaining nuts (arrowed)

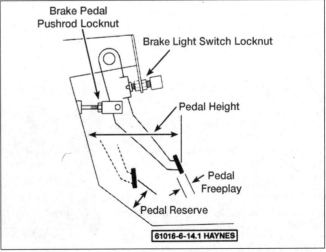

11.1 Brake pedal height, freeplay and reserve travel details

12.5 The check valve (arrowed) is integral with the servo vacuum hose

12.8 Remove the clip (arrowed) and pull out the servo pushrod clevis pin

12.9 Servo retaining nuts (arrowed)

exhaust the vacuum, then start the engine whilst keeping the pedal firmly depressed. As the engine starts, there should be a noticeable 'give' in the brake pedal as the vacuum builds-up. Allow the engine to run for at least two minutes, then switch it off. If the brake pedal is now depressed it should feel normal, but further applications should result in the pedal feeling firmer, with the pedal stroke decreasing with each application.

2 If the servo does not operate as described, first inspect the servo unit check valve as described in Section 13.

3 If the servo unit still fails to operate satisfactorily, the fault lies within the unit itself. Repairs to the unit are not possible – if faulty, the servo unit must be renewed.

Removal

4 Servo units shouldn't be disassembled. They require special tools not normally found in most automotive repair workshops. Because of its critical relationship to brake performance, the servo should be replaced with a new or rebuilt one.

5 Disconnect the vacuum hose/check valve leading from the engine to the servo **(see illustration)**. Be careful not to damage the hose when removing it from the servo fitting.

6 Remove the brake master cylinder (see Section 10).

7 Undo the screws and remove the trim panel beneath the steering column.

8 Locate the pushrod clevis connecting the servo to the brake pedal **(see illustration)**. Remove the R-clip from the clevis pin with pliers and pull out the clevis pin.

9 Remove the four nuts holding the brake servo to the bulkhead **(see illustration)**.

10 Slide the servo straight out from the bulkhead until the studs clear the holes. Be careful not to tear or damage the brake servo gasket between the bulkhead and the servo.

Refitting

11 Refitting is basically the reverse of removal. Tighten the servo mounting nuts to the specified torque. Be sure to use a new clevis retaining clip if the old clip is loose.

12 When refitting the servo unit vacuum hose/

check valve, be sure to fit the vacuum hose/ check valve with the arrows on the vacuum hose toward the engine.

13 If the servo unit is being renewed, the clearance between the master cylinder piston and the pushrod in the servo unit must be measured and, if necessary, adjusted.
Caution: This step applies to non-ABS models only. Vehicles equipped with ABS require special measuring tools to set the clearance accurately. If your vehicle is equipped with ABS, have the adjustment done by a Mazda dealer or other qualified repairer.

14 Using a depth micrometer or vernier caliper, calculate the distance from the pocket of the primary piston to the master cylinder mounting flange. Next, with the engine running for vacuum applied to the servo unit (or vacuum applied by a vacuum pump, if desired), measure the distance from the end of the servo pushrod to the mounting face of the servo where the master cylinder mounting flange seats. Subtract the depth of the piston pocket from the protrusion of the pushrod to calculate the clearance and compare your findings with the values listed (see Specifications). If not, turn the adjusting screw on the end of the servo unit pushrod until the clearance is within the specified limit.

15 After the final installation of the master cylinder and brake hoses and pipes, the brake pedal height and freeplay must be adjusted and the brake system must be bled.

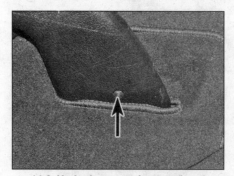

14.2 Undo the screw (arrowed) and remove the handbrake lever cover

13 Vacuum servo unit check valve –
removal, testing and refitting

Removal

1 Before starting, depress the brake pedal several times, to collapse any vacuum in the servo.

2 Working in the engine compartment, release the clamps and disconnect the hose from the intake manifold to the servo unit **(see illustration 12.5)**. The check valve is integral with the hose.

Testing

3 Examine the check valve for signs of damage, and renew if necessary.

4 The valve may be tested by blowing through it in both directions; air should flow through the valve in one direction only – when blown through from the servo unit end of the hose. Renew the valve and hose assembly if this is not the case.

Refitting

5 Reconnect the hose securely to the servo unit and intake manifold.

14 Handbrake –
adjustment

1 The handbrake lever, when properly adjusted, should travel the number of clicks listed (see Chapter 1 Section 13), when a moderate pulling force is applied. If it travels less than the specified minimum number of clicks, the handbrake may not be releasing completely and could cause the rear brakes to drag. If the lever can be pulled up more than the specified maximum number of clicks, the handbrake may not hold adequately on an incline, allowing the car to roll.

2 To gain access to the handbrake cable adjuster, remove the lever cover **(see illustration)**.

3 Securely block the front wheels so the vehicle won't roll. Jack up the rear end just until the tyres are off the ground, then place it securely on axle stands (see *Jacking and vehicle support*). Place the transmission in Neutral and release the handbrake completely.

4 Turn the adjusting nut until the desired travel is attained **(see illustration)**.

5 Pull the handbrake lever one click. The handbrake warning light should come on. Release the lever and make sure the rear wheels turn freely.

6 Refit the cover and lower the vehicle.

15 Handbrake cables – removal and refitting

1 Slacken the rear roadwheel nuts, raise the rear of the vehicle and support it securely on axle stands (see *Jacking and vehicle support*). Remove the rear roadwheel.

Equaliser-to-brake lever cable

2 Make sure the handbrake is completely released, then undo the screw and remove the lever cover **(see illustration 14.2)**.

3 Remove the handbrake lever adjusting nut.

4 Under the vehicle, it is best to remove the exhaust and heat shield components in the area of the handbrake cable connection to the handbrake lever. Remove the return spring **(see illustration)**.

5 Prise out the rubber grommet from the floor and pull the front cable out.

6 Refitting is the reverse of removal. Apply a light coat of grease to the portion of the cable end that engages with the equaliser. Also coat the sealing edge of the rubber grommet with silicone to ensure that it remains watertight.

Equaliser-to-handbrake cable

7 Remove the handbrake cable mounting bolts located along the vehicle chassis.

8 Remove the handbrake cable retaining clips at the equaliser **(see illustration)**.

9 Detach the handbrake cable from the caliper **(see illustration)**. Free the cable ends from the equaliser and pull the cable out from under the vehicle.

10 Refitting is the reverse of removal. Apply a light coat of grease to the portion of the cable end that engages with the equaliser.

11 Adjust the handbrake as described in Section 14.

16 Brake light switch – removal and refitting

Removal

1 Undo the screws and remove the trim panel from beneath the steering column **(see illustration)**.

2 Disconnect the wiring plug from the switch.

3 Slacken the locknut, then unscrew the switch from the pedal bracket **(see illustration)**.

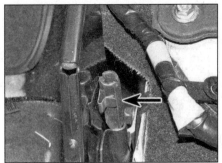

14.4 Handbrake adjuster nut (arrowed)

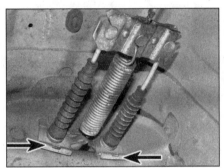

15.8 Slide sown the cable retaining clips (arrowed)

Refitting

4 Fit the switch to the pedal bracket, turning it until it lightly contacts the pedal stopper, then turn the switch an additional ½ turn. Tighten the locknut.

5 Reconnect the switch wiring plug.

6 Check the operation of the brake lights, then refit the trim panel.

17 Anti-lock braking system (ABS) – general information

1 ABS is fitted to some models only. The system comprises a hydraulic block which contains the hydraulic solenoid valves and the electrically-driven pump, the four roadwheel sensors (one fitted to each wheel), and the electronic control unit (ECU). The purpose of the system is to prevent the wheel(s) locking

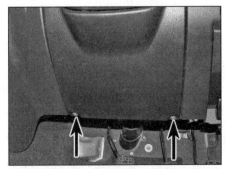

16.1 Undo the screws (arrowed) and remove the panel beneath the steering column

15.4 Handbrake front cable return spring

15.9 Undo the lock nut (arrowed) and detach the cable from the caliper

during heavy braking. This is achieved by automatic release of the brake on the relevant wheel, followed by re-application of the brake.

2 The solenoids are controlled by the ECU, which itself receives signals from the four wheel sensors (one fitted on each hub), which monitor the speed of rotation of each wheel. By comparing these signals, the ECU can determine the speed at which the vehicle is travelling. It can then use this speed to determine when a wheel is decelerating at an abnormal rate, compared to the speed of the vehicle, and therefore predicts when a wheel is about to lock. During normal operation, the system functions in the same way as a non-ABS braking system.

3 If the ECU senses that a wheel is about to lock, it operates the relevant solenoid valve in the hydraulic unit, which then isolates the brake caliper on the wheel which is about

16.3 Undo the locknut and unscrew the brake light switch

18.10 Front wheel speed sensor retaining bolt (arrowed)

18.18 Rear wheel speed sensor bolts (arrowed)

to lock from the master cylinder, effectively sealing-in the hydraulic pressure.

4 If the speed of rotation of the wheel continues to decrease at an abnormal rate, the ECU switches on the electrically-driven pump operates, and pumps the hydraulic fluid back into the master cylinder, releasing pressure on the brake caliper so that the brake is released. Once the speed of rotation of the wheel returns to an acceptable rate, the pump stops; the solenoid valve opens, allowing the hydraulic master cylinder pressure to return to the caliper, which then re-applies the brake. This cycle can be carried out at up to 10 times a second.

5 The action of the solenoid valves and return pump creates pulses in the hydraulic circuit. When the ABS system is functioning, these pulses can be felt through the brake pedal.

6 The operation of the ABS system is entirely dependent on electrical signals. To prevent the system responding to any inaccurate signals, a built-in safety circuit monitors all signals received by the ECU. If an inaccurate signal or low battery voltage is detected, the ABS system is automatically shut down, and the warning light on the instrument panel is illuminated, to inform the driver that the ABS system is not operational. Normal braking should still be available, however.

7 If a fault does develop in the ABS system, the vehicle must be taken to a Mazda dealer

or suitably-equipped specialist for fault diagnosis and repair.

18 Anti-lock braking system (ABS) components – removal and refitting

Hydraulic unit

1 Although it is possible for the home mechanic to remove the hydraulic unit, the unit's self-diagnosis system must be interrogated by dedicated test equipment before and after removal. Consequently, we recommend that removal and refitting the hydraulic unit should be entrusted to a Mazda dealer or suitably-equipped specialist.

Electronic control unit (ECU)

Note: *On 1998-on models (Mk 2 and Mk 2.5), the ECU is integral with the hydraulic control unit.*

2 Disconnect the battery negative lead as described in Chapter 5A, Section 4.

3 Roll back the carpet on the passenger's side to access the ECU.

4 Undo the retaining bolt/nuts and remove the cover panel.

5 Disconnect the wiring plug and withdraw the ECU.

6 Refitting is a reversal of removal.

Front wheel sensor

7 Chock the rear wheels, then firmly apply the handbrake, jack up the front of the vehicle and support on axle stands (see *Jacking and vehicle support*). Remove the appropriate front roadwheel.

8 Trace the wiring back from the sensor to the connector which is situated in the engine compartment.

9 Undo the screws/clip and release the wiring harness/guide.

10 Slacken and remove the bolt securing the sensor to the hub carrier, and remove the sensor and lead assembly from the vehicle **(see illustration)**.

11 Ensure that the sensor and hub carrier sealing faces are clean, then fit the sensor to the hub. Refit the retaining bolt and tighten it to the specified torque.

12 Ensure that the sensor wiring is correctly routed and retained by all the necessary clips, and reconnect it to its wiring connector. Refit the sensor wiring harness guide.

13 Refit the roadwheel, then lower the vehicle to the ground and tighten the roadwheel nuts to the specified torque.

Rear wheel sensor

14 Chock the front wheels, then jack up the rear of the vehicle and support it on axle stands (see *Jacking and vehicle support*). Remove the appropriate roadwheel.

15 If removing the left-hand sensor, remove the fuel filler pipe protector.

16 If removing the right-hand sensor, remove the spare wheel.

17 Trace the wiring back from the sensor to the connector which is situated in the luggage compartment. Release the wiring harness from any retaining clips/brackets.

18 Slacken and remove the bolt securing the sensor to the hub carrier, and remove the sensor and lead assembly from the vehicle **(see illustration)**.

19 Refit the sensor as described above in paragraphs 11 to 13.

Chapter 10
Suspension and steering

Contents

Degrees of difficulty

Easy, suitable for novice with little experience	**Fairly easy,** suitable for beginner with some experience	**Fairly difficult,** suitable for competent DIY mechanic	**Difficult,** suitable for experienced DIY mechanic	**Very difficult,** suitable for expert DIY or professional

Specifications

Front suspension
Type .... Independent, with MacPherson struts incorporating coil springs and telescopic shock absorbers. Anti-roll bar fitted to all models

Rear suspension
Type .... Independent, with MacPherson struts incorporating coil springs and telescopic shock absorbers. Anti-roll bar fitted to all models

Steering
Type .... Rack and pinion. Power assistance available on some models

Wheel alignment and steering angles
Vehicle must be unladen but have a full fuel tank
Front wheels:
  Camber angle:
    1997 and earlier .... 0°24' ± 45'
    1998-on .... 0°06' ± 1°
    Maximum difference between sides .... 1°
  Castor angle:
    1997 and earlier .... 4°30' ± 45'
    1998-on .... 5°48' ± 1°
    Maximum difference between sides .... 1°30'
  Toe setting (total) .... 0°18' ± 18' (3.0 ± 3.0 mm)
Rear wheels:
  Camber angle:
    1997 and earlier .... -0°43' ± 30'
    1998-on .... -0°47' ± 1°
    Maximum difference between sides .... 1°
  Toe setting (total) .... 0°18' ± 18' (3.0 ± 3.0 mm)

Torque wrench settings

	Nm	lbf ft
Front suspension		
Anti-roll bar mounting clamp bolts	25	18
Anti-roll bar-to-link rod nuts	50	37
Hub/bearing assembly locknut*	200	148
Lower balljoint mounting bolts	90	66
Lower balljoint nut	70	52
Lower wishbone/arm bolts:		
Rear	100	74
Front	90	66
Strut brace bolts	22	16
Strut damper/piston rod nut:		
1997 and earlier	45	33
1998-on	22	16
Strut mounting-to-body nuts	34	25
Strut to wishbone/arm	90	66
Upper balljoint nut	60	44
Upper wishbone/arm bolt	130	96
Rear suspension		
Anti-roll bar clamps	25	18
Anti-roll bar link	50	37
Lower wishbone/arm bolts	90	66
Strut damper/piston rod nut:		
1997 and earlier	45	33
1998-on	22	16
Strut lower mounting bolt	90	66
Strut mounting-to-body	34	25
Upper wishbone/arm bolts	63	46
Steering		
Power steering pipe union nuts	40	30
Power steering pump bolts	43	32
Steering column bolts/nuts	22	16
Steering column universal joint clamp/pinch-bolt	22	16
Steering rack mounting bolts:		
1997 and earlier	56	41
1998-on	90	66
Steering wheel	45	33
Track rod end balljoint retaining nut:		
1997 and earlier	40	30
1998-on	50	37
Roadwheels		
Roadwheel nuts	110	81

* Do not re-use

1 General information

The independent front and rear suspension is of the MacPherson strut type, incorporating coil springs and integral telescopic shock absorbers. The MacPherson struts are located by a lower wishbone/arm suspension arms, which use rubber inner mounting bushes, and incorporate a balljoint at the outer ends. The upper wishbone/arm suspension arms also use rubber inner mounting bushes and incorporate a balljoint at the outer ends. The hub carriers, which carry the brake calipers and the hub/disc assemblies, are connected to the upper and lower wishbone/arms

through the balljoints. Front and rear anti-roll bars are fitted to all models. The anti-roll bar is rubber-mounted and is connected to both suspension lower wishbone/arms by connecting links.

The steering column is connected to the steering rack by an intermediate shaft, which incorporates a universal joint.

The steering rack is mounted onto the front subframe, and is connected by two track rods, with balljoints at their outer ends, to the steering arms projecting forwards from the hub carriers. The track rod ends are threaded, to facilitate adjustment.

Power-assisted steering is fitted to some models. The hydraulic steering system is powered by a belt-driven pump, which is driven off the crankshaft pulley.

2 Front hub assembly – removal and refitting

Removal

1 Remove the brake caliper, caliper bracket and brake disc as described in Chapter 9.
2 Place a dial indicator against the hub **(see illustration)**. Push the hub all the way in and set the indicator to zero. Pull the hub out as far as it will go and note the reading (hub endplay). If it exceeds 0.5 mm, undo the locknut as described below and try retightening it to the specified torque. If this doesn't bring endplay within the specified range, you'll need to renew the entire hub.

2.2 Mount a DTI gauge against the front hub face

2.3 Prise the grease cap from the hub

2.4 Use a small punch to 'un-stake' the locknut

2.5 Slide the hub and bearing from the stub axle

2.6 Disc shield retaining bolts (arrowed)

2.7 Use a punch to 'stake' the nut to the axle

⚠ *Warning: If retightening the locknut does correct excessive endplay, don't re-use the locknut – remove it and fit a new one.*

3 Remove the grease cap from the hub **(see illustration)**. If it's not too distorted, it may be possible to re-use the cap.

4 Bend back the staked portion of the locknut with a hammer and punch, then undo the locknut **(see illustration)**. **Note:** *If you're planning to try retightening the locknut to correct excessive end play, file away all of the staked portion after the nut is removed. Otherwise you won't be able to torque it accurately.*

5 Pull the hub and bearing assembly off the stub axle **(see illustration)**. If necessary, use a puller.

6 If necessary, unbolt and remove the brake disc shield **(see illustration)**.

Refitting

7 Refitting is the reverse of removal. Be sure to clean off the stub axle and lubricate it with wheel bearing grease. Fit a new locknut, tighten it to the specified torque, then stake the locknut with a hammer and punch **(see illustration)**.

3 Front hub carrier –
removal and refitting

Removal

1 Slacken the front roadwheel nuts, raise the front of the vehicle and support it securely on axle stands (see *Jacking and vehicle support*). Remove the wheel.

2 If the hub carrier is to be renewed, remove the hub and bearing assembly as described in Section 2.

3 If the vehicle is equipped with ABS, remove the bolt and detach the ABS wheel sensor from the hub carrier.

4 Disconnect the track rod end from the hub carrier as described in Section 21.

5 Disconnect the balljoints from the hub carrier as described in Section 6, then remove the hub carrier from the vehicle.

6 Examine the hub carrier for signs of wear or damage, and renew if necessary.

Refitting

7 Refitting is the reverse of removal. Tighten all fasteners to their specified torque, and use new split pins on the balljoint nuts.

4 Front strut –
removal, overhaul and refitting

Removal

1 Chock the rear wheels, apply the handbrake, then jack up the front of the car and support on axle stands (see *Jacking and vehicle support*). Remove the appropriate roadwheel.

2 Undo the fasteners and remove the engine undershield (where fitted).

3 Mark the spring with paint so the assembly can be refitted with the correct orientation **(see illustration)**.

4 Undo the nuts and detach the anti-roll bar from the link rod on the lower wishbone on each side of the vehicle **(see illustration)**.

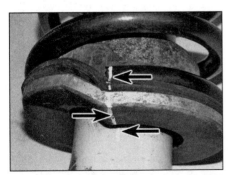

4.3 Paint alignment marks (arrowed) to aid refitting

4.4 Use an Allen key to counterhold the anti-roll bar link rod balljoint whilst slackening the nut

4.5a Shock absorber lower mounting bolt (arrowed)

4.5b ABS sensor wiring harness bracket retaining bolt (arrowed)

4.6a Undo the bolt (arrowed) securing the ABS sensor harness to the underside of the upper wishbone

4.6b Undo the nut and slide the pivot bolt forwards to release the wishbone (arrowed)

4.7 Shock absorber upper mounting nuts (arrowed)

Use an Allen key to counterhold the link rod balljoint shank.

5 Remove the shock absorber's lower bolt and nut, then undo the bolt securing the ABS wheel speed sensor wiring harness bracket

4.13 Use spring compressors

4.15b ... washer ...

4.15c ... rubber mounting ...

(where fitted) to the shock absorber **(see illustrations)**.

6 Undo the bolt securing the ABS wheel speed sensor wiring harness (where fitted) to the upper wishbone, then undo the nut, recover

the washer and slide the upper wishbone/arm pivot bolt forward, releasing the arm from the subframe **(see illustration)**.

7 Working in the engine compartment, remove the shock absorber's upper mounting nuts **(see illustration)**. Lever down on the lower wishbone/arm, lower the shock absorber/coil spring assembly free of the wheelarch/wing and remove it from the vehicle.

8 Check the shock absorber body for leaking fluid, dents, cracks and other obvious damage which would warrant renewal.

9 Check the coil spring for chips or cracks in the spring coating (this will cause premature spring failure due to corrosion). Inspect the spring seat for cuts and general deterioration.

10 If any undesirable conditions exist, renew the unit using the information in this Section.

Overhaul

⚠️ **Warning: Before attempting to dismantle the front suspension strut, a suitable tool to hold the coil spring in compression must be obtained. Adjustable coil spring compressors are readily available, and are recommended for this operation. Any attempt to dismantle the strut without such a tool is likely to result in damage or personal injury.**

11 With the strut removed from the car, clean away all external dirt, then mount it upright in a vice.

12 Prise the cap (where fitted) from the top centre of the shock/coil spring assembly. Slacken the damper shaft nut(s) beneath the cap, but DO NOT remove it/them yet. Use an Allen key to counterhold the damper rod whilst slackening the nuts.

13 Following the tool manufacturer's instructions, fit the spring compressor on the spring and compress it sufficiently to relieve all pressure from the upper spring seat **(see illustration)**. This can be verified by wiggling the spring.

14 Remove the damper shaft nut(s) and washer. It may be necessary to hold the shaft from turning while slackening the nut.

15 Mark the outer side of the spring and mounting plates so they can be refitted in the same orientation to the spring. Remove the nut, washer, rubber mounting, and mounting plate (as applicable) **(see illustrations)**. Check

4.15d ... and mounting plate

4.16a Lift off the rubber mounting, washer ...

4.16b ... gaiter ...

the mounting plate for cracking and general deterioration. If there is any doubt about its condition, renew it.

16 Lift the rubber mounting, washer, gaiter and bump stop (as applicable) from the damper shaft **(see illustrations)**. Check the rubber for cracking and hardness, renewing it if necessary.

17 Carefully lift the compressed spring from the assembly and set it in a safe place **(see illustration)**.

 Warning: Keep the ends of the spring pointed away from your body.

18 With the strut assembly now completely dismantled, examine all the components for wear, damage or deformation, and check the upper mounting bearing for smoothness of operation. Renew any of the components as necessary.

19 Examine the strut for signs of fluid leakage. Check the strut piston for signs of pitting along its entire length, and check the strut body for signs of damage.

Reassembly

20 Place the coil spring onto the lower spring seat, with the end of the spring resting in the step (lowest part of the seat) **(see illustration)**.

21 Extend the damper rod to its full length and refit the bump stop, gaiter, washer and rubber mounting.

22 Refit the mounting plate, rubber mounting and washer. Align the mounting plate with marks made on removal **(see illustration)**.

1997 and earlier models

23 Refit the damper shaft nut and partially tighten it.

24 Remove the spring compressor tool.

25 Tighten the damper shaft nut to the specified torque.

1998-on models

26 Refit the lower piston rod nut, and tighten it until 15.7 to 17.7 mm of piston rod is protruding above the nut **(see illustration)**.

27 Refit the upper piston rod nut, and tighten it to the specified torque.

28 Remove the spring compressor tool.

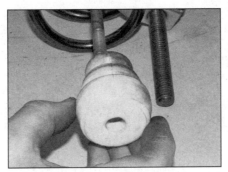

4.16c ... and bump stop

Refitting

29 Refitting is a reversal of removal, noting the following points:

a) *Tighten all fasteners to their specified torque where given.*

4.20 Ensure the end of the spring locates in the step of the seat (arrowed)

4.26 Measure the distance from the top of the nut to the end of the rod

4.17 Carefully lift the compressed spring from the damper

b) *Don't forget to fit the plastic gasket between the upper mounting plate and the vehicle body (see illustration).*

c) *We recommend the front wheel alignment is checked at the earliest opportunity.*

4.22 Align the marks made on removal

4.29 Fit the plastic gasket between the mounting plate the vehicle body

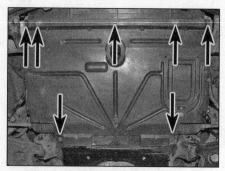

5.1a Undershield fasteners beneath (arrowed) ...

5.1b ... and each side (arrowed)

5.2 Insert an Allen key into the balljoint shank (arrowed) to counterhold the anti-roll bar link

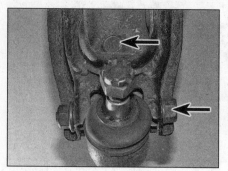

5.4 Balljoint through-bolt and upper bolt (arrowed) – hub carrier removed for clarity

5.5a Make alignment marks between the pivot bolt head eccentric washer and the subframe ...

5.5b ... then remove the pivot bolts (arrowed)

5 Front wishbones/arms – removal, overhaul and refitting

Note: *New lower arm front balljoint nuts will be required on refitting.*

Lower wishbone/arm

Removal

1 Chock the rear wheels, firmly apply the handbrake, then jack up the front of the car and support on axle stands (see *Jacking and vehicle support*). Remove the appropriate front roadwheel. Undo the fasteners and remove the engine undershield (where fitted) **(see illustrations)**.

2 Disconnect the anti-roll bar link rod from the lower wishbone/arm **(see illustration)**.
3 Remove the shock absorber lower bolt as described in Section 4.
4 Remove the balljoint through-bolt and the upper bolt that secures it to the wishbone/arm **(see illustration)**.
5 Make alignment marks between the bolt head eccentric washers and the subframe, then remove the inner pivot bolts that secure the lower wishbone/arm to the subframe **(see illustrations)**. Note that the eccentric washers are integral with the bolts. Lower the inner end of the wishbone/arm away from the subframe, pull it away from the balljoint and remove it from under the vehicle.

Overhaul

6 Inspect the front and rear bushings in the lower control arm. If either bushing is torn or cracked, renew them as follows.
7 Ideally, use a hydraulic press to remove the bushes from the arm. However, they can be removed using a combination of suitable spacers, threaded rod, nuts and washers **(see illustrations)**.
8 Position the new bushes in the arm, and press them into place, reversing the method of removal **(see illustrations)**. Ensure the bore in the arm is clean and smooth – use plenty of warm soapy water as lubrication when pressing in the bushes.

Refitting

9 Refitting is the reverse of the removal

5.7a Cut away the rubber flanges ...

5.7b ... and press out the bushes using a combination of spacers, threaded rod, nuts and washers

5.8a Using warm, soapy water as a lubricant ...

5.8b ... press the new bushes into place ...

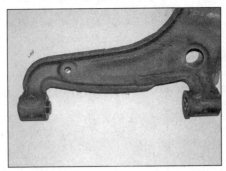

5.8c ... in the suspension arm/wishbone

5.15a Undo the nut (arrowed) ...

procedure. Tighten the balljoint bolts to the specified torque while the vehicle is still raised. Tighten the remaining fasteners (lower arm pivots, anti-roll bar link rod, shock absorber lower bolt) loosely at first, then refit the wheels and lower the vehicle. Tighten the fasteners to the specified torque with the vehicle's weight resting on the wheels.

10 Have front end alignment checked at the earliest opportunity.

Upper wishbone/arm

Removal

11 Chock the rear wheels, firmly apply the handbrake, then jack up the front of the car and support on axle stands (see *Jacking and vehicle support*). Remove the appropriate front roadwheel. Undo the fasteners and remove the engine undershield (where fitted) (see illustrations 5.1a and 5.1b).

12 On models with ABS, release the clip that secures the wheel speed sensor harness.

13 Remove the shock absorber lower mounting bolt. Support the lower wishbone/ arm from below.

14 Pull out the split pin, undo the nut, and detach the upper balljoint from the hub carrier using a balljoint separator tool.

15 Undo the nut and remove the inner pivot bolt (see illustrations). Withdraw the arm from the vehicle.

Overhaul

16 Inspect the front and rear bushings in the wishbone/arm. If any bushing is torn or cracked, renew them as follows.

17 Ideally, use a hydraulic press to remove the bushes from the arm. However, they can be removed using a combination of suitable spacers, threaded rod, nuts and washers (see illustration 5.7a and 5.7b).

18 Position the new bushes in the arm, and press them into place, reversing the method of removal (see illustration).

19 Ensure the bore in the arm is clean and smooth – use plenty of warm soapy water as lubrication when pressing in the bushes.

Refitting

20 Refitting is the reverse of the removal procedure. Tighten the balljoint nut to the specified torque while the vehicle is still

5.15b ... and slide the pivot bolt (arrowed) forwards

raised, then install a new split pin. Tighten the remaining fasteners (pivot bolt, shock absorber lower bolt) loosely at first, then install the wheels and lower the vehicle. Tighten the fasteners to the specified torques with the vehicle's weight resting on the wheels.

21 Have front end alignment checked at the earliest opportunity.

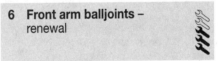

6 Front arm balljoints – renewal

Upper balljoint

1 The upper balljoint is integral with the upper wishbone (see Section 5). However, the balljoint rubber boot can be renewed separately. Remove the upper wishbone as

6.1 Prise the old boot from the balljoint ...

5.18 Press the upper arm bushes with the flanges (arrowed) to the outside

described in Section 5, then prise the old boot from the balljoint (see illustration).

2 Position the new boot over the balljoint, and press it squarely into place using a 30 mm socket, until the gap between the boot ring and the seat is less than 1.0 mm (see illustration).

3 Refit the upper wishbone as described in Section 5.

Lower balljoint

4 Chock the rear wheels, firmly apply the handbrake, then jack up the front of the car and support on axle stands (see *Jacking and vehicle support*). Remove the appropriate front roadwheel.

5 Undo the nut and pull out the shock absorber lower mounting bolt (see illustration 4.5a).

6 Support the lower wishbone/arm with a workshop jack, then pull out the split pin, and slacken the balljoint nut. Do not completely remove the nut at this stage (see illustration).

6.2 ... and press the new one into place

6.6 Remove the lower balljoint split pin (arrowed) and slacken the nut

6.7 Detach the balljoint from the hub carrier using a balljoint separator tool

4 Withdrawn the anti-roll bar from under the vehicle and remove the rubber bushings.

5 Check the rubber bushings and link rod grommets for cracks and tears. Renew all damaged bushings; renew the links if the grommets are damaged.

Refitting

6 Align the rubber bushings with the marks on the anti-roll bar, then position the anti-roll bar, refit the clamps and tighten the retaining bolts to the specified torque.

7 Reconnect the link rods and tighten the bolts to the specified torque.

8 Refit the engine undershield.

9 Refit the roadwheels and lower the vehicle to the ground.

7 Detach the balljoint from the hub carrier using a balljoint separator tool **(see illustration)**. Lift the hub carrier over the balljoint stud.

8 Undo the balljoint retaining bolts and remove it **(see illustration 5.4)**.

9 Insert the new balljoint stud into the hole in the base of the hub carrier and refit the nut. Do not tighten the nut at this stage.

10 Refit the balljoint mounting bolts and tighten them to the specified torque.

11 Tighten the balljoint stud nut to the specified torque, and secure it with a new split pin.

12 Refit the shock absorber lower mounting bolt and tighten the nut to the specified torque.

13 Refit the roadwheel and lower the vehicle to the ground. Have the front wheel alignment checked at the earliest opportunity.

7 Front anti-roll bar – removal and refitting

Removal

1 Chock the rear wheels, firmly apply the handbrake, then jack up the front of the car and support on axle stands (see *Jacking and vehicle support*). Remove the appropriate front roadwheel. Undo the fasteners and remove the radiator undershield (where fitted) **(see illustration 5.1a and 5.1b)**.

2 Disconnect the anti-roll bar link rod from the lower wishbone/arm **(see illustration 5.2)**. Use an Allen key to counterhold the link rod balljoint shank.

3 Undo the retaining bolts and remove the anti-roll bar clamps **(see illustration)**.

8 Front strut brace – removal and refitting

Note: *A strut brace is only fitted on sports suspension models from 2000.*

1 Undo the bolts at each end of the strut brace and manoeuvre it from position **(see illustration)**.

2 If required, undo the nuts and remove the mounting brackets.

3 Refitting is a reversal of removal. Tighten the fasteners to their specified torque where given.

9 Rear hub and bearing – removal and refitting

Note: *The hub assembly should not be removed unless it, or the hub bearing, is to be renewed. The hub is a press-fit in the bearing inner race, and removal of the hub will damage the bearings. If the hub is to be removed, be prepared to renew the hub bearing at the same time.*

Removal

1 Remove the hub carrier assembly as described in Section 11.

2 Prise the oil seal from the inner face of the hub carrier.

3 Use a hydraulic press and suitable sized spacers to force the hub from the centre of the bearing **(see illustration)**.

4 Remove the circlip, then press the bearing from the hub carrier **(see illustration)**. Do not remove the disc shield unless absolutely necessary.

5 If the hub is to be re-used, remove the bearing inner race using a chisel, or bearing remover **(see illustration)**.

Refitting

6 Thoroughly clean the hub carrier bore, removing all traces of dirt and grease, and polish away any burrs or raised edges which might hinder reassembly. Renew the circlip if there is any doubt about its condition.

7.3 Anti-roll bar right-hand clamp bolts (arrowed)

8.1 Undo the bolts (arrowed) at each end of the strut brace

9.3 Press the hub from the centre of the wheel bearing

9.4 Remove the circlip and press the bearing from the hub carrier

9.5 Ideally, remove the bearing inner race using a bearing remover

9.8 Press the new bearing squarely into the hub carrier

9.12 Fit the new oil seal into the inner face of the hub carrier

7 On reassembly, apply a light film of clean engine oil to the bearing outer race to aid installation.

8 Locate the bearing in the hub carrier and press it into position, ensuring that it enters the carrier squarely, using a suitable tubular spacer which bears only on the bearing outer race **(see illustration)**.

9 Secure the bearing in position with the new circlip, making sure it is correctly located in the hub carrier groove.

10 Apply a smear of oil to the hub surface, and locate it in the bearing inner race.

11 Press the hub into place supporting the bearing with a spacer that bears only on the bearing inner race. **Note:** *Do not be tempted to knock the hub into position with a hammer and drift, as this will almost certainly damage the bearing.*

12 Press the new oil seal squarely into position on the inner face of the hub carrier **(see illustration)**.

13 Refit the hub carrier as described in Section 11.

10 Rear strut –
removal, overhaul and refitting

Removal

1 Chock the front wheels, then jack up the rear of the car and support on axle stands (see *Jacking and vehicle support*). Remove the rear roadwheels.

2 Support the lower wishbone/arm from

below, then detach the anti-roll bar link rod from the wishbone/arm so it can drop below its normal position.

Caution: Don't let the lower arm strain the brake hose when it drops.

3 If you're working on the left side of the vehicle, remove the protection shield for the fuel tank filler pipe from within the luggage compartment **(see illustration)**.

4 Remove the shock absorber's lower bolt and nut **(see illustration)**.

5 Working in the luggage compartment, remove the upper mounting nuts **(see illustration)**. Lower the shock absorber from place and manoeuvre it from under the vehicle.

Overhaul

6 Inspection and renewal of the damper unit or coil spring are the same as for front shock absorber/coil spring assemblies (Section 4).

Refitting

7 Refitting is the reverse of removal. Tighten all fasteners to their specified torque. Tighten the anti-roll bar lower link rod bolt and roadwheel nuts loosely, then lower the vehicle and tighten them to their specified torque.

11 Rear hub carrier –
removal, overhaul and refitting

Removal

1 Chock the front wheels, then jack up the

rear of the car and support it on axle stands (see *Jacking and vehicle support*). Remove the relevant roadwheel.

2 Remove the brake disc and ABS wheel speed sensor (where applicable) as described in Chapter 9, Section 7 and 18.

3 Remove the driveshaft/hub nut, and release the driveshaft from the hub splines, as described in Chapter 8, Section 4.

4 Support the lower wishbone/arm from below with a workshop jack, then remove the outer pivot bolts from the upper and lower wishbones/arms, and withdrawn the hub carrier from place **(see illustrations 12.4, 12.14a and 12.14b)**. Support the driveshaft so as not to damage the gaiter. **Note:** *Only remove the disc shield if it is absolutely necessary.*

Overhaul

5 Examine the upper rubber bush for cracks, damage and deterioration. If necessary, remove the bush using a combination of spacers, threaded rod, washers and nuts.

6 Ensure the bore of the hub carrier is clean and free from burrs/rust.

7 Coat the new bush liberally with soapy water, then draw it into position in the hub carrier, again using suitable spacers, threaded rod, etc **(see illustration)**.

Refitting

8 Refitting is a reversal of removal, noting the following points:
  a) Tighten all fasteners to their specified torque.
  b) Before tightening any fastener that runs

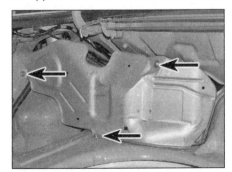

10.3 Undo the bolts (arrowed) and remove the protection shield

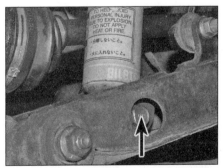

10.4 Rear shock absorber lower mounting bolt (arrowed)

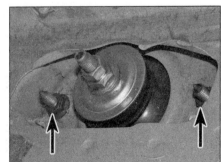

10.5 Shock absorber upper mounting bolts (arrowed)

11.7 The bush should be central in the hub carrier

through a rubber bushing, raise the hub carrier with a trolley jack to simulate normal ride height.
c) *Have the rear wheel alignment checked at the earliest opportunity.*

12 Rear wishbones/arms – removal, overhaul and refitting

Lower wishbone/arm

Removal

1 Chock the front wheels, firmly apply the handbrake, then jack up the rear of the car and support on axle stands (see *Jacking and vehicle support*). Remove the appropriate roadwheel.

2 Disconnect the anti-roll bar link rod from the lower wishbone/arm **(see illustration)**.
3 Remove the shock absorber lower bolt as described in Section 10.
4 Remove the outer pivot bolt that secures the wishbone/arm to the hub carrier **(see illustration)**.
5 Make alignment marks between the inner pivot bolt heads eccentric washers and the subframe, then remove the inner pivot bolts that secure the lower wishbone/arm to the subframe **(see illustrations)**. Lower the inner end of the wishbone/arm away from the subframe and remove it from under the vehicle.

Overhaul

6 Inspect the inner and outer bushings in the wishbone/arm. If any bushing is torn or cracked, renew them as described in Section 5.

Refitting

7 Install the wishbone/arm inner pivot bolts. Line up the bolt head eccentric washers in the positions marked on removal.
8 Refit the outer pivot through bolt, then raise the hub carrier to simulate normal ride height, and tighten the inner and outer pivot bolts to their specified torque.
9 Refit the lower suspension strut mounting bolt, and the anti-roll bar link rod bolt and tighten them to the specified torque.
10 Refit the roadwheel and lower the vehicle to the ground.

11 Have rear wheel alignment checked and adjusted if necessary at the earliest opportunity.

Upper wishbone/arm

Removal

12 Chock the front wheels, firmly apply the handbrake, then jack up the rear of the car and support on axle stands (see *Jacking and vehicle support*). Remove the appropriate roadwheel.
13 Support the lower wishbone/arm with a trolley jack.
14 Remove the inner and outer pivot bolts and manoeuvre the wishbone/arm from the vehicle **(see illustrations)**.

Overhaul

15 Inspect the inner bushings in the wishbone/arm. If any bushing is torn or cracked, renew them as described in Section 5.

Refitting

16 Manoeuvre the wishbone/arm into position, refit the inner and outer pivots bolts, but do not tighten them at this stage.
17 Raise the hub carrier to simulate normal ride height, then tighten the pivot bolts to the specified torque.
18 Refit the roadwheel and lower the vehicle to the ground.
19 Have the rear wheel alignment checked at the earliest opportunity.

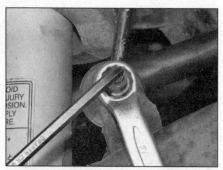

12.2 Use an Allen key to counterhold the anti-roll bar link rod balljoint whilst slackening the nut

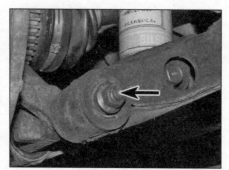

12.4 Lower wishbone outer pivot bolt (arrowed)

12.5a Make alignment marks between the pivot bolt eccentric washer and the subframe (arrowed) ...

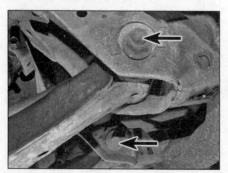

12.5b ... then remove the inner pivot bolts (arrowed)

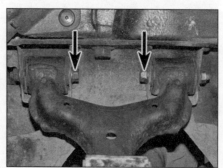

12.14a Upper arm inner pivot bolts (arrowed) ...

12.14b ... and outer pivot bolt (arrowed)

13 Rear anti-roll bar – removal and refitting

Removal

1 Chock the front wheels, then jack up the rear of the car and support on axle stands (see *Jacking and vehicle support*). Remove the rear roadwheels.

2 Unbolt the anti-roll bar bushing clamps from the body **(see illustration)**.

3 Unbolt the anti-roll bar from the upper ends of the link rods **(see illustration)**. The anti-roll bar can now be removed from the vehicle. Pull the bushings off the anti-roll bar using a rocking motion.

4 Unbolt the lower ends of the anti-roll link rod on each side of the vehicle and remove the rods.

5 Check the bushings for wear, hardness, distortion, cracking and other signs of deterioration, renewing them if necessary. Also check the anti-roll bar link rod bushings for the same conditions, and renew if necessary.

6 Using a wire brush, clean the areas of the bar where the bushings ride.

Refitting

7 Refitting is the reverse of the removal procedure. Apply rubber lubricant to the bushings prior to installation.

Caution: Do not use petroleum-based products or brake fluid, as these will damage the rubber.

8 Install the bushings at the anti-roll bar clamps with the bushing flat bottom/split facing the crossmember, and with the bushing located on the installation position line painted on the anti-roll bar. On the left side of the vehicle, centre the inner edge of the bushing in the light-coloured paint mark between the two dark paint marks. On the right side, position the inner end of the bushing just inside the dark paint mark.

9 Refit and tighten the anti-roll bar clamp bolts and link rod bolts. Tighten them loosely at first. Refit the road wheel and retaining nuts then tighten them loosely.

10 Lower the vehicle. Tighten the anti-roll bar

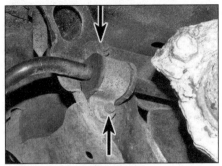

13.2 Rear anti-roll bar left-hand clamp nuts (arrowed)

fasteners and roadwheel nuts to the specified torque.

14 Steering wheel – removal and refitting

Removal

1 Set the front wheels in the straight-ahead position.

2 Remove the airbag unit (where fitted) from the centre of the steering wheel, referring to Chapter 12, Section 20. On models without an airbag prise up the plastic cap to reveal the steering wheel retaining nut. Disconnect any wiring as the cap is removed.

3 Slacken and remove the steering wheel retaining nut. Disconnect the steering wheel wiring plug(s) where fitted **(see illustration)**.

4 Make alignment marks between the steering wheel and the column shaft to aid refitting.

5 Lift the steering wheel off the column splines. If it is tight, tap it up near the centre, using the palm of your hand, or twist it from side to side, whilst pulling upwards to release it from the shaft splines. If the steering wheel is still reluctant to release, bolt a length of steel strip across the end of the column (using the holes provided in the steering wheel centre), and gradually tighten the bolts, whilst gently tapping the end of the shaft **(see illustration)**. Use adhesive tape to secure the airbag rotary contact unit; do not attempt to rotate it whilst the wheel is removed.

13.3 Rear anti-roll bar link rod-to-bar retaining nut (arrowed)

Refitting

6 Refitting is the reverse of removal, noting the following points.

  a) *On models with an airbag, if the contact unit has been rotated with the wheel removed, centralise it by rotating its centre fully anti-clockwise. From this position, rotate the centre back through 2.75 complete rotations in a clockwise direction.*

  b) *Engage the wheel with the column splines, aligning the previously-made marks.*

  c) *Where applicable, ensure the lugs on the indicator cancelling sleeve locate correctly with the holes on the front of the steering wheel boss.*

  d) *Tighten the steering wheel retaining nut to the specified torque.*

  e) *Refit the airbag unit (see Chapter 12, Section 20).*

15 Steering column – removal, inspection and refitting

Removal

1 Remove the steering column combination switch assembly as described in Chapter 12, Section 4.

2 Disconnect any remaining wiring plugs and release any wiring harnesses from the column assembly.

3 Unclip and remove the plastic boot around the base of the column adjacent to the pedals **(see illustration)**.

14.3 Depress the clip (arrowed) and disconnect the wiring plug

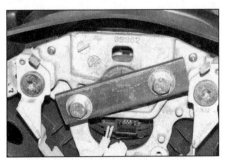

14.5 Attach a strip of steel over the end of the shaft using the holes provided in the steering wheel centre

15.3 Pull the plastic boot from the base of the steering column

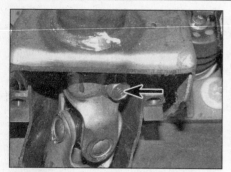

15.4 Remove the clamp bolt (arrowed)

15.5b ... and 2 nuts (arrowed) at the base

4 Slacken and remove the clamp bolt, make alignment marks and disengage the universal joint from the steering column shaft **(see illustration)**.
5 Undo the mounting bolts/nuts and pull the column to the rear **(see illustrations)**.

Inspection

6 The steering column incorporates a telescopic safety feature. In the event of a front-end crash, the shaft collapses and prevents the steering wheel injuring the driver. Before refitting the steering column, examine the column and mountings for damage and deformation, and renew as necessary.
7 Check the steering shaft for signs of free play in the column bushes. If any damage or wear is found on the steering column bushes, the column should be overhauled. Overhaul of the column is a complex task requiring several

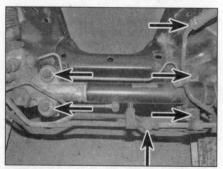

17.3 Power steering rack mounting bolts and fluid pressure/return pipe connections (arrowed – engine removed for clarity)

15.5a The column is secured by 2 bolts (arrowed) at the top ...

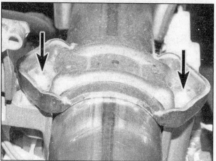

16.2 The steering column lock is secured by 2 shear bolts (arrowed)

special tools, and should be entrusted to a Mazda dealer.

Refitting

8 Manoeuvre the column into position and engage it with the steering rack pinion splines, aligning the marks made prior to removal.
9 Locate the column in position and screw in the mounting bolts. Tighten them to the specified torque.
10 The remainder of refitting is a reversal of removal.

16 Steering column lock – removal and refitting

1 Remove the steering column combination switch as described in Chapter 12, Section 4,

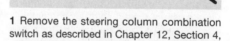

17.4 Steering column universal joint pinch-bolt (arrowed)

then disconnect the wiring plug from the lock/ switch assembly.
2 The steering column lock is secured by shear bolts. Use a sharp chisel on the bolt heads to undo them **(see illustration)**.
3 Remove the upper bracket followed by the lock assembly.
4 Position the steering lock assembly on the column, refit the upper bracket, then fit the new shear bolts and tighten them until the heads shear off.
5 Refit the steering column as described in Section 15.

17 Steering rack assembly – removal and refitting

Removal

1 Chock the rear wheels, firmly apply the handbrake, then jack up the front of the car and support on axle stands (see *Jacking and vehicle support*). Remove both front roadwheels, undo the fasteners and remove the engine undershield.
2 Set the steering in the 'straight-ahead' position and engage the steering lock. Disconnect the battery negative lead as described in Chapter 5A, Section 4.
3 If equipped with power steering, place a container under the steering rack, then disconnect the power steering pressure and return pipes **(see illustration)**. Cap or cover the ends to prevent excessive fluid loss and contamination.
4 Mark the relationship of the steering column universal joint at the steering rack pinion. Remove the steering column universal joint pinch-bolt **(see illustration)**.
5 Separate the track rod ends from the hub carrier as described in Section 21.
6 Support the steering rack and remove the steering rack mounting bolts **(see illustration 17.3)**. Separate the steering column shaft from the steering rack pinion and remove the rack assembly.

⚠ *Warning: Do NOT turn the steering wheel while the steering rack is removed. If the steering wheel is inadvertently turned, check the airbag rotary connector for damage and adjust as necessary (see Chapter 12, Section 20).*

7 Check the steering rack mounting grommets for excessive wear or deterioration, renewing them if necessary.

Refitting

8 Raise the steering rack into position and connect the pinion to the universal joint, aligning the marks.
9 Install the steering rack mounting brackets and bolts and tighten them to the specified torque.
10 Connect the track rod ends to the hub carriers and tighten them to the specified torque.
11 Fit the universal joint pinch-bolt and tighten it to the specified torque.

12 If equipped with power steering, connect the power steering pressure and return hoses to the steering rack and fill the power steering pump reservoir with the recommended fluid (see *Lubricants and fluids*).

13 Lower the vehicle and bleed the steering system (see Section 19).

14 We recommend having the front wheel alignment checked at the earliest opportunity.

18 Power steering pump – removal and refitting

Removal

1 Remove the auxiliary drivebelt as described in Chapter 1, Section 6.

2 Using a large syringe or old poultry baster, remove as much fluid out of the power steering fluid reservoir as possible. Place a container under the vehicle to catch any fluid that spills out when the hoses are disconnected. Cap or cover the hoses to prevent entry of dirt or other contaminants.

3 Slacken the clamp and disconnect the fluid return hose from the pump **(see illustration)**. Detach the electrical connector from the pressure sensor on the pump, if applicable.

4 Disconnect the pressure pipe from the pump, and detach the support bracket **(see illustration 18.3)**.

5 Check the pressure pipe O-rings and renew if necessary.

6 Raise the front of the vehicle and place it securely on axle stands (see *Jacking and vehicle support*).

7 Remove the pivot, adjuster and mounting bolts/nuts, then remove the pump from the vehicle.

8 If access to engine components is required, remove the pump mounting bracket mounting bolts and remove the mounting bracket.

Refitting

9 Refitting is the reverse of removal. Be sure to tighten the pressure pipe fitting to the specified torque.

10 Refit the auxiliary drivebelt as described in Chapter 1, Section 6.

11 Top off the fluid level in the reservoir (see *Weekly checks*) and bleed the system (see Section 19).

19 Power steering system – bleeding

1 Following any operation in which the power steering fluid lines have been disconnected, the power steering system must be bled to remove all air and obtain proper steering performance.

2 Before starting the engine and with the front wheels in the straight-ahead position, check the power steering fluid level and, if low, add fluid until it reaches the L (Low) mark on the dipstick.

18.3 Power steering pump return hose and pressure pipe (arrowed)

3 Without starting the engine, turn the steering wheel from lock to lock, then recheck the fluid level.

4 Start the engine and allow it to run at a fast idle. Recheck the fluid level and add more power steering fluid if necessary to reach the L mark on the dipstick.

5 Bleed the system by turning the wheels from side to side, without hitting the stops. This will remove the air from the system. Continuously check the reservoir and keep the reservoir full of fluid as this is done.

6 When the air is removed from the system, return the wheels to the straight-ahead position and keep the engine running for several more minutes before turning it off, or road test as follows before turning the engine off.

7 Road test the vehicle to ensure the steering system is functioning normally and is noise-free.

8 Recheck and top-up the power steering fluid level to the F (Full) mark on the dipstick while the engine is at normal operating temperature. Add fluid if necessary (see *Weekly checks*).

20 Steering rack rubber gaiters – renewal

1 Remove the track rod end from the steering rack as described in Section 21.

2 Release the clamps securing the gaiter to the steering rack, and pull the gaiter over the track rod **(see illustration)**.

3 Thoroughly clean the track rod and the steering rack housing, using fine abrasive

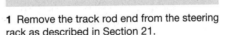

21.2 Remove the split pin (arrowed) from the balljoint shank

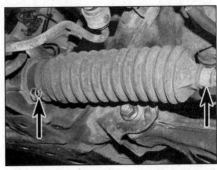

20.2 Steering rack gaiter clamps (arrowed)

paper to polish off any corrosion, burrs or sharp edges, which might damage the new gaiter's sealing lips on installation. Scrape off all the grease from the old gaiter, and apply it to the track rod inner balljoint. (This assumes that grease has not been lost or contaminated as a result of damage to the old gaiter. Use fresh grease if in doubt – consult a Mazda dealer or parts specialist.)

4 Apply a little grease to the track rod so the gaiter will slide, then carefully fit the new gaiter (with the retaining clips in place) over the track rod, and locate it on the steering rack housing. Position the outer edge of the gaiter on the track rod.

5 Secure the gaiter to the rack and track rod with the retaining clamps.

6 Refit the track rod end as described in Section 21.

21 Track rod end – removal and refitting
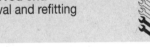

Removal

1 Apply the handbrake, then jack up the front of the car and support it on axle stands (see *Jacking and vehicle support*). Remove the appropriate front roadwheel.

2 Remove the split pin **(see illustration)** and slacken the nut on the track rod end stud.

3 Hold the track rod end with a pair of locking pliers or spanner and slacken the locknut enough to mark the position of the track rod end end in relation to the threads **(see illustration)**.

21.3 Slacken the track rod end locknut (arrowed)

21.4 Use a balljoint separator tool to detach the track rod end from the hub carrier

4 Use a balljoint separator to detach the track rod end from the hub carrier (see illustration).

5 Unscrew the track rod end from the track rod.

Refitting

6 Thread the track rod end to the marked position on the track rod and insert the track rod end stud into the hub carrier. Tighten the locknut securely.

7 Fit the castellated nut on the stud and tighten it to the specified torque. Install a new

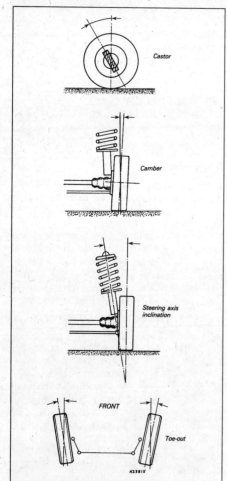

22.1 Steering geometry details

split pin. If the hole for the split pin does not line up with one of the slots in the nut, tighten the nut an additional amount until it slides through easily; do not slacken the nut.

8 Have the wheel alignment checked at the earliest opportunity.

22 Wheel alignment and steering angles – general information

Definitions

1 A car's steering and suspension geometry is defined in four basic settings (see illustration) – all angles are usually expressed in degrees (toe settings are also expressed as a measurement); the steering axis is defined as an imaginary line drawn through the axis of the suspension strut, extended where necessary to contact the ground.

2 Camber is the angle between each roadwheel and a vertical line drawn through its centre and tyre contact patch, when viewed from the front or rear of the car. Positive camber is when the roadwheels are tilted outwards from the vertical at the top; negative camber is when they are tilted inwards.

3 The front camber angle is not adjustable, and is given for reference only. The rear camber angle is adjustable and can be adjusted using a camber angle gauge.

4 Castor is the angle between the steering axis and a vertical line drawn through each roadwheel's centre and tyre contact patch, when viewed from the side of the car. Positive castor is when the steering axis is tilted so that it contacts the ground ahead of the vertical; negative castor is when it contacts the ground behind the vertical.

5 Castor is not adjustable, and is given for reference only; while it can be checked using a castor checking gauge, if the figure obtained is significantly different from that specified, the car must be taken for careful checking by a professional, as the fault can only be caused by wear or damage to the body or suspension components.

6 Toe is the difference, viewed from above, between lines drawn through the roadwheel centres and the car's centre-line. 'Toe-in' is when the roadwheels point inwards, towards each other at the front, while 'toe-out' is when they splay outwards from each other at the front.

7 The front wheel toe setting is adjusted by screwing the track rod in or out of the tack rod end, to alter the effective length of the track rod assembly.

8 Rear wheel toe setting is not adjustable.

Checking and adjustment

Front wheel toe setting

9 Due to the special measuring equipment necessary to check the wheel alignment, and the skill required to use it properly, the checking and adjustment of these settings is

best left to a Mazda dealer or similar expert. Note that most tyre-fitting shops now possess sophisticated checking equipment.

10 To check the toe setting, a tracking gauge must first be obtained. Two types of gauge are available, and can be obtained from motor accessory shops. The first type measures the distance between the front and rear inside edges of the roadwheels, as previously described, with the car stationary. The second type, known as a 'scuff plate', measures the actual position of the contact surface of the tyre, in relation to the road surface, with the car in motion. This is achieved by pushing or driving the front tyre over a plate, which then moves slightly according to the scuff of the tyre, and shows this movement on a scale. Both types have their advantages and disadvantages, but either can give satisfactory results if used correctly and carefully.

11 Make sure that the steering is in the straight-ahead position when making measurements.

12 If adjustment is necessary, apply the handbrake then jack up the front of the car and support it securely on axle stands.

13 First clean the track rod threads; if they are corroded, apply penetrating fluid before starting adjustment. Release the rubber gaiter outer clips, peel back the gaiters and apply a smear of grease so that both are free and will not be twisted or strained as their respective track rods are rotated.

14 Retain the track rod with a suitable spanner and slacken the balljoint locknut. Alter the length of the track rod, by screwing them into or out of track rod ends, rotating the track rod using an open-ended spanner fitted to the track rod flats provided; shortening the track rods (screwing them onto their balljoints) will reduce toe-in/increase toe-out.

15 When the setting is correct, hold the track rod and tighten the balljoint locknut to the specified torque setting. If after adjustment, the steering wheel spokes are no longer horizontal when the wheels are in the straight-ahead position, remove the steering wheel and reposition it (see Section 14).

16 Check that the toe setting has been correctly adjusted by lowering the car to the ground and rechecking the toe setting; re-adjust if necessary. Ensure that the rubber gaiters are seated correctly and are not twisted or strained, and secure them in position with the retaining clips; where necessary fit a new retaining clip (see Section 20).

Wheel camber angle

17 Checking and adjusting of the camber angle should be entrusted to a Mazda dealer or other suitably-equipped specialist. Note that most tyre-fitting shops now possess sophisticated checking equipment. For reference, adjustments are made by slackening the lower wishbone/arm pivot bolts, and rotating the eccentric washer. Once adjustment is correct, tighten the bolts to the specified torque.

Chapter 11
Bodywork and fittings

Contents

Degrees of difficulty

Easy, suitable for novice with little experience	Fairly easy, suitable for beginner with some experience	Fairly difficult, suitable for competent DIY mechanic	Difficult, suitable for experienced DIY mechanic	Very difficult, suitable for expert DIY or professional

Specifications

Torque wrench settings	Nm	lbf ft
Crossbrace bolts	78	58
Seat belt mounting bolts	60	44
Seat mounting bolts	44	32

1 General information

The bodyshell is made of pressed-steel with an aluminium bonnet. Most components are welded together, but some use is made of structural adhesives.

The door and some other vulnerable panels are made of zinc-coated metal, and are further protected by being coated with an anti-chip primer before being sprayed.

Extensive use is made of plastic materials, mainly in the interior, but also in exterior components. The front and rear bumpers are injection-moulded from a synthetic material that is very strong and yet light.

2 Maintenance – bodywork and underframe

1 The condition of a vehicle's bodywork is the one thing that significantly affects its value. Maintenance is easy, but needs to be regular. Neglect, particularly after minor damage, can lead quickly to further deterioration and costly repair bills. It is important also to keep watch on those parts of the vehicle not immediately visible, for instance the underside, inside all the wheel arches, and the lower part of the engine compartment.

2 The basic maintenance routine for the bodywork is washing – preferably with a lot of water, from a hose. This will remove all the loose solids which may have stuck to the vehicle. It is important to flush these off in such a way as to prevent grit from scratching the finish. The wheel arches and underframe need washing in the same way, to remove any accumulated mud which will retain moisture and tend to encourage rust. Oddly enough, the best time to clean the underframe and wheel arches is in wet weather, when the mud is thoroughly wet and soft. In very wet weather, the underframe is usually cleaned of large accumulations automatically, and this is a good time for inspection.

3 Periodically, except on vehicles with a wax-based underbody protective coating, it is a good idea to have the whole of the underframe of the vehicle steam-cleaned, engine compartment included, so that a

thorough inspection can be carried out to see what minor repairs and renovations are necessary. Steam cleaning is available at many garages, and is necessary for the removal of the accumulation of oily grime, which sometimes is allowed to become thick in certain areas. If steam-cleaning facilities are not available, there are some excellent grease solvents available which can be brush-applied; the dirt can then be simply hosed off. Note that these methods should not be used on vehicles with wax-based underbody protective coating, or the coating will be removed. Such vehicles should be inspected annually, preferably just before Winter, when the underbody should be washed down, and repair any damage to the wax coating. Ideally, a completely fresh coat should be applied. It would also be worth considering the use of such wax-based protection for injection into door panels, sills, box sections, etc, as an additional safeguard against rust damage, where such protection is not provided by the vehicle manufacturer.

4 After washing paintwork, wipe off with a chamois leather to give an unspotted clear finish. A coat of clear protective wax polish will give added protection against chemical pollutants in the air. If the paintwork sheen has dulled or oxidised, use a cleaner/polisher combination to restore the brilliance of the shine. This requires a little effort, but such dulling is usually caused because regular washing has been neglected. Care needs to be taken with metallic paintwork, as special non-abrasive cleaner/polisher is required to avoid damage to the finish. Always check that the door and ventilator opening drain holes and pipes are completely clear, so that water can be drained out. Brightwork should be treated in the same way as paintwork. Windscreens and windows can be kept clear of the smeary film which often appears, by proprietary glass cleaner. Never use any form of wax or other body or chromium polish on glass.

3 Maintenance – upholstery and carpets

Mats and carpets should be brushed or vacuum-cleaned regularly, to keep them free of grit. If they are badly stained, remove them from the vehicle for scrubbing or sponging, and make quite sure they are dry before refitting. Seats and interior trim panels can be kept clean by wiping with a damp cloth and a proprietary brand of cleaner. If they do become stained (which can be more apparent on light-coloured upholstery), use a little liquid detergent and a soft nail brush to scour the grime out of the grain of the material. Do not forget to keep the headlining clean in the same way as the upholstery. When using liquid cleaners inside the vehicle, do not over-wet the surfaces being cleaned. Excessive damp

could get into the seams and padded interior, causing stains, offensive odours or even rot. If the inside of the vehicle gets wet accidentally, it is worthwhile taking some trouble to dry it out properly, particularly where carpets are involved. *Do not leave oil or electric heaters inside the vehicle for this purpose.*

4 Minor body damage – repair

Minor scratches

1 If the scratch is very superficial, and does not penetrate to the metal of the bodywork, repair is very simple. Lightly rub the area of the scratch with a paintwork renovator or a very fine cutting paste to remove loose paint from the scratch, and to clear the surrounding bodywork of wax polish. Rinse the area with clean water.

2 Apply touch-up paint to the scratch using a fine paint brush; continue to apply fine layers of paint until the surface of the paint in the scratch is level with the surrounding paintwork. Allow the new paint at least two weeks to harden, then blend it into the surrounding paintwork by rubbing the scratch area with a paintwork renovator or a very fine cutting paste. Finally, apply wax polish.

3 Where the scratch has penetrated right through to the metal of the bodywork, causing the metal to rust, a different repair technique is required. Remove any loose rust from the bottom of the scratch with a penknife, then apply rust-inhibiting paint to prevent the formation of rust in the future. Using a rubber or nylon applicator, fill the scratch with bodystopper paste. If required, this paste can be mixed with cellulose thinners to provide a very thin paste which is ideal for filling narrow scratches. Before the stopper-paste in the scratch hardens, wrap a piece of smooth cotton rag around the top of a finger. Dip the finger in cellulose thinners, and quickly sweep it across the surface of the stopper-paste in the scratch; this will ensure that the surface of the stopper-paste is slightly hollowed. The scratch can now be painted over as described earlier in this Section.

Dents

4 When deep denting of the vehicle's bodywork has taken place, the first task is to pull the dent out, until the affected bodywork almost attains its original shape. There is little point in trying to restore the original shape completely, as the metal in the damaged area will have stretched on impact, and cannot be reshaped fully to its original contour. It is better to bring the level of the dent up to a point which is about 3 mm below the level of the surrounding bodywork. In cases where the dent is very shallow anyway, it is not worth trying to pull it out at all. If the underside of the dent is accessible, it can be hammered

out gently from behind, using a mallet with a wooden or plastic head. Whilst doing this, hold a suitable block of wood firmly against the outside of the panel, to absorb the impact from the hammer blows and thus prevent a large area of the bodywork from being 'belled-out'.

5 Should the dent be in a section of the bodywork which has a double skin, or some other factor making it inaccessible from behind, a different technique is called for. Drill several small holes through the metal inside the area – particularly in the deeper section. Then screw long self-tapping screws into the holes, just sufficiently for them to gain a good purchase in the metal. Now the dent can be pulled out by pulling on the protruding heads of the screws with a pair of pliers.

6 The next stage of the repair is the removal of the paint from the damaged area, and from an inch or so of the surrounding 'sound' bodywork. This is accomplished most easily by using a wire brush or abrasive pad on a power drill, although it can be done just as effectively by hand, using sheets of abrasive paper. To complete the preparation for filling, score the surface of the bare metal with a screwdriver or the tang of a file, or alternatively, drill small holes in the affected area. This will provide a good 'key' for the filler paste.

7 To complete the repair, see the Section on filling and respraying.

Rust holes or gashes

8 Remove all paint from the affected area, and from an inch or so of the surrounding 'sound' bodywork, using an abrasive pad or a wire brush on a power drill. If these are not available, a few sheets of abrasive paper will do the job most effectively. With the paint removed, you will be able to judge the severity of the corrosion, and therefore decide whether to renew the whole panel (if this is possible) or to repair the affected area. New body panels are not as expensive as most people think, and it is often quicker and more satisfactory to fit a new panel than to attempt to repair large areas of corrosion.

9 Remove all fittings from the affected area, except those which will act as a guide to the original shape of the damaged bodywork (eg, headlamp shells, etc). Then, using tin snips or a hacksaw blade, remove all loose metal and any metal badly affected by corrosion. Hammer the edges of the hole inwards, to create a slight depression for the filler paste.

10 Wire-brush the affected area to remove the powdery rust from the surface of the remaining metal. Paint the affected area with rust-inhibiting paint; if the back of the rusted area is accessible, treat this also.

11 Before filling can take place, it will be necessary to block the hole in some way. This can be achieved with aluminium or plastic mesh, or aluminium tape.

12 Aluminium or plastic mesh, or glass-fibre matting, is probably the best material to use for a large hole. Cut a piece to the approximate size and shape of the hole to be filled, then position it in the hole so that its edges are below the level of the surrounding bodywork. It can be retained in position by several blobs of filler paste around its periphery.

13 Aluminium tape should be used for small or very narrow holes. Pull a piece off the roll, trim it to the approximate size and shape required, then pull off the backing paper (if used) and stick the tape over the hole; it can be overlapped if the thickness of one piece is insufficient. Burnish down the edges of the tape with the handle of a screwdriver or similar, to ensure that the tape is securely attached to the metal underneath.

Filling and respraying

14 Before using this Section, see the Sections on dent, deep scratch, rust holes and gash repairs.

15 Many types of bodyfiller are available, but generally speaking, those proprietary kits which contain a tin of filler paste and a tube of resin hardener are best for this type of repair which can be used directly from the tube. A wide, flexible plastic or nylon applicator will be found invaluable for imparting a smooth and well-contoured finish to the surface of the filler.

16 Mix up a little filler on a clean piece of card or board – measure the hardener carefully (follow the maker's instructions on the pack), otherwise the filler will set too rapidly or too slowly. Using the applicator, apply the filler paste to the prepared area; draw the applicator across the surface of the filler to achieve the correct contour and to level the surface. When a contour that approximates to the correct one is achieved, stop working the paste – if you carry on too long, the paste will become sticky and begin to 'pick-up' on the applicator. Continue to add thin layers of filler paste at 20-minute intervals, until the level of the filler is just proud of the surrounding bodywork.

17 Once the filler has hardened, the excess can be removed using a metal plane or file. From then on, progressively-finer grades of abrasive paper should be used, starting with a 40-grade production paper, and finishing with a 400-grade wet-and-dry paper. Always wrap the abrasive paper around a flat rubber, cork, or wooden block – otherwise the surface of the filler will not be completely flat. During the smoothing of the filler surface, the wet-and-dry paper should be periodically rinsed in water. This will ensure that a very smooth finish is imparted to the filler at the final stage.

18 At this stage, the 'dent' should be surrounded by a ring of bare metal, which in turn should be encircled by the finely 'feathered' edge of the good paintwork. Rinse the repair area with clean water, until all the dust produced by the rubbing-down operation has gone.

19 Spray the whole area with a light coat of primer – this will show up any imperfections in the surface of the filler. Repair these

imperfections with fresh filler paste or bodystopper, and again smooth the surface with abrasive paper. If bodystopper is used, it can be mixed with cellulose thinners, to form a thin paste which is ideal for filling small holes. Repeat this spray-and-repair procedure until you are satisfied that the surface of the filler, and the feathered edge of the paintwork, are perfect. Clean the repair area with clean water, and allow to dry fully.

20 The repair area is now ready for final spraying. Paint spraying must be carried out in a warm, dry, windless and dust-free atmosphere. This condition can be created artificially if you have access to a large indoor working area, but if you are forced to work in the open, you will have to pick your day very carefully. If you are working indoors, dousing the floor in the work area with water will help to settle the dust which would otherwise be in the atmosphere. If the repair area is confined to one body panel, mask off the surrounding panels; this will help to minimise the effects of a slight mis-match in paint colours. Bodywork fittings (eg chrome strips, door handles etc) will also need to be masked off. Use genuine masking tape, and several thickness of newspaper, for the masking operations.

21 Before starting to spray, agitate the aerosol can thoroughly, then spray a test area (an old tin, or similar) until the technique is mastered. Cover the repair area with a thick coat of primer; the thickness should be built up using several thin layers of paint, rather than one thick one. Using 400 grade wet-and-dry paper, rub down the surface of the primer until it is smooth. While doing this, the work area should be thoroughly doused with water, and the wet-and-dry paper periodically rinsed in water. Allow to dry before spraying on more paint.

22 Spray on the top coat, again building up the thickness by using several thin layers of paint. Start spraying at the top of the repair area, and then, using a side to side motion, work downwards until the whole repair area and about 2 inches of the surrounding original paintwork is covered. Remove all masking material 10 to 15 minutes after spraying on the final coat of paint.

23 Allow the new paint at least two weeks to harden, then, using a paintwork renovator or a very fine cutting paste, blend the edges of the paint into the existing paintwork. Finally, apply wax polish.

Plastic components

24 With the use of more and more plastic body components by the vehicle manufacturers (eg, bumpers. spoilers, and in some cases major body panels), rectification of more serious damage to such items has become a matter of either entrusting repair work to a specialist in this field, or renewing complete components. Repair of such damage by the DIY owner is not feasible, owing to the cost of the equipment and materials required for effecting such repairs. The basic technique

involves making a groove along the line of the crack in the plastic, using a rotary burr in a power drill. The damaged part is then welded back together, using a hot air gun to heat up and fuse a plastic filler rod into the groove. Any excess plastic is then removed, and the area rubbed down to a smooth finish. It is important that a filler rod of the correct plastic is used, as body components can be made of different types (eg, polycarbonate, ABS, polypropylene).

25 Damage of a less serious nature (abrasions, minor cracks etc) can be repaired by the DIY owner using a two-part epoxy filler repair material which can be used directly from the tube. Once mixed in equal proportions, this is used in similar fashion to the bodywork filler used on metal panels. The filler is usually cured in twenty to thirty minutes, ready for sanding and painting.

26 If the owner is renewing a complete component himself, or if he has repaired it with epoxy filler, he will be left with the problem of finding a suitable paint for finishing which is compatible with the type of plastic used. At one time, the use of a universal paint was not possible, owing to the complex range of plastics met with in body component applications. Standard paints, generally speaking, will not bond to plastic or rubber satisfactorily, but professional matched paints, to match any plastic or rubber finish, can be obtained from some dealers. However, it is now possible to obtain a plastic body parts finishing kit which consists of a pre-primer treatment, a primer and coloured top coat. Full instructions are normally supplied with a kit, but basically the method of use is to first apply the pre-primer to the component concerned, and allow it to dry for up to 30 minutes. Then the primer is applied, and left to dry for about an hour before finally applying the special-coloured top coat. The result is a correctly coloured component, where the paint will flex with the plastic or rubber, a property that standard paint does not normally possess.

---

5 Major body damage – repair

Where serious damage has occurred, or large areas need renewal due to neglect, it means that complete new panels will need welding-in, and this is best left to professionals. If the damage is due to impact, it will also be necessary to check completely the alignment of the bodyshell, and this can only be carried out accurately by a Mazda dealer or specialist using jigs. If the body is left misaligned, it is primarily dangerous, as the car will not handle properly, and secondly, uneven stresses will be imposed on the steering, suspension and possibly transmission, causing abnormal wear, or complete failure, particularly to such items as the tyres.

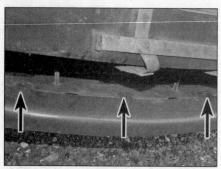

6.5 Clip locations (arrowed) at the lower edge of the air intake aperture

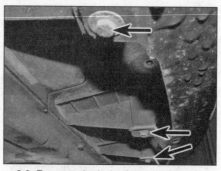

6.6 Remove the bolts (arrowed) at the lower edge of the bumper

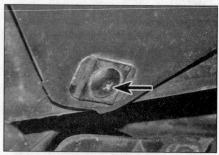

6.7 Undo the screws (arrowed) and prise out the fasteners at the upper edge of the air intake aperture

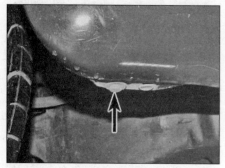

6.8a Lower support strap retaining bolt (arrowed)

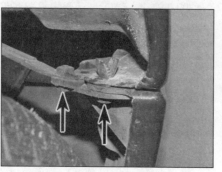

6.8b Upper support strap bolt, and bumper-to-wing bolt (arrowed)

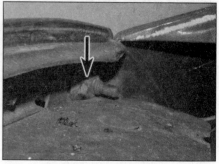

6.9 Undo the nut (arrowed) each side, just in front of the headlight

6 Front bumper – removal and refitting

Removal

1997 and earlier models

1 Raise the headlights. Apply the handbrake, raise the vehicle and support it securely on axle stands (see *Jacking and vehicle support*). Remove the engine undershield (where fitted), and open the bonnet.
2 Disconnect the battery negative lead as described in Chapter 5A, Section 4.
3 Remove the direction indicator as described in Chapter 12, Section 7.
4 Release the fasteners and remove the panel

(where fitted) at the top of the bumper, in front of the radiator.
5 Prise out the plastic clips (where fitted) at the lower edge of the air intake aperture **(see illustration)**.
6 Remove the lower bolts that secure the front bumper to the reinforcement **(see illustration)**.
7 Along the upper edge of the air intake opening, remove the bumper screws and the number plate bracket bolts or fasteners (as applicable) **(see illustration)**.
8 Under each side of the vehicle, undo the bolts/nuts, detach the support straps and the bolt securing the bumper to the wing **(see illustrations)**.
9 Remove the bumper-to-wing nut on each side and withdraw the bumper **(see illustration)**.

1998-on models

10 Undo the centre screws, lever out the 3 plastic expansion rivets each side securing the bumper in the wheel arch area, then pull the wheel arch liner away a little, and remove the screw securing the bumper to the wing **(see illustrations)**.
11 Undo the screws each side on the underside of the bumper **(see illustration)**.
12 Undo the 4 bolts on the top edge of the bumper **(see illustration)**.
13 Undo the screws and prise out the 2 plastic expansion rivets in the radiator inlet aperture **(see illustration)**.
14 Prise out the 3 plastic clips in the lower part of the radiator inlet aperture **(see illustration)**.
15 With the help of an assistant, pull the

6.10a Undo the centre screws and remove the plastic expansion rivets (arrowed)

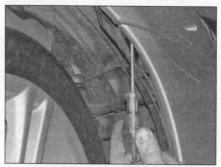

6.10b Undo the screw securing the bumper to the wing each side

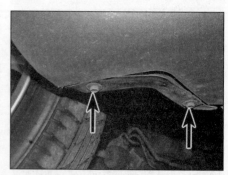

6.11 Remove the screws on the underside of the bumper each side (arrowed)

6.12 Bumper upper retaining bolts (arrowed)

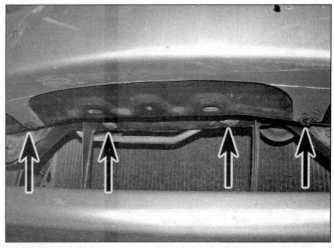

6.13 Undo the screws and remove the plastic expansion rivets (arrowed)

rear edges of the bumper outwards a little to release the retaining clips, and manoeuvre the bumper forwards from place. Disconnect any wiring plugs as the bumper is withdrawn **(see illustration)**.

Refitting

16 Refitting is a reversal of removal.

| 7 | **Rear bumper –** removal and refitting |

Removal

1997 and earlier models

1 Apply the handbrake, raise the vehicle and support it securely on axle stands (see *Jacking and vehicle support*).

2 Under the vehicle, remove the fasteners securing the bumper to the wheel arch liner and wing each side **(see illustration)**. Soak the bumper fasteners is releasing spray prior to removal.

3 Remove the fasteners on the underside of the bumper each side **(see illustration)**.

4 Undo the bumper mounting nuts **(see illustration)**, and with the help of an assistant, manoeuvre the bumper rearwards.

5 Refitting is the reversal of removal.

1998-on models

6 Remove the rear lights as described in Chapter 12, Section 7.

7 Undo the screws/scrivets, and remove the mudguard each side **(see illustrations)**.

8 Remove the scrivet, pull away the wheel arch liner, then undo the screw(s) each side in the wheel arch area **(see illustration)**.

9 Remove the number plate, then undo the screw each side of the number plate area **(see illustration)**.

10 Undo the screws and prise out the 2 scrivets on the underside of the bumper **(see illustration)**.

6.14 Prise out the clips in the lower part of the radiator inlet aperture

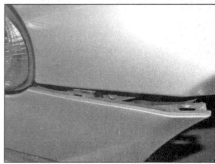

6.15 Pull the rear edges outwards a little

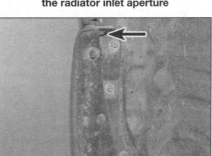

7.2 Undo the bumper-to-wheel arch liner screws, then the screw (arrowed) securing the bumper to the wing

7.3 Remove the screw each side (arrowed) on the bumper underside

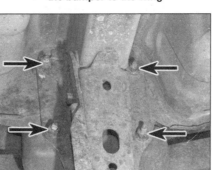

7.4 The bumper is secured to the vehicle by 4 nuts (arrowed) each side

7.7a Remove the fasteners in the wheel arch area (arrowed) ...

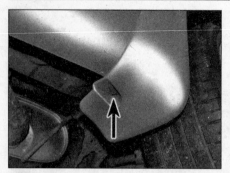

7.7b ... the screw underneath (arrowed) ...

7.7c ... and remove the mudguard each side

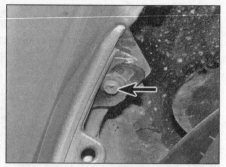

7.8 Undo the screw securing the bumper to the rear wing each side (arrowed)

7.9 Undo the screws in the number plate area

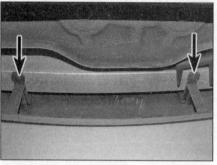

7.10 Undo the centre screw, and prise out the scrivet underneath the bumper (arrowed)

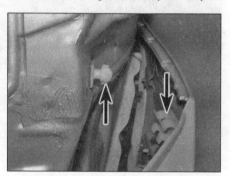

7.11 Pull the front edge outwards to release the clips (arrowed)

11 Pull the front edges of the bumper outwards a little to release the clips, then with the help of an assistant, manoeuvre the bumper rearwards **(see illustration)**. Disconnect any wiring plugs as the bumper is withdrawn.

Refitting

12 Refitting is a reverse of the removal procedure ensuring that the bumper ends are correctly positioned.

8 Bonnet –
removal, refitting and adjustment

Removal and refitting

1 Make alignment marks around the hinges to ensure proper alignment during refitting.

2 Disconnect the windscreen washer tube **(see illustration)**.
3 Have an assistant support the bonnet, then undo the hinge-to-bonnet nuts and remove it from the vehicle **(see illustration)**.
4 Refitting is the reverse of removal.

Adjustment

5 Fore-and-aft and side-to-side adjustment of the bonnet is achieved by moving the hinge plate slot after slackening the nuts.
6 Make alignment marks around the entire hinge plate so you can judge the amount of movement.
7 Slacken the nuts and move the bonnet into correct alignment. Move it only a little at a time. Tighten the hinge bolts and carefully lower the bonnet to check the position.

8 If necessary after installation, the entire bonnet lock assembly can be adjusted up-and-down as well as from side-to-side on the radiator support so the bonnet closes securely, and is flush with the wings. To make the adjustment, scribe or felt tip mark a line around the bonnet lock mounting bolts to aid alignment when refitting, then loosen the bolts and reposition the lock assembly to align with the striker on the bonnet, as necessary **(see illustration)**. Following adjustment, retighten the mounting bolts. On later models, the bonnet height can be adjusted by rotating the rubber buffers at the front corners.
9 The bonnet lock assembly, as well as the hinges, should be periodically lubricated with white lithium-base grease to prevent binding and wear.

8.2 Disconnect the washer tube (arrowed)

8.3 Undo the bonnet-to-hinge nuts

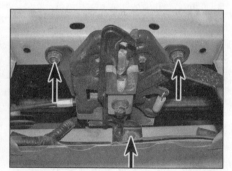

8.8 Bonnet lock mounting bolts (arrowed)

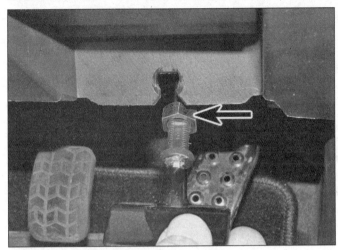

9.6 Slacken the locknut, rotate the release handle slightly, and lower it from the facia

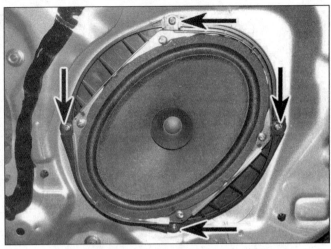

10.4 Speaker retaining screws (arrowed)

9 Bonnet lock and release cable – removal and refitting

Lock

1 Make a mark around the lock to aid alignment when refitting, then remove the bonnet lock mounting bolts **(see illustration 8.8)**. Remove the lock.
2 Disconnect the bonnet release cable by removing the cable retaining clip near the bonnet lock and disengaging the cable from the lock assembly.
3 Refitting is the reverse of removal. **Note:** *Adjust the lock so the bonnet engages securely when closed and the bonnet buffers are slightly compressed.*

Cable

4 Disconnect the bonnet release cable from the lock as described previously.
5 Attach a piece of thin wire or string to the end of the cable and unfasten all remaining cable retaining clips.
6 Slacken the locknut and detach the bonnet release lever from the trim panel below the steering column **(see illustration)**.
7 Pull the cable and grommet rearward into the passenger compartment until you can see

10.7 Door check strap pin (arrowed)

the wire or string. Ensure that the new cable has a grommet attached, then remove the old cable from the wire or string and replace it with the new cable.
8 Working in the engine compartment, pull the wire or string back through the bulkhead, pulling the cable with it.
9 The remainder of refitting is a reversal of removal. **Note:** *Push the cable grommet with your fingers from inside the passenger compartment to seat the grommet into the bulkhead correctly.*

10 Door – removal, refitting and adjustment

Removal and refitting

1 Lower the window completely then disconnect the battery negative lead as described in Chapter 5A, Section 4.
2 Open the door all the way and support it on jacks or blocks covered with rags to prevent damaging the paint.
3 Remove the door trim panel and weatherproof membrane as described in Section 11.
4 Remove the door speaker **(see illustration)**.
5 Label them to aid refitting, then unplug all electrical connectors, and release the wiring harnesses from the door.
6 Working through the door speaker hole and the door opening, detach the rubber conduit between the body and the door. Then pull the wiring harness through the conduit and remove it from the door.
7 Pull out the pin out of the door check strap **(see illustration)**. Remove the nuts and detach the check strap from the door.
8 Mark around the door hinges and hinge bolts to aid alignment when refitting **(see illustration)**.
9 Remove the hinge-to-door bolts and carefully withdraw the door.
10 Refitting is the reverse of removal. Adjust

and securely tighten the door hinge bolts and striker bolts, if removed, as described below.

Adjustment

11 Following refitting, locate the alignment marks made during door removal. Make sure the door is aligned properly and adjust it if necessary as follows:
a) *Up-and-down and forward-and-backward adjustments are made by loosening the hinge-to-body bolts and moving the door, as necessary. A special offset tool may be required to reach some of the bolts.*
b) *In-and-out and up-and-down adjustments are made by loosening the door side hinge bolts and moving the door, as necessary. A special offset tool may be required to reach some of the bolts.*
c) *The door lock striker can also be adjusted both up-and-down and sideways to provide a positive engagement with the locking mechanism. This is done by loosening the screws and moving the striker by hand or by lightly tapping with a soft-faced hammer, as necessary.*
d) *Check the alignment of the wedge attached to the lower part of the doorjamb with the dovetail in the door. Adjust if necessary by loosening the wedge screws and moving the wedge up or down.*

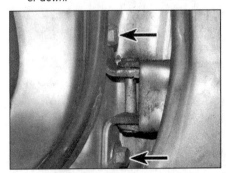

10.8 Door hinge bolts (arrowed)

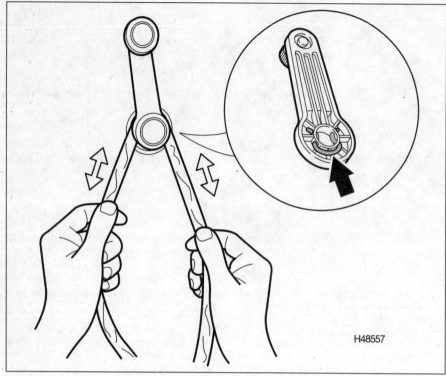

11.1 Release the winder handle clip with a cloth

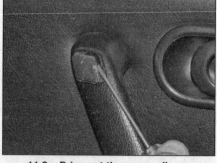

11.2a Prise out the upper clip ...

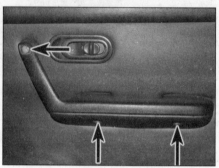

11.2b ... then undo the armrest screws (arrowed)

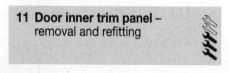

11 Door inner trim panel – removal and refitting

Removal

1997 and earlier models

1 On manual window models, remove the window winder handle by working a cloth back-and-forth behind the handle to dislodge the retaining clip **(see illustration)**. A special tool is available for this purpose, but it is not essential. With the retaining clip removed, pull off the handle.

2 Prise the trim cap from the upper armrest screw, then remove the screws and armrest **(see illustrations)**.

3 Remove the screw from the interior door handle cover **(see illustration)**.

4 Lift up the interior door handle and remove the trim cover.

5 Use a flat-bladed blunt tool between the speaker cover and door, and prise the cover from place. Use the same method to remove the door trim panel. Work around the outer edge to release the retaining clips **(see illustrations)**.

6 Make sure all of the door trim retaining clips are disengaged. Remove the door trim panel from the vehicle by gently pulling it upwards and out, while disconnecting any electrical connectors.

7 For access to inside the door, remove the plastic weatherproof membrane. Peel back the membrane, taking care not to tear it. To remove the weatherproof membrane completely, you'll need to remove the inside handle and peel back the separate handle weatherproof membrane **(see illustration)**.

1998-on models

8 On manual window models, remove the window winder handle by working a cloth back-and-forth behind the handle to dislodge the retaining clip **(see illustration 11.1)**. A special tool is available for this purpose, but it is not essential. With the retaining clip removed, pull off the handle.

9 Undo the screw and remove the interior release handle cover **(see illustrations)**.

10 Prise up the centre pins, then lever out the plastic expansion rivets at the rear and front edges of the panel **(see illustrations)**.

11 Undo the screw(s) securing the pull handle **(see illustrations)**.

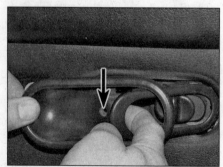

11.3 Undo the screw (arrowed), pull the handle, and slide the cover forwards

11.5a Prise the speaker cover from place

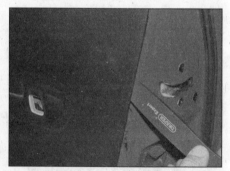

11.5b Use a blunt, flat-bladed tool to prise between the trim panel and door, and release the clips

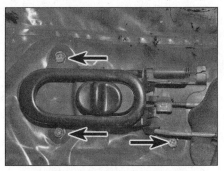

11.7 Undo the screws (arrowed) and detach the interior release handle

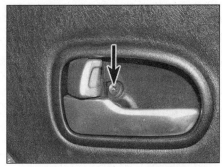

11.9a Undo the screw (arrowed) ...

11.9b ... and remove the cover

11.10a Prise up the centre pin and remove the plastic rivet at the front edge of the panel ...

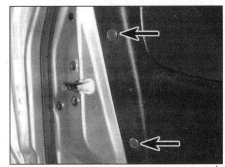

11.10b ... and the 2 (arrowed) at the rear

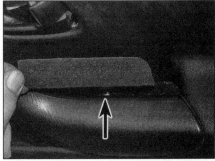

11.11a On some models, lift out the mat to access the lower armrest screw (arrowed)

12 Use a flat-bladed blunt tool between the door trim panel and door to disengage the door trim retaining clips. Work around the outer edge until the panel is released **(see illustration 11.5b)**.

13 Make sure all of the door trim retaining clips are disengaged. Remove the door trim panel from the vehicle by gently pulling it upwards and out, while disconnecting any electrical connectors.

14 For access to the interior of the door, remove the plastic weatherproof membrane.

Undo the screw and remove the interior release handle, then peel back the membrane, taking care not to tear it. If required, remove the polystyrene block, turn the handle over and disconnect the cables/rods **(see illustrations)**.

11.11b Undo the upper armrest screw

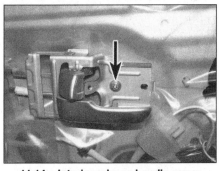

11.14a Interior release handle screw (arrowed)

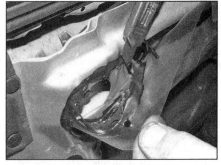

11.14b Use a sharp knife to cut through the membrane sealant

11.14c Where fitted, undo the screws and remove the polystyrene block

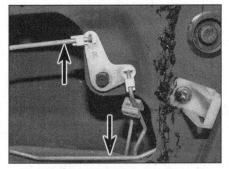

11.14d Disconnect the operating rods (arrowed) ...

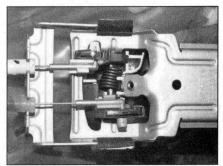

11.14e ... or cables (as applicable)

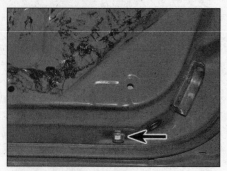

12.3a Undo the nut (arrowed) at the base of the window rear guide ...

12.3b ... and the nut at the top

12.4a Pull the clip (arrowed) to release the exterior handle control rod

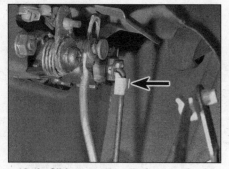

12.4b Slide away the clip (arrowed) and disconnect the lock cylinder rod

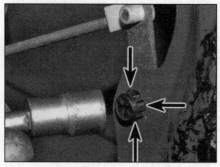

12.5 Use a suitable socket to compress the pivot clips (arrowed)

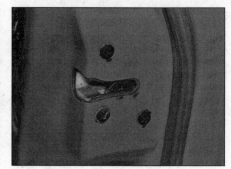

12.6 Lock retaining screws

Refitting

15 To refit the door trim panel, first press the weatherproof membrane back into place. If necessary, add more sealant to hold it in place. Refit the interior release handle and polystyrene block if it was removed.

16 Prior to refitting the door trim panel, be sure to refit any clips which may have come out of the door trim panel during removal.

17 Place the door trim panel in position, making sure that any door panel electrical connectors are connected or routed through the panel as necessary. Press the door trim panel into place until the clips are seated.

18 The remainder of refitting is the reverse of the removal steps. If the vehicle has manual windows, place the clip on the window winder handle, then push the handle onto the shaft until the clip engages.

12 Door handle and lock components – removal and refitting

Door lock

1 Remove the door trim panel and the weatherproof membrane as described in Section 11.

1997 and earlier models

2 Remove the window glass as described in Section 13.

3 Undo the 2 nuts and remove the window glass rear guide **(see illustrations)**.

4 Disconnect the exterior handle control rod from the lock, and the lock cylinder rod from the cylinder lever **(see illustrations)**.

5 Squeeze together the clips and detach the interior handle pivot bracket from the door **(see illustration)**.

6 Remove the lock retaining screws from the end of the door, and manoeuvre the lock from place **(see illustration)**.

1998-on models

7 Remove the window glass as described in Section 13.

8 Undo the 2 nuts and remove the window glass rear guide **(see illustrations 12.3a and 12.3b)**.

9 Note their fitted positions, then undo the 2 nuts and remove the polystyrene pads from the door frame (where fitted) **(see illustration)**.

10 Reach inside the door, undo the nut, prise up the centre pin, lever out the expansion rivet and remove the plastic cover (where fitted) over the exterior handle **(see illustrations)**.

12.9 Undo the nuts (arrowed) and remove the polystyrene pads

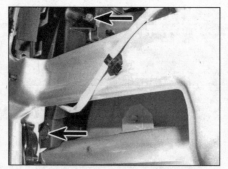

12.10a Undo the nut, remove the expansion rivet (arrowed) ...

12.10b ... and manoeuvre the plastic cover from place

12.11 Rotate the clips (arrowed) and disconnect the control rods

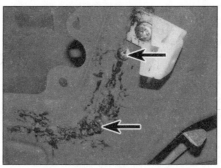

12.12 Lock motor screws (arrowed) – 1998 and 1999 models

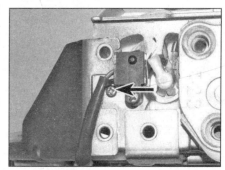

12.14a Undo the screw (arrowed) ...

12.14b ... and remove the plastic cover ...

12.14c ... to access the control cables

12.14d Lock control rods (arrowed)

11 Release the clips and disconnect the control rods from the lock cylinder and exterior handle **(see illustration)**.

12 On models from 1998 to 1999, undo the 2 screws securing the lock motor to the door **(see illustration)**.

13 On all models, remove the lock retaining screws from the end of the door, and manoeuvre the lock from place **(see illustration 12.6)**. Disconnect any wiring plugs as the lock is withdrawn.

14 If required, undo the screw, remove the plastic cover (where fitted), then disconnect the control cables/rods from the lock **(see illustrations)**.

All models

15 Refitting is a reversal of removal.

Exterior handle

16 Remove the door trim panel and the weatherproof membrane as described in Section 11.

1997 and earlier models

17 Remove the window glass as described in Section 13. Undo the 2 nuts and remove the window glass rear guide **(see illustrations 12.3a and 12.3b)**. Disconnect the exterior handle control rod from the lock, and the lock cylinder rod from the cylinder lever **(see illustrations 12.4a and 12.4b)**.

18 Undo the retaining nuts and manoeuvre the exterior handle assembly from the door **(see illustration)**.

19 If required, prise out the clip and slide the lock cylinder from the exterior handle assembly **(see illustrations)**.

1998-on models

20 Remove the window glass as described in Section 13.

21 Undo the 2 nuts and remove the window glass rear guide **(see illustrations 12.3a and 12.3b)**.

22 Undo the 2 nuts and remove the 2 polystyrene pads from the door frame (where fitted) **(see illustration 12.9)**.

23 Reach inside the door, undo the nut, prise up the centre pin, lever out the expansion rivet and remove the plastic cover (where fitted) over the exterior handle **(see illustrations 12.10a and 12.10b)**.

24 Release the clips and disconnect the control rods from the lock cylinder and exterior handle **(see illustration 12.11)**.

25 Prise out the grommet, then working through the door access hole, remove

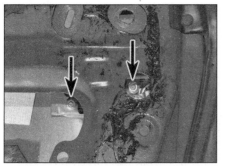

12.18 Exterior handle retaining nuts (arrowed)

12.19a Prise out the clip ...

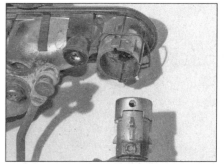

12.19b ... and remove the lock cylinder

12.25a Prise out the grommet ...

12.25b ... to access the handle retaining nut (arrowed)

12.26a Release the clip each side and remove the switch

12.26b The centre of the switch aligns with the end of the lock barrel

12.27 Lock cylinder retaining clip (arrowed)

All models

28 Refitting is a reversal of removal.

Interior release handle

29 Refer to Section 11 for removal and refitting.

13 Door window glass – removal, refitting and adjustment

Removal and refitting

1 Open the window to approximately 190 mm (1997 and earlier models) or 225 mm (1998-on models) from the fully open position.
2 Remove the door trim panel and weatherproof membrane as described in Section 11.

1997 and earlier

3 Prise out the clip at each end and remove the exterior weatherstrip from the top edge of the door (see illustrations).

All models

4 Note their fitted positions, then undo the bolts and remove the glass 'stops' from the door (see illustrations).
5 Undo the 3 screws securing the glass to the regulator (see illustration).
6 Manoeuvre the glass upwards and out of the door (see illustration).
7 Refitting is the reverse of removal.

the exterior handle retaining nut (see illustrations). Manoeuvre the exterior handle from the door.
26 If required, unclip the switch (where fitted) from the lock cylinder (see illustrations). Note

how the centre of the switch aligns with the end of the lock barrel.
27 Use a pliers or screwdriver to prise the retaining clip, and slide the barrel from place (see illustration).

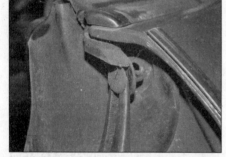

13.3a Prise out the clip at the rear ...

13.3b ... the clip at the front ...

13.3c ... and remove the exterior weatherstrip

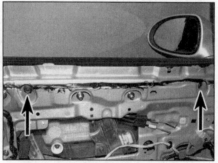

13.4a Undo the bolts (arrowed) ...

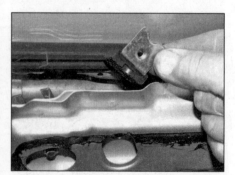

13.4b ... and remove the window 'stops'

Adjustment

8 Window glass vertical adjustment is by means of the upper stoppers mounted in the door frame (1997 and earlier models) or the lower edge of the glass (1998-on). Loosen the stopper screws, position and hold the glass fully closed in the door frame, and lightly tighten the adjustment screws. Slowly lower the window, checking for smooth travel. Adjust vertically and horizontally to obtain full closure with smooth travel as the window is wound up and down.

9 Window glass in-and-out adjustment is done by moving the lower ends of the rear channel and regulator in or out. To do this, loosen the channel and regulator nuts in the bottom of the door. Move the channel and regulator in or out as necessary to obtain correct alignment of the glass when the window is closed, then tighten the nuts.

14 Door window regulator – removal and refitting

1 Remove the door window glass as described in Section 13.

2 Make alignment marks around the lower nuts/bolts, pull out the rubber insert from the channel, then undo the nuts/bolts and remove the front window guide channel **(see illustrations)**.

3 Make alignment marks around the regulator mounting bolts/nuts to aid refitting.

4 On models with electric windows,

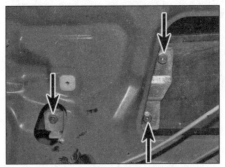

13.5 Window glass securing screws (arrowed)

disconnect the motor wiring plug, and unclip the wiring harness as necessary.

5 Undo the retaining bolts/nuts and manoeuvre the regulator and motor (where fitted) through the door frame access hole **(see illustrations)**. Release the cables from any clips as necessary.

6 Refitting is the reverse of removal. During installation, apply multipurpose grease to the regulator rollers, ensuring they rotate freely.

15 Boot lid – removal, refitting and adjustment

⚠ **Warning: The boot lid is heavy enough to cause injury if the balance spring isn't in position. If you need to remove the balance spring, remove the boot lid first.**

13.6 Manoeuvre the glass from the door

Removal and refitting

1 Disconnect any cables or wire harness connectors attached to the boot lid that would interfere with removal.

2 Make alignment marks around the hinge mounting nuts with a marking pen or paint **(see illustration)**.

3 While an assistant supports the boot lid, remove the lid-to-hinge nuts on both sides and remove it.

4 If you need to remove the balance spring, wrap a screwdriver with tape to protect the paint, then insert it through the end of the balance spring and prise it out of the notch.

5 Refitting is the reverse of removal. **Note:** *When refitting the boot lid, align the hinges with the marks made during removal.*

Adjustment

6 Fore-and-aft and side-to-side adjustment

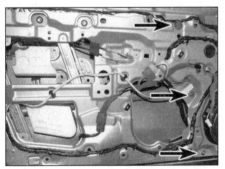

14.2a Front glass guide channel retaining nuts/bolts (arrowed)

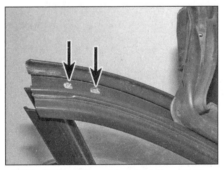

14.2b Pull up the rubber insert, undo the screws (arrowed) …

14.2c … and remove the guide channel

14.5a Undo the nuts underneath …

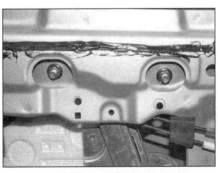

14.5b … at the top …

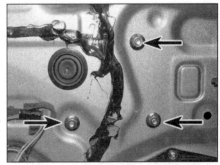

14.5c … and in the centre (arrowed)

15.2 Make alignment marks around the hinge nuts

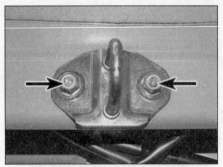

15.9 Boot lid striker bolts (arrowed)

of the boot lid is accomplished by moving the lid in relation to the hinge after loosening the bolts or nuts.

7 Scribe a line around the entire hinge plate as described earlier in this Section so you can determine the amount of movement.

8 Loosen the nuts and move the boot lid into correct alignment. Move it only a little at a time. Tighten the hinge nuts and carefully lower the boot lid to check the alignment.

9 If necessary after refitting, the entire boot lid striker assembly can be adjusted up and down as well as from side to side on the boot lid so the lid closes securely and is flush with the rear quarter panels. To do this, scribe a line around the boot striker assembly to provide a reference point. Then loosen the bolts and reposition the striker as necessary **(see illustration)**. Following adjustment, retighten the mounting bolts.

16 Boot lid lock components – removal and refitting

Boot lid lock

1 Open the boot, prise up the centre pins, lever out the plastic expansion rivets and remove the rear trim panel **(see illustrations)**.

2 Make alignment marks between the lock and the panel, then undo the retaining bolts and remove the lock **(see illustration)**. Disconnect any wiring plugs as the lock is withdrawn.

3 Disconnect the boot release cable or link rod from the lock **(see illustration)**.

4 To remove the striker, unbolt it from the boot lid **(see illustration 15.9)**.

5 Refitting is the reverse of removal. See Section 15 for adjustment procedures.

Boot lock cylinder

6 Open the boot, prise up the centre pins, lever out the plastic expansion rivets and remove the rear trim panel **(see illustrations 16.1a and 16.1b)**.

7 Prise the retaining clip loose from the actuator rod, separate the actuator rod from the lock cylinder, and disconnect the wiring plug (where applicable) **(see illustration)**.

8 On 1997 and earlier models, remove the number plate, then undo the nuts and remove the rear panel exterior trim.

9 On 1998-on models, remove the rear bumper as described in Section 7.

10 On all models, remove the retaining bolts and take the lock cylinder out of the rear body panel **(see illustration)**.

11 Refitting is the reverse of removal.

Boot lid release cable

12 Remove the centre console as described in Section 27.

13 Remove the boot lid lock and disconnect the release cable as previously described in this Section.

14 Undo the screw, and lift out the storage compartment from the left-hand side of the boot **(see illustration)**.

15 Prise up the centre pins, lever out the plastic expansion rivets and remove the left-hand side trim panel from the boot (where fitted).

16 Undo the bolts and remove the panel from

16.1a Prise up the centre pins ...

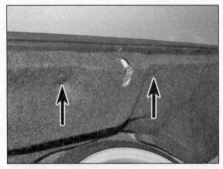

16.1b ... and remove the plastic expansion rivets

16.2 Undo the boot lid lock bolts (arrowed) ...

16.3 ... and disconnect the release cable and/or link rod

16.7 Pivot the clip and disconnect the link rod

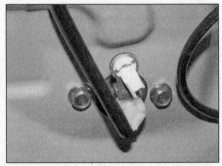

16.10 Undo the bolts and remove the lock cylinder assembly

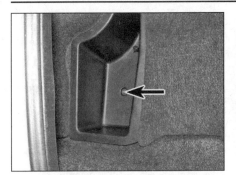

16.14 Undo the screw (arrowed) and lift out the storage compartment

16.16 Remove the panel from the boot (arrowed)

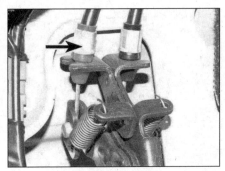

16.17 Pull the boot lid release outer cable (arrowed) from the bracket

the front left-hand corner of the boot (see illustration).

17 Pull the outer cable from the support bracket behind the release lever, and detach the cable end fitting (see illustration).

18 Note the fitted routing of the cable, release any retaining clips along its length.

19 Tie a length of string to the front end of the cable, release the bulkhead sealing grommet, then pull the cable from place. Untie the string, leaving it in place, to assist upon refitting.

20 Tie the string to the cable, and pull the cable into place.

21 The remainder of refitting is a reversal of removal. Check for correct operation of the lock release before closing the boot lid.

17 Central locking components – removal and refitting

Door/boot lock actuators

1998 to 1999 models

1 Remove the door lock assembly as described in Section 12.

2 Disengage the actuator from the control rod (see illustration).

2000-on models

3 The actuators are integral with the door/boot locks. Refer to Section 12.

All models

4 Refitting is the reverse of removal. Prior to refitting any trim panels removed for access thoroughly check the operation of the central locking system.

Door/boot lock timer unit

5 Unlock the doors, then disconnect the battery negative lead as described in Chapter 5A, Section 4. Undo the 2 screws and remove the driver's side lower facia panel (see illustration).

6 Disconnect the wiring plug, then unclip the timer unit from the mounting bracket (see illustration).

7 Refitting is the reverse of removal. Prior to refitting any trim panels removed for access thoroughly check the operation of the central locking system.

Lock cylinder switch

8 Remove the door trim panel and weatherproof membrane as described in Section 11. Disconnect the exterior handle and lock cylinder link rods.

9 Disconnect the switch wiring plug, then unclip the switch from the lock cylinder (see illustration 12.26a).

10 Refitting is the reverse of removal. Prior to refitting any trim panels removed for access thoroughly check the operation of the central locking system.

Keyless entry unit

11 Ensure the doors are unlocked, then disconnect the battery negative lead as described in Chapter 5A, Section 4. Remove the glovebox as described in Section 26.

12 Disconnect the wiring plug, then undo the nut and remove the unit, complete with mounting bracket (see illustration).

17.2 Unhook the lock actuator from the link rod

17.6 The door/boot lock timer unit is in front of the immobiliser unit (arrowed)

13 If required, undo the screw and detach the bracket from the keyless entry unit.

14 Refitting is the reverse of removal. Prior to refitting any trim panels removed for access thoroughly check the operation of the central locking system.

Remote transmitter battery

15 Battery renewal is described in Chapter 1, Section 27.

18 Exterior mirrors – removal and refitting

1997 and earlier models

1 Carefully prise and the plastic trim around the mirror mounting with a blunt, flat-bladed tool to expose the mounting screws (see illustration).

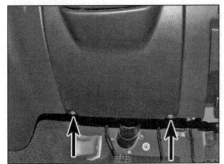

17.5 Undo the screws (arrowed) and remove the lower panel

17.12 Keyless entry unit

18.1 Prise up the plastic trim

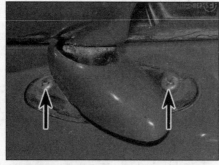

18.2 Mirror mounting screws (arrowed) – 1997 and earlier

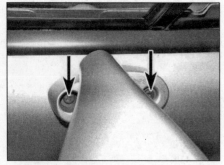

18.6 Twist the mirror to expose the mounting screws (arrowed) – 1998-on

2 Slightly rotate the mirror, then undo the mounting screws **(see illustration)**. Remove the mirror assembly

3 Refitting is a reversal of removal.

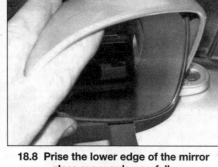

18.8 Prise the lower edge of the mirror glass rearwards carefully

1998-on models

Power mirrors

4 Remove the door main speaker as described in Chapter 12, Section 16.

5 Reach into the door and unplug the mirror wiring connector – clipped to the inside of the door above the main speaker aperture.

All mirrors

6 Rotate the mirror to expose the mounting screws **(see illustration)**. Undo the screws and remove the mirror.

7 Refitting is the reverse of removal.

Mirror glass

8 Push in the top edge of the mirror, then using a flat-bladed tool, carefully prise the lower edge rearwards to release the retaining clip **(see illustration)**. Disconnect any wiring as the mirror is removed.

9 To refit, reconnect any wiring plugs, insert the lower edge of the mirror glass holder (with the mirror) into the frame, then press the upper edge forwards to engage the retaining clips.

19 Windscreen and quarter light glass – removal and refitting

Windscreen

1 These areas of glass are secured by the tight fit of the weatherstrip in the body aperture, and are bonded in position with a special adhesive. Renewal of such fixed glass is a difficult, messy and time-consuming task, which is beyond the scope of the home mechanic. It is difficult, unless one has plenty of practice, to obtain a secure, waterproof fit. Furthermore, the task carries a high risk of breakage; this applies especially to the laminated glass windscreen. In view of this, owners are strongly advised to have this sort of work carried out by one of the many specialist windscreen fitters.

Door quarter glass

2 Remove the door window glass as described in Section 13.

3 Carefully pull the quarter glass and rubber insert rearwards from the front frame, then separate the glass from the rubber **(see illustrations)**.

4 Refitting is a reversal of removal.

20 Convertible roof – removal, refitting and adjustment

19.3a Pull the quarter glass and rubber insert rearwards from the frame

19.3b Separate the glass from the rubber insert

Removal and refitting

1 Unzip the rear window on 1997 and earlier models. On all models, pad the rear window on both sides with towels to protect it from scratches, then lower the top.

2 Remove the rear quarter trim each side, as described in Section 26.

3 Prise open the plastic panel and disconnect the aeroboard speakers (where fitted) wiring plug **(see illustration)**.

4 Remove the rear parcel shelf as described in Section 26.

5 Undo the nuts and remove the roof retaining strips at the lower edges **(see illustrations)**.

20.3 Open the panel and disconnect the aeroboard speakers wiring plug

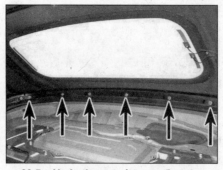

20.5a Undo the nuts (arrowed) at the centre ...

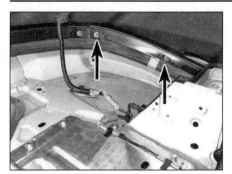

20.5b ... and each side (arrowed)

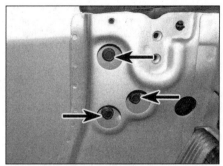

20.8a Undo the mounting bolts each side (arrowed)

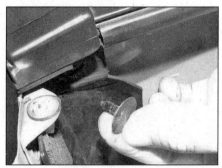

20.8b Prise out the clip at each front corner

6 Disconnect the heated rear window wiring plug (where fitted).

7 Prise up the centre pins, lever out the plastic expansion rivets and remove the plastic trim panel (where fitted) above the hinge each side.

8 Remove the mounting bolts at each front corner, prise out the push-in clip at each front corner, disengage the roof from the mounting studs and moulding lip **(see illustrations)**. With the help of an assistant, lift the top off the vehicle, being careful not to scratch the window.

9 Take the opportunity to clean out the drain holes each side **(see illustration)**.

10 Refitting is the reverse of the removal steps. Ensure the rain rail and moulding lip engages correctly.

Adjustment

11 Lift the cover to expose the top latch adjusting nut **(see illustration)**. Turn the nut clockwise to decrease the clearance between the top and the windscreen header, or anti-clockwise to increase it.

21 Detachable hard top –
removal, refitting and adjustment

Note: *The hard top is heavy and somewhat awkward to remove and refit – enlist the help of an assistant.*

Removal and refitting

1 Fully lower the door windows.

2 Disconnect the heated rear window (where fitted) connector.

3 Lower the sunvisors and release the catches at the top of the windscreen.

4 Release the catch on each side of the top at the lower corner.

5 Hold the forward part of the top with one hand and have an assistant do the same on the other side. Press down on the rear deck catches to free the top from the mounting studs on the rear deck. Move the top back just enough to clear the studs and lift it straight up and off the vehicle.

6 Refitting is the reverse of removal. Make sure the convertible top is lowered all the way before you install the hard top.

Adjustment

7 The side and top catches are adjusted in the same way as the convertible top catches **(see illustration 20.11)**.

8 To adjust the mounting studs on the rear deck, loosen their bolts. Move the plates forward, backward or sideways as needed and tighten the bolts securely.

22 Body exterior fittings –
removal and refitting

Wheel arch liners and body under-panels

1 The various plastic covers fitted to the underside of the vehicle are secured in position by a mixture of screws, nuts and retaining clips and removal will be fairly obvious on inspection. Work methodically around, removing its retaining screws and releasing its retaining clips until the panel is free and can be removed from the underside of the vehicle. Most clips used on the vehicle are simply prised out of position. Other clips can be released by unscrewing/prising out the centre pins and then removing the clip.

2 Where fitted, disconnect the tyre pressure transmitter wiring plug as the wheel arch liner is withdrawn.

3 On refitting, renew any retaining clips that may have been broken on removal, and ensure that the panel is securely retained by all the relevant clips and screws.

Body trim strips and badges

4 The various body trim strips and badges

20.9 Clean out the drain holes (arrowed)

20.11 Lift the cover to access the top latch adjusting nut (arrowed)

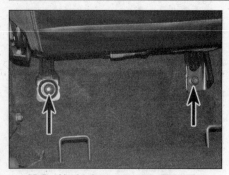

23.2a Undo the seat mounting bolts (arrowed) at the rear ...

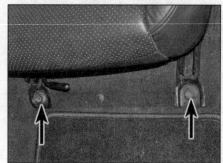

23.2b ... and the front

are held in position with a special adhesive tape. Removal requires the trim/badge to be heated, to soften the adhesive, and then cut away from the surface. Due to the high risk of damage to the vehicle's paintwork during this operation, it is recommended that this task should be entrusted to a Mazda dealer or suitably-equipped specialist.

23 Seats –
removal and refitting

 Warning: Read Section 24 before proceeding.

1 On models with airbags and seat belt pretensioners, disconnect the battery negative lead as described in Chapter 5A, Section 4, then wait at least 1 minute for any residual electrical energy to dissipate.
2 Remove the seat rail retaining bolts at the floor, disconnect the electrical connector(s) at the front lower edge, and lift the seat from the vehicle **(see illustrations)**.
3 Refitting is the reverse of removal. Tighten the bolts to the specified torque.

24 Seat belt tensioning
mechanism –
general information

1 Some models (1998-on) are fitted with a front seat belt tensioner system. The system is designed to instantaneously take up any slack in the seat belt in the case of a sudden frontal impact, therefore reducing the possibility of injury to the seat occupants. The pretensioner function is integral with the inertia reel seat belt retractors.
2 The seat belt tensioner is triggered by a frontal impact above a predetermined force. Lesser impacts, including impacts from behind, will not trigger the system.
3 When the system is triggered, a pyrotechnic device is detonated which acts on the inertia reel mechanism, and keeps the occupant in position in the seat. Once the tensioner has been triggered, the seat belt will be permanently locked and the assembly must be renewed.
4 There is a risk of injury if the system is triggered inadvertently when working on the vehicle. If any work is to be carried out on the seat/seat belt, disable the tensioner by disconnecting the battery negative lead (see Chapter 5A, Section 4), and waiting at least 1 minute before proceeding.
5 Also note the following warnings before contemplating any work on a seat.

 Warning: If the tensioner mechanism is dropped, it must be renewed, even it has suffered no apparent damage.
• **Do not allow any solvents to come into contact with the tensioner mechanism.**
• **Do not subject the seat to any form of shock as this could accidentally trigger the seat belt tensioner.**

25 Seat belt components –
removal and refitting

 Warning: Read Section 24 before proceeding.

Removal

Seat belt/inertia reel

1 On models from 1994, prise up the covers, undo the retaining bolts and remove the cross brace (where fitted) behind the seat backrests
2 Remove the relevant rear quarter trim panel as described in Section 26.
3 Remove the lower anchorage bolt **(see illustration)**. Note the fitted location of any spacers/washers to aid refitting.
4 Undo the inertia reel retaining bolts **(see illustration)**. Where applicable, disconnect the inertia reel wiring plug.

Seat belt stalk

5 Undo the retaining bolt and detach the stalk from the seat base. Note the positions of the washers/spacers to aid refitting. Disconnect any wiring plugs as the stalk is withdrawn **(see illustration)**. To improve access, remove the relevant seat as described in Section 23.

Refitting

6 Refitting is a reversal of the removal procedure, ensuring that all fasteners are tightened to their specified torque where given. Apply a little thread-locking compound to the mounting bolts.

26 Interior trim –
removal and refitting

Interior trim panels

1 The interior trim panels are secured using either screws or various types of trim fasteners, usually studs or clips.
2 Check that there are no other panels overlapping the one to be removed; usually there is a sequence that has to be followed that will become obvious on close inspection.

25.3 Note the spacers and washers fitted to the lower anchorage bolt

25.4 Inertia reel retaining bolts (arrowed)

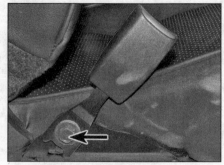

25.5 Seat belt stalk retaining bolt (arrowed)

26.6 Hood locating cup screws (arrowed)

26.7a Prise off the cover ...

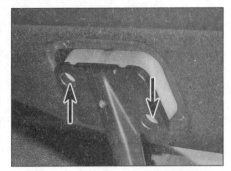

26.7b ... and undo the mirror mounting bolts (arrowed)

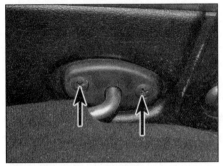

26.8a Sunvisor mounting screws (arrowed)

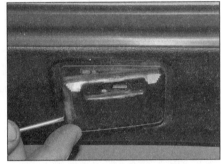

26.8b Prise away the interior light lens ...

26.8c ... and undo the retaining screws (arrowed)

3 Remove all obvious fasteners, such as screws. If the panel will not come free, it is held by hidden clips or fasteners. These are usually situated around the edge of the panel and can be prised up to release them; note, however that they can break quite easily so renewals should be available. The best way of releasing such clips without the correct type of tool, is to use a large flat-bladed screwdriver. Note that some panels are secured by plastic expanding rivets, where the centre pin must be prised up before the rivet can be removed. Note in many cases that the adjacent sealing strip must be prised back to release a panel.

4 When removing a panel, never use excessive force or the panel may be damaged; always check carefully that all fasteners have been removed or released before attempting to withdraw a panel.

5 Refitting is the reverse of the removal

procedure; secure the fasteners by pressing them firmly into place and ensure that all disturbed components are correctly secured to prevent rattles.

Upper windscreen trim

6 Make alignment marks around the hood locating cups, then undo the screws and remove them **(see illustration)**.

7 On 1997 and earlier models, prise off the plastic cover, then undo the bolts and remove the interior mirror **(see illustrations)**.

8 Undo the screws and remove the sunvisor assembly each side, then where applicable, remove the interior light lens, undo the screws securing the light unit **(see illustrations)**.

9 Carefully pull the trim away from the windscreen surround to release the retaining clips, noting how the ends of the trim engage with the tops of the A-pillar trims **(see**

illustration). Unplug the interior light unit as the trim panel is withdrawn (as applicable).

10 Refitting is a reversal of removal.

A-pillar trim

11 Remove the upper windscreen trim as previously described in this Section.

12 Pull the rubber weatherstrip from the door pillar in the area of the pillar trim.

13 Pull the trim to the centre of the vehicle, starting at the top. Note the lugs at the base of the trim panel **(see illustrations)**.

14 Refitting is the reverse of the removal procedure; secure the fasteners by pressing them firmly into place and ensure that all disturbed components are correctly secured to prevent rattles.

Steering column shrouds

15 Undo the screws and remove the steering column lower shroud **(see illustrations)**.

26.9 Note the clip (arrowed) securing the windscreen trim to the A-pillar trim

26.13a Pull the A-pillar trim inwards to release the clips

26.13b Note the lug (arrowed) at the base of the pillar trim

26.15a On early models, the lower shroud is secured by 4 screws (arrowed) …

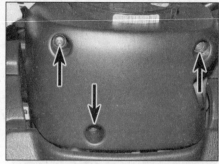

26.15b … whilst on later models, only 3 screws are used (arrowed)

26.16 Pull the upper shroud from the lower shroud (steering wheel removed for clarity)

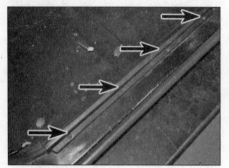

26.18a Undo the screws (arrowed) securing the door sill trim panel – 1997 and earlier

26.18b Pull the door sill trim panel upwards to release the clips – 1998-on

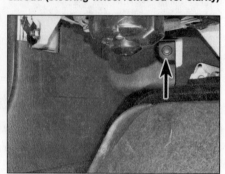

26.20 Prise up the centre pin and remove the plastic expansion rivet (arrowed)

16 Carefully prise the upper shroud from the lower shroud, and manoeuvre the shrouds from position (see illustration).

17 Refitting is a reversal of removal.

Front side trim

18 Undo the retaining screws (1997 and earlier models), pull the door sill trim panel upwards to release the retaining clips (see illustrations).

19 Pull away the rubber weatherstrip from the door aperture adjacent to the side trim panel.

20 Lever out the plastic expansion rivet at the front upper edge of the side trim (see illustration).

21 Pull the side trim inwards to release the retaining clips.

22 Refitting is the reverse of the removal procedure; secure the fasteners by pressing them firmly into place and ensure that all disturbed components are correctly secured to prevent rattles. If necessary, prise the retaining clips from the door sill and refit them to the sill trim prior to refitting.

Rear quarter trim

23 Undo the screws (models up to 1998 only) and pull the door sill trim panel upwards to release the retaining clips (see illustrations 26.18a and 26.18b).

24 Pull away the rubber weatherstrip from the door aperture adjacent to the rear quarter trim panel.

25 Undo the screws and remove the roof striker plate (where fitted) each side (see illustration).

26 Prise up the seat belt guide trim and cover, then undo the seat belt upper anchorage bolt (see illustrations). Note the fitted positions of any washers/spacers.

27 Undo the screws/prise out the pin (as applicable) and remove the trim at the corner of the panel (see illustrations).

28 Where fitted, undo the screws and remove the aeroboard (see illustration). Disconnect the wiring plug (see illustration 20.3).

29 Undo the screws/prise up the centre

26.25 Roof striker plate bolts (arrowed)

26.26a Prise up the cover to access the seat belt upper anchorage bolt

26.26b Undo the upper anchorage bolt, noting the locations of the various washers/spacers

26.26c Unclip the seat belt guide trim

26.27a Undo the screw (arrowed) ...

26.27b ... and prise out the pin

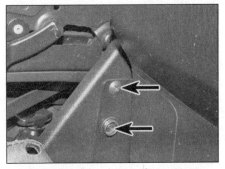

26.28 Aeroboard mounting screws (arrowed)

26.29a Prise up the centre pin and remove the plastic expansion rivet (arrowed) ...

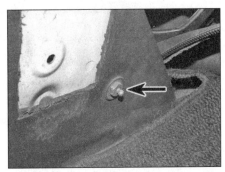

26.29b ... or undo the screw (arrowed)

26.30 Disengage the seat belt as the trim panel is withdrawn

pin (as applicable), and lever out the plastic expansion rivet securing the rear quarter trim **(see illustrations)**.

30 Pull the rear quarter trim panel inwards to release the retaining clips **(see illustration)**. Disengage the seat belt as the trim is withdrawn.

31 Refitting is the reverse of the removal procedure; secure the fasteners by pressing them firmly into place and ensure that all disturbed components are correctly secured to prevent rattles.

Rear parcel shelf

32 Remove the rear quarter trim panels as previously described in this Section, then undo the screws and remove the hood bump stop each side **(see illustration)**.

33 The rear parcel shelf is secured by a combination of push-on clips, screws and plastic expansion rivets. Prise up the centre pins, lever out the plastic expansion rivets, undo the screws and prise the push-in clips out as necessary **(see illustrations)**. Manoeuvre the shelf from position.

34 Refitting is the reverse of the removal procedure; secure the fasteners by pressing them firmly into place and ensure that all disturbed components are correctly secured to prevent rattles.

Luggage area trim panels

35 The various luggage compartment trim panels are secured by plastic expansion rivets. Prise up the centre pin, and lever out the rivets **(see illustrations 16.1a and 16.1b)**. Manoeuvre the relevant panel from position.

36 Refitting is a reversal of removal.

Driver's side lower facia panel

37 Undo the 2 screws at the lower edge, then pull the panel rearwards to release the retaining clips **(see illustration 17.5)**.

38 Refitting is a reversal of removal.

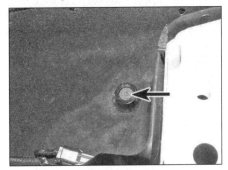

26.32 Undo the screw (arrowed) and remove the bump stop

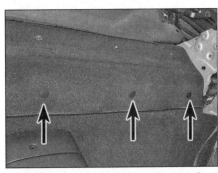

26.33b ... and front edges (arrowed)

Glovebox

1997 and earlier models

39 Open the glovebox, undo the hinge screws on the lower edge, and remove the glovebox **(see illustration)**.

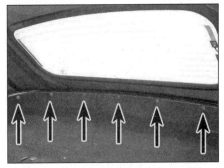

26.33a The parcel shelf is secured by various clips rear (arrowed) ...

26.39 Undo the screws (arrowed) and remove the glovebox – 1997 and earlier

26.40 Press the top edges inwards to disengage the 'stops'

1998-on models

40 Open the glovebox, and press the top edge of the glovebox inwards to disengage the 'stops' (see illustration).
41 Slide the glovebox to the centre and

27.2 Rotate the gearchange lever knob anti-clockwise to remove it

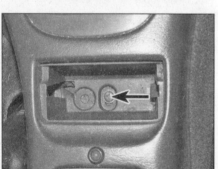

27.3b ... and 1998/1999 models (arrowed)

27.5b Remove the rubber seal around the boot lid/fuel flap release levers

26.41 Slide the glovebox to the centre to disengage the pivot pin

disengage the pivot pin (see illustration). Withdraw the glovebox from position.

All models

42 Refitting is a reversal of removal.

27.3a Lift the ashtray and undo the screw (arrowed) – 1997 and earlier ...

27.4 Prise out the window switch and undo the screw beneath

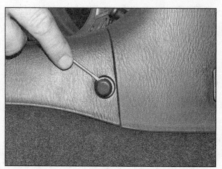

27.6a Prise up the plastic covers each side ...

Carpets

43 The passenger compartment floor carpet is in one piece, secured at its edges by screws or clips, usually the same fasteners used to secure the various adjoining trim panels.
44 Carpet removal and refitting is reasonably straightforward but very time-consuming because all adjoining trim panels must be removed first, as must components such as the seats, the centre console and seat belt lower anchorages.

27 Centre console – removal and refitting

Removal

1 Disconnect the negative battery lead as described in Chapter 5A, Section 4.
2 Unscrew the gearchange lever knob (see illustration).
3 On 1999 and earlier models, lift out the ashtray assembly and remove the screw beneath it (see illustrations).
4 On 2000-on models, prise out the electric window switch, and undo the screw beneath it (see illustration).
5 Open the storage compartment, undo the screws at the base, and remove the rubber seal (where applicable) around the boot lid/fuel flap release levers (see illustrations).
6 Prise up the plastic cover (where fitted) and remove the screw at the lower front of the console on each side (see illustrations).

27.5a Remove the 2 screws in the base of the storage compartment

27.6b ... and remove the screws

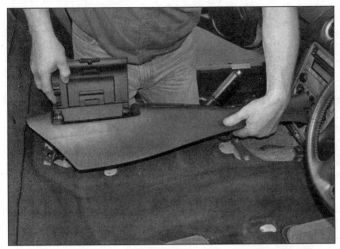

27.7 Lift up the console and release any wiring from the underside

28.11 Remove the screws (arrowed) securing the fusebox to the facia

7 Lift the console up and release any wiring **(see illustration)**. Lift the console over the gearchange lever and manoeuvre it from position.

Refitting

8 Manoeuvre the centre console over the gearchange lever. The remainder of refitting is the reverse of removal making sure all fasteners are securely tightened.

28 Facia panel assembly – removal and refitting

HAYNES HiNT *Label each wiring connector as it is disconnected from its relevant component. The labels will prove useful on refitting, when routing the wiring and feeding the wiring through the facia apertures.*

Removal

1 Disconnect the battery negative lead as described in Chapter 5A, Section 4.
2 Remove the centre console as described in Section 27.
3 Remove the A-pillar trim panel each side as described in Section 26.

4 Remove the steering column as described in Chapter 10, Section 15.
5 Remove the passenger's airbag (where fitted) as described in Chapter 12, Section 20.
6 Remove the facia mounted audio unit (where applicable) as described in Chapter 12, Section 15.
7 Remove the heater control assembly as described in Chapter 3, Section 9.
8 Remove the instrument cluster as described in Chapter 12, Section 9.
9 Remove the glovebox as described in Section 26 (if not already done so).
10 Detach the bonnet release knob or lever from the facia **(see illustration 9.6)**.
11 On 1998-on models, unclip the fusebox cover, then undo the screws securing the fusebox to the facia **(see illustration)**.
12 Prise out the centre hole cover on the top of the facia at the windscreen vent panel **(see illustration)**. Remove the bolt exposed.
13 Prise out the covers in the right and left side panels at the ends of the facia as well as at the bottom of the centre panel each side **(see illustrations)**. Remove the facia retaining bolts exposed.
14 With the help of an assistant, carefully remove the facia while disconnecting any remaining electrical connectors. Note the routing of the wiring harnesses to aid refitting.

Refitting

15 Refitting is a reversal of the removal procedure, noting the following points:
a) *Manoeuvre the facia into position and ensure that the wiring is correctly routed and securely retained by its facia clips.*
b) *Clip the facia back into position, making sure all the wiring connectors are fed through their respective apertures, then refit all the facia fasteners, and tighten them securely.*
c) *On completion, reconnect the battery and check that all the electrical components and switches function correctly.*

29 Fuel filler flap release cable – renewal

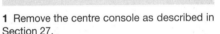

1 Remove the centre console as described in Section 27.
2 Undo the screw and lift out the storage compartment (where fitted) from the left-hand side of the boot **(see illustration 16.14)**.
3 Prise up the centre pins, lever out the plastic expansion rivets and remove the left-hand trim panel from the boot.
4 Undo the bolts and remove the metal panel from the front, left-hand corner of the boot **(see illustration 16.16)**.

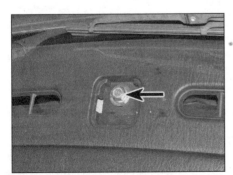

28.12 Prise up the cover in the centre of the facia and undo the bolt

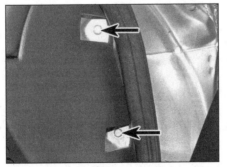

28.13a Prise out the covers and remove the bolts at each end of the facia (arrowed) ...

28.13b ... and the bolts each side of the centre panel (arrowed)

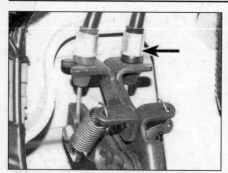

29.5 Slide the outer cable from the bracket (arrowed)

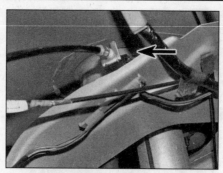

29.6a Reach up to the underside of the filler flap area (arrowed) …

29.6b … and pull the lever (arrowed) to release the flap – removed for clarity

29.7 Undo the nut and pull the release mechanism into the boot

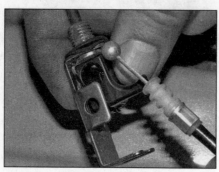

29.8 Note which groove on the outer cable was fitted on the bracket

5 Slide the outer cable from the support bracket at the release lever, and detach the cable end fitting **(see illustration)**.

6 Reach up to the underside of the fuel filler flap and pull the lever to release the flap **(see illustrations)**.

7 Undo the retaining nut and pull the mechanism into the boot **(see illustration)**.

8 Note its fitted position, then slide the outer cable from the support bracket and detach the cable end fitting **(see illustration)**.

9 Refitting is a reversal of removal. Check for correct operation before closing the fuel filler flap.

Chapter 12
Body electrical systems

Contents

Degrees of difficulty

Easy, suitable for novice with little experience 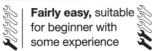	**Fairly easy,** suitable for beginner with some experience	**Fairly difficult,** suitable for competent DIY mechanic	**Difficult,** suitable for experienced DIY mechanic	**Very difficult,** suitable for expert DIY or professional

Specifications

System type...	12 volt negative earth
Fuses..	See fusebox lid

Bulbs	**Wattage**
Exterior lights	
Direction indicator side repeater	5 capless
Direction indicator:	
Front...	21
Rear:	
1997 and earlier models................................	21
1998-on models	21 capless
Front foglight	55 (H11 type)
Headlight:	
Eunos models.....................................	Sealed beam
1999 and earlier models................................	55/60 H4
2000-on models:	
Main beam	60 HB3
Dipped beam	51 HB4
Sidelight	5 capless
High-level brake light	21
Number plate light	5 capless
Rear foglight:	
1997 and earlier models..............................	21
1998-on models	21 capless
Reversing light:	
1997 and earlier models..............................	21
1998-on models	21 capless
Brake/tail light:	
1997 and earlier models..............................	21/5
1998-on models	21/5 capless

Bulbs (continued)

Interior lights

	Wattage
Interior lights	8 festoon
Instrument panel/warning lights:	
Directional indicator	3.4 capless
Illumination	3.4 capless
Warning lights	1.4 capless
Heater control panel	1.4 capless

Torque wrench settings

	Nm	lbf ft
Airbag system fixings:		
Driver's airbag:		
Nuts	5	4
Bolts	10	7
Passenger's airbag retaining bolts/nuts:		
1997 and earlier models	22	16
1998-on models	12	9

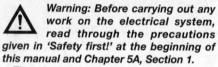

1 General information and precautions

⚠ **Warning: Before carrying out any work on the electrical system, read through the precautions given in 'Safety first!' at the beginning of this manual and Chapter 5A, Section 1.**

The electrical system is of the 12 volt negative earth type. Power for the lights and all electrical accessories is supplied by a lead-acid type battery which is charged by the alternator.

This Chapter covers repair and service procedures for the various electrical components not associated with engine. Information on the battery, alternator and starter motor can be found in Chapter 5A.

It should be noted that prior to working on any component in the electrical system, the battery negative terminal should first be disconnected to prevent the possibility of electrical short circuits and/or fires (see Chapter 5A, Section 4).

2 Electrical fault finding – general information

Note: *Refer to the precautions given in 'Safety first!' and in Section 1 of this Chapter before starting work. The following tests relate to testing of the main electrical circuits, and should not be used to test delicate electronic circuits (such as anti-lock braking systems), particularly where an electronic control module/unit (ECM/ECU) is used.*

General

1 A typical electrical circuit consists of an electrical component, any switches, relays, motors, fuses, fusible links or circuit breakers related to that component, and the wiring and connectors which link the component to both the battery and the chassis. To help to pin-point a problem in an electrical circuit, wiring diagrams are included at the end of this Chapter.

2 Before attempting to diagnose an electrical fault, first study the appropriate wiring diagram to obtain a complete understanding of the components included in the particular circuit concerned. The possible sources of a fault can be narrowed down by noting if other components related to the circuit are operating properly. If several components or circuits fail at one time, the problem is likely to be related to a shared fuse or earth connection.

3 Electrical problems usually stem from simple causes, such as loose or corroded connections, a faulty earth connection, a blown fuse, a melted fusible link, or a faulty relay. Visually inspect the condition of all fuses, wires and connections in a problem circuit before testing the components. Use the wiring diagrams to determine which terminal connections will need to be checked in order to pin-point the trouble spot.

4 The basic tools required for electrical fault finding include a circuit tester or voltmeter (a 12 volt bulb with a set of test leads can also be used for certain tests); a self-powered test light (sometimes known as a continuity tester); an ohmmeter (to measure resistance); a battery and set of test leads; and a jumper wire, preferably with a circuit breaker or fuse incorporated, which can be used to bypass suspect wires or electrical components. Before attempting to locate a problem with test instruments, use the wiring diagram to determine where to make the connections.

5 To find the source of an intermittent wiring fault (usually due to a poor or dirty connection, or damaged wiring insulation), a 'wiggle' test can be performed on the wiring. This involves wiggling the wiring by hand to see if the fault occurs as the wiring is moved. It should be possible to narrow down the source of the fault to a particular section of wiring. This method of testing can be used in conjunction with any of the tests described in the following sub-Sections.

6 Apart from problems due to poor connections, two basic types of fault can occur in an electrical circuit – open circuit, or short circuit.

7 Open circuit faults are caused by a break somewhere in the circuit, which prevents current from flowing. An open circuit fault will prevent a component from working, but will not cause the relevant circuit fuse to blow.

8 Short circuit faults are caused by a 'short' somewhere in the circuit, which allows the current flowing in the circuit to 'escape' along an alternative route, usually to earth. Short circuit faults are normally caused by a breakdown in wiring insulation, which allows a feed wire to touch either another wire, or an earthed component such as the bodyshell. A short circuit fault will normally cause the relevant circuit fuse to blow.

Finding an open circuit

9 To check for an open circuit, connect one lead of a circuit tester or voltmeter to either the negative battery terminal or a known good earth.

10 Connect the other lead to a connector in the circuit being tested, preferably nearest to the battery or fuse.

11 Switch on the circuit, bearing in mind that some circuits are live only when the ignition switch is moved to a particular position.

12 If voltage is present (indicated either by the tester bulb lighting or a voltmeter reading, as applicable), this means that the section of the circuit between the relevant connector and the battery is problem-free.

13 Continue to check the remainder of the circuit in the same fashion.

14 When a point is reached at which no voltage is present, the problem must lie between that point and the previous test point with voltage. Most problems can be traced to a broken, corroded or loose connection.

Finding a short circuit

15 To check for a short circuit, first disconnect the load(s) from the circuit (loads are the components which draw current from a circuit, such as bulbs, motors, heating elements, etc).

16 Remove the relevant fuse from the circuit, and connect a circuit tester or voltmeter to the fuse connections.

17 Switch on the circuit, bearing in mind that some circuits are live only when the ignition switch is moved to a particular position.

18 If voltage is present (indicated either by the tester bulb lighting or a voltmeter reading, as applicable), this means that there is a short circuit.

19 If no voltage is present, but the fuse still blows with the load(s) connected, this indicates an internal fault in the load(s).

Finding an earth fault

20 The battery negative terminal is connected to 'earth' – the metal of the engine/transmission and the car body – and most systems are wired so that they only receive a positive feed, the current returning through the metal of the car body. This means that the component mounting and the body form part of that circuit. Loose or corroded mountings can therefore cause a range of electrical faults, ranging from total failure of a circuit, to a puzzling partial fault. In particular, lights may shine dimly (especially when another circuit sharing the same earth point is in operation), motors (eg, wiper motors or the radiator cooling fan motor) may run slowly, and the operation of one circuit may have an apparently unrelated effect on another. Note that on many vehicles, earth straps are used between certain components, such as the engine/transmission and the body, usually where there is no metal-to-metal contact between components due to flexible rubber mountings, etc **(see illustrations)**.

21 To check whether a component is properly earthed, disconnect the battery and connect one lead of an ohmmeter to a known good earth point. Connect the other lead to the wire or earth connection being tested. The resistance reading should be zero; if not, check the connection as follows.

22 If an earth connection is thought to be faulty, dismantle the connection and clean back to bare metal both the bodyshell and the wire terminal or the component earth connection mating surface. Be careful to remove all traces of dirt and corrosion, then use a knife to trim away all paint, so that a clean metal-to-metal joint is made. On reassembly, tighten the joint fasteners securely; if a wire terminal is being refitted, use serrated washers between the terminal and the bodyshell to ensure a clean and secure connection. When the connection is remade, prevent the onset of corrosion in the future by applying a coat of petroleum jelly or silicone-based grease or by spraying on (at regular intervals) a proprietary ignition sealer or a water dispersant lubricant.

2.20a The earth strap from the battery is attached to the vehicle body in the boot (arrowed) ...

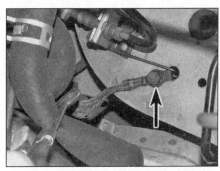

2.20b ... whilst the engine earth strap is attached to the left-hand side of the engine compartment bulkhead (arrowed)

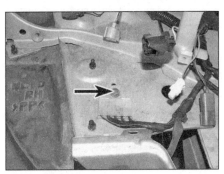

2.20c Other earth locations maybe under the headlight (arrowed) ...

2.20d ... under the wiper motor mounting bolt (arrowed) ...

2.20e ... on the rear of the cylinder head (arrowed) ...

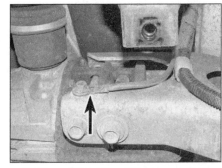

2.20f ... at the rear of the power plant frame (arrowed) ...

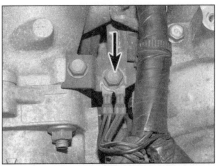

2.20g ... between the intake manifold and cylinder head cover (arrowed) ...

2.20h ... the reverse of the facia crossmember (arrowed)

3.1a Main fusebox under the right-hand side of the facia – late models ...

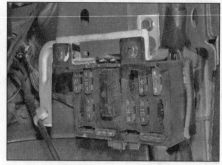

3.1b ... and early models

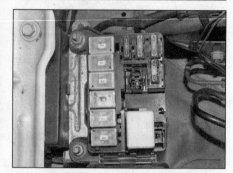

3.1c The engine compartment fusebox is located on the right-hand side

3 Fuses and relays – general information

Main fuses

1 The fuses are located in the engine compartment on the right-hand side, whilst some others are located underneath the facia on the driver's side (see illustrations).

2 A list of the circuits each fuse protects is given on fusebox cover. A pair of tweezers for removing the fuses is also clipped to the fusebox. High amperage fuses are located in the main fusebox in the engine compartment.

3 To remove a fuse, first switch off the circuit concerned (or the ignition), then pull the fuse out of its terminals. The wire within the fuse should be visible; if the fuse is blown it will be broken or melted.

4 Always renew a fuse with one of an identical rating; never use a fuse with a different rating from the original or substitute anything else. Never renew a fuse more than once without tracing the source of the trouble. The fuse rating is stamped on top of the fuse; note that the fuses are also colour-coded for easy recognition.

5 If a new fuse blows immediately, find the cause before renewing it again; a short to earth as a result of faulty insulation is most likely. Where a fuse protects more than one circuit, try to isolate the defect by switching on each circuit in turn (if possible) until the fuse blows again. Always carry a supply of spare fuses of each relevant rating on the vehicle, a spare of each rating should be clipped into the base of the fusebox.

Relays

6 Many electrical accessories in the vehicle use relays to switch the electrical supply to the component. If the relay is defective, that component will not operate properly. Relay locations vary by model year.

7 The main relays are located on the left- and right-hand sides of the engine compartment, whilst others are located under the driver's side of the facia, and in the boot (see illustrations).

8 If a circuit or system controlled by a relay develops a fault and the relay is suspect, operate the system; if the relay is functioning it should be possible to hear it click as it is energised. If this is the case the fault lies with the components or wiring of the system. If the relay is not being energised then either the relay is not receiving a main supply or a switching voltage or the relay itself is faulty. Testing is by the substitution of a known good unit but be careful; while some relays are identical in appearance and in operation, others look similar but perform different functions.

9 To renew a relay first ensure that the ignition switch is off. The relay can then simply be pulled out from the socket and the new relay pressed in.

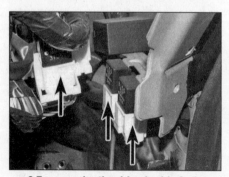

3.7a Relays can be located on the right-hand side (arrowed) ...

3.7b ... or left-hand side of the engine compartment (arrowed) ...

3.7c ... under the driver's side facia (arrowed) ...

3.7d ... or in the boot

4 Switches – removal and refitting

Note: Disconnect the battery negative lead (see Chapter 5A, Section 4) before removing any switch, and reconnect the lead after refitting the switch.

Ignition switch

1 Remove the steering column upper and lower shrouds as described in Chapter 11, Section 26.

2 Disconnect the electrical connector from the switch.

3 Remove the screw and separate the switch from the steering lock assembly (see illustration).

4 Refitting is the reverse of removal.

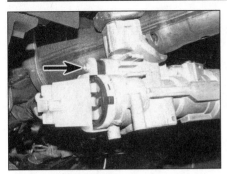

4.3 Ignition switch retaining screw (arrowed)

4.6a On early models, the lower steering column shroud is secured by 4 screws (arrowed) ...

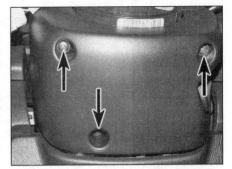

4.6b ... whilst on later models, 3 screws (arrowed) are used

Steering column combination switch

5 Remove the steering wheel as described in Chapter 10, Section 14.

6 Undo the screws, then unclip the upper and lower steering column shrouds, then undo the screws and remove the trim panel beneath the steering column (see illustrations).

Models without driver's airbag

7 Slacken the clamp screw on the underside of the switch, then lift the locking pin and slide the assembly from the column (see illustrations). Disconnect the wiring plugs as the switch assembly is withdrawn.

Models with driver's airbag

8 Remove the combination switch retaining screws (see illustration).

9 Disconnect the electrical connectors and slide the combination switch off the column (see illustration).

⚠️ **Warning: Handle the combination switch/rotary contact unit assembly very carefully. Damage to the rotary contact unit could cause an airbag system failure, resulting in serious personal injury.**

All models

10 Refitting is the reverse of removal. Ensure the rotary contact unit is centred properly before refitting the combination switch/rotary contact unit assembly onto the steering column as follows:

a) Position the front wheels pointing straight-ahead.

b) Gently rotate the rotary contact unit inner

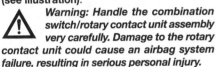

4.6c Unclip the upper and lower shrouds

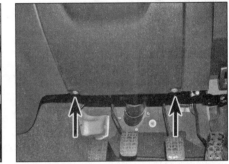

4.6d Undo the screws and remove the panel beneath the steering column (arrowed)

hub clockwise to the end of its stop. Do not force it against the stop.

c) Rotate the rotary contact unit 2 3/4 turns anti-clockwise.

d) Align the mark on the inner hub with the mark on the housing (see illustration).

4.7a Slacken the clamp screw (arrowed) underneath ...

Hazard warning switch and headlight retractor switch

1997 and earlier models

11 Remove the centre console as described in Chapter 11, Section 27.

4.7b ... then lift the locking pin

4.8 Undo the combination switch retaining screws (arrowed) ...

4.9 ... and with a sharp pull, remove the switch assembly

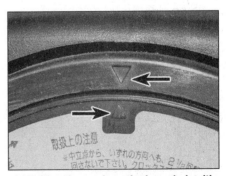

4.10 Align the mark on the inner hub with the mark on the housing (arrowed)

4.12 Prise out the vents from the centre panel

4.13a Undo the screws (arrowed) in the vent apertures ...

4.13b ... and the screw at the base (arrowed) ...

4.13c ... then pull the panel rearwards

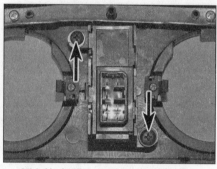

4.14 Undo the screws (arrowed) and remove the hazard/headlight switch

4.17 Press the hazard warning switch from the facia

12 Carefully prise out the air ducts from the facia centre panel **(see illustration)**.

13 Undo the screw in the duct apertures and the screw at the base of the panel. Manoeuvre the panel rearwards, disconnecting the wiring pugs as the panel is withdrawn **(see illustrations)**.

14 Undo the screws and remove the switch from the panel **(see illustration)**.

15 Refitting is the reverse of removal.

1998-on models

16 Remove the electrical unit below the hazard switch. On some models this may be the clock (Section 10), on others this maybe the audio unit (Section 15).

17 Reach through the aperture, and press the switch from the facia **(see illustration)**. Disconnect the wiring plug as the switch is withdrawn.

18 Refitting is a reversal of removal.

Electric window switches

1999 and earlier models

19 Remove the centre console as described in Chapter 11, Section 27.

20 On early models, the switch is retained by 2 screws, whilst on later models, the switch is clipped into place. Remove the screw/release the clips and remove the switch **(see illustrations)**.

21 Refitting is a reversal of removal.

2000-on models

22 Using a blunt, flat-bladed tool, carefully prise the switch assembly from the centre console **(see illustration)**. Disconnect the wiring plug as the switch is withdrawn.

23 Refitting is a reversal of removal.

Exterior mirror switches

24 Using a blunt, flat-bladed tool, carefully prise the switch from the facia **(see illustration)**. Disconnect the wiring plug as the switch is withdrawn.

25 Refitting is a reversal of removal.

Clutch pedal switch

26 Refer to Chapter 6, Section 8.

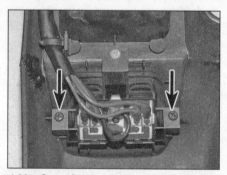

4.20a On early models, the electric window switch is retained by screws (arrowed) ...

4.20b ... whilst on later models, clips are used (arrowed)

4.22 Prise the window switch from the console – 2000-on

4.24 Prise the mirror adjustment switch from the facia

4.28 Reach up and press the switches from the facia

4.31a Undo the screws (arrowed) at the lower edge ...

4.31b ... and pull the centre panel rearwards

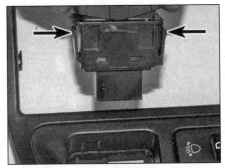

4.32 Squeeze the clips (arrowed) and remove the switch

4.35 Reach up through the fusebox aperture and press out the switch(es)

4.37 Undo the screws and withdraw the courtesy light switch

Rear foglight and heated rear window switches

1997 and earlier models

27 Undo the screws and remove the panel beneath the steering column **(see illustration 4.6d)**.
28 Reach up and press the switch(es) from place **(see illustration)**. Disconnect the wiring plugs as the switch(es) are withdrawn.
29 Refitting is the reverse of removal.

1998 to 1999 models

Note: *On these models the heated rear window switch is integral with the heater control panel.*
30 Remove the centre console as described in Chapter 11, Section 27.
31 Undo the screws at the lower edge, and pull the facia centre panel rearwards to release the clips **(see illustrations)**.
32 Disconnect the wiring plug(s), squeeze

together the retaining clips and push the switch from the panel **(see illustration)**.
33 Refitting is a reversal of removal.

2000-on models

Note: *This also applies to the instrument panel illumination switch.*
34 Remove the fusebox cover from the facia.
35 Reach up behind the facia, squeeze together the clips each side, and press the switch assembly from the facia **(see illustration)**. Disconnect the wiring plug as the switch assembly is withdrawn.
36 Refitting is a reversal of removal.

Courtesy light switches

37 Undo the retaining screw, and pull the light switch from the door aperture **(see illustration)**. Disconnect the wiring plug as the switch is withdrawn.
38 Refitting is a reversal of removal.

Headlight levelling and heated seat switches

1998 to 2000 models

39 Remove the centre console as described in Chapter 11, Section 27.
40 Undo the screws at the lower edge, and pull the facia centre panel rearwards to release the clips **(see illustration 4.31a and 4.31b)**.
41 Disconnect the wiring plug(s), squeeze together the retaining clips and push the switch from the panel **(see illustration)**.
42 Refitting is a reversal of removal.

2000-on models

43 Carefully prise the switch panel from the centre panel **(see illustration)**.
44 Squeeze together the clips and remove the relevant switch from the panel **(see illustration)**. Disconnect the wiring plug as the switch is withdrawn.
45 Refitting is a reversal of removal.

4.41 Squeeze the clips (arrowed) and remove the headlight levelling switch

4.43 Prise the switch panel from the centre panel

4.44 Squeeze the clips (arrowed) and remove the switch

5.3 Undo the 2 screws (arrowed) each side of the headlight bezel

5.4a Slacken the screws (arrowed) ...

5.4b ... rotate the retaining ring anti-clockwise and remove it

5.5 Pull the wiring plug from the sealed beam unit

5.6 Press the headlight in a little, then rotate it to align the retaining screws (arrowed) with the larger holes

5 Bulbs (exterior lights) – renewal

General

1 Whenever a bulb is renewed, note the following points.
  a) *Remember that if the light has just been in use the bulb may be extremely hot.*
  b) *Always check the bulb contacts and holder, ensuring that there is clean metal-to-metal contact between the bulb and its live(s) and earth. Clean off any corrosion or dirt before fitting a new bulb.*
  c) *Wherever bayonet-type bulbs are fitted ensure that the live contact(s) bear firmly against the bulb contact.*
  d) *Always ensure that the new bulb is of the*

correct rating and that it is completely clean before fitting it; this applies particularly to headlight/foglight bulbs (see below).
  e) *When handling the new bulb, use a tissue or clean cloth to avoid touching the glass with the fingers; moisture and grease from the skin can cause blackening and rapid failure of the bulb. If the glass is accidentally touched, wipe it clean using methylated spirit.*

Headlight – 1997 and earlier models

2 Operate the switch to raise the headlights, then disconnect the negative battery cable as described in Chapter 5A, Section 4.
3 Remove the screws at each side of the headlight bezel, then remove the bezel **(see illustration)**.

Eunos models

4 Remove the headlight retaining ring **(see illustrations)**.
5 Pull the sealed beam unit out of the housing and unplug its wiring connector **(see illustration)**.

Mk 1 models

6 Press the headlight inwards a little, rotate it anti-clockwise and pull the headlight from the housing. Disconnect the wiring plug and remove the rubber boot **(see illustration)**.
7 Release the retaining clip and remove the bulb. Note how the lugs on the bulb flange engage with the locating slots in the reflector **(see illustrations)**.

All models

8 Reverse the removal steps to fit the new bulb.

Headlight – 1998 and 1999 models

9 Reach behind the headlight, and pull the wiring plug from the bulb.
10 Note its fitted position, then pull the rubber boot from the rear of the headlight **(see illustration)**.
11 Release the retaining clip and remove the headlight bulb **(see illustration)**.
12 Note how the bulb locating lugs engage with the slots in headlight reflector, then fit the new bulb and secure it with the retaining clip **(see illustration)**.
13 Refit the rubber boot, and reconnect the wiring plug.

5.7a Release the retaining clip (arrowed)

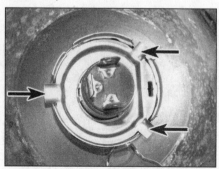

5.7b Note how the lugs engage with the reflector (arrowed)

5.10 Remove the rubber boot from the rear of the headlight

5.11 Press and lift to release the clip (arrowed)

5.12 Engage the lugs on the bulb flange with the slots in the reflector

5.14 Rotate the bulbholder assembly anti-clockwise and remove it

5.19 Pull the capless sidelight bulb from the holder

5.21a Rotate the bulbholder anti-clockwise and pull it from the reflector – 1998/1999 models ...

5.21b ... and 2000-on models (arrowed)

Headlight – 2000-on models

14 Although on these models the main beam is provided by a bulb separate from the dipped beam, the renewal procedure for both bulbs is identical. Reach behind the headlight, hold the rubber boot stationary, and rotate the bulbholder approximately 90° anti-clockwise and pull it from the reflector **(see illustration)**. Note that the outer bulb is for the dipped beam, and the bulbs are integral with the holders.

15 Depress the tab and disconnect the wiring plug.

16 Refitting is a reversal of removal.

Front sidelight

1997 and earlier models

17 Remove the sidelight/indication assembly as described in Section 7.

18 Rotate the bulbholder anti-clockwise, and pull it from the light unit.

19 Pull the capless bulb from the holder **(see illustration)**.

20 Refitting is a reversal of removal.

1998-on models

21 Rotate the bulbholder anti-clockwise and remove it from the reflector **(see illustrations)**. Pull the capless bulb from the holder.

22 Refitting is a reversal of removal.

Front direction indicator

1997 and earlier models

23 Remove the sidelight/indicator assembly as described in Section 7.

24 Rotate the bulbholder anti-clockwise

and remove it from the rear of the light **(see illustration)**.

25 The bulb is a bayonet fitting in the holder. Push the bulb in slightly, then rotate it anti-clockwise and pull it from the holder.

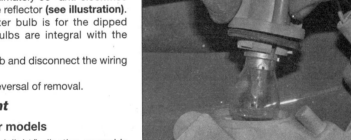

5.24 Direction indicator bulbholder – 1997 and earlier

5.27b Push the bulb in, and twist it anti-clockwise

26 Refitting is a reversal of removal.

1998-on models

27 Rotate the bulbholder anti-clockwise and remove it from the rear of the headlight **(see illustrations)**.

5.27a Rotate the bulbholder anti-clockwise to remove it – 1998 and 1999

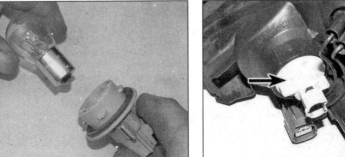

5.27c Direction indicator (arrowed) – 2000-on

5.31 Pull the capless side repeater bulb from the holder

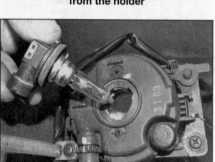

5.34b Rotate the bulbholder/bulb anti-clockwise and remove it

28 The bulb is a bayonet fitting in the holder. Push the bulb in slightly, then rotate it anti-clockwise and pull it from the holder.
29 Refitting is a reverse of the removal procedure.

5.36 Twist the direction indicator bulbholder (arrowed) anti-clockwise and remove it

5.37b Twist, and remove the relevant bulb

5.34a Release the clip from the rear of the foglight

5.35 Foglight aim adjusting screw (arrowed)

Side repeater

30 Remove the side repeater light assembly as described in Section 7.
31 Rotate the bulbholder anti-clockwise and

5.37a Squeeze together the clips and remove the bulbholder assembly

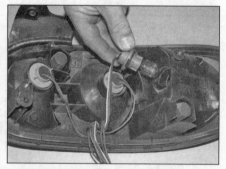

5.40 Twist the relevant bulbholder anti-clockwise – 1998-on

pull it from the lens, pull the capless bulb from the holder **(see illustration)**.
32 Refitting is a reverse of the removal procedure.

Front foglight

33 Undo the screws and pull back the front, lower section of the front wheel arch liner. To improve access, raise the front of the vehicle, support it securely on axle stands (see *Jacking and vehicle support*). Remove the relevant front roadwheel.
34 Disconnect the wiring from the bulbholder, release the clip, then rotate the bulbholder anti-clockwise and pull it from the foglight. Note that the bulb is integral with the holder **(see illustrations)**.
35 Refitting is a reversal of removal. If necessary, adjust the aim of the light by rotating the adjusting screw on the rear of the unit **(see illustration)**.

Rear light cluster

1997 and earlier models

36 To remove the indicator bulb, twist the bulbholder anti-clockwise, and pull it from the light unit **(see illustration)**. Press the bulb in slightly, twist it anti-clockwise and remove it from the bulbholder.
37 To remove the brake/tail or reverse bulbs, squeeze together the retaining clips and pull the bulbholder assembly from the rear of the light unit **(see illustrations)**. Press the relevant bulb in slightly, twist it anti-clockwise and remove it from the bulbholder.
38 Refitting is a reversal of removal.

1998-on models

39 Remove the light unit as described in Section 7.
40 Twist the relevant bulbholder anti-clockwise and pull it from the rear of the light unit **(see illustration)**. Pull the capless bulb from the holder.
41 Refitting is a reversal of removal.

Rear foglight

1997 and earlier models

42 Undo the 2 screws and remove the foglight lens.
43 Press the bulb in slightly, twist it anti-clockwise and remove it from the bulbholder.
44 Refitting is a reversal of removal.

High-level brake light

45 Rotate the bulbholder anti-clockwise, and remove it from the light unit **(see illustration)**. Press the bulb in slightly, twist it anti-clockwise and remove it from the bulbholder.
46 Refitting is a reversal of removal.

Number plate light

1997 and earlier models

47 Prise out the clips and pull away the trim panel from the lights.

48 Rotate the bulbholder anti-clockwise and detach it from the light unit **(see illustration)**. Remove the bulb.
49 Refitting is a reversal of removal.

1998-on models

50 Carefully push the light unit in the direction of the arrow to compress the retaining spring, then remove the lens unit **(see illustration)**. If the lens is reluctant to release, remove the high-level brake light as described in Section 7, then reach through the aperture, compress the clip at the arrowed end and push the light unit from place.
51 Rotate the bulbholder anti-clockwise and remove it from the light unit **(see illustration)**. Pull the capless bulb from the holder.
52 Refitting is a reversal of removal.

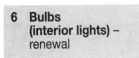

6 Bulbs (interior lights) – renewal

General

1 Refer to Section 5, paragraph 1.

Courtesy lights

2 Using a wooden or plastic spatula, carefully prise the lower edge (1997 and earlier) or side edge (1998-on) of the interior light lens and remove it **(see illustrations)**.
3 Pull the festoon bulb from the contacts **(see illustration)**.
4 Refitting is a reversal of removal.

Luggage compartment light

5 Using a wooden or plastic spatula, carefully prise down the side edge of the interior light lens and remove it.
6 Pull the festoon bulb from the contacts.
7 Refitting is a reversal of removal.

Instrument illumination and warning lights

8 Remove the instrument cluster as described in Section 9.
9 Rotate the bulbholder anti-clockwise and remove it from the rear of the unit **(see illustration)**.
10 Pull the capless bulb from the holder **(see illustration)**.
11 Refitting is a reversal of removal.

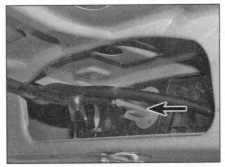

5.45 Rotate the high-level brake light bulbholder (arrowed) anti-clockwise

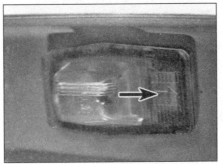

5.50 Push the number plate light lens in the direction of the cast-in arrow

Heater control panel illumination

12 Remove the heater control panel as described in Chapter 3, Section 9.

6.2a Prise out the lower edge – 1997 and earlier ...

6.3 Prise out the festoon bulb from the contacts

5.48 Number plate bulbholder (arrowed) – 1997 and earlier

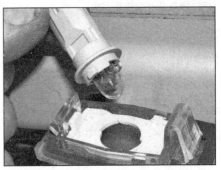

5.51 Rotate the bulbholder anti-clockwise and pull the capless bulb from place

13 Rotate the bulbholder anti-clockwise and remove it. Pull the capless bulb from the holder.
14 Refitting is a reversal of removal.

6.2b ... or side edge of the courtesy light lens – 1998-on

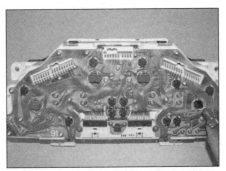

6.9 Rotate the illumination/warning light bulbholder anti-clockwise to remove it

6.10 Pull the capless bulb from the holder

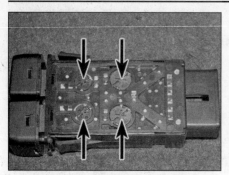

6.16 Switch illumination bulbholders (arrowed)

Switch illumination

15 Many of the switches are fitted with renewable illumination bulbs. Remove the relevant switch as described in Section 4.

16 Rotate the bulbholder anti-clockwise and pull it from the switch. Small, thin-nosed pliers may be needed **(see illustration)**.

17 Pull the capless bulb from the holder.

18 Refitting is a reversal of removal.

---

7 Exterior light units –
   removal and refitting

Headlight

1997 and earlier models

1 Remove the headlight bulb/sealed beam unit as described in Section 5.

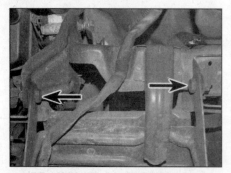

7.3a Undo the 2 bolts (arrowed) ...

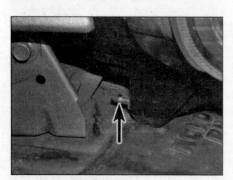

7.6b Pull the headlight forwards to release the locating pin (arrowed)

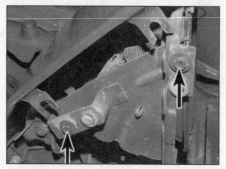

7.2 Slacken the screws (arrowed) each side, the lift away the 'lid'

2 Slacken the 2 screws each side and lift away the 'lid' of the headlight **(see illustration)**.

3 Unclip the wiring harness, then undo the bolt each side, prise the link rod from the retractor motor arm, and remove the headlight **(see illustrations)**.

4 Refitting is the reverse of removal.

1998-on models

5 Remove the front bumper as described in Chapter 11, Section 6.

6 The headlight is secured by 2 screws at the upper edge. Undo the screws, and pull the headlight forwards a little to release the locating pin **(see illustrations)**.

7 Disconnect the headlight wiring plug(s), and release the wiring loom from the retaining clips (where fitted).

8 Refitting is a direct reversal of the removal procedure. Lightly tighten the retaining screws and check the alignment of the headlight with the bumper and bonnet. Once the light

7.3b ... use pliers to prise the retractor arm from the link rod

7.11 Slacken the locknut and adjust the position of the 'stopper'

unit is correctly positioned, securely tighten the retaining screws and check the headlight beam alignment using the information given in Section 8.

Headlight retractor motor

Adjustment

9 Raise the headlights and disconnect the negative cable from the battery as described in Chapter 5A, Section 4.

10 Prise the link on the retractor motor free from the arm on the headlight lid **(see illustration 7.3b)**.

11 Lower the headlight lid by hand until it rests against the stopper **(see illustration)**. The lid should be flush with the body. If it isn't, raise the lid and adjust the stopper as necessary.

12 Reconnect the actuator link to the arm and reconnect the battery lead. Operate the headlights with the switch and check the adjustment again.

Renewal

13 To remove the retractor motor, unplug its wiring connector and prise the link off the arm **(see illustration 7.3b)**. Unbolt the motor and remove it **(see illustration)**.

14 Refitting is a reversal of removal.

Front direction indicator and sidelight

1997 and earlier models

15 Undo the 2 screws and pull the light unit from the front of the vehicle **(see illustration)**.

7.6a Headlight retaining screws (arrowed)

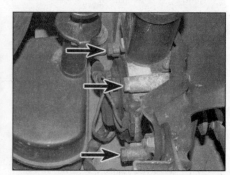

7.13 Retractor motor mounting bolts (arrowed)

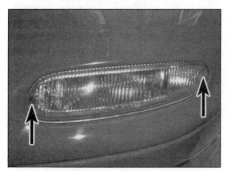

7.15 Undo the screws (arrowed) and remove the direction indicator/sidelight unit

7.18a Depress the clip at the rear edge of the side repeater ...

7.18b ... and prise it from the wing

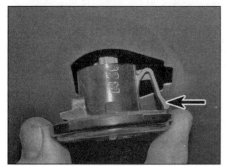

7.20 Push the side repeater rearwards to compress the clip (arrowed)

7.23 Front foglight mounting bolts (arrowed)

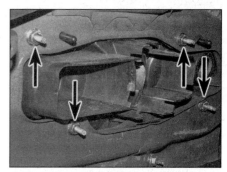

7.27a Rear light cluster retaining nuts (arrowed) – 1997 and earlier

16 Twist the bulbholders anti-clockwise and remove them from the light unit.
17 Refitting is a reversal of removal.

Front indicator side repeater

1997 and earlier models

18 Insert a blunt, flat-bladed tool, into the slot on the rear edge of the light unit, depress the clip and carefully prise the side repeater from the wing **(see illustrations)**. Rotate the bulbholder anti-clockwise and remove it.
19 Refitting is a reversal of removal.

1998-on models

20 Using finger pressure, push the side repeater lens gently rearwards. Pull out the front edge of the lens and withdraw it from the wing **(see illustration)**. Disconnect the wiring plug as the unit is withdrawn.
21 Refitting is a reverse of the removal procedure.

Front foglight

22 Undo the screws and pull back the front section of the wheel arch liner.
23 Undo the mounting bolts, and remove the foglight. Disconnect the wiring plug as the light is withdrawn **(see illustration)**.
24 Refitting is a reversal of removal. If required, the foglight aim can be adjusted by rotating the adjuster screw **(see illustration 5.35)**.

Rear light cluster

1997 and earlier models

25 Remove the tail light bulbs as described in Section 5.
26 Release the wiring harness from the clips on the rear of the light unit.
27 Undo the 4 retaining nuts and carefully pull the light unit from position. Take care not to damage the foam seal between the light unit and the vehicle body **(see illustrations)**.

28 Refitting is a reversal of removal.

1998-on models

29 Working in the luggage compartment, prise out the clips and pull away the trim panel in front of the rear light unit(s) **(see illustration)**.
30 Undo the retaining screw at the top edge, and the 2 retaining nuts on the rear of the light unit **(see illustrations)**. Remove the light unit. Disconnect the wiring plug as the light unit is withdrawn.
31 Refitting is a reversal of removal.

High-level brake light

1997 and earlier models

32 Disconnect the wiring plug from the rear of the unit.
33 Undo the nut at each end and detach the light unit from the boot lid **(see illustration)**.
34 Refitting is a reversal of removal.

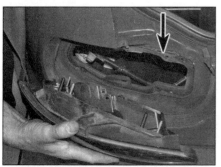

7.27b Check the condition of the foam seal (arrowed)

7.29 Prise up the centre pins, and lever out the plastic expansion rivets

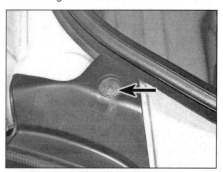

7.30a Undo the screw (arrowed) at the top edge ...

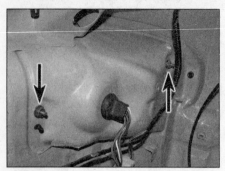

7.30b ... the nuts in the boot (arrowed) ...

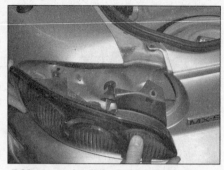

7.30c ... and pull the light unit from place

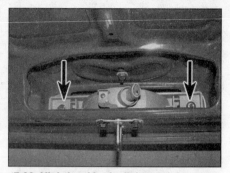

7.33 High-level brake light retaining nuts (arrowed) – 1997 and earlier

7.35 Pull the wiring harness clips from the studs (arrowed) and undo the retaining nuts

7.36a Insert a screwdriver into the slot ...

7.36b ... and release the clip – unit removed for clarity

1998-on models

35 Disconnect the wiring plug from the rear of the unit, pull the harness clips from the mounting studs, then undo the retaining nuts **(see illustration)**.

36 Insert a small screwdriver into the slot in the rear of the light unit, and compress the retaining clip **(see illustrations)**. Pull the light unit from the boot lid.

37 Refitting is a reversal of removal.

8 Headlight beam alignment – general information

1 Accurate adjustment of the headlight beam is only possible using optical beam setting equipment and this work should therefore be carried out by a Mazda dealer or suitably-equipped workshop.

2 For reference, the headlights can be adjusted by rotating the adjuster screws:

- *1997 and earlier models have a vertical adjustment screw at the base of the headlight, and a horizontal adjustment screw at the side of the headlight (see illustration).*
- *1998-on models have adjustment screws are on the rear of the headlight (see illustration).*

3 Some models have an electrically-operated headlight beam adjustment system which is controlled through the switch in the facia. On these models ensure that the switch is set to the Off position before adjusting the headlight aim.

9 Instrument cluster – removal and refitting

Removal

1 Remove the steering wheel as described in Chapter 10, Section 14.

2 Undo the screws securing the lower steering column shroud, then unclip the upper shroud and remove them – see Chapter 11, Section 26.

1997 and earlier models

3 Undo the 2 screws and pull the instrument cluster surround rearwards to release the clips **(see illustration)**.

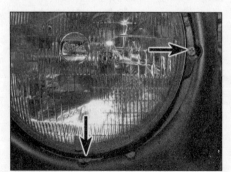

8.2a Headlight aim adjusting screws (arrowed) – 1997and earlier ...

8.2b ... and 1998-on (arrowed)

9.3 Instrument cluster surround retaining screws (arrowed)

9.4 Pull the instrument cluster surround rearwards – 1998-on

9.5 Undo the screws (arrowed) and pull the instrument cluster rearwards

9.6 Disconnect the speedometer cable from the instrument cluster (arrowed)

1998-on models

4 Pull the instrument cluster surround rearwards to release the clips **(see illustration)**.

All models

5 Remove the retaining screws and pull the instrument cluster rearwards a little **(see illustration)**.

6 Unscrew the speedometer cable (where fitted), and disconnect the wiring plugs **(see illustration)**. Manoeuvre the instrument cluster from position.

Refitting

7 Refitting is the reverse of removal, making sure the instrument panel wiring is correctly reconnected and securely held in position by any retaining clips. On completion reconnect the battery and check the operation of the panel warning lights to ensure that they are functioning correctly.

10 Clock (1998-on models) – removal and refitting

1 Remove the centre console as described in Chapter 11, Section 27.

2 Undo the 2 screws at the lower edge, and pull the facia centre panel rearwards to release the retaining clips **(see illustrations 4.31a and 4.31b)**.

3 Carefully prise the clock from the facia **(see illustration)**. Disconnect the wiring plugs as the clock is withdrawn.

4 Refitting is a reversal of removal.

11 Horn – removal and refitting

1 The horn is adjacent to the bonnet lock.

2 Undo the retaining bolt and remove the horn, disconnecting the wiring connector as it becomes accessible.

3 Refitting is the reverse of removal.

12 Wiper arm – removal and refitting

Removal

1 Operate the wiper motor, then switch it off so that the wiper arms return to the 'at rest' position. Open the bonnet

2 Stick a piece of masking tape on the windscreen alongside the edge of the wiper blade to use as an alignment aid on refitting.

3 Prise off the wiper arm spindle nut cover(s) then slacken and remove the spindle nut(s). Lift the blade off the glass and pull the wiper arm off its spindle. If necessary the arm can be levered off the spindle using a suitable flat-bladed screwdriver or suitable puller **(see illustrations)**.

Refitting

4 Ensure that the wiper arm and spindle splines are clean and dry then refit the arm to

10.3 Prise the clock from the facia

the spindle, aligning the wiper blade with the tape fitted on removal. Refit the spindle nut, tightening securely, and clip the nut cover back in position.

5 If the position of the front wiper arms has been lost, set the arms so the end of the blade is approximately 25 mm above the edge of the windscreen trim **(see illustration)**.

13 Windscreen wiper motor and linkage – removal and refitting

Removal

Linkage

1 Remove the wiper arms as described in Section 12.

2 Working at the rear of the engine

12.3a Prise off the cover, undo the spindle nut ...

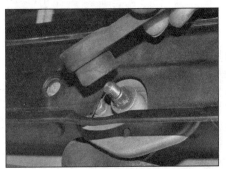

12.3b ... and lever the wiper arm from the spindle

12.5 The end of the blade should be 25 mm above the windscreen trim (arrowed)

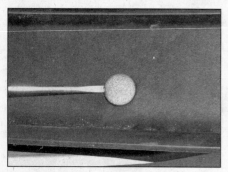

13.2a Prise up the plastic covers …

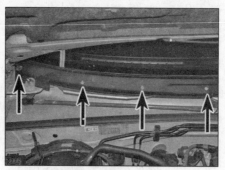

13.2b … undo the screws (right-hand screws arrowed) …

13.2c … and pull up the scuttle trim panel

compartment, prise up the plastic covers, undo the screws, and remove the scuttle trim panel **(see illustrations)**.

3 Prise up the centre pins, lever out the plastic expansion rivets, undo the screws and remove the trim cover over the linkage **(see illustration)**.

4 Use a screwdriver to prise the linkage rod from the motor arm **(see illustration)**.

5 Undo the mounting bolts and remove the linkage assembly **(see illustration)**.

Motor

6 Disconnect the motor wiring plug.

7 Use a screwdriver to prise the linkage rod from the motor arm **(see illustration 13.4)**.

8 Undo the mounting bolts and manoeuvre the motor from position **(see illustration)**.

Refitting

9 Refitting is the reverse of removal.

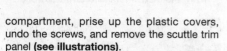

14 Windscreen washer system components – removal and refitting

Washer system reservoir

1 The windscreen washer reservoir is located in the engine compartment.

2 Empty the contents of the reservoir or be prepared for fluid spillage.

3 Undo the reservoir retaining screw(s) **(see illustrations)**.

4 Manoeuvre the reservoir from position, and disconnect the wiring connector(s) from the reservoir level switch (where fitted) and pump, then note their fitted locations, and disconnect the various hoses from the reservoir.

5 Refitting is a reversal of removal. Ensure the locating lugs on the base of the reservoir engage

correctly with the corresponding slots in the inner wing. Refill the reservoir and check for leakage.

Windscreen washer pump

6 Remove the fluid reservoir as previously described in this Section.

7 Carefully pull the pump from the grommet in the side of the reservoir **(see illustration)**.

8 Refitting is the reverse of removal, using a new sealing grommet if the original one shows signs of damage or deterioration. Refill the reservoir and check the pump grommet for leaks.

Washer reservoir level switch

9 Some models are fitted with a fluid level switch. Remove the fluid reservoir as described previously in this Section.

10 Carefully pull the switch from the grommet in the base of the reservoir.

11 Refitting is the reverse of removal, using a

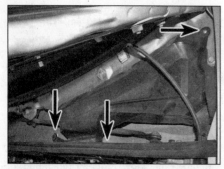

13.3 Remove the fasteners (arrowed) and lift out the trim cover

13.4 Prise the linkage rod from the motor arm

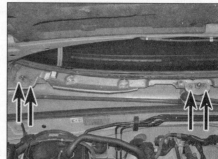

13.5 Wiper linkage retaining bolts (arrowed)

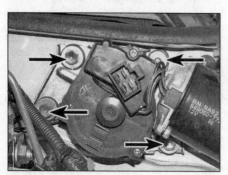

13.8 The wiper motor is secured by 3 bolts at the front, and 1 at the rear (arrowed)

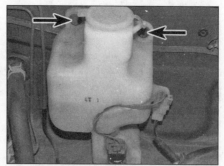

14.3a Washer reservoir retaining screws (arrowed) – 1999 and earlier …

14.3b … and 2000-on (arrowed)

new sealing grommet if the original one shows signs of damage or deterioration. Refill the reservoir and check for leaks.

Windscreen washer jets

12 Open the bonnet and disconnect the washer hose(s) from the base of the jet.
13 Squeeze together the clip each side of the jet and manoeuvre it out the top of the bonnet **(see illustration)**.
14 On refitting, push the jet back into position in the bonnet, and securely connect the jet to the hose. If necessary insert a needle into the jet nozzle and adjust the aim.

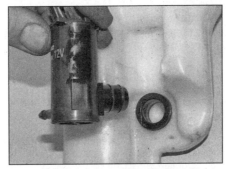

14.7 Pull the washer pump from the grommet

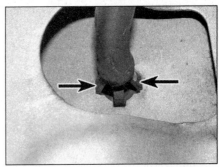

14.13 Squeeze together the clips (arrowed) and push the washer jet from the bonnet

---

15 Audio unit – removal and refitting

Note: *The following procedure is for the unit fitted to the project vehicle. Removal and refitting procedures of other units will differ slightly.*

Removal

1 Disconnect the battery negative lead as described in Chapter 5A, Section 4.
2 Using a blunt, flat-bladed tool, carefully prise the trim from each side of the audio unit **(see illustration)**. Ensure the trims are prised squarely rearwards to prevent damage to the locating pins.
3 Insert Mazda special tools or equivalent, into the holes each side, release the clips and pull the audio unit rearwards. Disconnect the wiring plugs as the unit is withdrawn **(see illustration)**. Note that audio unit removal tools are generally available from automotive parts retailers or audio system specialists.

Refitting

4 Refitting is a reversal of removal.

16 Loudspeakers – removal and refitting

Door main loudspeaker

1997 and earlier models

1 Carefully pull the speaker grille from the door **(see illustration)**.

16.1 Prise the speaker grille from the door

15.2 Carefully prise the trim away each side

2 Undo the retaining screws and remove the speaker. Disconnect the wiring plug as the speaker is withdrawn.
3 Refitting is the reverse of removal.

1998-on models

4 Remove the door inner trim panel as described in Chapter 11, Section 11.
5 Undo the retaining screws and remove the speaker **(see illustration)**. Disconnect the wiring plug as the speaker is withdrawn.
6 Refitting is the reverse of removal.

Door upper loudspeaker

7 Remove the door inner trim panel as described in Chapter 11, Section 11.
8 Undo the retaining screws and detach the speaker from the door trim.
9 Refitting is a reversal of removal.

Headrest speakers

10 Remove the seat (see Chapter 11,

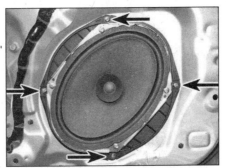

16.5 Speaker retaining screws (arrowed)

15.3 Insert the removal tools, and pull the unit rearwards

Section 23). Remove the seatback portion of the seat cover.
11 Remove the speaker grille, then remove the speaker retaining screws/nuts. Unplug the electrical connector and remove the speaker.
12 Refitting is the reverse of removal.

17 Radio aerial – removal and refitting

1 Open the boot and disconnect the aerial wiring plug **(see illustration)**. **Note:** *The aerial may be tested if desired, by checking continuity at the aerial wiring plug end. The aerial should have full continuity (no resistance).*
2 Place masking tape around the aerial base to protect the paint.
3 On models with a manual aerial, unscrew and remove the mast.

17.1 Aerial wiring plugs and retaining nut (arrowed)

17.4 Use a pair of circlip pliers (or similar) to unscrew the aerial base

4 On all models, unscrew and remove the aerial base **(see illustration)**.

5 On models with powered aerials, turn the ignition key to On, turn the radio switch to On, then, after the aerial fully extends, gently pull on the mast – the mast and nylon rack gear will pull out of the aerial assembly.

6 To remove the aerial assembly, remove the boot side trim on the side with the aerial. Disconnect the aerial wiring plug(s) and bolt or nut, then lift out the aerial assembly.

7 Refitting is the reverse of removal. To refit the mast on power aerial models:

 a) *Turn the ignition switch and radio to On.*
 b) *Wait until the power aerial stops operating (you hear no more noise from it).*
 c) *Insert the aerial mast into the power aerial assembly.*
 d) *Make sure the aerial mast rack gear fits into the pinion gear within the power aerial assembly.*
 e) *Turn the ignition switch to LOCK. The power aerial will operate, retracting the mast.*
 f) *After the aerial mast is retracted, refit and tighten the mounting nut securely.*

18 Anti-theft alarm system –
general information

The MX5 models are equipped with a sophisticated anti-theft alarm and immobiliser system. Should a fault develop, the system's self-diagnosis facility should be interrogated using dedicated test equipment. Consult your Mazda dealer or suitably-equipped specialist.

19 Airbag system –
general information and precautions

The models covered by this manual may be equipped with a driver's airbag mounted in the centre of the steering wheel, and a passenger's airbag located behind the facia. The airbag system comprises of the airbag unit(s) (complete with gas generators), impact sensor, the control unit and a warning light in the instrument panel.

The airbag system is triggered in the event of a heavy frontal or side impact above a predetermined force; depending on the point of impact. The airbag(s) is inflated within milliseconds and forms a safety cushion between the cabin occupants and the cabin interior, and therefore greatly reduces the risk of injury. The airbag then deflates almost immediately.

Every time the ignition is switched on, the airbag control unit performs a self-test. The self-test takes approximately 2 to 6 seconds and during this time the airbag warning light on the facia is illuminated. After the self-test has been completed the warning light should go out. If the warning light fails to come on, remains illuminated after the initial period, or comes on at any time when the vehicle is being driven, there is a fault in the airbag system. The vehicle should be taken to a Mazda dealer for examination at the earliest possible opportunity.

⚠️ *Warning: Before carrying out any operations on the airbag system, disconnect the battery negative terminal, and wait for at least 1 minute. This will allow the capacitors in the system to discharge. When operations are complete, make sure no one is inside the vehicle when the battery is reconnected.*
• *Note that the airbag(s) must not be subjected to temperatures in excess of 90°C. When the airbag is removed, ensure that it is stored the correct way up to prevent possible inflation (padded surface uppermost).*
• *Do not allow any solvents or cleaning agents to contact the airbag assemblies. They must be cleaned using only a damp cloth.*

• *The airbags and control unit are both sensitive to impact. If either is dropped or damaged they should be renewed.*
• *Disconnect the airbag control unit wiring plug prior to using arc-welding equipment on the vehicle.*

20 Airbag system components –
removal and refitting

Note: *Refer to the warnings in Section 19 before carrying out the following operations.*
1 Disconnect the battery negative terminal (see Chapter 5A, Section 4), then continue as described under the relevant heading.

Driver's airbag

1997 and earlier models

2 Ensure the steering wheel is in the straight-ahead position, then undo the 2 screws at the lower edge, and pull the lower panel rearwards to release the retaining clips **(see illustration)**.
3 Working under the facia, disconnect the orange and blue rotary contact unit wiring plug.
4 Undo the 4 airbag retaining nuts on the front of the steering wheel boss, and withdraw the airbag from the steering wheel. Disconnect the wiring plugs as the airbag is withdrawn. Note that the airbag must not be knocked or dropped and should be stored the correct way up with its padded surface uppermost.
5 On refitting reconnect the wiring connector(s) and seat the airbag unit in the steering wheel, making sure the wire does not become trapped. Tighten the nuts to the specified torque. Reconnect the battery as described in Chapter 5A, Section 4.

1998-on models

6 With the wheel in the straight-ahead position, prise out the plastic cover each side (where fitted), then undo the airbag retaining bolts **(see illustration)**.
7 Carefully lift the airbag assembly away from the steering wheel. Note their fitted positions and disconnect the wiring plug(s) from the airbag unit **(see illustration)**. Note that the airbag must not be knocked or dropped and

20.2 Undo the screws (arrowed) and pull the panel rearwards

20.6 Prise out the cover and undo the airbag retaining bolt each side of the steering wheel boss

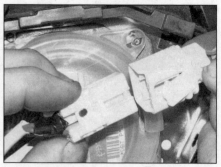

20.7 Depress the clip and disconnect the airbag wiring plug

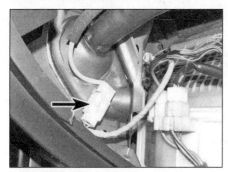

20.10 Disconnect the airbag wiring plug (arrowed)

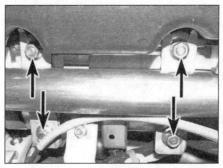

20.11a Undo the nuts/bolts (arrowed) ...

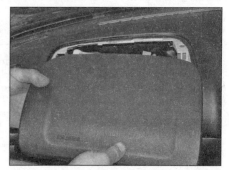

20.11b ... and manoeuvre the passenger's airbag rearwards

20.16 Rotary contact unit retaining screws (arrowed)

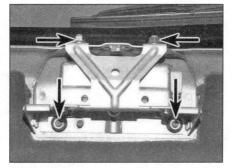

20.22 Airbag control unit retaining nuts (arrowed)

20.23 The arrow on the control unit must point forwards

should be stored the correct way up with its padded surface uppermost.

8 On refitting reconnect the wiring connector(s) and seat the airbag unit in the steering wheel, making sure the wire does not become trapped. Tighten the bolts to the specified torque. Reconnect the battery as described in Chapter 5A, Section 4.

Passenger airbag

9 Remove the passenger's glovebox as described in Chapter 11, Section 26.

10 Release the locking catch(es), and disconnect the airbag wiring plug(s) **(see illustration)**.

11 Undo the 4 retaining nuts/bolts and manoeuvre the airbag rearwards (not upwards) from the facia **(see illustrations)**.

12 Refitting is a reversal of removal. Tighten the airbag retaining nuts/bolts to the specified torque, and reconnect the battery negative terminal.

Rotary contact assembly

1997 and earlier models

13 The rotary contact unit is integral with the steering column combination switch assembly. Removal and refitting of the switch is described in Section 4.

1998-on models

14 Remove the steering wheel as described in Chapter 10, Section 14.

15 Undo the screws, then unclip the lower and upper steering column shrouds **(see illustrations 4.6b and 4.6c)**.

16 Undo the 3 screws and remove the rotary contact unit **(see illustration)**.

17 Refitting is the reverse of removal. If the contact unit has been rotated with the wheel removed, centralise it by rotating its centre fully clockwise until it stops. From this position, rotate the centre back through 2.75 complete rotations in an anti-clockwise direction until the marks align **(see illustration 4.10)**.

Control unit

1994 to 1997 models

18 The control unit is located under the right-hand side of the facia. Remove the complete facia as described in Chapter 11, Section 28.

19 Undo the retaining nuts and remove the control unit complete with mounting bracket. Disconnect the wiring plugs as the unit is withdrawn.

20 Refitting is the reverse of removal.

1998-on models

21 Remove the complete facia as described in Chapter 11, Section 28.

22 Undo the nuts and remove the control unit along with the mounting bracket **(see illustration)**. Disconnect the wiring plug as the unit is withdrawn. If required, undo the screws and detach the bracket from the control unit.

23 Refitting is a reversal of removal. Note arrow on the control unit must face forwards **(see illustration)**.

Impact sensors

1997 and earlier models only

24 The D sensors are bolted to the front panel. To remove the outer sensors, release the fasteners and remove the front wheel arch liner. Disconnect the sensor(s) wiring plug.

25 The S sensor is located centrally under the facia. Remove the complete facia as described in Chapter 11, Section 28.

26 With bolt type sensors, undo the retaining bolts/nuts and withdrawn the sensor and mounting bracket. Handle the sensor with care – they are easily damaged.

27 Refitting is a reversal of removal. Tighten the retaining bolts/nuts securely.

Mazda MX5 (1989-1997) wiring diagrams

Diagram 1

 WARNING: *This vehicle is fitted with a supplemental restraint system (SRS) consisting of a combination of driver (and passenger) airbag(s), side impact protection airbags and seatbelt pre-tensioners. The use of electrical test equipment on any SRS wiring systems may cause the seatbelt pre-tensioners to abruptly retract and airbags to explosively deploy, resulting in potentially severe personal injury. Extreme care should be taken to correctly identify any circuits to be tested to avoid choosing any of the SRS wiring in error.*

For further information see airbag system precautions in body electrical systems chapter.

Note: The SRS wiring harness can normally be identified by yellow and/or orange harness or harness connectors.

Key to symbols

Solenoid actuator		Bulb		Wire splice, soldered joint, or unspecified connector
Earth point		Switch		Connecting wires
Wire colour (blue with white tracer)	L/W	Fuse/Fusible link and current rating	F4 40A	Diode
Dashed outline denotes part of a larger item, containing in this case an electronic or solid state device.		Resistor		Light-emitting diode
		Variable resistor		Item number
				Motor/pump
		Variable resistor		Heating element

Engine compartment fusebox ⑤

F1	30A	Fuel injection circuits, alternator
F2	30A	Headlights
F3	80A	Main circuit protection
F4	40A	Ignition circuits
F5	60A	Anti-lock brakes
F6	30A	Engine cooling fan
F7	20A	Additional cooling fan
F8	15A	Foglights
F9	10A	Fuel injection circuits
F10	30A	Headlight retractor

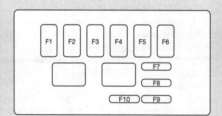

Passenger compartment fusebox ⑥

F1	15A	Engine cooling fan
F2	10A	Instrument cluster
F3	–	Spare
F4	30A	Heater blower
F5	–	Spare
F6	30A	Electric windows
F7	20A	Wash/wipe
F8	–	Spare
F9	10A	Tail lights
F10	–	Spare
F11	10A	Horn, stop lights
F12	10A	Hazard warning lights
F13	–	Spare
F14	–	Spare
F15	15A	Cigar lighter
F16	–	Spare
F17	10A	Interior lights

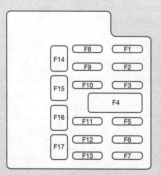

Luggage compartment fusebox ⑬

F1	10A	Heated rear window (if fitted)
F2	10A	Electric aerial (if fitted)

H47487

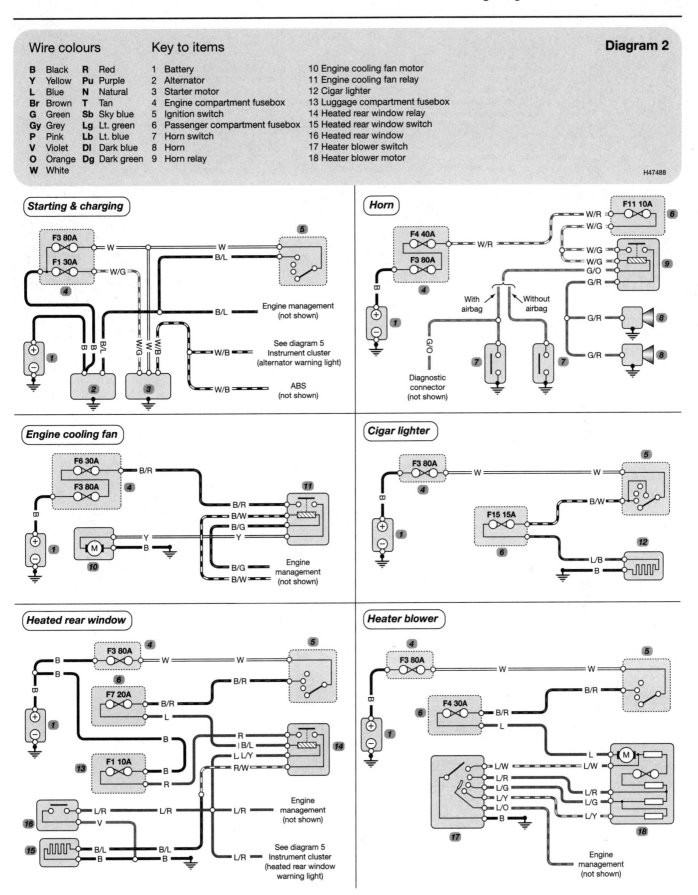

Wire colours

B	Black	**R**	Red
Y	Yellow	**Pu**	Purple
L	Blue	**N**	Natural
Br	Brown	**T**	Tan
G	Green	**Sb**	Sky blue
Gy	Grey	**Lg**	Lt. green
P	Pink	**Lb**	Lt. blue
V	Violet	**Dl**	Dark blue
O	Orange	**Dg**	Dark green
W	White		

Key to items

1 Battery
2 Alternator
3 Starter motor
4 Engine compartment fusebox
5 Ignition switch
6 Passenger compartment fusebox
7 Horn switch
8 Horn
9 Horn relay
10 Engine cooling fan motor
11 Engine cooling fan relay
12 Cigar lighter
13 Luggage compartment fusebox
14 Heated rear window relay
15 Heated rear window switch
16 Heated rear window
17 Heater blower switch
18 Heater blower motor

Diagram 2

H47488

Starting & charging

Horn

Engine cooling fan

Cigar lighter

Heated rear window

Heater blower

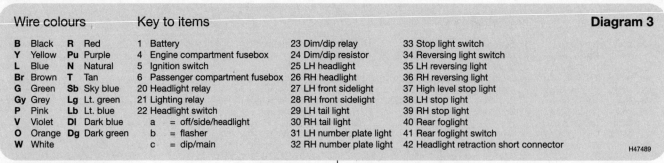

Wire colours

B	Black	R	Red
Y	Yellow	Pu	Purple
L	Blue	N	Natural
Br	Brown	T	Tan
G	Green	Sb	Sky blue
Gy	Grey	Lg	Lt. green
P	Pink	Lb	Lt. blue
V	Violet	Dl	Dark blue
O	Orange	Dg	Dark green
W	White		

Key to items

1 Battery
4 Engine compartment fusebox
5 Ignition switch
6 Passenger compartment fusebox
20 Headlight relay
21 Lighting relay
22 Headlight switch
  a = off/side/headlight
  b = flasher
  c = dip/main
23 Dim/dip relay
24 Dim/dip resistor
25 LH headlight
26 RH headlight
27 LH front sidelight
28 RH front sidelight
29 LH tail light
30 RH tail light
31 LH number plate light
32 RH number plate light
33 Stop light switch
34 Reversing light switch
35 LH reversing light
36 RH reversing light
37 High level stop light
38 LH stop light
39 RH stop light
40 Rear foglight
41 Rear foglight switch
42 Headlight retraction short connector

Diagram 3

H47489

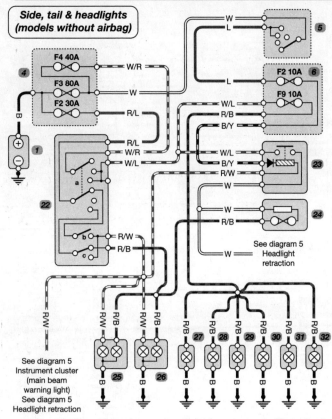

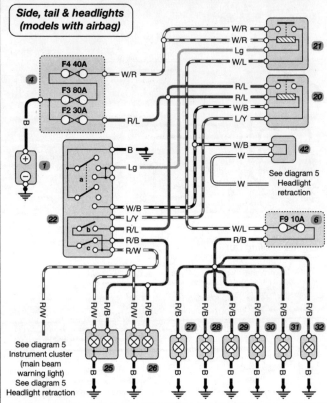

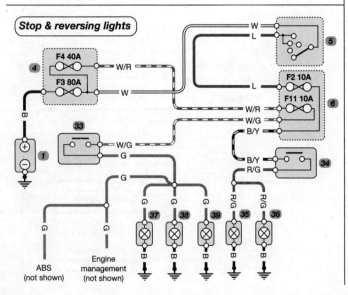

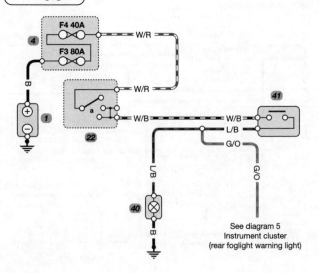

Wire colours

B	Black	R	Red
Y	Yellow	Pu	Purple
L	Blue	N	Natural
Br	Brown	T	Tan
G	Green	Sb	Sky blue
Gy	Grey	Lg	Lt. green
P	Pink	Lb	Lt. blue
V	Violet	Dl	Dark blue
O	Orange	Dg	Dark green
W	White		

Key to items

1 Battery
4 Engine compartment fusebox
5 Ignition switch
6 Passenger compartment fusebox
13 Luggage compartment fusebox
21 Lighting relay
22 Headlight switch
  a = off/side/headlight
45 LH Interior light
46 RH interior light
47 LH door switch

48 RH door switch
49 Direction indicator switch
50 Direction indicator relay
51 Hazard warning light switch
52 LH front direction indicator
53 LH indicator side repeater
54 LH rear direction indicator
55 RH front direction indicator
56 RH indicator side repeater
57 RH rear direction indicator
58 Switch illumination dimmer control

59 Wiper motor
60 Wash/wipe switch
  a = flick wipe
  b = wiper
  c = washer
61 Washer pump
62 Audio unit
63 Electric aerial
64 LH door speaker
65 RH door speaker

Diagram 4

H47490

Direction indicators & hazard warning lights

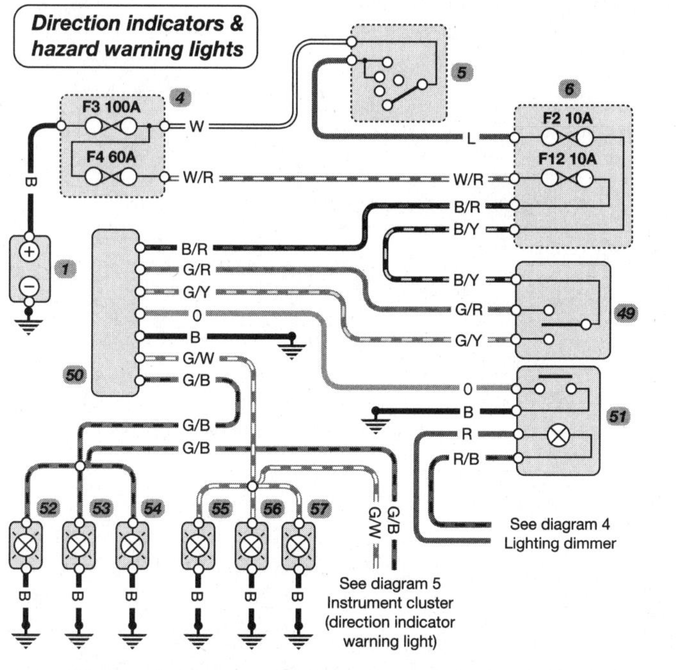

Wash/wipe

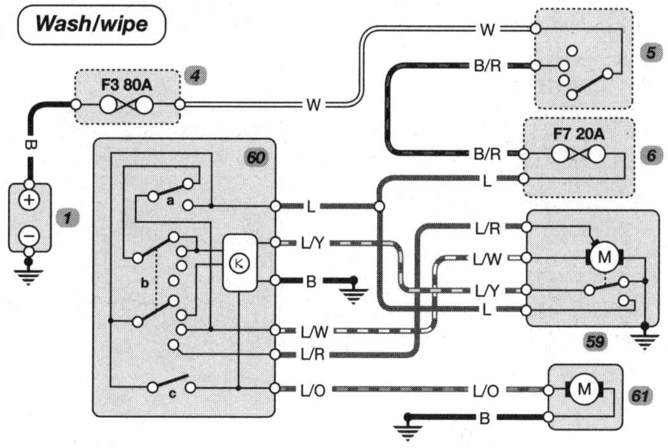

Interior light

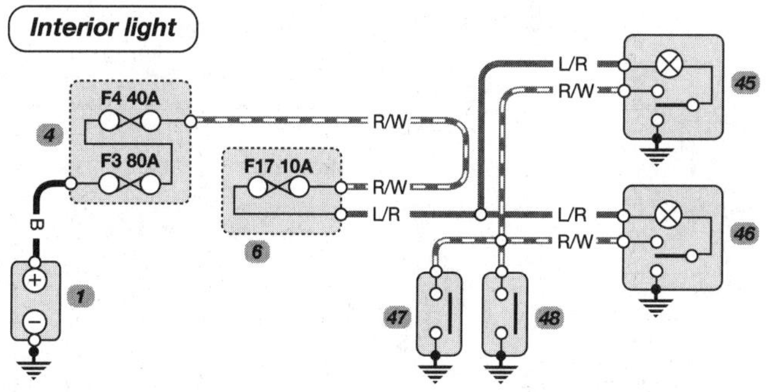

lighting dimmer (without airbag)

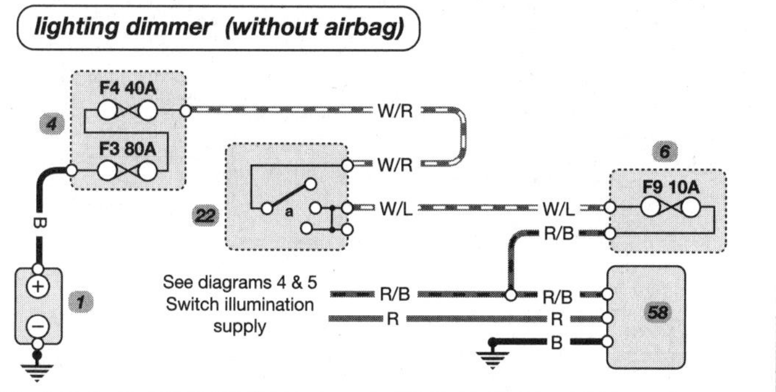

Audio system

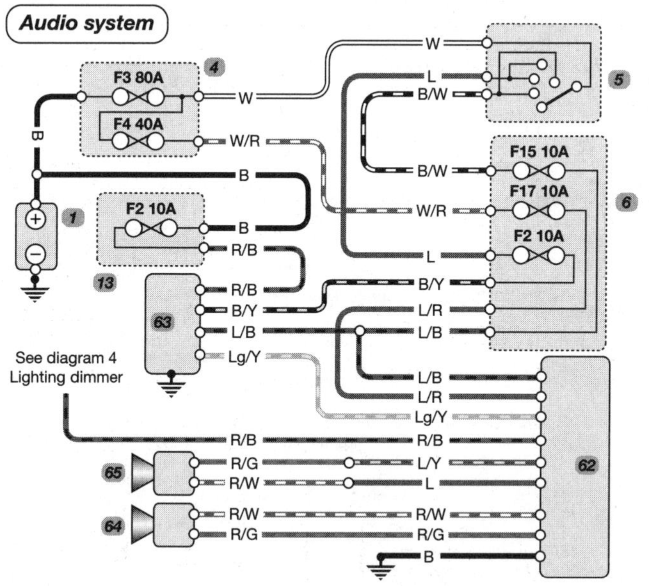

lighting dimmer (with airbag)

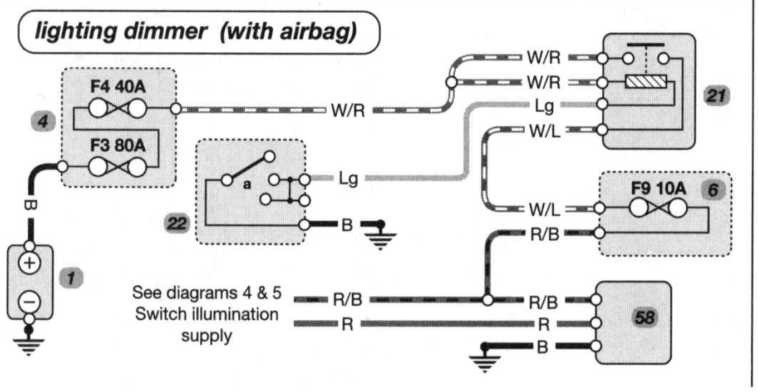

See diagram 4
Lighting dimmer

See diagram 5
Instrument cluster
(direction indicator
warning light)

See diagrams 4 & 5
Switch illumination
supply

See diagrams 4 & 5
Switch illumination
supply

See diagram 4
Lighting dimmer

Wire colours

B	Black	R	Red
Y	Yellow	Pu	Purple
L	Blue	N	Natural
Br	Brown	T	Tan
G	Green	Sb	Sky blue
Gy	Grey	Lg	Lt. green
P	Pink	Lb	Lt. blue
V	Violet	Dl	Dark blue
O	Orange	Dg	Dark green
W	White		

Key to items

1   Battery
4   Engine compartment fusebox
5   Ignition switch
6   Passenger compartment fusebox
70 Fuel gauge sender unit/fuel pump
71 Engine coolant temp. sensor
72 Oil pressure sensor
73 Low brake fluid switch
74 Handbrake switch
75 Low washer fluid sensor
76 Instrument cluster
  a = heated rear window warning light
  b = ABS warning light
  c = brake system warning light
  d = low washer fluid warning light
  e = alternator warning light
  f = airbag warning light
  g = oil pressure gauge
  h = coolant temperature gauge
  i = fuel gauge
  j = tachometer
  k = illumination
  l = headlight retraction warning light
  m = RH indicator warning light
  n = LH indicator warning light
  o = main beam warning light
  p = rear foglight warning light
  q = speed sensor
80 Electric window control switch
81 LH window motor
82 RH window motor
83 Electric mirror control switch
84 LH mirror assembly
85 RH mirror assembly
86 Retractable headlight unit
87 Retractable headlight switch
88 LH retractable headlight actuator
89 RH retractable headlight actuator

Diagram 5

H47491

Instrument cluster

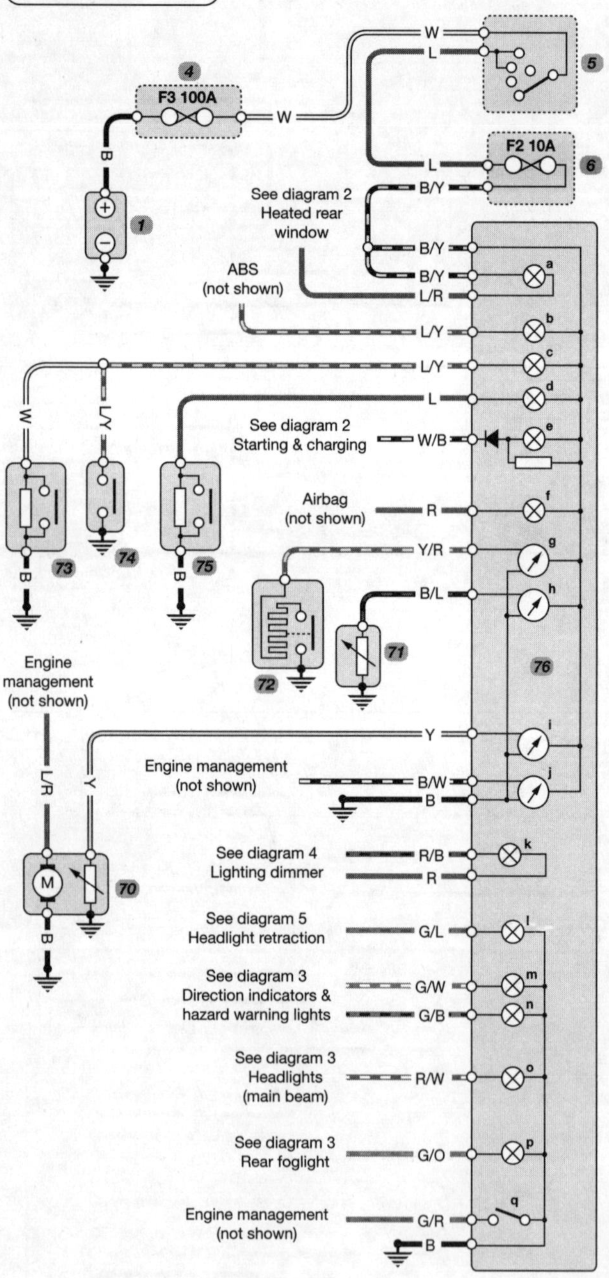

Electric windows

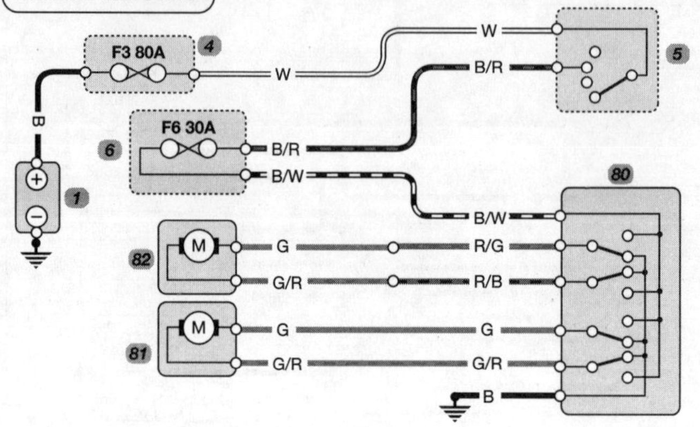

Electric mirrors

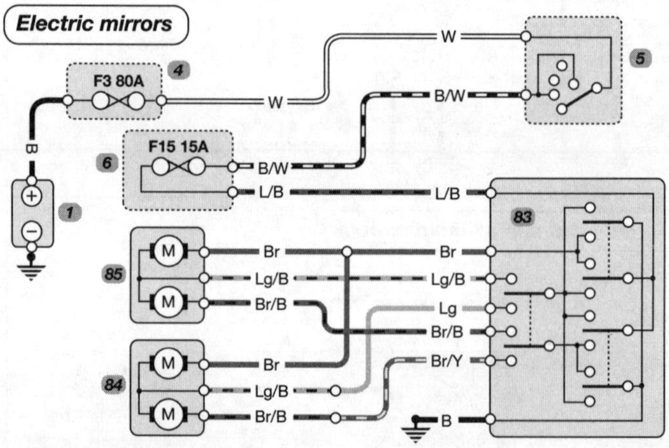

Headlight retraction

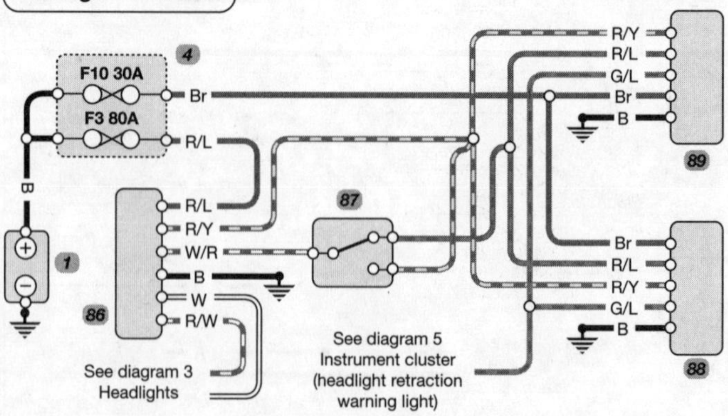

Mazda MX5 (1998-1999) wiring diagrams

Diagram 6

WARNING: *This vehicle is fitted with a supplemental restraint system (SRS) consisting of a combination of driver (and passenger) airbag(s), side impact protection airbags and seatbelt pre-tensioners. The use of electrical test equipment on any SRS wiring systems may cause the seatbelt pre-tensioners to abruptly retract and airbags to explosively deploy, resulting in potentially severe personal injury. Extreme care should be taken to correctly identify any circuits to be tested to avoid choosing any of the SRS wiring in error.*

For further information see airbag system precautions in body electrical systems chapter.

Note: The SRS wiring harness can normally be identified by yellow and/or orange harness or harness connectors.

Key to symbols

Symbol		Symbol		Symbol	
Solenoid actuator		Bulb		Wire splice, soldered joint, or unspecified connector	
Earth point		Switch		Connecting wires	
Wire colour (blue with white tracer)	L/W	Fuse/Fusible link and current rating	**F4 40A**	Diode	
		Resistor		Light-emitting diode	
Dashed outline denotes part of a larger item, containing in this case an electronic or solid state device.		Variable resistor		Item number	12
		Variable resistor		Motor/pump	M
				Heating element	

Engine compartment fusebox ⑤

F1	40A	Headlights & heated rear window
F2	30A	Fuel injection circuits
F3	80A	Main circuit protection
F4	40A	Ignition circuits
F5	30A	Heater blower motor
F6	30A	Engine cooling fan
F7	20A	Tail lights, instrument cluster illumination
F8	20A	Central locking
F9	20A	Anti-lock brakes
F10	15A	Stop lights, horn & shift lock

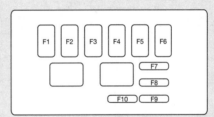

Passenger compartment fusebox ⑥

F1	20A	Wash/wipe
F2	30A	Electric windows
F3	10A	Air conditioning
F4	10A	Direction indicators
F5	10A	Central locking
F6	-	Spare
F7	15A	Heated rear window
F8	10A	Interior light, electric aerial & audible warning
F9	20A	Cigar lighter
F10	10A	Audio system
F11	-	Spare
F12	15A	Tail lights, parking lights
F13	15A	Engine management
F14	15A	Instrument cluster
F15	10A	Direction indicators
F16	10A	SRS & ABS
F17	30A	Cooling fan motor, magnetic clutch
F18	-	Spare
F19	10A	Rear foglight
F20	15A	RH headlight
F21	15A	LH headlight
F22	-	Spare

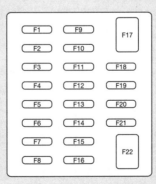

Wire colours

B	Black	R	Red
Y	Yellow	Pu	Purple
L	Blue	N	Natural
Br	Brown	T	Tan
G	Green	Sb	Sky blue
Gy	Grey	Lg	Lt. green
P	Pink	Lb	Lt. blue
V	Violet	Dl	Dark blue
O	Orange	Dg	Dark green
W	White		

Key to items

1 Battery
2 Alternator
3 Starter motor
4 Engine compartment fusebox
5 Ignition switch
6 Passenger compartment fusebox
7 Horn switch
8 Horn
9 Steering wheel clock spring
10 Horn relay
11 Engine cooling fan motor
12 Engine cooling fan relay
13 Cigar lighter
14 Air conditioning relay
15 Air conditioning cooling fan
16 Compressor clutch relay
17 Compressor clutch
18 Heated rear window relay
19 Heated rear window switch
20 Heated rear window
21 Condenser
22 Thermal protection

Diagram 7

H47493

Starting & charging

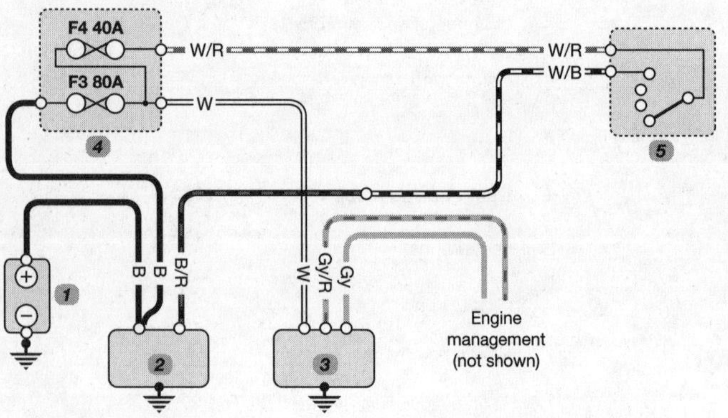

Horn

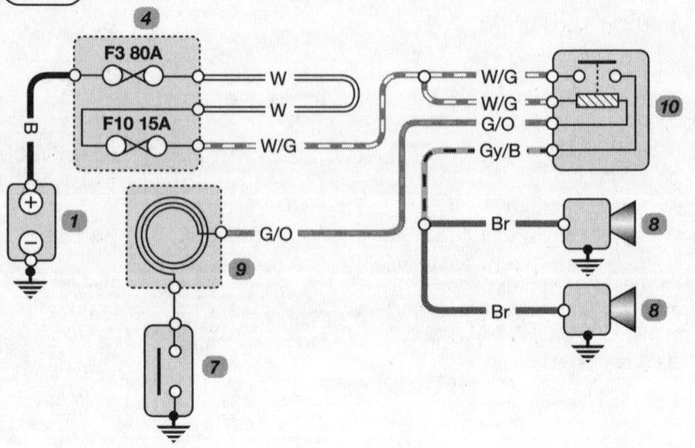

Engine cooling fan

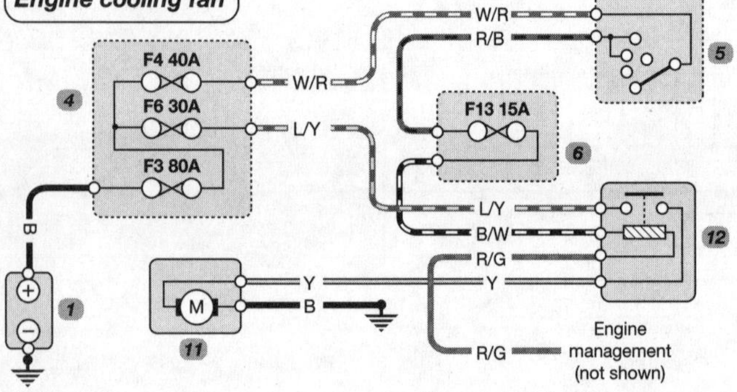

Cigar lighter

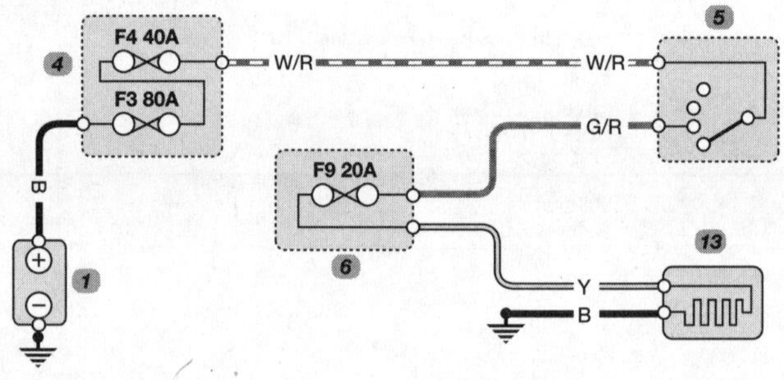

Compressor clutch & air conditioning engine cooling fan

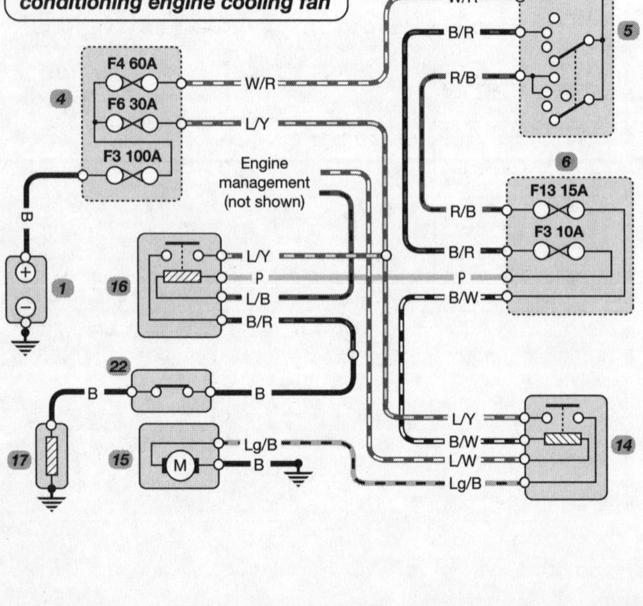

Heated rear window

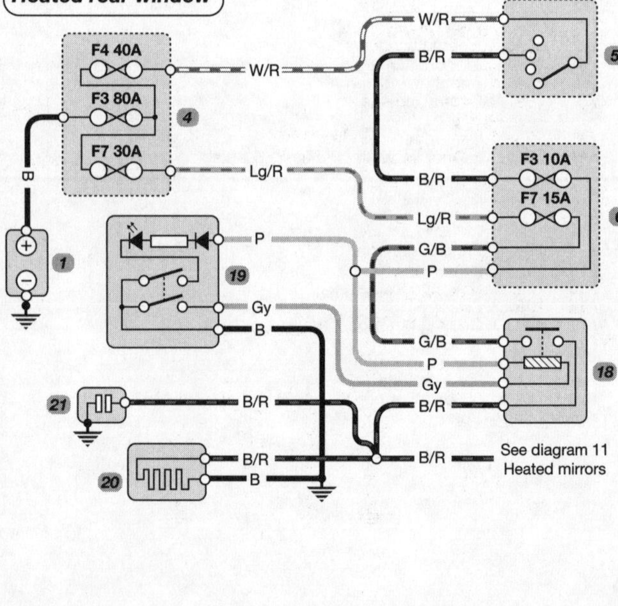

See diagram 11
Heated mirrors

Wire colours

B	Black	**R**	Red
Y	Yellow	**Pu**	Purple
L	Blue	**N**	Natural
Br	Brown	**T**	Tan
G	Green	**Sb**	Sky blue
Gy	Grey	**Lg**	Lt. green
P	Pink	**Lb**	Lt. blue
V	Violet	**Dl**	Dark blue
O	Orange	**Dg**	Dark green
W	White		

Key to items

1 Battery
4 Engine compartment fusebox
5 Ignition switch
6 Passenger comp. fusebox
24 Headlight relay
25 Lighting relay
26 Headlight switch
  a = main/dip/flash
  b = off/side/headlight
27 LH headlight dip beam
28 RH headlight dip beam
29 LH headlight main beam
30 RH headlight main beam
31 LH front sidelight
32 RH front sidelight
33 LH tail light
34 RH tail light
35 Stop light switch
36 Reversing light switch
37 Reversing light
38 LH stop light
39 RH stop light
40 High level stop light
41 Direction indicator flasher unit
42 Direction indicator switch
43 Hazard warning light switch
44 LH front direction indicator
45 LH rear direction indicator
46 LH indicator side repeater
47 RH front direction indicator
48 RH rear direction indicator
49 RH indicator side repeater
50 LH number plate light
51 RH number plate light
52 Rear foglight switch
53 Rear foglight relay
54 Rear foglight

Diagram 8

H47494

Side, tail & headlights

Direction indicators & hazard warning lights

Stop & reversing lights

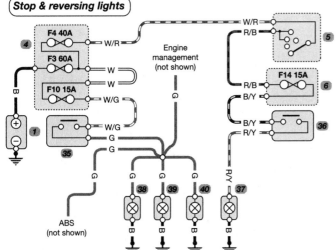

Rear foglights

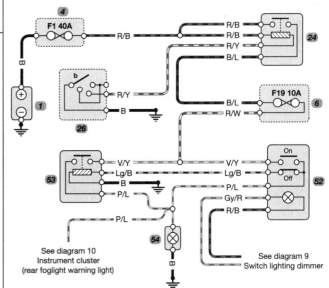

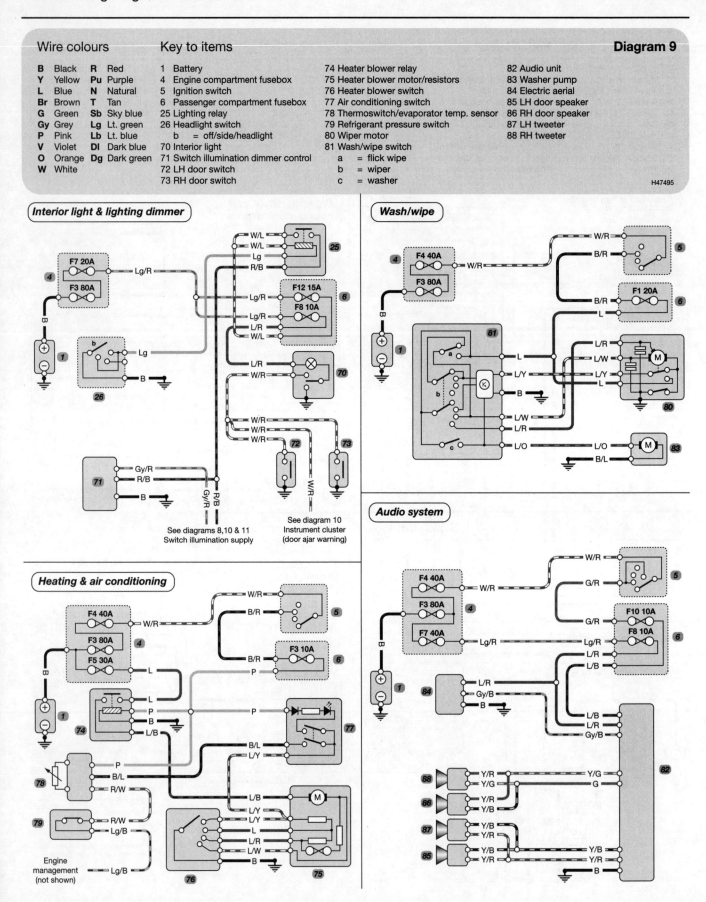

Wire colours

B	Black	**R**	Red
Y	Yellow	**Pu**	Purple
L	Blue	**N**	Natural
Br	Brown	**T**	Tan
G	Green	**Sb**	Sky blue
Gy	Grey	**Lg**	Lt. green
P	Pink	**Lb**	Lt. blue
V	Violet	**Dl**	Dark blue
O	Orange	**Dg**	Dark green
W	White		

Key to items

1 Battery
4 Engine compartment fusebox
5 Ignition switch
6 Passenger compartment fusebox
25 Lighting relay
26 Headlight switch
  b = off/side/headlight
70 Interior light
71 Switch illumination dimmer control
72 LH door switch
73 RH door switch

74 Heater blower relay
75 Heater blower motor/resistors
76 Heater blower switch
77 Air conditioning switch
78 Thermoswitch/evaporator temp. sensor
79 Refrigerant pressure switch
80 Wiper motor
81 Wash/wipe switch
  a = flick wipe
  b = wiper
  c = washer

82 Audio unit
83 Washer pump
84 Electric aerial
85 LH door speaker
86 RH door speaker
87 LH tweeter
88 RH tweeter

Diagram 9

H47495

Interior light & lighting dimmer

Wash/wipe

See diagrams 8,10 & 11
Switch illumination supply

See diagram 10
Instrument cluster
(door ajar warning)

Audio system

Heating & air conditioning

Engine
management
(not shown)

Wire colours

B	Black	R	Red
Y	Yellow	Pu	Purple
L	Blue	N	Natural
Br	Brown	T	Tan
G	Green	Sb	Sky blue
Gy	Grey	Lg	Lt. green
P	Pink	Lb	Lt. blue
V	Violet	Dl	Dark blue
O	Orange	Dg	Dark green
W	White		

Key to items

1 Battery
4 Engine compartment fusebox
5 Ignition switch
6 Passenger compartment fusebox
95 Fuel gauge sender unit
96 Engine coolant temp. sensor
97 Oil pressure switch
98 Low brake fluid switch
99 Handbrake switch
100 Vehicle speed sensor
101 Instrument cluster
  a = alarm
  b = trip computer
  c = SRS warning light
  d = ABS warning light
  e = brake warning light
  f = fuel gauge
  g = coolant temp. gauge
  h = oil pressure gauge
  i = main beam warning light
  j = speedometer
  k = tachometer
  l = rear foglight warning light
  m = RH indicator warning light
  n = LH indicator warning light
  o = alternator warning light
  p = airbag off warning light
  q = low fuel warning light
  r = illumination

Diagram 10

H47496

Instrument cluster

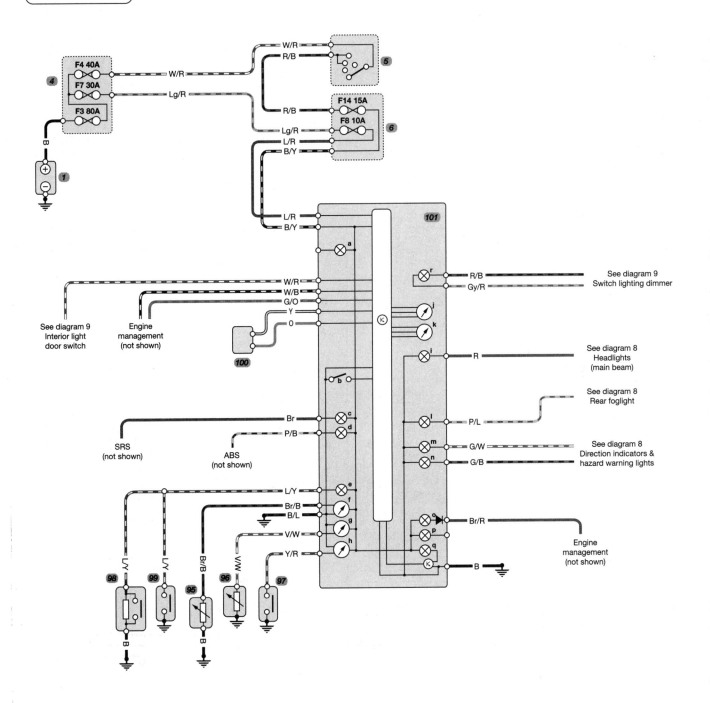

Wire colours

B	Black	R	Red
Y	Yellow	Pu	Purple
L	Blue	N	Natural
Br	Brown	T	Tan
G	Green	Sb	Sky blue
Gy	Grey	Lg	Lt. green
P	Pink	Lb	Lt. blue
V	Violet	Dl	Dark blue
O	Orange	Dg	Dark green
W	White		

Key to items

1 Battery
4 Engine compartment fusebox
5 Ignition switch
6 Passenger compartment fusebox
24 Headlight relay
26 Headlight switch
  a = main/dip/flash
  b = off/side/headlight
105 Electric window control switch
106 LH window motor

107 RH window motor
108 Electric mirror control switch
109 LH mirror assembly
110 RH mirror assembly
112 Central locking control unit
113 Door locking motor
114 Door locking switch
115 Headlight levelling switch
116 LH headlight levelling actuator
117 RH headlight levelling actuator

Diagram 11

H47497

Electric windows

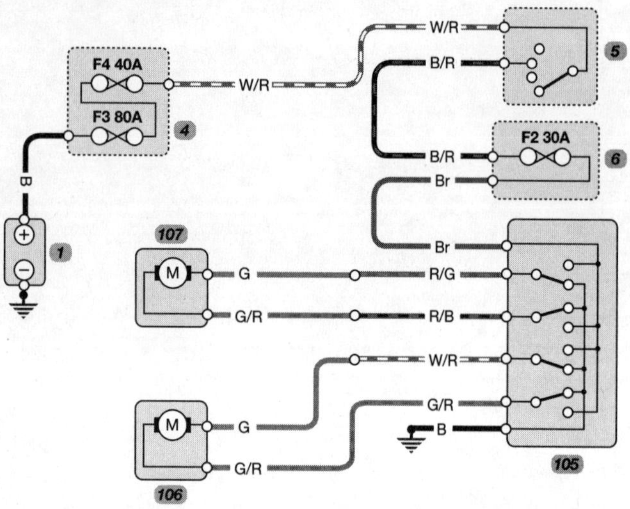

Central locking

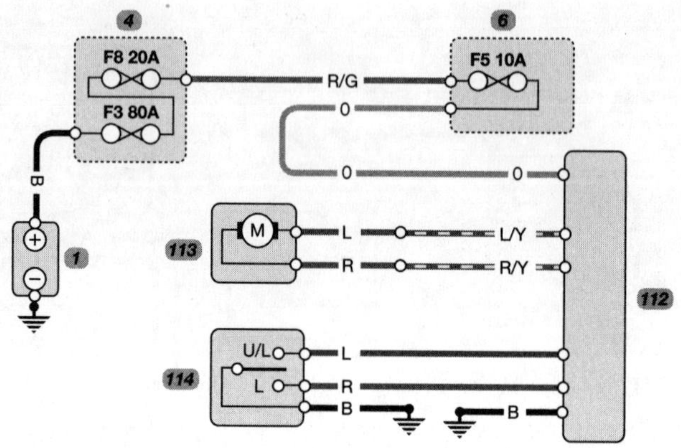

Electric mirrors

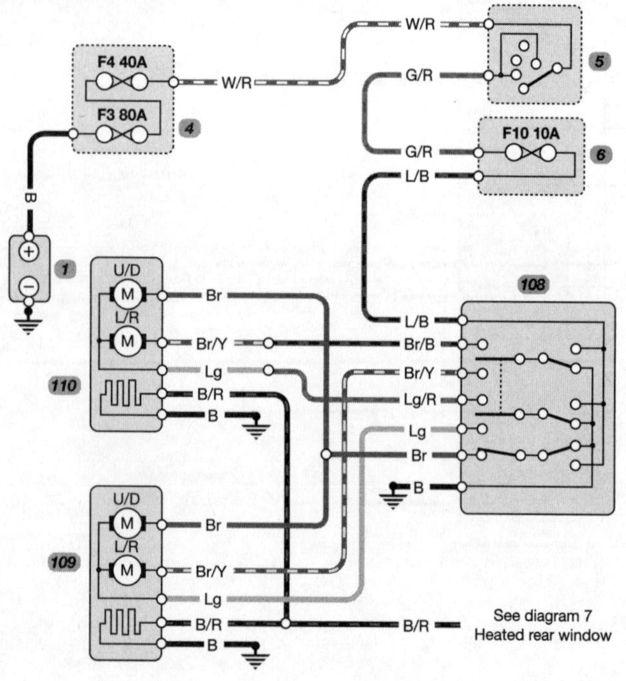

Headlight levelling

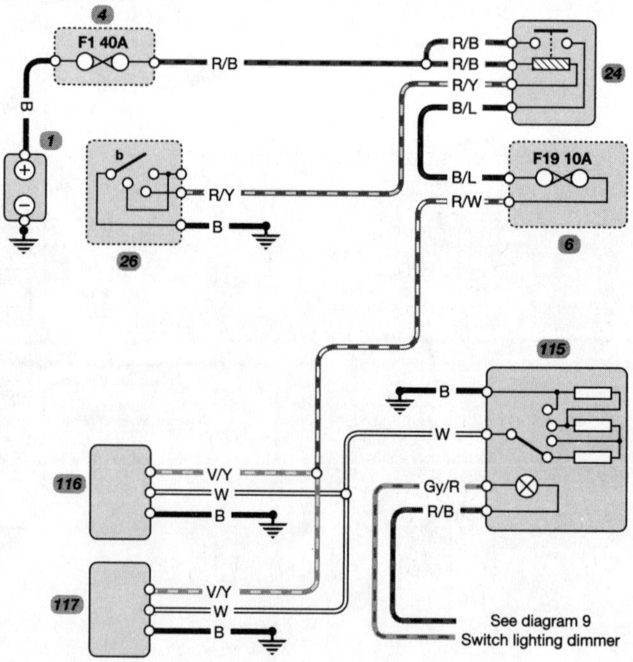

See diagram 7
Heated rear window

See diagram 9
Switch lighting dimmer

Mazda MX5 (2000-on) wiring diagrams

Diagram 12

 WARNING: *This vehicle is fitted with a supplemental restraint system (SRS) consisting of a combination of driver (and passenger) airbag(s), side impact protection airbags and seatbelt pre-tensioners. The use of electrical test equipment on any SRS wiring systems may cause the seatbelt pre-tensioners to abruptly retract and airbags to explosively deploy, resulting in potentially severe personal injury. Extreme care should be taken to correctly identify any circuits to be tested to avoid choosing any of the SRS wiring in error.*

For further information see airbag system precautions in body electrical systems chapter.

Note: The SRS wiring harness can normally be identified by yellow and/or orange harness or harness connectors.

Key to symbols

Symbol	Symbol	Symbol
Solenoid actuator	Bulb	Wire splice, soldered joint, or unspecified connector
Earth point	Switch	Connecting wires
Wire colour (blue with white tracer) — L/W	Fuse/Fusible link and current rating **F4 60A**	Diode
	Resistor	Light-emitting diode
Dashed outline denotes part of a larger item, containing in this case an electronic or solid state device.	Variable resistor	Item number **12**
	Variable resistor	Motor/pump
		Heating element

Engine compartment fusebox 5

F1	40A	Headlights & heated rear window
F2	30A	Fuel injection circuits
F3	100A	Main circuit protection
F4	60A	Ignition circuits
F5	30A	Heater blower motor
F6	30A	Engine cooling fan
F7	30A	Tail lights, instrument cluster illumination
F8	20A	Central locking
F9	20A	Anti-lock brakes
F10	15A	Stop lights, horn & shift lock

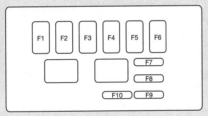

Passenger compartment fusebox 6

F1	20A	Wash/wipe
F2	30A	Electric windows
F3	7.5A	Air conditioning
F4	10A	Direction indicators
F5	10A	Central locking
F6	-	Spare
F7	15A	Heated rear window
F8	10A	Interior light, electric aerial & audible warning
F9	20A	Cigar lighter
F10	10A	Audio system
F11	15A	Front fog lights
F12	15A	Tail lights, parking lights
F13	15A	Engine management
F14	15A	Instrument cluster
F15	7.5A	Direction indicators
F16	10A	SRS & ABS
F17	20A	Cooling fan motor, magnetic clutch
F18	20A	Heated seats
F19	10A	Rear foglight
F20	15A	RH headlight
F21	15A	LH headlight
F22	-	Spare

H47498

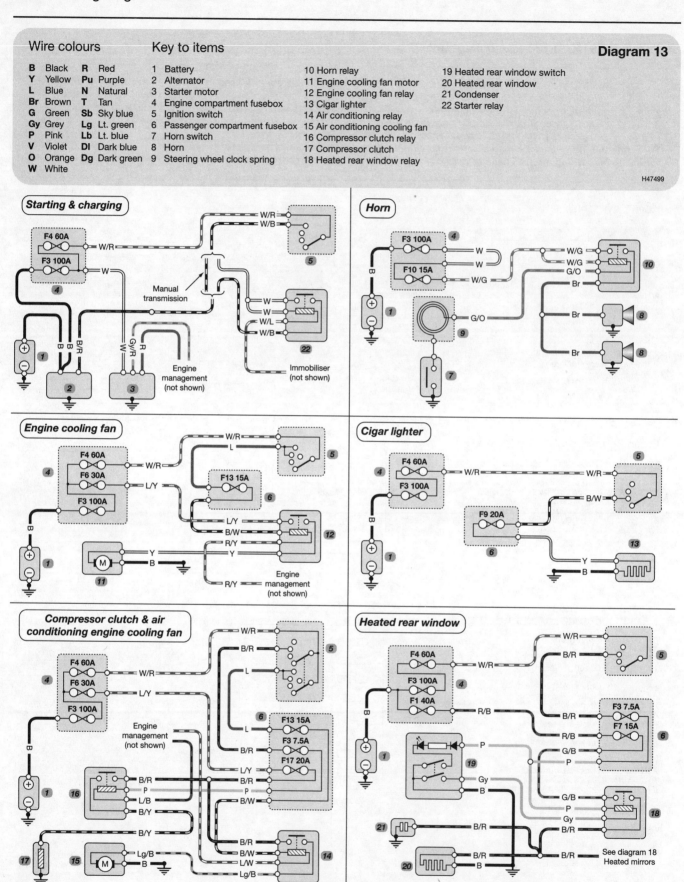

Wire colours

B	Black	R	Red
Y	Yellow	Pu	Purple
L	Blue	N	Natural
Br	Brown	T	Tan
G	Green	Sb	Sky blue
Gy	Grey	Lg	Lt. green
P	Pink	Lb	Lt. blue
V	Violet	Dl	Dark blue
O	Orange	Dg	Dark green
W	White		

Key to items

1 Battery
2 Alternator
3 Starter motor
4 Engine compartment fusebox
5 Ignition switch
6 Passenger compartment fusebox
7 Horn switch
8 Horn
9 Steering wheel clock spring
10 Horn relay
11 Engine cooling fan motor
12 Engine cooling fan relay
13 Cigar lighter
14 Air conditioning relay
15 Air conditioning cooling fan
16 Compressor clutch relay
17 Compressor clutch
18 Heated rear window relay
19 Heated rear window switch
20 Heated rear window
21 Condenser
22 Starter relay

Diagram 13

H47499

Starting & charging

Horn

Engine cooling fan

Cigar lighter

Compressor clutch & air conditioning engine cooling fan

Heated rear window

Wire colours

B	Black	R	Red
Y	Yellow	Pu	Purple
L	Blue	N	Natural
Br	Brown	T	Tan
G	Green	Sb	Sky blue
Gy	Grey	Lg	Lt. green
P	Pink	Lb	Lt. blue
V	Violet	Dl	Dark blue
O	Orange	Dg	Dark green
W	White		

Key to items

1 Battery
4 Engine compartment fusebox
5 Ignition switch
6 Passenger comp. fusebox
24 Headlight relay
25 Lighting relay
26 Headlight switch
  a = main/dip/flash
  b = off/side/headlight
27 LH headlight dip beam
28 RH headlight dip beam
29 LH headlight main beam
30 RH headlight main beam
31 LH front sidelight
32 RH front sidelight
33 LH tail light
34 RH tail light
35 Stop light switch
36 Reversing light switch
37 Reversing light
38 LH stop light
39 RH stop light
40 High level stop light
41 Direction indicator flasher unit
42 Direction indicator switch
43 Hazard warning light switch
44 LH front direction indicator
45 LH rear direction indicator
46 LH indicator side repeater
47 RH front direction indicator
48 RH rear direction indicator
49 RH indicator side repeater
50 Rear foglight control unit
51 LH front foglight
52 RH front foglight
53 Front foglight relay
54 Front foglight switch
55 Automatic transmission
  selector switch illumination

Diagram 14

H47500

Side, tail & headlights

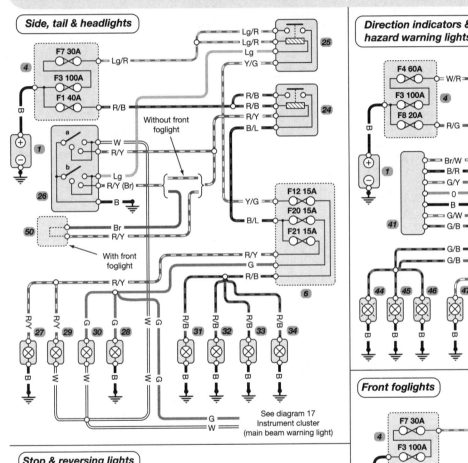

See diagram 17
Instrument cluster
(main beam warning light)

Stop & reversing lights

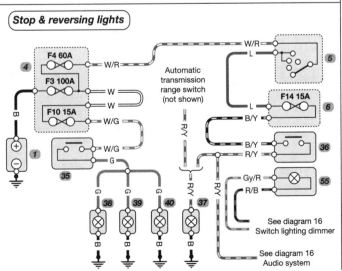

See diagram 16
Switch lighting dimmer

See diagram 16
Audio system

Direction indicators & hazard warning lights

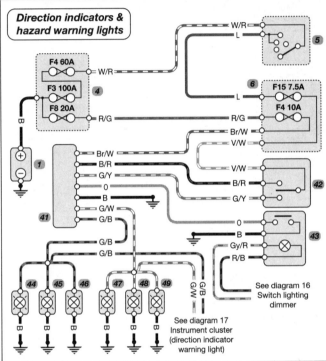

See diagram 16
Switch lighting
dimmer

See diagram 17
Instrument cluster
(direction indicator
warning light)

Front foglights

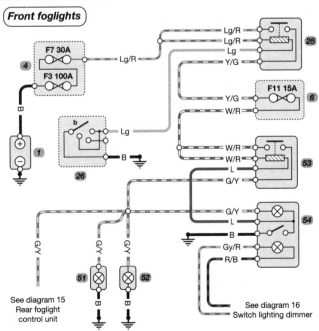

See diagram 15
Rear foglight
control unit

See diagram 16
Switch lighting dimmer

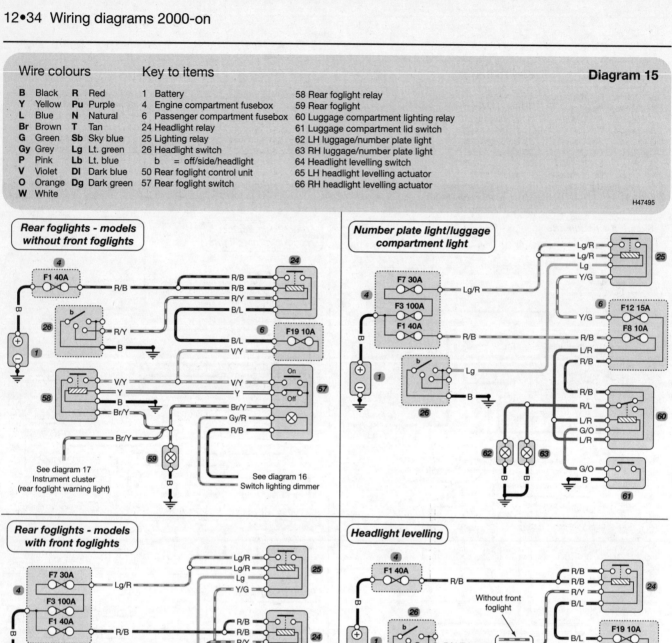

Wire colours

B	Black	R	Red
Y	Yellow	Pu	Purple
L	Blue	N	Natural
Br	Brown	T	Tan
G	Green	Sb	Sky blue
Gy	Grey	Lg	Lt. green
P	Pink	Lb	Lt. blue
V	Violet	Dl	Dark blue
O	Orange	Dg	Dark green
W	White		

Key to items

1 Battery
4 Engine compartment fusebox
6 Passenger compartment fusebox
24 Headlight relay
25 Lighting relay
26 Headlight switch
  b = off/side/headlight
50 Rear foglight control unit
57 Rear foglight switch

58 Rear foglight relay
59 Rear foglight
60 Luggage compartment lighting relay
61 Luggage compartment lid switch
62 LH luggage/number plate light
63 RH luggage/number plate light
64 Headlight levelling switch
65 LH headlight levelling actuator
66 RH headlight levelling actuator

Diagram 15

H47495

Rear foglights - models without front foglights

Number plate light/luggage compartment light

See diagram 17
Instrument cluster
(rear foglight warning light)

See diagram 16
Switch lighting dimmer

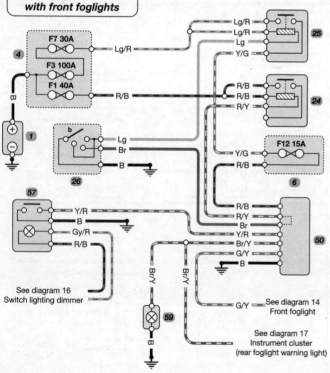

Rear foglights - models with front foglights

See diagram 16
Switch lighting dimmer

See diagram 16
Front foglight

See diagram 17
Instrument cluster
(rear foglight warning light)

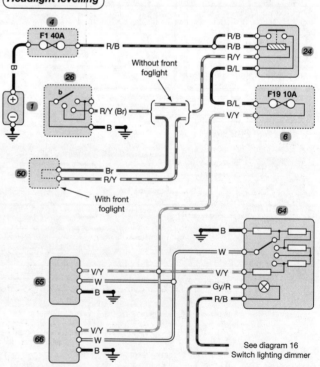

Headlight levelling

Without front foglight

With front foglight

See diagram 16
Switch lighting dimmer

Wire colours

B	Black	R	Red
Y	Yellow	Pu	Purple
L	Blue	N	Natural
Br	Brown	T	Tan
G	Green	Sb	Sky blue
Gy	Grey	Lg	Lt. green
P	Pink	Lb	Lt. blue
V	Violet	Dl	Dark blue
O	Orange	Dg	Dark green
W	White		

Key to items

1 Battery
4 Engine compartment fusebox
5 Ignition switch
6 Passenger compartment fusebox
25 Lighting relay
26 Headlight switch
　b = off/side/headlight
70 Interior light
71 Switch illumination dimmer control
72 LH door switch
73 RH door switch
74 Heater blower relay
75 Heater blower motor/resistors
76 Heater blower switch
77 Air conditioning switch
78 Thermoswitch/evaporator temp. sensor
79 Refrigerant pressure switch
80 Wiper motor
81 Wash/wipe switch
　a = flick wipe
　b = wiper
　c = washer
82 Audio unit
83 Washer pump
84 Electric aerial
85 LH door speaker
86 RH door speaker
87 LH tweeter
88 RH tweeter
89 LH aeroboard speaker
90 RH aeroboard speaker

Diagram 16

H47502

Interior light & lighting dimmer

Wash/wipe

Heating & air conditioning

Audio system

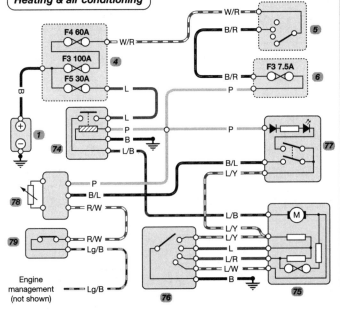

See diagrams 14,15 & 17
Switch illumination supply

See diagram 17
Instrument cluster
(door ajar warning)

Engine
management
(not shown)

See diagram 17
Instrument cluster

See diagram 14
Reversing light/
transmission switch

Engine
management
(not shown)

Wire colours

B	Black	**R**	Red
Y	Yellow	**Pu**	Purple
L	Blue	**N**	Natural
Br	Brown	**T**	Tan
G	Green	**Sb**	Sky blue
Gy	Grey	**Lg**	Lt. green
P	Pink	**Lb**	Lt. blue
V	Violet	**Dl**	Dark blue
O	Orange	**Dg**	Dark green
W	White		

Key to items

1	Battery
4	Engine compartment fusebox
5	Ignition switch
6	Passenger compartment fusebox
95	Fuel gauge sender unit
96	Engine coolant temp. sensor
97	Oil pressure switch
98	Low brake fluid switch
99	Handbrake switch
100	Buckle switch
101	Seatbelt warning light
102	Vehicle speed sensor

103	Instrument cluster
a =	alarm
b =	trip computer
c =	seatbelt warning light
d =	SRS warning light
e =	ABS warning light
f =	brake warning light
g =	fuel gauge
h =	coolant temp. gauge
i =	oil pressure gauge
j =	main beam warning light
k =	speedometer

l =	tachometer
m =	rear foglight warning light
n =	RH indicator warning light
o =	LH indicator warning light
p =	auto. trans. hold warning light
q =	MIL warning light
r =	alternator warning light
s =	airbag off warning light
t =	low fuel warning light
u =	illumination

Diagram 17

H47503

Instrument cluster

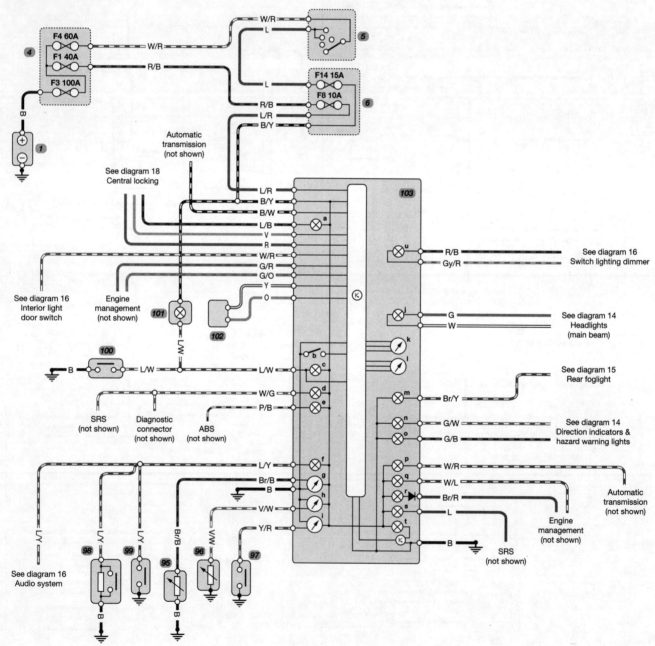

Wire colours

B	Black	R	Red
Y	Yellow	Pu	Purple
L	Blue	N	Natural
Br	Brown	T	Tan
G	Green	Sb	Sky blue
Gy	Grey	Lg	Lt. green
P	Pink	Lb	Lt. blue
V	Violet	Dl	Dark blue
O	Orange	Dg	Dark green
W	White		

Key to items

1 Battery
4 Engine compartment fusebox
5 Ignition switch
6 Passenger compartment fusebox
105 Electric window control switch
106 LH window motor
107 RH window motor
108 Electric mirror control switch
109 LH mirror assembly
110 RH mirror assembly
111 Key reminder switch
112 Central locking control unit
113 LH door locking motor
114 RH door locking motor
115 LH door key cylinder switch
116 RH door key cylinder switch

Diagram 18

H47504

Electric windows

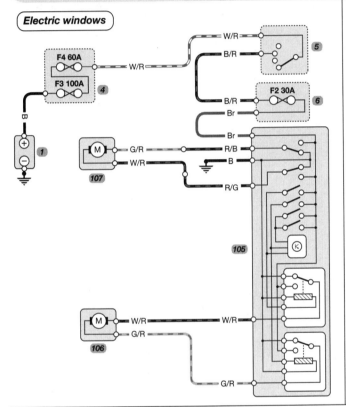

Electric mirrors

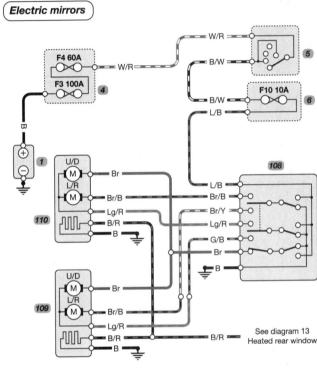

Central locking

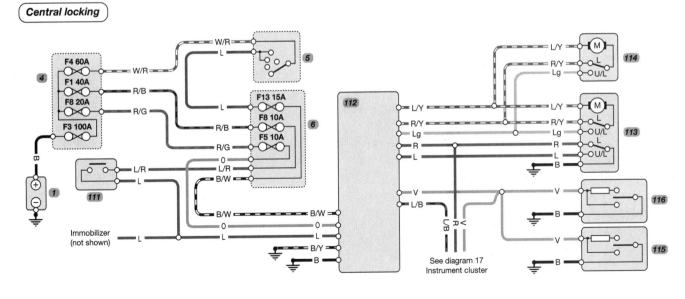

Dimensions

Note: *All figures are approximate, and may vary according to model. Refer to manufacturer's data for exact figures.*

Overall length:
    1997 and earlier models. . . . .   3948 mm
    1998-on models . . . .   3975 mm
Overall width:
    1997 and earlier models. . . . .   1676 mm
    1998-on models . . . .   1680 mm
Overall height. . . . .   1225 mm
Wheelbase . . . .   2266 mm

(handwritten annotations:)
2005 ONWARD.
3995mm = +20mm
1720mm = +40mm
1245mm = +20mm
2330mm = +64mm

Fuel economy

Although depreciation is still the biggest part of the cost of motoring for most car owners, the cost of fuel is more immediately noticeable. These pages give some tips on how to get the best fuel economy.

Working it out

Manufacturer's figures

Car manufacturers are required by law to provide fuel consumption information on all new vehicles sold. These 'official' figures are obtained by simulating various driving conditions on a rolling road or a test track. Real life conditions are different, so the fuel consumption actually achieved may not bear much resemblance to the quoted figures.

How to calculate it

Many cars now have trip computers which will

display fuel consumption, both instantaneous and average. Refer to the owner's handbook for details of how to use these.

To calculate consumption yourself (and maybe to check that the trip computer is accurate), proceed as follows.

1. Fill up with fuel and note the mileage, or zero the trip recorder.
2. Drive as usual until you need to fill up again.
3. Note the amount of fuel required to refill the tank, and the mileage covered since the previous fill-up.
4. Divide the mileage by the amount of fuel used to obtain the consumption figure.

For example:

Mileage at first fill-up (a) = 27,903
Mileage at second fill-up (b) = 28,346
Mileage covered (b - a) = 443
Fuel required at second fill-up = 48.6 litres

The half-completed changeover to metric units in the UK means that we buy our fuel

in litres, measure distances in miles and talk about fuel consumption in miles per gallon. There are two ways round this: the first is to convert the litres to gallons before doing the calculation (by dividing by 4.546, or see Table 1). So in the example:

48.6 litres ÷ 4.546 = 10.69 gallons
443 miles ÷ 10.69 gallons = 41.4 mpg

The second way is to calculate the consumption in miles per litre, then multiply that figure by 4.546 (or see Table 2).

So in the example, fuel consumption is:

443 miles ÷ 48.6 litres = 9.1 mpl
9.1 mpl x 4.546 = 41.4 mpg

The rest of Europe expresses fuel consumption in litres of fuel required to travel 100 km (l/100 km). For interest, the conversions are given in Table 3. In practice it doesn't matter what units you use, provided you know what your normal consumption is and can spot if it's getting better or worse.

Table 1: conversion of litres to Imperial gallons

litres	1	2	3	4	5	10	20	30	40	50	60	70
gallons	0.22	0.44	0.66	0.88	1.10	2.24	4.49	6.73	8.98	11.22	13.47	15.71

Table 2: conversion of miles per litre to miles per gallon

miles per litre	5	6	7	8	9	10	11	12	13	14
miles per gallon	23	27	32	36	41	46	50	55	59	64

Table 3: conversion of litres per 100 km to miles per gallon

litres per 100 km	4	4.5	5	5.5	6	6.5	7	8	9	10
miles per gallon	71	63	56	51	47	43	40	35	31	28

Maintenance

A well-maintained car uses less fuel and creates less pollution. In particular:

Filters

Change air and fuel filters at the specified intervals.

Oil

Use a good quality oil of the lowest viscosity specified by the vehicle manufacturer (see *Lubricants and fluids*). Check the level often and be careful not to overfill.

Spark plugs

When applicable, renew at the specified intervals.

Tyres

Check tyre pressures regularly. Under-inflated tyres have an increased rolling resistance. It is generally safe to use the higher pressures specified for full load conditions even when not fully laden, but keep an eye on the centre band of tread for signs of wear due to over-inflation.

When buying new tyres, consider the 'fuel saving' models which most manufacturers include in their ranges.

Driving style

Acceleration

Acceleration uses more fuel than driving at a steady speed. The best technique with modern cars is to accelerate reasonably briskly to the desired speed, changing up through the gears as soon as possible without making the engine labour.

Air conditioning

Air conditioning absorbs quite a bit of energy from the engine – typically 3 kW (4 hp) or so. The effect on fuel consumption is at its worst in slow traffic. Switch it off when not required.

Anticipation

Drive smoothly and try to read the traffic flow so as to avoid unnecessary acceleration and braking.

Automatic transmission

When accelerating in an automatic, avoid depressing the throttle so far as to make the transmission hold onto lower gears at higher speeds. Don't use the 'Sport' setting, if applicable.

When stationary with the engine running, select 'N' or 'P'. When moving, keep your left foot away from the brake.

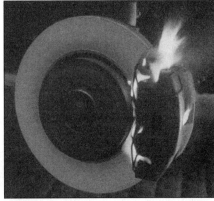

Braking

Braking converts the car's energy of motion into heat – essentially, it is wasted. Obviously some braking is always going to be necessary, but with good anticipation it is surprising how much can be avoided, especially on routes that you know well.

Carshare

Consider sharing lifts to work or to the shops. Even once a week will make a difference.

Electrical loads

Electricity is 'fuel' too; the alternator which charges the battery does so by converting some of the engine's energy of motion into electrical energy. The more electrical accessories are in use, the greater the load on the alternator. Switch off big consumers like the heated rear window when not required.

Freewheeling

Freewheeling (coasting) in neutral with the engine switched off is dangerous. The effort required to operate power-assisted brakes and steering increases when the engine is not running, with a potential lack of control in emergency situations.

In any case, modern fuel injection systems automatically cut off the engine's fuel supply on the overrun (moving and in gear, but with the accelerator pedal released).

Gadgets

Bolt-on devices claiming to save fuel have been around for nearly as long as the motor car itself. Those which worked were rapidly adopted as standard equipment by the vehicle manufacturers. Others worked only in certain situations, or saved fuel only at the expense of unacceptable effects on performance, driveability or the life of engine components.

The most effective fuel saving gadget is the driver's right foot.

Journey planning

Combine (eg) a trip to the supermarket with a visit to the recycling centre and the DIY store, rather than making separate journeys.

When possible choose a travelling time outside rush hours.

Load

The more heavily a car is laden, the greater the energy required to accelerate it to a given speed. Remove heavy items which you don't need to carry.

One load which is often overlooked is the contents of the fuel tank. A tankful of fuel (55 litres / 12 gallons) weighs 45 kg (100 lb) or so. Just half filling it may be worthwhile.

Lost?

At the risk of stating the obvious, if you're going somewhere new, have details of the route to hand. There's not much point in achieving record mpg if you also go miles out of your way.

Parking

If possible, carry out any reversing or turning manoeuvres when you arrive at a parking space so that you can drive straight out when you leave. Manoeuvering when the engine is cold uses a lot more fuel.

Driving around looking for free on-street parking may cost more in fuel than buying a car park ticket.

Premium fuel

Most major oil companies (and some supermarkets) have premium grades of fuel which are several pence a litre dearer than the standard grades. Reports vary, but the consensus seems to be that if these fuels improve economy at all, they do not do so by enough to justify their extra cost.

Roof rack

When loading a roof rack, try to produce a wedge shape with the narrow end at the front. Any cover should be securely fastened – if it flaps it's creating turbulence and absorbing energy.

Remove roof racks and boxes when not in use – they increase air resistance and can create a surprising amount of noise.

Short journeys

The engine is at its least efficient, and wear is highest, during the first few miles after a cold start. Consider walking, cycling or using public transport.

Speed

The engine is at its most efficient when running at a steady speed and load at the rpm where it develops maximum torque. (You can find this figure in the car's handbook.) For most cars this corresponds to between 55 and 65 mph in top gear.

Above the optimum cruising speed, fuel consumption starts to rise quite sharply. A car travelling at 80 mph will typically be using 30% more fuel than at 60 mph.

Supermarket fuel

It may be cheap but is it any good? In the UK all supermarket fuel must meet the relevant British Standard. The major oil companies will say that their branded fuels have better additive packages which may stop carbon and other deposits building up. A reasonable compromise might be to use one tank of branded fuel to three or four from the supermarket.

Switch off when stationary

Switch off the engine if you look like being stationary for more than 30 seconds or so. This is good for the environment as well as for your pocket. Be aware though that frequent restarts are hard on the battery and the starter motor.

Windows

Driving with the windows open increases air turbulence around the vehicle. Closing the windows promotes smooth airflow and

reduced resistance. The faster you go, the more significant this is.

And finally . . .

Driving techniques associated with good fuel economy tend to involve moderate acceleration and low top speeds. Be considerate to the needs of other road users who may need to make brisker progress; even if you do not agree with them this is not an excuse to be obstructive.

Safety must always take precedence over economy, whether it is a question of accelerating hard to complete an overtaking manoeuvre, killing your speed when confronted with a potential hazard or switching the lights on when it starts to get dark.

Conversion factors

Length (distance)
Inches (in)	x 25.4	= Millimetres (mm)	x 0.0394	=	Inches (in)
Feet (ft)	x 0.305	= Metres (m)	x 3.281	=	Feet (ft)
Miles	x 1.609	= Kilometres (km)	x 0.621	=	Miles

Volume (capacity)
Cubic inches (cu in; in³)	x 16.387	= Cubic centimetres (cc; cm³)	x 0.061	=	Cubic inches (cu in; in³)
Imperial pints (Imp pt)	x 0.568	= Litres (l)	x 1.76	=	Imperial pints (Imp pt)
Imperial quarts (Imp qt)	x 1.137	= Litres (l)	x 0.88	=	Imperial quarts (Imp qt)
Imperial quarts (Imp qt)	x 1.201	= US quarts (US qt)	x 0.833	=	Imperial quarts (Imp qt)
US quarts (US qt)	x 0.946	= Litres (l)	x 1.057	=	US quarts (US qt)
Imperial gallons (Imp gal)	x 4.546	= Litres (l)	x 0.22	=	Imperial gallons (Imp gal)
Imperial gallons (Imp gal)	x 1.201	= US gallons (US gal)	x 0.833	=	Imperial gallons (Imp gal)
US gallons (US gal)	x 3.785	= Litres (l)	x 0.264	=	US gallons (US gal)

Mass (weight)
Ounces (oz)	x 28.35	= Grams (g)	x 0.035	=	Ounces (oz)
Pounds (lb)	x 0.454	= Kilograms (kg)	x 2.205	=	Pounds (lb)

Force
Ounces-force (ozf; oz)	x 0.278	= Newtons (N)	x 3.6	=	Ounces-force (ozf; oz)
Pounds-force (lbf; lb)	x 4.448	= Newtons (N)	x 0.225	=	Pounds-force (lbf; lb)
Newtons (N)	x 0.1	= Kilograms-force (kgf; kg)	x 9.81	=	Newtons (N)

Pressure
Pounds-force per square inch (psi; lbf/in²; lb/in²)	x 0.070	= Kilograms-force per square centimetre (kgf/cm²; kg/cm²)	x 14.223	=	Pounds-force per square inch (psi; lbf/in²; lb/in²)
Pounds-force per square inch (psi; lbf/in²; lb/in²)	x 0.068	= Atmospheres (atm)	x 14.696	=	Pounds-force per square inch (psi; lbf/in²; lb/in²)
Pounds-force per square inch (psi; lbf/in²; lb/in²)	x 0.069	= Bars	x 14.5	=	Pounds-force per square inch (psi; lbf/in²; lb/in²)
Pounds-force per square inch (psi; lbf/in²; lb/in²)	x 6.895	= Kilopascals (kPa)	x 0.145	=	Pounds-force per square inch (psi; lbf/in²; lb/in²)
Kilopascals (kPa)	x 0.01	= Kilograms-force per square centimetre (kgf/cm²; kg/cm²)	x 98.1	=	Kilopascals (kPa)
Millibar (mbar)	x 100	= Pascals (Pa)	x 0.01	=	Millibar (mbar)
Millibar (mbar)	x 0.0145	= Pounds-force per square inch (psi; lbf/in²; lb/in²)	x 68.947	=	Millibar (mbar)
Millibar (mbar)	x 0.75	= Millimetres of mercury (mmHg)	x 1.333	=	Millibar (mbar)
Millibar (mbar)	x 0.401	= Inches of water (inH₂O)	x 2.491	=	Millibar (mbar)
Millimetres of mercury (mmHg)	x 0.535	= Inches of water (inH₂O)	x 1.868	=	Millimetres of mercury (mmHg)
Inches of water (inH₂O)	x 0.036	= Pounds-force per square inch (psi; lbf/in²; lb/in²)	x 27.68	=	Inches of water (inH₂O)

Torque (moment of force)
Pounds-force inches (lbf in; lb in)	x 1.152	= Kilograms-force centimetre (kgf cm; kg cm)	x 0.868	=	Pounds-force inches (lbf in; lb in)
Pounds-force inches (lbf in; lb in)	x 0.113	= Newton metres (Nm)	x 8.85	=	Pounds-force inches (lbf in; lb in)
Pounds-force inches (lbf in; lb in)	x 0.083	= Pounds-force feet (lbf ft; lb ft)	x 12	=	Pounds-force inches (lbf in; lb in)
Pounds-force feet (lbf ft; lb ft)	x 0.138	= Kilograms-force metres (kgf m; kg m)	x 7.233	=	Pounds-force feet (lbf ft; lb ft)
Pounds-force feet (lbf ft; lb ft)	x 1.356	= Newton metres (Nm)	x 0.738	=	Pounds-force feet (lbf ft; lb ft)
Newton metres (Nm)	x 0.102	= Kilograms-force metres (kgf m; kg m)	x 9.804	=	Newton metres (Nm)

Power
Horsepower (hp)	x 745.7	= Watts (W)	x 0.0013	=	Horsepower (hp)

Velocity (speed)
Miles per hour (miles/hr; mph)	x 1.609	= Kilometres per hour (km/hr; kph)	x 0.621	=	Miles per hour (miles/hr; mph)

Fuel consumption*
Miles per gallon, Imperial (mpg)	x 0.354	= Kilometres per litre (km/l)	x 2.825	=	Miles per gallon, Imperial (mpg)
Miles per gallon, US (mpg)	x 0.425	= Kilometres per litre (km/l)	x 2.352	=	Miles per gallon, US (mpg)

Temperature
Degrees Fahrenheit = (°C x 1.8) + 32   Degrees Celsius (Degrees Centigrade; °C) = (°F - 32) x 0.56

It is common practice to convert from miles per gallon (mpg) to litres/100 kilometres (l/100km), where mpg x l/100 km = 282

Spare parts are available from many sources, including maker's appointed garages, accessory shops, and motor factors. To be sure of obtaining the correct parts, it will sometimes be necessary to quote the vehicle identification number. If possible, it can also be useful to take the old parts along for positive identification. Items such as starter motors and alternators may be available under a service exchange scheme – any parts returned should be clean.

Our advice regarding spare parts is as follows.

Officially appointed garages

This is the best source of parts which are peculiar to your car, and which are not otherwise generally available (eg, badges, interior trim, certain body panels, etc). It is also the only place at which you should buy parts if the car is still under warranty.

Accessory shops

These are very good places to buy materials and components needed for the maintenance of your car (oil, air and fuel filters, light bulbs, drivebelts, greases, brake pads, touch-up paint, etc). Components of this nature sold by a reputable shop are usually of the same standard as those used by the car manufacturer.

Besides components, these shops also sell tools and general accessories, usually have convenient opening hours, charge lower prices, and can often be found close to home. Some accessory shops have parts counters where components needed for almost any repair job can be purchased or ordered.

Motor factors

Good factors will stock all the more important components which wear out comparatively quickly, and can sometimes supply individual components needed for the overhaul of a larger assembly (eg, brake seals and hydraulic parts, bearing shells, pistons, valves). They may also handle work such as cylinder block reboring, crankshaft regrinding, etc.

Engine reconditioners

These specialise in engine overhaul and can also supply components. It is recommended that the establishment is a member of the Federation of Engine Re-Manufacturers, or a similar society.

Tyre and exhaust specialists

These outlets may be independent, or members of a local or national chain. They frequently offer competitive prices when compared with a main dealer or local garage, but it will pay to obtain several quotes before making a decision. When researching prices, also ask what extras may be added – for instance fitting a new valve, balancing the wheel and tyre disposal all both commonly charged on top of the price of a new tyre.

Other sources

Beware of parts or materials obtained from market stalls, car boot sales, on-line auctions or similar outlets. Such items are not invariably sub-standard, but there is little chance of compensation if they do prove unsatisfactory. In the case of safety-critical components such as brake pads, there is the risk not only of financial loss, but also of an accident causing injury or death.

Second-hand components or assemblies obtained from a car breaker can be a good buy in some circumstances, but this sort of purchase is best made by the experienced DIY mechanic.

Vehicle identification numbers

Modifications are a continuing and unpublicised process in vehicle manufacture, quite apart from major model changes. Spare parts manuals and lists are compiled upon a numerical basis, the individual vehicle identification numbers being essential to correct identification of the component concerned.

When ordering spare parts, always give as much information as possible. Quote the vehicle type and year, vehicle identification number (VIN), and engine number, as appropriate.

The vehicle identification number (VIN) is stamped into the centre of the engine compartment bulkhead (see illustration). On some vehicles, a model plate is also located in the centre of the engine compartment bulkhead. The model plate also gives vehicle loading details, engine type, and various trim and colour codes.

The engine number is stamped on the right-hand (1.6 litre engines) or left-hand (1.8 litre engines) end of the cylinder block (see illustration).

The VIN number and model plate (arrowed)

Engine number location (arrowed) – 1.8 litre shown

Whenever servicing, repair or overhaul work is carried out on the car or its components, observe the following procedures and instructions. This will assist in carrying out the operation efficiently and to a professional standard of workmanship.

Joint mating faces and gaskets

When separating components at their mating faces, never insert screwdrivers or similar implements into the joint between the faces in order to prise them apart. This can cause severe damage which results in oil leaks, coolant leaks, etc upon reassembly. Separation is usually achieved by tapping along the joint with a soft-faced hammer in order to break the seal. However, note that this method may not be suitable where dowels are used for component location.

Where a gasket is used between the mating faces of two components, a new one must be fitted on reassembly; fit it dry unless otherwise stated in the repair procedure. Make sure that the mating faces are clean and dry, with all traces of old gasket removed. When cleaning a joint face, use a tool which is unlikely to score or damage the face, and remove any burrs or nicks with an oilstone or fine file.

Make sure that tapped holes are cleaned with a pipe cleaner, and keep them free of jointing compound, if this is being used, unless specifically instructed otherwise.

Ensure that all orifices, channels or pipes are clear, and blow through them, preferably using compressed air.

Oil seals

Oil seals can be removed by levering them out with a wide flat-bladed screwdriver or similar implement. Alternatively, a number of self-tapping screws may be screwed into the seal, and these used as a purchase for pliers or some similar device in order to pull the seal free.

Whenever an oil seal is removed from its working location, either individually or as part of an assembly, it should be renewed.

The very fine sealing lip of the seal is easily damaged, and will not seal if the surface it contacts is not completely clean and free from scratches, nicks or grooves. If the original sealing surface of the component cannot be restored, and the manufacturer has not made provision for slight relocation of the seal relative to the sealing surface, the component should be renewed.

Protect the lips of the seal from any surface which may damage them in the course of fitting. Use tape or a conical sleeve where possible. Where indicated, lubricate the seal lips with oil before fitting and, on dual-lipped seals, fill the space between the lips with grease.

Unless otherwise stated, oil seals must be fitted with their sealing lips toward the lubricant to be sealed.

Use a tubular drift or block of wood of the appropriate size to install the seal and, if the seal housing is shouldered, drive the seal down to the shoulder. If the seal housing is unshouldered, the seal should be fitted with its face flush with the housing top face (unless otherwise instructed).

Screw threads and fastenings

Seized nuts, bolts and screws are quite a common occurrence where corrosion has set in, and the use of penetrating oil or releasing fluid will often overcome this problem if the offending item is soaked for a while before attempting to release it. The use of an impact driver may also provide a means of releasing such stubborn fastening devices, when used in conjunction with the appropriate screwdriver bit or socket. If none of these methods works, it may be necessary to resort to the careful application of heat, or the use of a hacksaw or nut splitter device. Before resorting to extreme methods, check that you are not dealing with a left-hand thread!

Studs are usually removed by locking two nuts together on the threaded part, and then using a spanner on the lower nut to unscrew the stud. Studs or bolts which have broken off below the surface of the component in which they are mounted can sometimes be removed using a stud extractor.

Always ensure that a blind tapped hole is completely free from oil, grease, water or other fluid before installing the bolt or stud. Failure to do this could cause the housing to crack due to the hydraulic action of the bolt or stud as it is screwed in.

For some screw fastenings, notably cylinder head bolts or nuts, torque wrench settings are no longer specified for the latter stages of tightening, "angle-tightening" being called up instead. Typically, a fairly low torque wrench setting will be applied to the bolts/nuts in the correct sequence, followed by one or more stages of tightening through specified angles.

When checking or retightening a nut or bolt to a specified torque setting, slacken the nut or bolt by a quarter of a turn, and then retighten to the specified setting. However, this should not be attempted where angular tightening has been used.

Locknuts, locktabs and washers

Any fastening which will rotate against a component or housing during tightening should always have a washer between it and the relevant component or housing.

Spring or split washers should always be renewed when they are used to lock a critical component such as a big-end bearing retaining bolt or nut. Locktabs which are folded over to retain a nut or bolt should always be renewed.

Self-locking nuts can be re-used in non-critical areas, providing resistance can be felt when the locking portion passes over the bolt or stud thread. However, it should be noted that self-locking stiffnuts tend to lose their effectiveness after long periods of use, and should then be renewed as a matter of course.

Split pins must always be replaced with new ones of the correct size for the hole.

When thread-locking compound is found on the threads of a fastener which is to be re-used, it should be cleaned off with a wire brush and solvent, and fresh compound applied on reassembly.

Special tools

Some repair procedures in this manual entail the use of special tools such as a press, two or three-legged pullers, spring compressors, etc. Wherever possible, suitable readily-available alternatives to the manufacturer's special tools are described, and are shown in use. In some instances, where no alternative is possible, it has been necessary to resort to the use of a manufacturer's tool, and this has been done for reasons of safety as well as the efficient completion of the repair operation. Unless you are highly-skilled and have a thorough understanding of the procedures described, never attempt to bypass the use of any special tool when the procedure described specifies its use. Not only is there a very great risk of personal injury, but expensive damage could be caused to the components involved.

Environmental considerations

When disposing of used engine oil, brake fluid, antifreeze, etc, give due consideration to any detrimental environmental effects. Do not, for instance, pour any of the above liquids down drains into the general sewage system, or onto the ground to soak away. Many local council refuse tips provide a facility for waste oil disposal, as do some garages. You can find your nearest disposal point by calling the Environment Agency on 08708 506 506 or by visiting www.oilbankline.org.uk.

Note: It is illegal and anti-social to dump oil down the drain. To find the location of your local oil recycling bank, call 08708 506 506 or visit www.oilbankline.org.uk.

The jack supplied by Mazda should **only** be used for changing the roadwheels in an emergency. When carrying out any other kind of work, raise the vehicle using a heavy-duty hydraulic (or 'trolley') jack, and always supplement the jack with axle stands positioned under the vehicle jacking points. If the roadwheels do not have to be removed, consider using wheel ramps – if wished, these can be placed under the wheels once the vehicle has been raised using a hydraulic jack, and the vehicle lowered onto the ramps so that it is resting on its wheels.

Only ever jack the vehicle up on a solid, level surface. If there is even a slight slope, take great care that the vehicle cannot move as the wheels are lifted off the ground. Jacking up on an uneven or gravelled surface is not recommended, as the weight of the vehicle will not be evenly distributed, and the jack may slip as the vehicle is raised.

As far as possible, do not leave the vehicle unattended once it has been raised, particularly if children are playing nearby.

Before jacking up the front of the car, ensure that the handbrake is firmly applied. When jacking up the rear of the car, place wooden chocks in front of the front wheels, and engage first gear.

When using a hydraulic jack or axle stands, always position the jack head or axle stand head under the relevant jacking points. These are situated directly underneath the vehicle jack location holes in the sill. Note that the vehicle may also be lifted using a hydraulic 'trolley' jack under the rear final drive casing, and the front crossmember **(see illustrations)**.

Ensure that the jack head is correctly engaged before attempting to raise the vehicle.

Never work under, around, or near a raised vehicle, unless it is adequately supported in at least two places.

When jacking or supporting the vehicle at these points, always use a block of wood between the jack head or axle stand, and the vehicle body. It is also considered good practice to use a large block of wood when supporting under other areas, to spread the load over a wider area, and reduce the risk of damage to the underside of the car (it also helps to prevent the underbody coating from being damaged by the jack or axle stand). **Do not** jack the vehicle under any other part of the sill, engine sump, floor pan, subframe, or directly under any of the steering or suspension components.

Never work under, around, or near a raised vehicle, unless it is adequately supported on stands. Do not rely on a jack alone, as even a hydraulic jack could fail under load. Makeshift methods should not be used to lift and support the car during servicing work.

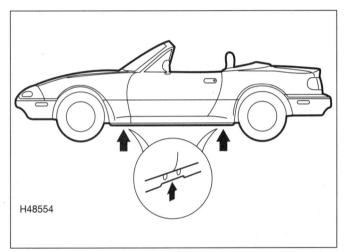

Jacking points under the sills each side (vehicle supplied jack)

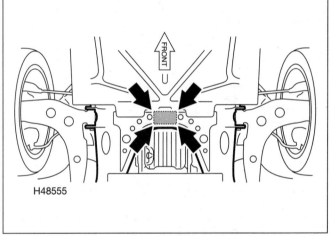

A workshop (trolley) jack can be placed under the front crossmember ...

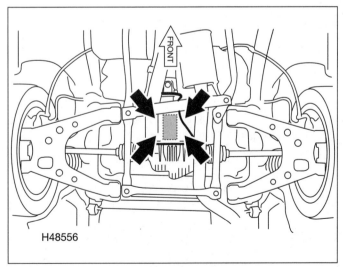

... or under the final drive unit

Introduction

A selection of good tools is a fundamental requirement for anyone contemplating the maintenance and repair of a motor vehicle. For the owner who does not possess any, their purchase will prove a considerable expense, offsetting some of the savings made by doing-it-yourself. However, provided that the tools purchased meet the relevant national safety standards and are of good quality, they will last for many years and prove an extremely worthwhile investment.

To help the average owner to decide which tools are needed to carry out the various tasks detailed in this manual, we have compiled three lists of tools under the following headings: *Maintenance and minor repair, Repair and overhaul*, and *Special*. Newcomers to practical mechanics should start off with the *Maintenance and minor repair* tool kit, and confine themselves to the simpler jobs around the vehicle. Then, as confidence and experience grow, more difficult tasks can be undertaken, with extra tools being purchased as, and when, they are needed. In this way, a *Maintenance and minor repair* tool kit can be built up into a *Repair and overhaul* tool kit over a considerable period of time, without any major cash outlays. The experienced do-it-yourselfer will have a tool kit good enough for most repair and overhaul procedures, and will add tools from the *Special* category when it is felt that the expense is justified by the amount of use to which these tools will be put.

Maintenance and minor repair tool kit

The tools given in this list should be considered as a minimum requirement if routine maintenance, servicing and minor repair operations are to be undertaken. We recommend the purchase of combination spanners (ring one end, open-ended the other); although more expensive than open-ended ones, they do give the advantages of both types of spanner.

- [ ] *Combination spanners:*
  Metric - 8 to 19 mm inclusive
- [ ] *Adjustable spanner - 35 mm jaw (approx.)*
- [ ] *Spark plug spanner (with rubber insert) - petrol models*
- [ ] *Spark plug gap adjustment tool - petrol models*
- [ ] *Set of feeler gauges*
- [ ] *Brake bleed nipple spanner*
- [ ] *Screwdrivers:*
  Flat blade - 100 mm long x 6 mm dia
  Cross blade - 100 mm long x 6 mm dia
  Torx - various sizes (not all vehicles)
- [ ] *Combination pliers*
- [ ] *Hacksaw (junior)*
- [ ] *Tyre pump*
- [ ] *Tyre pressure gauge*
- [ ] *Oil can*
- [ ] *Oil filter removal tool (if applicable)*
- [ ] *Fine emery cloth*
- [ ] *Wire brush (small)*
- [ ] *Funnel (medium size)*
- [ ] *Sump drain plug key (not all vehicles)*

Repair and overhaul tool kit

These tools are virtually essential for anyone undertaking any major repairs to a motor vehicle, and are additional to those given in the *Maintenance and minor repair* list. Included in this list is a comprehensive set of sockets. Although these are expensive, they will be found invaluable as they are so versatile - particularly if various drives are included in the set. We recommend the half-inch square-drive type, as this can be used with most proprietary torque wrenches.

The tools in this list will sometimes need to be supplemented by tools from the *Special* list:

- [ ] *Sockets to cover range in previous list (including Torx sockets)*
- [ ] *Reversible ratchet drive (for use with sockets)*
- [ ] *Extension piece, 250 mm (for use with sockets)*
- [ ] *Universal joint (for use with sockets)*
- [ ] *Flexible handle or sliding T "breaker bar" (for use with sockets)*
- [ ] *Torque wrench (for use with sockets)*
- [ ] *Self-locking grips*
- [ ] *Ball pein hammer*
- [ ] *Soft-faced mallet (plastic or rubber)*
- [ ] *Screwdrivers:*
  Flat blade - long & sturdy, short (chubby), and narrow (electrician's) types
  Cross blade – long & sturdy, and short (chubby) types
- [ ] *Pliers:*
  Long-nosed
  Side cutters (electrician's)
  Circlip (internal and external)
- [ ] *Cold chisel - 25 mm*
- [ ] *Scriber*
- [ ] *Scraper*
- [ ] *Centre-punch*
- [ ] *Pin punch*
- [ ] *Hacksaw*
- [ ] *Brake hose clamp*
- [ ] *Brake/clutch bleeding kit*
- [ ] *Selection of twist drills*
- [ ] *Steel rule/straight-edge*
- [ ] *Allen keys (inc. splined/Torx type)*
- [ ] *Selection of files*
- [ ] *Wire brush*
- [ ] *Axle stands*
- [ ] *Jack (strong trolley or hydraulic type)*
- [ ] *Light with extension lead*
- [ ] *Universal electrical multi-meter*

Sockets and reversible ratchet drive

Brake bleeding kit

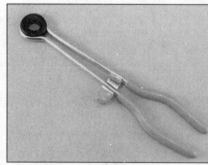

Torx key, socket and bit

Hose clamp

Angular-tightening gauge

Special tools

The tools in this list are those which are not used regularly, are expensive to buy, or which need to be used in accordance with their manufacturers' instructions. Unless relatively difficult mechanical jobs are undertaken frequently, it will not be economic to buy many of these tools. Where this is the case, you could consider clubbing together with friends (or joining a motorists' club) to make a joint purchase, or borrowing the tools against a deposit from a local garage or tool hire specialist.

The following list contains only those tools and instruments freely available to the public, and not those special tools produced by the vehicle manufacturer specifically for its dealer network. You will find occasional references to these manufacturers' special tools in the text of this manual. Generally, an alternative method of doing the job without the vehicle manufacturers' special tool is given. However, sometimes there is no alternative to using them. Where this is the case and the relevant tool cannot be bought or borrowed, you will have to entrust the work to a dealer.

- [ ] Angular-tightening gauge
- [ ] Valve spring compressor
- [ ] Valve grinding tool
- [ ] Piston ring compressor
- [ ] Piston ring removal/installation tool
- [ ] Cylinder bore hone
- [ ] Balljoint separator
- [ ] Coil spring compressors (where applicable)
- [ ] Two/three-legged hub and bearing puller
- [ ] Impact screwdriver
- [ ] Micrometer and/or vernier calipers
- [ ] Dial gauge
- [ ] Tachometer
- [ ] Fault code reader
- [ ] Cylinder compression gauge
- [ ] Hand-operated vacuum pump and gauge
- [ ] Clutch plate alignment set
- [ ] Brake shoe steady spring cup removal tool
- [ ] Bush and bearing removal/installation set
- [ ] Stud extractors
- [ ] Tap and die set
- [ ] Lifting tackle

Buying tools

Reputable motor accessory shops and superstores often offer excellent quality tools at discount prices, so it pays to shop around.

Remember, you don't have to buy the most expensive items on the shelf, but it is always advisable to steer clear of the very cheap tools. Beware of 'bargains' offered on market stalls, on-line or at car boot sales. There are plenty of good tools around at reasonable prices, but always aim to purchase items which meet the relevant national safety standards. If in doubt, ask the proprietor or manager of the shop for advice before making a purchase.

Care and maintenance of tools

Having purchased a reasonable tool kit, it is necessary to keep the tools in a clean and serviceable condition. After use, always wipe off any dirt, grease and metal particles using a clean, dry cloth, before putting the tools away. Never leave them lying around after they have been used. A simple tool rack on the garage or workshop wall for items such as screwdrivers and pliers is a good idea. Store all normal spanners and sockets in a metal box. Any measuring instruments, gauges, meters, etc, must be carefully stored where they cannot be damaged or become rusty.

Take a little care when tools are used. Hammer heads inevitably become marked, and screwdrivers lose the keen edge on their blades from time to time. A little timely attention with emery cloth or a file will soon restore items like this to a good finish.

Working facilities

Not to be forgotten when discussing tools is the workshop itself. If anything more than routine maintenance is to be carried out, a suitable working area becomes essential.

It is appreciated that many an owner-mechanic is forced by circumstances to remove an engine or similar item without the benefit of a garage or workshop. Having done this, any repairs should always be done under the cover of a roof.

Wherever possible, any dismantling should be done on a clean, flat workbench or table at a suitable working height.

Any workbench needs a vice; one with a jaw opening of 100 mm is suitable for most jobs. As mentioned previously, some clean dry storage space is also required for tools, as well as for any lubricants, cleaning fluids, touch-up paints etc, which become necessary.

Another item which may be required, and which has a much more general usage, is an electric drill with a chuck capacity of at least 8 mm. This, together with a good range of twist drills, is virtually essential for fitting accessories.

Last, but not least, always keep a supply of old newspapers and clean, lint-free rags available, and try to keep any working area as clean as possible.

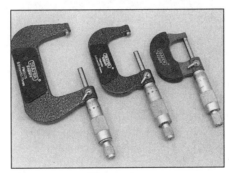

Micrometers

Dial test indicator ("dial gauge")

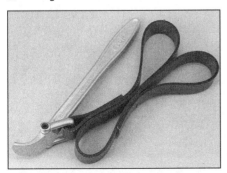

Oil filter removal tool (strap wrench type)

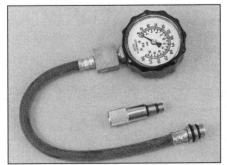

Compression tester

Bearing puller

This is a guide to getting your vehicle through the MOT test. Obviously it will not be possible to examine the vehicle to the same standard as the professional MOT tester. However, working through the following checks will enable you to identify any problem areas before submitting the vehicle for the test.

It has only been possible to summarise the test requirements here, based on the regulations in force at the time of printing. Test standards are becoming increasingly stringent, although there are some exemptions for older vehicles.

An assistant will be needed to help carry out some of these checks.

The checks have been sub-divided into four categories, as follows:

1 Checks carried out **FROM THE DRIVER'S SEAT**

2 Checks carried out **WITH THE VEHICLE ON THE GROUND**

3 Checks carried out **WITH THE VEHICLE RAISED AND THE WHEELS FREE TO TURN**

4 Checks carried out on **YOUR VEHICLE'S EXHAUST EMISSION SYSTEM**

1 Checks carried out **FROM THE DRIVER'S SEAT**

Handbrake (parking brake)

☐ Test the operation of the handbrake. Excessive travel (too many clicks) indicates incorrect brake or cable adjustment.

☐ Check that the handbrake cannot be released by tapping the lever sideways. Check the security of the lever mountings.

☐ If the parking brake is foot-operated, check that the pedal is secure and without excessive travel, and that the release mechanism operates correctly.

☐ Where applicable, test the operation of the electronic handbrake. The brake should engage and disengage without excessive delay. If the warning light does not extinguish when the brake is disengaged, this could indicate a fault which will need further investigation.

Footbrake

☐ Depress the brake pedal and check that it does not creep down to the floor, indicating a master cylinder fault. Release the pedal, wait a few seconds, then depress it again. If the pedal travels nearly to the floor before firm resistance is felt, brake adjustment or repair is necessary. If the pedal feels spongy, there is air in the hydraulic system which must be removed by bleeding.

☐ Check that the brake pedal is secure and in good condition. Check also for signs of fluid leaks on the pedal, floor or carpets, which would indicate failed seals in the brake master cylinder.

☐ Check the servo unit (when applicable) by operating the brake pedal several times, then keeping the pedal depressed and starting the engine. As the engine starts, the pedal will move down slightly. If not, the vacuum hose or the servo itself may be faulty.

Steering wheel and column

☐ Examine the steering wheel for fractures or looseness of the hub, spokes or rim.

☐ Move the steering wheel from side to side and then up and down. Check that the steering wheel is not loose on the column, indicating wear or a loose retaining nut. Continue moving the steering wheel as before, but also turn it slightly from left to right.

☐ Check that the steering wheel is not loose on the column, and that there is no abnormal movement of the steering wheel, indicating wear in the column support bearings or couplings.

☐ Check that the ignition lock (where fitted) engages and disengages correctly.

☐ Steering column adjustment mechanisms (where fitted) must be able to lock the column securely in place with no play evident.

Windscreen, mirrors and sunvisor

☐ The windscreen must be free of cracks or other significant damage within the driver's field of view. (Small stone chips are acceptable.) Rear view mirrors must be secure, intact, and capable of being adjusted.

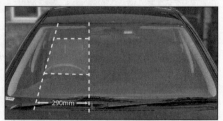

☐ The driver's sunvisor must be capable of being stored in the "up" position.

Seat belts and seats

Note: *The following checks are applicable to all seat belts, front and rear.*

☐ Examine the webbing of all the belts (including rear belts if fitted) for cuts, serious fraying or deterioration. Fasten and unfasten each belt to check the buckles. If applicable, check the retracting mechanism. Check the security of all seat belt mountings accessible from inside the vehicle, ensuring any height adjustable mountings lock securely in place.

☐ Seat belts with pre-tensioners, once activated, have a "flag" or similar showing on the seat belt stalk. This, in itself, is not a reason for test failure.

☐ The front seats themselves must be securely attached and the backrests must lock in the upright position.

Doors

☐ Both front doors must be able to be opened and closed from outside and inside, and must latch securely when closed.

Bonnet and boot/tailgate

☐ The bonnet and boot/tailgate must latch securely when closed.

2 Checks carried out WITH THE VEHICLE ON THE GROUND

Vehicle identification

☐ Number plates must be in good condition, secure and legible, with letters and numbers correctly spaced – spacing at (A) should be 33 mm and at (B) 11 mm. At the front, digits must be black on a white background and at the rear black on a yellow background. Other background designs (such as honeycomb) are not permitted.

☐ The VIN plate and/or homologation plate must be permanently displayed and legible.

Electrical equipment

☐ Switch on the ignition and check the operation of the horn.

☐ Check the windscreen washers and wipers, examining the wiper blades; renew damaged or perished blades. Also check the operation of the stop-lights.

☐ Check the operation of the sidelights and number plate lights. The lenses and reflectors must be secure, clean and undamaged.

☐ Check the operation and alignment of the headlights. The headlight reflectors must not be tarnished and the lenses must be undamaged.

☐ Switch on the ignition and check the operation of the direction indicators (including the instrument panel tell-tale) and the hazard warning lights. Operation of the sidelights and stop-lights must not affect the indicators - if it does, the cause is usually a bad earth at the rear light cluster. Indicators should flash at a rate of between 60 and 120 times per minute – faster or slower than this could indicate a fault with the flasher unit or a bad earth at one of the light units.

☐ Check the operation of the rear foglight(s), including the warning light on the instrument panel or in the switch.

☐ The ABS warning light must illuminate in accordance with the manufacturers' design. For most vehicles, the ABS warning light should illuminate when the ignition is switched on, and (if the system is operating properly) extinguish after a few seconds. Refer to the owner's handbook.

Footbrake

☐ Examine the master cylinder, brake pipes and servo unit for leaks, loose mountings, corrosion or other damage. If ABS is fitted, this unit should also be examined for signs of leaks or corrosion.

☐ The fluid reservoir must be secure and the fluid level must be between the upper (A) and lower (B) markings.

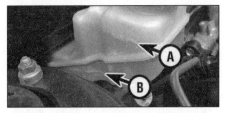

☐ Inspect both front brake flexible hoses for cracks or deterioration of the rubber. Turn the steering from lock to lock, and ensure that the hoses do not contact the wheel, tyre, or any part of the steering or suspension mechanism. With the brake pedal firmly depressed, check the hoses for bulges or leaks under pressure.

Steering and suspension

☐ Have your assistant turn the steering wheel from side to side slightly, up to the point where the steering gear just begins to transmit this movement to the roadwheels. Check for excessive free play between the steering wheel and the steering gear, indicating wear or insecurity of the steering column joints, the column-to-steering gear coupling, or the steering gear itself.

☐ Have your assistant turn the steering wheel more vigorously in each direction, so that the roadwheels just begin to turn. As this is done, examine all the steering joints, linkages, fittings and attachments. Renew any component that shows signs of wear or damage. On vehicles with power steering, check the security and condition of the steering pump, drivebelt and hoses.

☐ Check that the vehicle is standing level, and at approximately the correct ride height.

Shock absorbers

☐ Depress each corner of the vehicle in turn, then release it. The vehicle should rise and then settle in its normal position. If the vehicle continues to rise and fall, the shock absorber is defective. A shock absorber which has seized will also cause the vehicle to fail.

Exhaust system

☐ Start the engine. With your assistant holding a rag over the tailpipe, check the entire system for leaks. Repair or renew leaking sections.

3 Checks carried out **WITH THE VEHICLE RAISED AND THE WHEELS FREE TO TURN**

Jack up the front and rear of the vehicle, and securely support it on axle stands. Position the stands clear of the suspension assemblies. Ensure that the wheels are clear of the ground and that the steering can be turned from lock to lock.

Steering mechanism

☐ Have your assistant turn the steering from lock to lock. Check that the steering turns smoothly, and that no part of the steering mechanism, including a wheel or tyre, fouls any brake hose or pipe or any part of the body structure.
☐ Examine the steering rack rubber gaiters for damage or insecurity of the retaining clips. If power steering is fitted, check for signs of damage or leakage of the fluid hoses, pipes or connections. Also check for excessive stiffness or binding of the steering, a missing split pin or locking device, or severe corrosion of the body structure within 30 cm of any steering component attachment point.

Front and rear suspension and wheel bearings

☐ Starting at the front right-hand side, grasp the roadwheel at the 3 o'clock and 9 o'clock positions and rock gently but firmly. Check for free play or insecurity at the wheel bearings, suspension balljoints, or suspension mount-ings, pivots and attachments.
☐ Now grasp the wheel at the 12 o'clock and 6 o'clock positions and repeat the previous inspection. Spin the wheel, and check for roughness or tightness of the front wheel bearing.

☐ If excess free play is suspected at a component pivot point, this can be confirmed by using a large screwdriver or similar tool and levering between the mounting and the component attachment. This will confirm whether the wear is in the pivot bush, its retaining bolt, or in the mounting itself (the bolt holes can often become elongated).

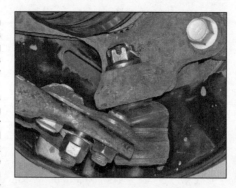

☐ Carry out all the above checks at the other front wheel, and then at both rear wheels.

Springs and shock absorbers

☐ Examine the suspension struts (when applicable) for serious fluid leakage, corrosion, or damage to the casing. Also check the security of the mounting points.
☐ If coil springs are fitted, check that the spring ends locate in their seats, and that the spring is not corroded, cracked or broken.
☐ If leaf springs are fitted, check that all leaves are intact, that the axle is securely attached to each spring, and that there is no deterioration of the spring eye mountings, bushes, and shackles.

☐ The same general checks apply to vehicles fitted with other suspension types, such as torsion bars, hydraulic displacer units, etc. Ensure that all mountings and attachments are secure, that there are no signs of excessive wear, corrosion or damage, and (on hydraulic types) that there are no fluid leaks or damaged pipes.
☐ Inspect the shock absorbers for signs of serious fluid leakage. Check for wear of the mounting bushes or attachments, or damage to the body of the unit.

Driveshafts (fwd vehicles only)

☐ Rotate each front wheel in turn and inspect the constant velocity joint gaiters for splits or damage. Also check that each driveshaft is straight and undamaged.

Braking system

☐ If possible without dismantling, check brake pad wear and disc condition. Ensure that the friction lining material has not worn excessively, (A) and that the discs are not fractured, pitted, scored or badly worn (B).

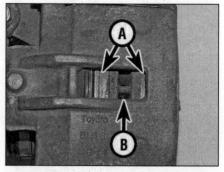

☐ Examine all the rigid brake pipes underneath the vehicle, and the flexible hose(s) at the rear. Look for corrosion, chafing or insecurity of the pipes, and for signs of bulging under pressure, chafing, splits or deterioration of the flexible hoses.
☐ Look for signs of fluid leaks at the brake calipers or on the brake backplates. Repair or renew leaking components.
☐ Slowly spin each wheel, while your assistant depresses and releases the footbrake. Ensure that each brake is operating and does not bind when the pedal is released.

☐ Examine the handbrake mechanism, checking for frayed or broken cables, excessive corrosion, or wear or insecurity of the linkage. Check that the mechanism works on each relevant wheel, and releases fully, without binding.

☐ It is not possible to test brake efficiency without special equipment, but a road test can be carried out later to check that the vehicle pulls up in a straight line.

Fuel and exhaust systems

☐ Inspect the fuel tank (including the filler cap), fuel pipes, hoses and unions. All components must be secure and free from leaks. Locking fuel caps must lock securely and the key must be provided for the MOT test.

☐ Examine the exhaust system over its entire length, checking for any damaged, broken or missing mountings, security of the retaining clamps and rust or corrosion.

Wheels and tyres

☐ Examine the sidewalls and tread area of each tyre in turn. Check for cuts, tears, lumps, bulges, separation of the tread, and exposure of the ply or cord due to wear or damage. Check that the tyre bead is correctly seated on the wheel rim, that the valve is sound and properly seated, and that the wheel is not distorted or damaged.

☐ Check that the tyres are of the correct size for the vehicle, that they are of the same size and type on each axle, and that the pressures are correct.

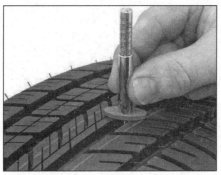

☐ Check the tyre tread depth. The legal minimum at the time of writing is 1.6 mm over the central three-quarters of the tread width. Abnormal tread wear may indicate incorrect front wheel alignment or wear in steering or suspension components.

☐ If the spare wheel is fitted externally or in a separate carrier beneath the vehicle, check that mountings are secure and free of excessive corrosion.

Body corrosion

☐ Check the condition of the entire vehicle structure for signs of corrosion in load-bearing areas. (These include chassis box sections, side sills, cross-members, pillars, and all suspension, steering, braking system and seat belt mountings and anchorages.) Any corrosion which has seriously reduced the thickness of a load-bearing area (or is within 30 cm of safety-related components such as steering or suspension) is likely to cause the vehicle to fail. In this case professional repairs are likely to be needed.

☐ Damage or corrosion which causes sharp or otherwise dangerous edges to be exposed will also cause the vehicle to fail.

Towbars

☐ Check the condition of mounting points (both beneath the vehicle and within boot/hatchback areas) for signs of corrosion, ensuring that all fixings are secure and not worn or damaged. There must be no excessive play in detachable tow ball arms or quick-release mechanisms.

4 Checks carried out on **YOUR VEHICLE'S EXHAUST EMISSION SYSTEM**

Petrol models

☐ The engine should be warmed up, and running well (ignition system in good order, air filter element clean, etc).

☐ Before testing, run the engine at around 2500 rpm for 20 seconds. Let the engine drop to idle, and watch for smoke from the exhaust. If the idle speed is too high, or if dense blue or black smoke emerges for more than 5 seconds, the vehicle will fail. Typically, blue smoke signifies oil burning (engine wear);

black smoke means unburnt fuel (dirty air cleaner element, or other fuel system fault).

☐ An exhaust gas analyser for measuring carbon monoxide (CO) and hydrocarbons (HC) is now needed. If one cannot be hired or borrowed, have a local garage perform the check.

CO emissions (mixture)

☐ The MOT tester has access to the CO limits for all vehicles. The CO level is measured at idle speed, and at 'fast idle' (2500 to 3000 rpm). The following limits are given as a general guide:

   At idle speed – Less than 0.5% CO
   At 'fast idle' – Less than 0.3% CO
   Lambda reading – 0.97 to 1.03

☐ If the CO level is too high, this may point to poor maintenance, a fuel injection system problem, faulty lambda (oxygen) sensor or catalytic converter. Try an injector cleaning treatment, and check the vehicle's ECU for fault codes.

HC emissions

☐ The MOT tester has access to HC limits for all vehicles. The HC level is measured at 'fast idle' (2500 to 3000 rpm). The following limits are given as a general guide:

   At 'fast idle' – Less then 200 ppm

☐ Excessive HC emissions are typically caused by oil being burnt (worn engine), or by a blocked crankcase ventilation system ('breather'). If the engine oil is old and thin, an oil change may help. If the engine is running badly, check the vehicle's ECU for fault codes.

Diesel models

☐ The only emission test for diesel engines is measuring exhaust smoke density, using a calibrated smoke meter. The test involves accelerating the engine at least 3 times to its maximum unloaded speed.

Note: *On engines with a timing belt, it is VITAL that the belt is in good condition before the test is carried out.*

☐ With the engine warmed up, it is first purged by running at around 2500 rpm for 20 seconds. A governor check is then carried out, by slowly accelerating the engine to its maximum speed. After this, the smoke meter is connected, and the engine is accelerated quickly to maximum speed three times. If the smoke density is less than the limits given below, the vehicle will pass:

   Non-turbo vehicles: 2.5m-1
   Turbocharged vehicles: 3.0m-1

☐ If excess smoke is produced, try fitting a new air cleaner element, or using an injector cleaning treatment. If the engine is running badly, where applicable, check the vehicle's ECU for fault codes. Also check the vehicle's EGR system, where applicable. At high mileages, the injectors may require professional attention.

Engine

☐ Engine fails to rotate when attempting to start
☐ Engine rotates, but will not start
☐ Engine difficult to start when cold
☐ Engine difficult to start when hot
☐ Starter motor noisy or excessively-rough in engagement
☐ Engine starts, but stops immediately
☐ Engine idles erratically
☐ Engine misfires at idle speed
☐ Engine misfires throughout the driving speed range
☐ Engine hesitates on acceleration
☐ Engine stalls
☐ Engine lacks power
☐ Engine backfires
☐ Oil pressure warning light illuminated with engine running
☐ Engine runs-on after switching off
☐ Engine noises

Cooling system

☐ Overheating
☐ Overcooling
☐ External coolant leakage
☐ Internal coolant leakage
☐ Corrosion

Fuel and exhaust systems

☐ Excessive fuel consumption
☐ Fuel leakage and/or fuel odour
☐ Excessive noise or fumes from exhaust system

Clutch

☐ Pedal travels to floor – no pressure or very little resistance
☐ Clutch fails to disengage (unable to select gears)
☐ Clutch slips (engine speed increases, with no increase in vehicle speed)
☐ Judder as clutch is engaged
☐ Noise when depressing or releasing clutch pedal

Manual transmission

☐ Noisy in neutral with engine running
☐ Noisy in one particular gear
☐ Difficulty engaging gears
☐ Jumps out of gear
☐ Vibration
☐ Lubricant leaks

Differential and propeller shaft

☐ Vibration when accelerating and decelerating
☐ Low-pitched whining, increasing with roadspeed

Driveshafts

☐ Vibration when accelerating or decelerating

Braking system

☐ Vehicle pulls to one side under braking
☐ Noise (grinding or high-pitched squeal) when brakes applied
☐ Excessive brake pedal travel
☐ Brake pedal feels spongy when depressed
☐ Excessive brake pedal effort required to stop vehicle
☐ Judder felt through brake pedal or steering wheel when braking
☐ Brakes binding
☐ Rear wheels locking under normal braking

Suspension and steering

☐ Vehicle pulls to one side
☐ Wheel wobble and vibration
☐ Excessive pitching and/or rolling around corners, or during braking
☐ Wandering or general instability
☐ Excessively-stiff steering
☐ Excessive play in steering
☐ Lack of power assistance
☐ Tyre wear excessive

Electrical system

☐ Battery will not hold a charge for more than a few days
☐ Ignition/no-charge warning light remains illuminated with engine running
☐ Ignition/no-charge warning light fails to come on
☐ Lights inoperative
☐ Instrument readings inaccurate or erratic
☐ Horn inoperative, or unsatisfactory in operation
☐ Windscreen wipers inoperative, or unsatisfactory in operation
☐ Windscreen washers inoperative, or unsatisfactory in operation
☐ Electric windows inoperative, or unsatisfactory in operation
☐ Central locking system inoperative, or unsatisfactory in operation

Introduction

The vehicle owner who does his or her own maintenance according to the recommended service schedules should not have to use this section of the manual very often. Modern component reliability is such that, provided those items subject to wear or deterioration are inspected or renewed at the specified intervals, sudden failure is comparatively rare. Faults do not usually just happen as a result of sudden failure, but develop over a period of time. Major mechanical failures in particular are usually preceded by characteristic symptoms over hundreds or even thousands of miles. Those components which do occasionally fail without warning are often small and easily carried in the vehicle.

With any fault finding, the first step is to decide where to begin investigations. Sometimes this is obvious, but on other occasions, a little detective work will be necessary. The owner who makes half a dozen haphazard adjustments or replacements may be successful in curing a fault (or its symptoms), but will be none the wiser if the fault recurs, and ultimately may have spent more time and money than was necessary. A calm and logical approach will be found to be more satisfactory in the long run. Always take into account any warning signs or abnormalities that may have been noticed in the period preceding the fault – power loss, high or low gauge readings, unusual smells,

etc – and remember that failure of components such as fuses or spark plugs may only be pointers to some underlying fault.

The pages which follow provide an easy-reference guide to the more common problems which may occur during the operation of the vehicle. These problems and their possible causes are grouped under headings denoting various components or systems, such as Engine, Cooling system, etc. The Chapter and/or Section which deals with the problem is also shown in brackets. Whatever the fault, certain basic principles apply. These are as follows:

Verify the fault. This is simply a matter of being sure that you know what the symptoms are before starting work. This is particularly important if you are investigating a fault for someone else, who may not have described it very accurately.

Don't overlook the obvious. For example, if the vehicle won't start, is there fuel in the tank? (Don't take anyone else's word on this particular point, and don't trust the fuel gauge either). If an electrical fault is indicated, look for loose or broken wires before digging out the test gear.

Cure the disease, not the symptom. Substituting a flat battery with a fully-charged one will get you off the hard shoulder, but if the underlying cause is not attended to, the new battery will go the same way. Similarly, changing oil-fouled spark plugs for a new set will get you moving again, but remember that the reason for the fouling (if it wasn't simply an incorrect grade of plug) will have to be established and corrected.

Don't take anything for granted. Particularly, don't forget that a 'new' component may itself be defective (especially if it's been rattling around in the boot for months), and don't leave components out of a fault diagnosis sequence just because they are new or recently-fitted. When you do finally diagnose a difficult fault, you'll probably realise that all the evidence was there from the start.

Consider what work, if any, has recently been carried out. Many faults arise through careless or hurried work. For instance, if any work has been performed under the bonnet, could some of the wiring have been dislodged or incorrectly routed, or a hose trapped? Have all the fasteners been properly tightened? Were new, genuine parts and new gaskets used? There is often a certain amount of detective work to be done in this case, as an apparently-unrelated task can have far-reaching consequences.

Engine

Engine fails to rotate when attempting to start

- [ ] Battery terminal connections loose or corroded (see *Weekly checks*)
- [ ] Battery discharged or faulty (Chapter 5A)
- [ ] Broken, loose or disconnected wiring in the starting circuit (Chapter 5A)
- [ ] Defective starter solenoid or ignition switch (Chapter 5A or 10)
- [ ] Defective starter motor (Chapter 5A)
- [ ] Starter pinion or flywheel ring gear teeth loose or broken (Chapter 2A or 5A)
- [ ] Engine earth strap broken or disconnected (Chapter 12)
- [ ] Engine suffering 'hydraulic lock' (eg, from water ingested after traversing flooded roads, or from a serious internal coolant leak) – consult a Mazda dealer for advice

Engine rotates, but will not start

- [ ] Fuel tank empty
- [ ] Battery discharged (engine rotates slowly) (Chapter 5A)
- [ ] Battery terminal connections loose or corroded (see *Weekly checks*)
- [ ] Ignition components damp or damaged (Chapter 1 or 5B)
- [ ] Immobiliser fault, or 'uncoded' ignition key being used (Chapter 12 or Roadside repairs)
- [ ] Crankshaft sensor fault (Chapter 4A)
- [ ] Broken, loose or disconnected wiring in the ignition circuit (Chapter 1 or 5B)
- [ ] Worn, faulty or incorrectly-gapped spark plugs (Chapter 1)
- [ ] Fuel injection system fault (Chapter 4A)
- [ ] Major mechanical failure (eg, timing belt snapped) (Chapter 2A)

Engine difficult to start when cold

- [ ] Battery discharged (Chapter 5A)
- [ ] Battery terminal connections loose or corroded (see *Weekly checks*)
- [ ] Worn, faulty or incorrectly-gapped spark plugs (Chapter 1)
- [ ] Other ignition system fault (Chapter 1 or 5B)
- [ ] Fuel injection system fault (Chapter 4A)
- [ ] Wrong grade of engine oil used (*Weekly checks*, Chapter 1)
- [ ] Low cylinder compression (Chapter 2A)

Engine difficult to start when hot

- [ ] Air filter element dirty or clogged (Chapter 1)
- [ ] Fuel injection system fault (Chapter 4A)
- [ ] Low cylinder compression (Chapter 2A)

Starter motor noisy or excessively-rough in engagement

- [ ] Starter pinion or flywheel ring gear teeth loose or broken (Chapter 2A or 5A)
- [ ] Starter motor mounting bolts loose or missing (Chapter 5A)
- [ ] Starter motor internal components worn or damaged (Chapter 5A)

Engine starts, but stops immediately

- [ ] Loose or faulty electrical connections in the ignition circuit (Chapter 1 or 5B)
- [ ] Vacuum leak at the throttle body or inlet manifold (Chapter 4A)
- [ ] Blocked injectors/fuel injection system fault (Chapter 4A)

Engine idles erratically

- [ ] Air filter element clogged (Chapter 1)
- [ ] Vacuum leak at the throttle body, inlet manifold or associated hoses (Chapter 4A)
- [ ] Worn, faulty or incorrectly-gapped spark plugs (Chapter 1)
- [ ] Valve clearances incorrect (Chapter 1)
- [ ] Uneven or low cylinder compression (Chapter 2A)
- [ ] Camshaft lobes worn (Chapter 2A)
- [ ] Timing belt incorrectly fitted (Chapter 2A)
- [ ] Blocked injectors/fuel injection system fault (Chapter 4A)

Engine misfires at idle speed

- [ ] Worn, faulty or incorrectly-gapped spark plugs (Chapter 1)
- [ ] Faulty spark plug HT leads (Chapter 1)
- [ ] Vacuum leak at the throttle body, inlet manifold or associated hoses (Chapter 4A)
- [ ] Blocked injectors/fuel injection system fault (Chapter 4A)
- [ ] Uneven or low cylinder compression (Chapter 2A)
- [ ] Disconnected, leaking, or perished crankcase ventilation hoses (Chapter 4B)

Engine (continued)

Engine misfires throughout the driving speed range

- ☐ Fuel filter choked (Chapter 1)
- ☐ Fuel pump faulty, or delivery pressure low (Chapter 4A)
- ☐ Fuel tank vent blocked, or fuel pipes restricted (Chapter 4A)
- ☐ Vacuum leak at the throttle body, inlet manifold or associated hoses (Chapter 4A)
- ☐ Worn, faulty or incorrectly-gapped spark plugs (Chapter 1)
- ☐ Faulty spark plug HT leads (Chapter 1)
- ☐ Faulty ignition coil (Chapter 5B)
- ☐ Uneven or low cylinder compression (Chapter 2A)
- ☐ Blocked injector/fuel injection system fault (Chapter 4A)
- ☐ Blocked catalytic converter (Chapter 4A)
- ☐ Engine overheating (Chapter 3)

Engine hesitates on acceleration

- ☐ Worn, faulty or incorrectly-gapped spark plugs (Chapter 1)
- ☐ Vacuum leak at the throttle body, inlet manifold or associated hoses (Chapter 4A)
- ☐ Blocked injectors/fuel injection system fault (Chapter 4A)

Engine stalls

- ☐ Vacuum leak at the throttle body, inlet manifold or associated hoses (Chapter 4A)
- ☐ Fuel filter choked (Chapter 1)
- ☐ Fuel pump faulty, or delivery pressure low (Chapter 4A)
- ☐ Fuel tank vent blocked, or fuel pipes restricted (Chapter 4A)
- ☐ Blocked injectors/fuel injection system fault (Chapter 4A)

Engine lacks power

- ☐ Air filter element blocked (Chapter 1)
- ☐ Fuel filter choked (Chapter 1)
- ☐ Fuel pipes blocked or restricted (Chapter 4A)
- ☐ Valve clearances incorrect (Chapter 1)
- ☐ Worn, faulty or incorrectly-gapped spark plugs (Chapter 1)
- ☐ Engine overheating (Chapter 3)
- ☐ Accelerator cable problem (Chapter 4A)
- ☐ Vacuum leak at the throttle body, inlet manifold or associated hoses (Chapter 4A)
- ☐ Blocked injectors/fuel injection system fault (Chapter 4A)
- ☐ Timing belt incorrectly fitted (Chapter 2A)
- ☐ Fuel pump faulty, or delivery pressure low (Chapter 4A)
- ☐ Uneven or low cylinder compression (Chapter 2A)
- ☐ Blocked catalytic converter (Chapter 4A)
- ☐ Brakes binding (Chapter 1 or 9)
- ☐ Clutch slipping (Chapter 6)

Engine backfires

- ☐ Timing belt incorrectly fitted (Chapter 2A)
- ☐ Vacuum leak at the throttle body, inlet manifold or associated hoses (Chapter 4A)
- ☐ Blocked injectors/fuel injection system fault (Chapter 4A)
- ☐ Blocked catalytic converter (Chapter 4A)
- ☐ Spark plug HT leads incorrectly fitted (Chapter 1 or 5B)
- ☐ Ignition coil unit faulty (Chapter 5B)

Oil pressure warning light illuminated with engine running

- ☐ Low oil level, or incorrect oil grade (see Weekly checks)
- ☐ Faulty oil pressure sensor, or wiring damaged (Chapter 2A)
- ☐ Worn engine bearings and/or oil pump (Chapter 2A)
- ☐ High engine operating temperature (Chapter 3)
- ☐ Oil pump pressure relief valve defective (Chapter 2A)
- ☐ Oil pump pick-up strainer clogged (Chapter 2A)

Engine runs-on after switching off

- ☐ Excessive carbon build-up in engine (Chapter 2B)
- ☐ High engine operating temperature (Chapter 3)
- ☐ Fuel injection system fault (Chapter 4A)

Engine noises

Pre-ignition (pinking) or knocking during acceleration or under load

- ☐ Ignition timing incorrect/ignition system fault (Chapter 1 or 5B)
- ☐ Incorrect grade of spark plug (Chapter 1)
- ☐ Incorrect grade of fuel (Chapter 4A)
- ☐ Knock sensor faulty – some petrol models (Chapter 5B)
- ☐ Vacuum leak at the throttle body, inlet manifold or associated hoses (Chapter 4A)
- ☐ Excessive carbon build-up in engine (Chapter 2B)
- ☐ Blocked injector/fuel injection system fault (Chapter 4A)

Whistling or wheezing noises

- ☐ Leaking inlet manifold or throttle body gasket – (Chapter 4A)
- ☐ Leaking exhaust manifold gasket or pipe-to-manifold joint (Chapter 4A)
- ☐ Leaking vacuum hose (Chapter 4A or 9)
- ☐ Blowing cylinder head gasket (Chapter 2A)
- ☐ Partially blocked or leaking crankcase ventilation system (Chapter 4B)

Tapping or rattling noises

- ☐ Valve clearances incorrect (Chapter 1)
- ☐ Worn valve gear or camshaft (Chapter 2A)
- ☐ Ancillary component fault (coolant pump, alternator, etc) (Chapter 3, 5A, etc)

Knocking or thumping noises

- ☐ Worn big-end bearings (regular heavy knocking, perhaps less under load) (Chapter 2B)
- ☐ Worn main bearings (rumbling and knocking, perhaps worsening under load) (Chapter 2B)
- ☐ Piston slap – most noticeable when cold, caused by piston/bore wear (Chapter 2B)
- ☐ Ancillary component fault (coolant pump, alternator, etc) (Chapter 3, 5A, etc)
- ☐ Engine mountings worn or defective (Chapter 2A)
- ☐ Front suspension or steering components worn (Chapter 10)

Cooling system

Overheating

- ☐ Insufficient coolant in system (see *Weekly checks*)
- ☐ Thermostat faulty (Chapter 3)
- ☐ Radiator core blocked, or grille restricted (Chapter 3)
- ☐ Cooling fan faulty, or resistor pack fault on models with twin fans (Chapter 3)
- ☐ Inaccurate coolant temperature sensor (Chapter 3)
- ☐ Airlock in cooling system (Chapter 3)
- ☐ Expansion tank pressure cap faulty (Chapter 3)
- ☐ Engine management system fault (Chapter 4A)

Overcooling

- ☐ Thermostat faulty (Chapter 3)
- ☐ Inaccurate coolant temperature sensor (Chapter 3)
- ☐ Cooling fan faulty (Chapter 3)
- ☐ Engine management system fault (Chapter 4A)

External coolant leakage

- ☐ Deteriorated or damaged hoses or hose clips (Chapter 1)
- ☐ Radiator core or heater matrix leaking (Chapter 3)
- ☐ Expansion tank pressure cap faulty (Chapter 1)
- ☐ Coolant pump internal seal leaking (Chapter 3)
- ☐ Coolant pump gasket leaking (Chapter 3)
- ☐ Boiling due to overheating (Chapter 3)
- ☐ Cylinder block core plug leaking (Chapter 2B)

Internal coolant leakage

- ☐ Leaking cylinder head gasket (Chapter 2)
- ☐ Cracked cylinder head or cylinder block (Chapter 2)

Corrosion

- ☐ Infrequent draining and flushing (Chapter 1)
- ☐ Incorrect coolant mixture or inappropriate coolant type (see *Weekly checks*)

Fuel and exhaust systems

Excessive fuel consumption

- ☐ Air filter element dirty or clogged (Chapter 1)
- ☐ Fuel injection system fault (Chapter 4A)
- ☐ Engine management system fault (Chapter 4A)
- ☐ Crankcase ventilation system blocked (Chapter 4B)
- ☐ Tyres under-inflated (see *Weekly checks*)
- ☐ Brakes binding (Chapter 1 or 9)
- ☐ Fuel leak, causing apparent high consumption (Chapter 1 or 4A)

Fuel leakage and/or fuel odour

- ☐ Damaged or corroded fuel tank, pipes or connections (Chapter 4A)
- ☐ Evaporative emissions system fault – petrol models (Chapter 4B)

Excessive noise or fumes from exhaust system

- ☐ Leaking exhaust system or manifold joints (Chapter 1A or 4A)
- ☐ Leaking, corroded or damaged silencers or pipe (Chapter 1 or 4A)
- ☐ Broken mountings causing body or suspension contact (Chapter 1)

Clutch

Pedal travels to floor – no pressure or very little resistance

- ☐ Air in hydraulic system/faulty master or slave cylinder (Chapter 6)
- ☐ Faulty hydraulic release system (Chapter 6)
- ☐ Clutch pedal return spring detached or broken (Chapter 6)
- ☐ Broken clutch release bearing or fork (Chapter 6)
- ☐ Broken diaphragm spring in clutch pressure plate (Chapter 6)

Clutch fails to disengage (unable to select gears)

- ☐ Air in hydraulic system/faulty master or slave cylinder (Chapter 6)
- ☐ Clutch pedal height incorrect (Chapter 1)
- ☐ Faulty hydraulic release system (Chapter 6)
- ☐ Clutch disc sticking on transmission input shaft splines (Chapter 6)
- ☐ Clutch disc sticking to flywheel or pressure plate (Chapter 6)
- ☐ Faulty pressure plate assembly (Chapter 6)
- ☐ Clutch release mechanism worn or incorrectly assembled (Chapter 6)

Clutch slips (engine speed increases, with no increase in vehicle speed)

- ☐ Faulty hydraulic release system (Chapter 6)
- ☐ Clutch pedal height incorrect (Chapter 1)
- ☐ Clutch disc linings excessively worn (Chapter 6)
- ☐ Clutch disc linings contaminated with oil or grease (Chapter 6)
- ☐ Faulty pressure plate or weak diaphragm spring (Chapter 6)

Judder as clutch is engaged

- ☐ Clutch disc linings contaminated with oil or grease (Chapter 6)
- ☐ Clutch disc linings excessively worn (Chapter 6)
- ☐ Faulty or distorted pressure plate or diaphragm spring (Chapter 6).
- ☐ Worn or loose engine or transmission mountings (Chapter 2A, 2B or 2C)
- ☐ Clutch disc hub or transmission input shaft splines worn (Chapter 6)

Noise when depressing or releasing clutch pedal

- ☐ Worn clutch release bearing (Chapter 6)
- ☐ Worn or dry clutch pedal bushes (Chapter 6)
- ☐ Worn or dry clutch master cylinder piston (Chapter 6)
- ☐ Faulty pressure plate assembly (Chapter 6)
- ☐ Pressure plate diaphragm spring broken (Chapter 6)
- ☐ Broken clutch disc cushioning springs (Chapter 6)

Manual transmission

Noisy in neutral with engine running

- ☐ Lack of oil (Chapter 1)
- ☐ Input shaft bearings worn (noise apparent with clutch pedal released, but not when depressed) (Chapter 7)*
- ☐ Clutch release bearing worn (noise apparent with clutch pedal depressed, possibly less when released) (Chapter 6)

Noisy in one particular gear

- ☐ Worn, damaged or chipped gear teeth (Chapter 7)*

Difficulty engaging gears

- ☐ Clutch fault (Chapter 6)
- ☐ Clutch pedal height incorrect (Chapter 1)
- ☐ Lack of oil (Chapter 1)
- ☐ Worn synchroniser units (Chapter 7)*

Jumps out of gear

- ☐ Worn synchroniser units (Chapter 7)*
- ☐ Worn selector forks (Chapter 7)*

Vibration

- ☐ Lack of oil (Chapter 1)
- ☐ Worn bearings (Chapter 7)*

Lubricant leaks

- ☐ Leaking driveshaft or selector shaft oil seal (Chapter 7)
- ☐ Leaking housing joint (Chapter 7)*
- ☐ Leaking input shaft oil seal (Chapter 7)*

Although the corrective action necessary to remedy the symptoms described is beyond the scope of the home mechanic, the above information should be helpful in isolating the cause of the condition, so that the owner can communicate clearly with a professional mechanic.

Differential and propshaft

Vibration when accelerating or decelerating

☐ Worn universal joint (Chapter 8)
☐ Bent or distorted propeller shaft (Chapter 8)

Low-pitched whining; increasing with roadspeed

☐ Worn differential (Chapter 8)

Driveshafts

Vibration when accelerating or decelerating

☐ Worn inner constant velocity joint (Chapter 8)
☐ Bent or distorted driveshaft (Chapter 8)

Braking system

Note: *Before assuming that a brake problem exists, make sure that the tyres are in good condition and correctly inflated, that the front wheel alignment is correct, and that the vehicle is not loaded with weight in an unequal manner. Apart from checking the condition of all pipe and hose connections, any faults occurring on the anti-lock braking system should be referred to a Mazda dealer for diagnosis.*

Vehicle pulls to one side under braking

☐ Worn, defective, damaged or contaminated brake pads on one side (Chapter 1 or 9)
☐ Seized or partially-seized brake caliper piston (Chapter 1 or 9)
☐ A mixture of brake pad materials fitted between sides (Chapter 1 or 9)
☐ Brake caliper mounting bolts loose (Chapter 9)
☐ Worn or damaged steering or suspension components (Chapter 1 or 10)

Noise (grinding or high-pitched squeal) when brakes applied

☐ Brake pad friction lining material worn down to metal backing (Chapter 1 or 9)
☐ Excessive corrosion of brake disc (may be apparent after the vehicle has been standing for some time (Chapter 1 or 9)
☐ Foreign object (stone chipping, etc) trapped between brake disc and shield (Chapter 1 or 9)

Excessive brake pedal travel

☐ Faulty master cylinder (Chapter 9)
☐ Brake pedal height incorrect (Chapter 9)
☐ Air in hydraulic system (Chapter 1 or 9)
☐ Faulty vacuum servo unit (Chapter 9)

Brake pedal feels spongy when depressed

☐ Air in hydraulic system (Chapter 1 or 9)
☐ Deteriorated flexible rubber brake hoses (Chapter 1 or 9)
☐ Master cylinder mounting nuts loose (Chapter 9)
☐ Faulty master cylinder (Chapter 9)

Excessive brake pedal effort required to stop vehicle

☐ Faulty vacuum servo unit (Chapter 9)
☐ Disconnected, damaged or insecure brake servo vacuum hose (Chapter 9)
☐ Primary or secondary hydraulic circuit failure (Chapter 9)
☐ Seized brake caliper piston (Chapter 9)
☐ Brake pads incorrectly fitted (Chapter 9)
☐ Incorrect grade of brake pads fitted (Chapter 9)
☐ Brake pad linings contaminated (Chapter 1 or 9)

Judder felt through brake pedal or steering wheel when braking

Note: *Under heavy braking on models equipped with ABS, vibration may be felt through the brake pedal. This is a normal feature of ABS operation, and does not constitute a fault.*

☐ Excessive run-out or distortion of discs (Chapter 1 or 9)
☐ Brake pad linings worn (Chapter 1 or 9)
☐ Brake caliper mounting bolts loose (Chapter 9)
☐ Wear in suspension or steering components or mountings (Chapter 1 or 10)
☐ Front wheels out of balance (see *Weekly checks*)

Brakes binding

☐ Seized brake caliper piston (Chapter 9)
☐ Incorrectly-adjusted handbrake mechanism (Chapter 9)
☐ Faulty master cylinder (Chapter 9)

Rear wheels locking under normal braking

☐ Rear brake pad linings contaminated or damaged (Chapter 1 or 9)
☐ Rear brake discs warped (Chapter 1 or 9)

Suspension and steering

Note: *Before diagnosing suspension or steering faults, be sure that the trouble is not due to incorrect tyre pressures, mixtures of tyre types, or binding brakes.*

Vehicle pulls to one side

- [ ] Defective tyre (see *Weekly checks*)
- [ ] Excessive wear in suspension or steering components (Chapter 1 or 10)
- [ ] Incorrect front wheel alignment (Chapter 10)
- [ ] Accident damage to steering or suspension components (Chapter 1)

Wheel wobble and vibration

- [ ] Front wheels out of balance (vibration felt mainly through the steering wheel) (see *Weekly checks*)
- [ ] Rear wheels out of balance (vibration felt throughout the vehicle) (see *Weekly checks*)
- [ ] Roadwheels damaged or distorted (see *Weekly checks*)
- [ ] Faulty or damaged tyre (see *Weekly checks*)
- [ ] Worn steering or suspension joints, bushes or components (Chapter 1 or 10)
- [ ] Wheel nuts loose (Chapter 1)

Excessive pitching and/or rolling around corners, or during braking

- [ ] Defective shock absorbers (Chapter 1 or 10)
- [ ] Broken or weak spring and/or suspension component (Chapter 1 or 10)
- [ ] Worn or damaged anti-roll bar or mountings (Chapter 1 or 10)

Wandering or general instability

- [ ] Incorrect front wheel alignment (Chapter 10)
- [ ] Worn steering or suspension joints, bushes or components (Chapter 1 or 10)
- [ ] Roadwheels out of balance (see *Weekly checks*)
- [ ] Faulty or damaged tyre (see *Weekly checks*)
- [ ] Wheel nuts loose (Chapter 1)
- [ ] Defective shock absorbers (Chapter 1 or 10)

Excessively-stiff steering

- [ ] Seized steering linkage balljoint or suspension balljoint (Chapter 1 or 10)
- [ ] Incorrect front wheel alignment (Chapter 10)
- [ ] Steering rack damaged (Chapter 10)
- [ ] Faulty steering column motor (Chapter 10)

Excessive play in steering

- [ ] Worn steering column/intermediate shaft joints (Chapter 10)
- [ ] Worn track rod balljoints (Chapter 1 or 10)
- [ ] Worn steering rack (Chapter 10)
- [ ] Worn steering or suspension joints, bushes or components (Chapter 1 or 10)

Lack of power assistance

- [ ] Faulty steering column motor (Chapter 10)

Tyre wear excessive

Tyres worn on inside or outside edges

- [ ] Tyres under-inflated (wear on both edges) (see *Weekly checks*)
- [ ] Incorrect camber or castor angles (wear on one edge only) (Chapter 10)
- [ ] Worn steering or suspension joints, bushes or components (Chapter 1 or 10)
- [ ] Excessively-hard cornering or braking
- [ ] Accident damage

Tyre treads exhibit feathered edges

- [ ] Incorrect toe-setting (Chapter 10)

Tyres worn in centre of tread

- [ ] Tyres over-inflated (see *Weekly checks*)

Tyres worn on inside and outside edges

- [ ] Tyres under-inflated (see *Weekly checks*)

Tyres worn unevenly

- [ ] Tyres/wheels out of balance (see *Weekly checks*)
- [ ] Excessive wheel or tyre run-out
- [ ] Worn shock absorbers (Chapter 1 or 10)
- [ ] Faulty tyre (see *Weekly checks*)

Electrical system

Note: *For problems associated with the starting system, refer to the faults listed under 'Engine' earlier in this Section.*

Battery will not hold a charge for more than a few days

- [ ] Battery defective internally (Chapter 5A)
- [ ] Battery terminal connections loose or corroded (see *Weekly checks*)
- [ ] Auxiliary drivebelt worn or incorrectly adjusted (Chapter 1)
- [ ] Alternator not charging at correct output (Chapter 5A)
- [ ] Alternator or voltage regulator faulty (Chapter 5A)
- [ ] Short-circuit causing continual battery drain (Chapter 5A or 12)

Ignition/no-charge warning light remains illuminated with engine running

- [ ] Auxiliary drivebelt broken, worn, or incorrectly adjusted (Chapter 1)
- [ ] Internal fault in alternator or voltage regulator (Chapter 5A)
- [ ] Broken, disconnected, or loose wiring in charging circuit (Chapter 5A or 12)

Ignition/no-charge warning light fails to come on

- [ ] Warning light bulb blown (Chapter 12)
- [ ] Broken, disconnected, or loose wiring in warning light circuit (Chapter 5A or 12)
- [ ] Alternator faulty (Chapter 5A)

Lights inoperative

- [ ] Bulb blown (Chapter 12)
- [ ] Corrosion of bulb or bulbholder contacts (Chapter 12)
- [ ] Blown fuse (Chapter 12)
- [ ] Faulty relay (Chapter 12)
- [ ] Broken, loose, or disconnected wiring (Chapter 12)
- [ ] Faulty switch (Chapter 12)

Instrument readings inaccurate or erratic

Fuel or temperature gauges give no reading

- [ ] Faulty level sensor unit (Chapter 3 or 4A)
- [ ] Wiring open-circuit (Chapter 12)
- [ ] Faulty gauge (Chapter 12)

Fuel or temperature gauges give continuous maximum reading

- [ ] Faulty level sensor unit (Chapter 3 or 4A)
- [ ] Wiring short-circuit (Chapter 12)
- [ ] Faulty gauge (Chapter 12)

Horn inoperative, or unsatisfactory in operation

Horn operates all the time

- [ ] Horn push either earthed or stuck down (Chapter 12)
- [ ] Horn cable-to-horn push earthed (Chapter 12)

Horn fails to operate

- [ ] Blown fuse (Chapter 12)
- [ ] Cable or connections loose, broken or disconnected (Chapter 12)
- [ ] Faulty horn (Chapter 12)

Horn emits intermittent or unsatisfactory sound

- [ ] Cable connections loose (Chapter 12)
- [ ] Horn mountings loose (Chapter 12)
- [ ] Faulty horn (Chapter 12)

Windscreen wipers inoperative, or unsatisfactory in operation

Wipers fail to operate, or operate very slowly

- [ ] Wiper blades stuck to screen, or linkage seized or binding (Chapter 12)
- [ ] Blown fuse (Chapter 12)
- [ ] Battery discharged (Chapter 5A)
- [ ] Cable or connections loose, broken or disconnected (Chapter 12)
- [ ] Faulty relay (Chapter 12)
- [ ] Faulty wiper motor (Chapter 12)

Wiper blades sweep over too large or too small an area of the glass

- [ ] Wiper blades incorrectly fitted, or wrong size used (see *Weekly checks*)
- [ ] Wiper arms incorrectly positioned on spindles (Chapter 12)
- [ ] Excessive wear of wiper linkage (Chapter 12)
- [ ] Wiper motor or linkage mountings loose or insecure (Chapter 12)

Wiper blades fail to clean the glass effectively

- [ ] Wiper blade rubbers dirty, worn or perished (see *Weekly checks*)
- [ ] Wiper blades incorrectly fitted, or wrong size used (see *Weekly checks*)
- [ ] Wiper arm tension springs broken, or arm pivots seized (Chapter 12)
- [ ] Insufficient windscreen washer additive to adequately remove road film (see *Weekly checks*)

Windscreen washers inoperative, or unsatisfactory in operation

One or more washer jets inoperative

- [ ] Blocked washer jet
- [ ] Disconnected, kinked or restricted fluid hose (Chapter 12)
- [ ] Insufficient fluid in washer reservoir (see *Weekly checks*)

Washer pump fails to operate

- [ ] Broken or disconnected wiring or connections (Chapter 12)
- [ ] Blown fuse (Chapter 12)
- [ ] Faulty washer switch (Chapter 12)
- [ ] Faulty washer pump (Chapter 12)

Washer pump runs for some time before fluid is emitted from jets

- [ ] Faulty one-way valve in fluid supply hose (Chapter 12)

Electric windows inoperative, or unsatisfactory in operation

Window glass will only move in one direction

- [ ] Faulty switch (Chapter 12)

Window glass slow to move

- [ ] Battery discharged (Chapter 5A)
- [ ] Regulator seized or damaged, or in need of lubrication (Chapter 12)
- [ ] Door internal components or trim fouling regulator (Chapter 11)
- [ ] Faulty motor (Chapter 11)

Window glass fails to move

- [ ] Blown fuse (Chapter 12)
- [ ] Faulty relay (Chapter 12)
- [ ] Broken or disconnected wiring or connections (Chapter 12)
- [ ] Faulty motor (Chapter 11)

Electrical system (continued)

Central locking system inoperative, or unsatisfactory in operation

Complete system failure

☐ Remote handset battery discharged, where applicable (Chapter 1)
☐ Blown fuse (Chapter 12)
☐ Faulty relay (Chapter 12)
☐ Broken or disconnected wiring or connections (Chapter 12)
☐ Faulty motor (Chapter 11)

Latch locks but will not unlock, or unlocks but will not lock

☐ Remote handset battery discharged, where applicable (Chapter 1)
☐ Faulty master switch (Chapter 12)
☐ Broken or disconnected latch operating rods or levers (Chapter 11)
☐ Faulty relay (Chapter 12)
☐ Faulty motor (Chapter 11)

One solenoid/motor fails to operate

☐ Broken or disconnected wiring or connections (Chapter 12)
☐ Faulty operating assembly (Chapter 11)
☐ Broken, binding or disconnected latch operating rods or levers (Chapter 11)
☐ Fault in door latch (Chapter 11)

A

ABS (Anti-lock brake system) A system, usually electronically controlled, that senses incipient wheel lockup during braking and relieves hydraulic pressure at wheels that are about to skid.

Air bag An inflatable bag hidden in the steering wheel (driver's side) or the dash or glovebox (passenger side). In a head-on collision, the bags inflate, preventing the driver and front passenger from being thrown forward into the steering wheel or windscreen.

Air cleaner A metal or plastic housing, containing a filter element, which removes dust and dirt from the air being drawn into the engine.

Air filter element The actual filter in an air cleaner system, usually manufactured from pleated paper and requiring renewal at regular intervals.

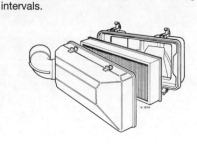

Air filter

Allen key A hexagonal wrench which fits into a recessed hexagonal hole.

Alligator clip A long-nosed spring-loaded metal clip with meshing teeth. Used to make temporary electrical connections.

Alternator A component in the electrical system which converts mechanical energy from a drivebelt into electrical energy to charge the battery and to operate the starting system, ignition system and electrical accessories.

Alternator (exploded view)

Ampere (amp) A unit of measurement for the flow of electric current. One amp is the amount of current produced by one volt acting through a resistance of one ohm.

Anaerobic sealer A substance used to prevent bolts and screws from loosening. Anaerobic means that it does not require oxygen for activation. The Loctite brand is widely used.

Antifreeze A substance (usually ethylene glycol) mixed with water, and added to a vehicle's cooling system, to prevent freezing of the coolant in winter. Antifreeze also contains chemicals to inhibit corrosion and the formation of rust and other deposits that

would tend to clog the radiator and coolant passages and reduce cooling efficiency.

Anti-seize compound A coating that reduces the risk of seizing on fasteners that are subjected to high temperatures, such as exhaust manifold bolts and nuts.

Anti-seize compound

Asbestos A natural fibrous mineral with great heat resistance, commonly used in the composition of brake friction materials. Asbestos is a health hazard and the dust created by brake systems should never be inhaled or ingested.

Axle A shaft on which a wheel revolves, or which revolves with a wheel. Also, a solid beam that connects the two wheels at one end of the vehicle. An axle which also transmits power to the wheels is known as a live axle.

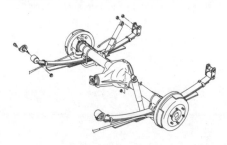

Axle assembly

Axleshaft A single rotating shaft, on either side of the differential, which delivers power from the final drive assembly to the drive wheels. Also called a driveshaft or a halfshaft.

B

Ball bearing An anti-friction bearing consisting of a hardened inner and outer race with hardened steel balls between two races.

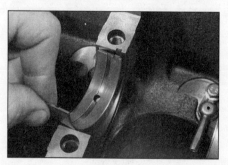

Bearing

Bearing The curved surface on a shaft or in a bore, or the part assembled into either, that permits relative motion between them with minimum wear and friction.

Big-end bearing The bearing in the end of the connecting rod that's attached to the crankshaft.

Bleed nipple A valve on a brake wheel cylinder, caliper or other hydraulic component that is opened to purge the hydraulic system of air. Also called a bleed screw.

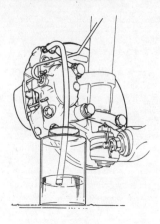

Brake bleeding

Brake bleeding Procedure for removing air from lines of a hydraulic brake system.

Brake disc The component of a disc brake that rotates with the wheels.

Brake drum The component of a drum brake that rotates with the wheels.

Brake linings The friction material which contacts the brake disc or drum to retard the vehicle's speed. The linings are bonded or riveted to the brake pads or shoes.

Brake pads The replaceable friction pads that pinch the brake disc when the brakes are applied. Brake pads consist of a friction material bonded or riveted to a rigid backing plate.

Brake shoe The crescent-shaped carrier to which the brake linings are mounted and which forces the lining against the rotating drum during braking.

Braking systems For more information on braking systems, consult the *Haynes Automotive Brake Manual*.

Breaker bar A long socket wrench handle providing greater leverage.

Bulkhead The insulated partition between the engine and the passenger compartment.

C

Caliper The non-rotating part of a disc-brake assembly that straddles the disc and carries the brake pads. The caliper also contains the hydraulic components that cause the pads to pinch the disc when the brakes are applied. A caliper is also a measuring tool that can be set to measure inside or outside dimensions of an object.

Camshaft A rotating shaft on which a series of cam lobes operate the valve mechanisms. The camshaft may be driven by gears, by sprockets and chain or by sprockets and a belt.

Canister A container in an evaporative emission control system; contains activated charcoal granules to trap vapours from the fuel system.

Canister

Carburettor A device which mixes fuel with air in the proper proportions to provide a desired power output from a spark ignition internal combustion engine.

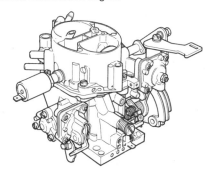

Carburettor

Castellated Resembling the parapets along the top of a castle wall. For example, a castellated balljoint stud nut.

Castellated nut

Castor In wheel alignment, the backward or forward tilt of the steering axis. Castor is positive when the steering axis is inclined rearward at the top.

Catalytic converter A silencer-like device in the exhaust system which converts certain pollutants in the exhaust gases into less harmful substances.

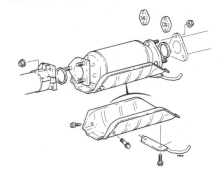

Catalytic converter

Circlip A ring-shaped clip used to prevent endwise movement of cylindrical parts and shafts. An internal circlip is installed in a groove in a housing; an external circlip fits into a groove on the outside of a cylindrical piece such as a shaft.

Clearance The amount of space between two parts. For example, between a piston and a cylinder, between a bearing and a journal, etc.

Coil spring A spiral of elastic steel found in various sizes throughout a vehicle, for example as a springing medium in the suspension and in the valve train.

Compression Reduction in volume, and increase in pressure and temperature, of a gas, caused by squeezing it into a smaller space.

Compression ratio The relationship between cylinder volume when the piston is at top dead centre and cylinder volume when the piston is at bottom dead centre.

Constant velocity (CV) joint A type of universal joint that cancels out vibrations caused by driving power being transmitted through an angle.

Core plug A disc or cup-shaped metal device inserted in a hole in a casting through which core was removed when the casting was formed. Also known as a freeze plug or expansion plug.

Crankcase The lower part of the engine block in which the crankshaft rotates.

Crankshaft The main rotating member, or shaft, running the length of the crankcase, with offset "throws" to which the connecting rods are attached.

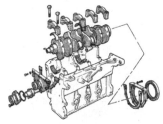

Crankshaft assembly

Crocodile clip See Alligator clip

D

Diagnostic code Code numbers obtained by accessing the diagnostic mode of an engine management computer. This code can be used to determine the area in the system where a malfunction may be located.

Disc brake A brake design incorporating a rotating disc onto which brake pads are squeezed. The resulting friction converts the energy of a moving vehicle into heat.

Double-overhead cam (DOHC) An engine that uses two overhead camshafts, usually one for the intake valves and one for the exhaust valves.

Drivebelt(s) The belt(s) used to drive accessories such as the alternator, water pump, power steering pump, air conditioning compressor, etc. off the crankshaft pulley.

Accessory drivebelts

Driveshaft Any shaft used to transmit motion. Commonly used when referring to the axleshafts on a front wheel drive vehicle.

Driveshaft

Drum brake A type of brake using a drum-shaped metal cylinder attached to the inner surface of the wheel. When the brake pedal is pressed, curved brake shoes with friction linings press against the inside of the drum to slow or stop the vehicle.

Drum brake assembly

E

EGR valve A valve used to introduce exhaust gases into the intake air stream.

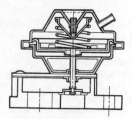

EGR valve

Electronic control unit (ECU) A computer which controls (for instance) ignition and fuel injection systems, or an anti-lock braking system. For more information refer to the *Haynes Automotive Electrical and Electronic Systems Manual.*

Electronic Fuel Injection (EFI) A computer controlled fuel system that distributes fuel through an injector located in each intake port of the engine.

Emergency brake A braking system, independent of the main hydraulic system, that can be used to slow or stop the vehicle if the primary brakes fail, or to hold the vehicle stationary even though the brake pedal isn't depressed. It usually consists of a hand lever that actuates either front or rear brakes mechanically through a series of cables and linkages. Also known as a handbrake or parking brake.

Endfloat The amount of lengthwise movement between two parts. As applied to a crankshaft, the distance that the crankshaft can move forward and back in the cylinder block.

Engine management system (EMS) A computer controlled system which manages the fuel injection and the ignition systems in an integrated fashion.

Exhaust manifold A part with several passages through which exhaust gases leave the engine combustion chambers and enter the exhaust pipe.

Exhaust manifold

F

Fan clutch A viscous (fluid) drive coupling device which permits variable engine fan speeds in relation to engine speeds.

Feeler blade A thin strip or blade of hardened steel, ground to an exact thickness, used to check or measure clearances between parts.

Feeler blade

Firing order The order in which the engine cylinders fire, or deliver their power strokes, beginning with the number one cylinder.

Flywheel A heavy spinning wheel in which energy is absorbed and stored by means of momentum. On cars, the flywheel is attached to the crankshaft to smooth out firing impulses.

Free play The amount of travel before any action takes place. The "looseness" in a linkage, or an assembly of parts, between the initial application of force and actual movement. For example, the distance the brake pedal moves before the pistons in the master cylinder are actuated.

Fuse An electrical device which protects a circuit against accidental overload. The typical fuse contains a soft piece of metal which is calibrated to melt at a predetermined current flow (expressed as amps) and break the circuit.

Fusible link A circuit protection device consisting of a conductor surrounded by heat-resistant insulation. The conductor is smaller than the wire it protects, so it acts as the weakest link in the circuit. Unlike a blown fuse, a failed fusible link must frequently be cut from the wire for replacement.

G

Gap The distance the spark must travel in jumping from the centre electrode to the side

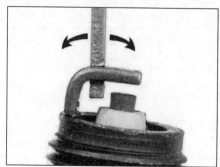

Adjusting spark plug gap

electrode in a spark plug. Also refers to the spacing between the points in a contact breaker assembly in a conventional points-type ignition, or to the distance between the reluctor or rotor and the pickup coil in an electronic ignition.

Gasket Any thin, soft material - usually cork, cardboard, asbestos or soft metal - installed between two metal surfaces to ensure a good seal. For instance, the cylinder head gasket seals the joint between the block and the cylinder head.

Gasket

Gauge An instrument panel display used to monitor engine conditions. A gauge with a movable pointer on a dial or a fixed scale is an analogue gauge. A gauge with a numerical readout is called a digital gauge.

H

Halfshaft A rotating shaft that transmits power from the final drive unit to a drive wheel, usually when referring to a live rear axle.

Harmonic balancer A device designed to reduce torsion or twisting vibration in the crankshaft. May be incorporated in the crankshaft pulley. Also known as a vibration damper.

Hone An abrasive tool for correcting small irregularities or differences in diameter in an engine cylinder, brake cylinder, etc.

Hydraulic tappet A tappet that utilises hydraulic pressure from the engine's lubrication system to maintain zero clearance (constant contact with both camshaft and valve stem). Automatically adjusts to variation in valve stem length. Hydraulic tappets also reduce valve noise.

I

Ignition timing The moment at which the spark plug fires, usually expressed in the number of crankshaft degrees before the piston reaches the top of its stroke.

Inlet manifold A tube or housing with passages through which flows the air-fuel mixture (carburettor vehicles and vehicles with throttle body injection) or air only (port fuel-injected vehicles) to the port openings in the cylinder head.

J

Jump start Starting the engine of a vehicle with a discharged or weak battery by attaching jump leads from the weak battery to a charged or helper battery.

L

Load Sensing Proportioning Valve (LSPV) A brake hydraulic system control valve that works like a proportioning valve, but also takes into consideration the amount of weight carried by the rear axle.

Locknut A nut used to lock an adjustment nut, or other threaded component, in place. For example, a locknut is employed to keep the adjusting nut on the rocker arm in position.

Lockwasher A form of washer designed to prevent an attaching nut from working loose.

M

MacPherson strut A type of front suspension system devised by Earle MacPherson at Ford of England. In its original form, a simple lateral link with the anti-roll bar creates the lower control arm. A long strut - an integral coil spring and shock absorber - is mounted between the body and the steering knuckle. Many modern so-called MacPherson strut systems use a conventional lower A-arm and don't rely on the anti-roll bar for location.

Multimeter An electrical test instrument with the capability to measure voltage, current and resistance.

N

NOx Oxides of Nitrogen. A common toxic pollutant emitted by petrol and diesel engines at higher temperatures.

O

Ohm The unit of electrical resistance. One volt applied to a resistance of one ohm will produce a current of one amp.

Ohmmeter An instrument for measuring electrical resistance.

O-ring A type of sealing ring made of a special rubber-like material; in use, the O-ring is compressed into a groove to provide the sealing action.

O-ring

Overhead cam (ohc) engine An engine with the camshaft(s) located on top of the cylinder head(s).

Overhead valve (ohv) engine An engine with the valves located in the cylinder head, but with the camshaft located in the engine block.

Oxygen sensor A device installed in the engine exhaust manifold, which senses the oxygen content in the exhaust and converts this information into an electric current. Also called a Lambda sensor.

P

Phillips screw A type of screw head having a cross instead of a slot for a corresponding type of screwdriver.

Plastigage A thin strip of plastic thread, available in different sizes, used for measuring clearances. For example, a strip of Plastigage is laid across a bearing journal. The parts are assembled and dismantled; the width of the crushed strip indicates the clearance between journal and bearing.

Plastigage

Propeller shaft The long hollow tube with universal joints at both ends that carries power from the transmission to the differential on front-engined rear wheel drive vehicles.

Proportioning valve A hydraulic control valve which limits the amount of pressure to the rear brakes during panic stops to prevent wheel lock-up.

R

Rack-and-pinion steering A steering system with a pinion gear on the end of the steering shaft that mates with a rack (think of a geared wheel opened up and laid flat). When the steering wheel is turned, the pinion turns, moving the rack to the left or right. This movement is transmitted through the track rods to the steering arms at the wheels.

Radiator A liquid-to-air heat transfer device designed to reduce the temperature of the coolant in an internal combustion engine cooling system.

Refrigerant Any substance used as a heat transfer agent in an air-conditioning system. R-12 has been the principle refrigerant for many years; recently, however, manufacturers have begun using R-134a, a non-CFC substance that is considered less harmful to the ozone in the upper atmosphere.

Rocker arm A lever arm that rocks on a shaft or pivots on a stud. In an overhead valve engine, the rocker arm converts the upward movement of the pushrod into a downward movement to open a valve.

Rotor In a distributor, the rotating device inside the cap that connects the centre electrode and the outer terminals as it turns, distributing the high voltage from the coil secondary winding to the proper spark plug. Also, that part of an alternator which rotates inside the stator. Also, the rotating assembly of a turbocharger, including the compressor wheel, shaft and turbine wheel.

Runout The amount of wobble (in-and-out movement) of a gear or wheel as it's rotated. The amount a shaft rotates "out-of-true." The out-of-round condition of a rotating part.

S

Sealant A liquid or paste used to prevent leakage at a joint. Sometimes used in conjunction with a gasket.

Sealed beam lamp An older headlight design which integrates the reflector, lens and filaments into a hermetically-sealed one-piece unit. When a filament burns out or the lens cracks, the entire unit is simply replaced.

Serpentine drivebelt A single, long, wide accessory drivebelt that's used on some newer vehicles to drive all the accessories, instead of a series of smaller, shorter belts. Serpentine drivebelts are usually tensioned by an automatic tensioner.

Serpentine drivebelt

Shim Thin spacer, commonly used to adjust the clearance or relative positions between two parts. For example, shims inserted into or under bucket tappets control valve clearances. Clearance is adjusted by changing the thickness of the shim.

Slide hammer A special puller that screws into or hooks onto a component such as a shaft or bearing; a heavy sliding handle on the shaft bottoms against the end of the shaft to knock the component free.

Sprocket A tooth or projection on the periphery of a wheel, shaped to engage with a chain or drivebelt. Commonly used to refer to the sprocket wheel itself.

Starter inhibitor switch On vehicles with an automatic transmission, a switch that prevents starting if the vehicle is not in Neutral or Park.

Strut See MacPherson strut.

T

Tappet A cylindrical component which transmits motion from the cam to the valve stem, either directly or via a pushrod and rocker arm. Also called a cam follower.

Thermostat A heat-controlled valve that regulates the flow of coolant between the cylinder block and the radiator, so maintaining optimum engine operating temperature. A thermostat is also used in some air cleaners in which the temperature is regulated.

Thrust bearing The bearing in the clutch assembly that is moved in to the release levers by clutch pedal action to disengage the clutch. Also referred to as a release bearing.

Timing belt A toothed belt which drives the camshaft. Serious engine damage may result if it breaks in service.

Timing chain A chain which drives the camshaft.

Toe-in The amount the front wheels are closer together at the front than at the rear. On rear wheel drive vehicles, a slight amount of toe-in is usually specified to keep the front wheels running parallel on the road by offsetting other forces that tend to spread the wheels apart.

Toe-out The amount the front wheels are closer together at the rear than at the front. On front wheel drive vehicles, a slight amount of toe-out is usually specified.

Tools For full information on choosing and using tools, refer to the *Haynes Automotive Tools Manual*.

Tracer A stripe of a second colour applied to a wire insulator to distinguish that wire from another one with the same colour insulator.

Tune-up A process of accurate and careful adjustments and parts replacement to obtain the best possible engine performance.

Turbocharger A centrifugal device, driven by exhaust gases, that pressurises the intake air. Normally used to increase the power output from a given engine displacement, but can also be used primarily to reduce exhaust emissions (as on VW's "Umwelt" Diesel engine).

U

Universal joint or U-joint A double-pivoted connection for transmitting power from a driving to a driven shaft through an angle. A U-joint consists of two Y-shaped yokes and a cross-shaped member called the spider.

V

Valve A device through which the flow of liquid, gas, vacuum, or loose material in bulk may be started, stopped, or regulated by a movable part that opens, shuts, or partially obstructs one or more ports or passageways. A valve is also the movable part of such a device.

Valve clearance The clearance between the valve tip (the end of the valve stem) and the rocker arm or tappet. The valve clearance is measured when the valve is closed.

Vernier caliper A precision measuring instrument that measures inside and outside dimensions. Not quite as accurate as a micrometer, but more convenient.

Viscosity The thickness of a liquid or its resistance to flow.

Volt A unit for expressing electrical "pressure" in a circuit. One volt that will produce a current of one ampere through a resistance of one ohm.

W

Welding Various processes used to join metal items by heating the areas to be joined to a molten state and fusing them together. For more information refer to the *Haynes Automotive Welding Manual*.

Wiring diagram A drawing portraying the components and wires in a vehicle's electrical system, using standardised symbols. For more information refer to the *Haynes Automotive Electrical and Electronic Systems Manual*.

Note: *References throughout this index are in the form* "**Chapter number**" • "**Page number**". *So, for example, 2C•15 refers to page 15 of Chapter 2C.*

Note: *References throughout this index are in the form* **"Chapter number"** • **"Page number"**. *So, for example, 2C•15 refers to page 15 of Chapter 2C.*

Note: *References throughout this index are in the form* "**Chapter number**" • "**Page number**". *So, for example, 2C•15 refers to page 15 of Chapter 2C.*

Note: *References throughout this index are in the form* **"Chapter number"** • **"Page number"**. *So, for example, 2C•15 refers to page 15 of Chapter 2C.*

Haynes Manuals – The Complete UK Car List

Title	Book No.
ALFA ROMEO Alfasud/Sprint (74 - 88) up to F *	0292
Alfa Romeo Alfetta (73 - 87) up to E *	0531
AUDI 80, 90 & Coupe Petrol (79 - Nov 88) up to F	0605
Audi 80, 90 & Coupe Petrol (Oct 86 - 90) D to H	1491
Audi 100 & 200 Petrol (Oct 82 - 90) up to H	0907
Audi 100 & A6 Petrol & Diesel (May 91 - May 97) H to P	3504
Audi A3 Petrol & Diesel (96 - May 03) P to 03	4253
Audi A4 Petrol & Diesel (95 - 00) M to X	3575
Audi A4 Petrol & Diesel (01 - 04) X to 54	4609
AUSTIN A35 & A40 (56 - 67) up to F *	0118
Austin/MG/Rover Maestro 1.3 & 1.6 Petrol (83 - 95) up to M	0922
Austin/MG Metro (80 - May 90) up to G	0718
Austin/Rover Montego 1.3 & 1.6 Petrol (84 - 94) A to L	1066
Austin/MG/Rover Montego 2.0 Petrol (84 - 95) A to M	1067
Mini (59 - 69) up to H *	0527
Mini (69 - 01) up to X	0646
Austin/Rover 2.0 litre Diesel Engine (86 - 93) C to L	1857
Austin Healey 100/6 & 3000 (56 - 68) up to G *	0049
BEDFORD CF Petrol (69 - 87) up to E	0163
Bedford/Vauxhall Rascal & Suzuki Supercarry (86 - Oct 94) C to M	3015
BMW 316, 320 & 320i (4-cyl) (75 - Feb 83) up to Y *	0276
BMW 320, 320i, 323i & 325i (6-cyl) (Oct 77 - Sept 87) up to E	0815
BMW 3- & 5-Series Petrol (81 - 91) up to J	1948
BMW 3-Series Petrol (Apr 91 - 99) H to V	3210
BMW 3-Series Petrol (Sept 98 - 03) S to 53	4067
BMW 520i & 525e (Oct 81 - June 88) up to E	1560
BMW 525, 528 & 528i (73 - Sept 81) up to X *	0632
BMW 5-Series 6-cyl Petrol (April 96 - Aug 03) N to 03	4151
BMW 1500, 1502, 1600, 1602, 2000 & 2002 (59 - 77) up to S *	0240
CHRYSLER PT Cruiser Petrol (00 - 03) W to 53	4058
CITROËN 2CV, Ami & Dyane (67 - 90) up to H	0196
Citroën AX Petrol & Diesel (87 - 97) D to P	3014
Citroën Berlingo & Peugeot Partner Petrol & Diesel (96 - 05) P to 55	4281
Citroën BX Petrol (83 - 94) A to L	0908
Citroën C15 Van Petrol & Diesel (89 - Oct 98) F to S	3509
Citroën C3 Petrol & Diesel (02 - 05) 51 to 05	4197
Citroen C5 Petrol & Diesel (01-08) Y to 08	4745
Citroën CX Petrol (75 - 88) up to F	0528
Citroën Saxo Petrol & Diesel (96 - 04) N to 54	3506
Citroën Visa Petrol (79 - 88) up to F	0620
Citroën Xantia Petrol & Diesel (93 - 01) K to Y	3082
Citroën XM Petrol & Diesel (89 - 00) G to X	3451
Citroën Xsara Petrol & Diesel (97 - Sept 00) R to W	3751
Citroën Xsara Picasso Petrol & Diesel (00 - 02) W to 52	3944
Citroen Xsara Picasso (03-08)	4784
Citroën ZX Diesel (91 - 98) J to S	1922
Citroën ZX Petrol (91 - 98) H to S	1881
Citroën 1.7 & 1.9 litre Diesel Engine (84 - 96) A to N	1379
FIAT 126 (73 - 87) up to E *	0305
Fiat 500 (57 - 73) up to M *	0090
Fiat Bravo & Brava Petrol (95 - 00) N to W	3572
Fiat Cinquecento (93 - 98) K to R	3501
Fiat Panda (81 - 95) up to M	0793
Fiat Punto Petrol & Diesel (94 - Oct 99) L to V	3251
Fiat Punto Petrol (Oct 99 - July 03) V to 03	4066
Fiat Punto Petrol (03-07) 03 to 07	4746
Fiat Regata Petrol (84 - 88) A to F	1167
Fiat Tipo Petrol (88 - 91) E to J	1625
Fiat Uno Petrol (83 - 95) up to M	0923
Fiat X1/9 (74 - 89) up to G *	0273
FORD Anglia (59 - 68) up to G *	0001
Ford Capri II (& III) 1.6 & 2.0 (74 - 87) up to E *	0283
Ford Capri II (& III) 2.8 & 3.0 V6 (74 - 87) up to E	1309
Ford Cortina Mk I & Corsair 1500 ('62 - '66) up to D*	0214
Ford Cortina Mk III 1300 & 1600 (70 - 76) up to P *	0070
Ford Escort Mk I 1100 & 1300 (68 - 74) up to N *	0171
Ford Escort Mk I Mexico, RS 1600 & RS 2000 (70 - 74) up to N *	0139
Ford Escort Mk II Mexico, RS 1800 & RS 2000 (75 - 80) up to W *	0735
Ford Escort (75 - Aug 80) up to V *	0280
Ford Escort Petrol (Sept 80 - Sept 90) up to H	0686
Ford Escort & Orion Petrol (Sept 90 - 00) H to X	1737
Ford Escort & Orion Diesel (Sept 90 - 00) H to X	4081
Ford Fiesta (76 - Aug 83) up to Y	0334
Ford Fiesta Petrol (Aug 83 - Feb 89) A to F	1030
Ford Fiesta Petrol (Feb 89 - Oct 95) F to N	1595
Ford Fiesta Petrol & Diesel (Oct 95 - Mar 02) N to 02	3397
Ford Fiesta Petrol & Diesel (Apr 02 - 07) 02 to 57	4170
Ford Focus Petrol & Diesel (98 - 01) S to Y	3759
Ford Focus Petrol & Diesel (Oct 01 - 05) 51 to 05	4167
Ford Galaxy Petrol & Diesel (95 - Aug 00) M to W	3984
Ford Granada Petrol (Sept 77 - Feb 85) up to B *	0481
Ford Granada & Scorpio Petrol (Mar 85 - 94) B to M	1245
Ford Ka (96 - 02) P to 52	3570
Ford Mondeo Petrol (93 - Sept 00) K to X	1923
Ford Mondeo Petrol & Diesel (Oct 00 - Jul 03) X to 03	3990
Ford Mondeo Petrol & Diesel (July 03 - 07) 03 to 56	4619
Ford Mondeo Diesel (93 - 96) L to N	3465
Ford Orion Petrol (83 - Sept 90) up to H	1009
Ford Sierra 4-cyl Petrol (82 - 93) up to K	0903
Ford Sierra V6 Petrol (82 - 91) up to J	0904
Ford Transit Petrol (Mk 2) (78 - Jan 86) up to C	0719
Ford Transit Petrol (Mk 3) (Feb 86 - 89) C to G	1468
Ford Transit Diesel (Feb 86 - 99) C to T	3019
Ford Transit Diesel (00-06)	4775
Ford 1.6 & 1.8 litre Diesel Engine (84 - 96) A to N	1172
Ford 2.1, 2.3 & 2.5 litre Diesel Engine (77 - 90) up to H	1606
FREIGHT ROVER Sherpa Petrol (74 - 87) up to E	0463
HILLMAN Avenger (70 - 82) up to Y	0037
Hillman Imp (63 - 76) up to R *	0022
HONDA Civic (Feb 84 - Oct 87) A to E	1226
Honda Civic (Nov 91 - 96) J to N	3199
Honda Civic Petrol (Mar 95 - 00) M to X	4050
Honda Civic Petrol & Diesel (01 - 05) X to 55	4611
Honda CR-V Petrol & Diesel (01-06)	4747
Honda Jazz (01 - Feb 08) 51 - 57	4735
HYUNDAI Pony (85 - 94) C to M	3398
JAGUAR E Type (61 - 72) up to L *	0140
Jaguar MkI & II, 240 & 340 (55 - 69) up to H *	0098
Jaguar XJ6, XJ & Sovereign; Daimler Sovereign (68 - Oct 86) up to D	0242
Jaguar XJ6 & Sovereign (Oct 86 - Sept 94) D to M	3261
Jaguar XJ12, XJS & Sovereign; Daimler Double Six (72 - 88) up to F	0478
JEEP Cherokee Petrol (93 - 96) K to N	1943
LADA 1200, 1300, 1500 & 1600 (74 - 91) up to J	0413
Lada Samara (87 - 91) D to J	1610
LAND ROVER 90, 110 & Defender Diesel (83 - 07) up to 56	3017
Land Rover Discovery Petrol & Diesel (89 - 98) G to S	3016
Land Rover Discovery Diesel (Nov 98 - Jul 04) S to 04	4606
Land Rover Freelander Petrol & Diesel (97 - Sept 03) R to 53	3929
Land Rover Freelander Petrol & Diesel (Oct 03 - Oct 06) 53 to 56	4623
Land Rover Series IIA & III Diesel (58 - 85) up to C	0529
Land Rover Series II, IIA & III 4-cyl Petrol (58 - 85) up to C	0314
MAZDA 323 (Mar 81 - Oct 89) up to G	1608
Mazda 323 (Oct 89 - 98) G to R	3455
Mazda 626 (May 83 - Sept 87) up to E	0929
Mazda B1600, B1800 & B2000 Pick-up Petrol (72 - 88) up to F	0267
Mazda RX-7 (79 - 85) up to C *	0460
MERCEDES-BENZ 190, 190E & 190D Petrol & Diesel (83 - 93) A to L	3450
Mercedes-Benz 200D, 240D, 240TD, 300D & 300TD 123 Series Diesel (Oct 76 - 85)	1114
Mercedes-Benz 250 & 280 (68 - 72) up to L *	0346
Mercedes-Benz 250 & 280 123 Series Petrol (Oct 76 - 84) up to B *	0677
Mercedes-Benz 124 Series Petrol & Diesel (85 - Aug 93) C to K	3253
Mercedes-Benz A-Class Petrol & Diesel (98-04) S to 54	4748
Mercedes-Benz C-Class Petrol & Diesel (93 - Aug 00) L to W	3511
Mercedes-Benz C-Class (00-06)	4780
MGA (55 - 62) *	0475
MGB (62 - 80) up to W	0111
MG Midget & Austin-Healey Sprite (58 - 80) up to W *	0265
MINI Petrol (July 01 - 05) Y to 05	4273
MITSUBISHI Shogun & L200 Pick-Ups Petrol (83 - 94) up to M	1944
MORRIS Ital 1.3 (80 - 84) up to B	0705
Morris Minor 1000 (56 - 71) up to K	0024
NISSAN Almera Petrol (95 - Feb 00) N to V	4053
Nissan Almera & Tino Petrol (Feb 00 - 07) V to 56	4612
Nissan Bluebird (May 84 - Mar 86) A to C	1223
Nissan Bluebird Petrol (Mar 86 - 90) C to H	1473
Nissan Cherry (Sept 82 - 86) up to D	1031
Nissan Micra (83 - Jan 93) up to K	0931
Nissan Micra (93 - 02) K to 52	3254
Nissan Micra Petrol (03-07) 52 to 57	4734
Nissan Primera Petrol (90 - Aug 99) H to T	1851
Nissan Stanza (82 - 86) up to D	0824
Nissan Sunny Petrol (May 82 - Oct 86) up to D	0895
Nissan Sunny Petrol (Oct 86 - Mar 91) D to H	1378
Nissan Sunny Petrol (Apr 91 - 95) H to N	3219
OPEL Ascona & Manta (B Series) (Sept 75 - 88) up to F *	0316
Opel Ascona Petrol (81 - 88)	3215
Opel Astra Petrol (Oct 91 - Feb 98)	3156
Opel Corsa Petrol (83 - Mar 93)	3160
Opel Corsa Petrol (Mar 93 - 97)	3159
Opel Kadett Petrol (Nov 79 - Oct 84) up to B	0634
Opel Kadett Petrol (Oct 84 - Oct 91)	3196
Opel Omega & Senator Petrol (Nov 86 - 94)	3157
Opel Rekord Petrol (Feb 78 - Oct 86) up to D	0543
Opel Vectra Petrol (Oct 88 - Oct 95)	3158
PEUGEOT 106 Petrol & Diesel (91 - 04) J to 53	1882
Peugeot 205 Petrol (83 - 97) A to P	0932
Peugeot 206 Petrol & Diesel (98 - 01) S to X	3757
Peugeot 206 Petrol & Diesel (02 - 06) 51 to 06	4613
Peugeot 306 Petrol & Diesel (93 - 02) K to 02	3073
Peugeot 307 Petrol & Diesel (01 - 04) Y to 54	4147
Peugeot 309 Petrol (86 - 93) C to K	1266
Peugeot 405 Petrol (88 - 97) E to P	1559
Peugeot 405 Diesel (88 - 97) E to P	3198
Peugeot 406 Petrol & Diesel (96 - Mar 99) N to T	3394
Peugeot 406 Petrol & Diesel (Mar 99 - 02) T to 52	3982

* Classic reprint

All the products featured on this page are available through most motor accessory shops, cycle shops and book stores. Our policy of continuous updating and development means that titles are being constantly added to the range. For up-to-date information on our complete list of titles, please telephone: (UK) +44 1963 442030 • (USA) +1 805 498 6703 • (Sweden) +46 18 124016 • (Australia) +61 3 9763 8100

CL24.08/09

Preserving Our Motoring Heritage

< *The Model J Duesenberg Derham Tourster. Only eight of these magnificent cars were ever built – this is the only example to be found outside the United States of America*

Almost every car you've ever loved, loathed or desired is gathered under one roof at the Haynes Motor Museum. Over 300 immaculately presented cars and motorbikes represent every aspect of our motoring heritage, from elegant reminders of bygone days, such as the superb Model J Duesenberg to curiosities like the bug-eyed BMW Isetta. There are also many old friends and flames. Perhaps you remember the 1959 Ford Popular that you did your courting in? The magnificent 'Red Collection' is a spectacle of classic sports cars including AC, Alfa Romeo, Austin Healey, Ferrari, Lamborghini, Maserati, MG, Riley, Porsche and Triumph.

A Perfect Day Out

Each and every vehicle at the Haynes Motor Museum has played its part in the history and culture of Motoring. Today, they make a wonderful spectacle and a great day out for all the family. Bring the kids, bring Mum and Dad, but above all bring your camera to capture those golden memories for ever. You will also find an impressive array of motoring memorabilia, a comfortable 70 seat video cinema and one of the most extensive transport book shops in Britain. The Pit Stop Cafe serves everything from a cup of tea to wholesome, home-made meals or, if you prefer, you can enjoy the large picnic area nestled in the beautiful rural surroundings of Somerset.

John Haynes O.B.E., Founder and Chairman of the museum at the wheel of a Haynes Light 12. >

< *Graham Hill's Lola Cosworth Formula 1 car next to a 1934 Riley Sports.*

The Museum is situated on the A359 Yeovil to Frome road at Sparkford, just off the A303 in Somerset. It is about 40 miles south of Bristol, and 25 minutes drive from the M5 intersection at Taunton.

Open 9.30am - 5.30pm (10.00am - 4.00pm Winter) 7 days a week, *except Christmas Day, Boxing Day and New Years Day*

Special rates available for schools, coach parties and outings Charitable Trust No. 292048